Transnational Philippines

Transnational Philippines

Cultural Encounters
in Philippine Literature in Spanish

Edited by Axel Gasquet
and Rocío Ortuño Casanova

University of Michigan Press
Ann Arbor

For questions or permissions, please contact um.press.perms@umich.edu

Published in the United States of America by the
University of Michigan Press
Manufactured in the United States of America
Printed on acid-free paper
First published February 2024

A CIP catalog record for this book is available from the British Library.

Library of Congress Cataloging-in-Publication Data

Names: Gasquet, Axel, 1966– editor. | Ortuño Casanova, Rocío, editor. |
   Michigan Publishing (University of Michigan), publisher.
Title: Transnational Philippines : cultural encounters in Philippine literature in Spanish /
   Edited by Axel Gasquet and Rocio Ortuño Casanova.
Other titles: Cultural encounters in Philippine literature in Spanish
Description: Ann Arbor, Michigan : University of Michigan Press, 2024. |
   Includes bibliographical references and index.
Identifiers: LCCN 2023039380 | ISBN 9780472133505 (hardcover) |
   ISBN 9780472039616 (paperback) | ISBN 9780472904020 (ebook other)
Subjects: LCSH: Philippine literature (Spanish)—History and criticism. | Postcolonialism in
   literature. | Postcolonialism—Philippines. | LCGFT: Literary criticism. | Essays.
Classification: LCC PQ8718 .T73 2024 | DDC 860.9/9599—dc23/eng/20231031
LC record available at https://lccn.loc.gov/2023039380

DOI: https://doi.org/10.3998/mpub.11959397

The University of Michigan Press's open access publishing program is made possible thanks
to additional funding from the University of Michigan Office of the Provost and the generous
support of contributing libraries.

Cover illustration: *Los mantones de Manila*, by Fernando Fader (1914).
Courtesy of Museo Nacional de Bellas Artes, Argentina.

CONTENTS

Part III. Modernity and Globalization

Part IV. Anti-Colonial Writings in the Colonial Language

Part V. Narratives of the Self and World War II

Digital materials related to this title can be found on
the Fulcrum platform via the following citable URL:
https://doi.org/10.3998/mpub.11959397

Introduction

Philippine Literature in Spanish at the Periphery of the Canon

Nationalism, Transnationalism, Postnationalism, and Genres

Rocío Ortuño Casanova and Axel Gasquet

The fifth centennial of the first circumnavigation of the globe (2019–21) brought with it an interesting situation. While Spain, Portugal, and the Philippines were all organizing events to commemorate the beginning of an interconnected world and the contact of distant cultures, each country was internally pursuing its own nationalist agenda. Spain and Portugal were competing to prove who the protagonist of the first circumnavigation had been—either the Basque Juan Sebastian Elcano or the Portuguese Ferdinand Magellan—as both countries were eager to add that point to their respective national feats.[1] On the other hand, while the Iberian countries whitewashed their colonial history by organizing events around the contact of cultures, the benefits of globalization, and, in the case of Spain, old ties of friendship with the Philippines,[2] the Philippines themselves approached the commemoration with harsh criticism of colonial imposition. This point of view challenged the Eurocentric account of events, not least by bringing to Spain the version of history that claimed the first global circumnavigation for the Malay Enrique de Malacca instead of Magellan or Elcano.[3]

These disputes show that the approach to global interconnectivity is still nationalistic and inclined to recycle colonialist discourses that assume hierarchies in the value of knowledge and the direction in which it was spread. This political approach has fed back the study methods traditionally used to teach and learn cultural expressions, so that they are also based on the compartmentalization of knowledge and the study of nationalistic literature. This

3

interest seems to surface in books such as Luis Mariñas's *La literatura filipina en castellano*, which explains some achievements in Fil-Hispanic literature as a result of Spanish influence (1974),[4] and Adam Lifshey's *Subversions of the American Century*, which claims Fil-Hispanic literature of the early 20th century as part of US national literature.

However, the study of national literatures in isolation clashes with the interconnected reality, in which we see diasporic literatures or travelogues that may challenge the idea of national adscriptions. It also creates a problem with Fil-Hispanic literature,[5] which has been marginalized in literary history and its teaching: partly due to the Eurocentric character that literature courses have had until recently in most educative institutions of Europe, America, and the Philippines themselves and partly to the compartmentalization of literary history into national categories. With this approach to literary history, Philippine literature in Spanish has had a difficult fit. It has also been further marginalized by the field of Hispanic studies, which has been traditionally divided into Spanish Peninsular literature and Latin American literature, leaving out cultural productions in Spanish from Africa and Asia.

This difficulty for Fil-Hispanic literature to find a fit into a nationalistic literary history is caused by two main circumstances. First, the Philippines were a colonial archipelago during the period of national identity formation in the 19th century. Yolanda Martínez-San Miguel suggests that during the time when the idea of the nation was formed in the Philippines and the Spanish-speaking Caribbean, intellectuals from both archipelagos were living in Spain, forming a diasporic community. Therefore, displacement and ambivalence toward the metropolis and the island where some of the colonial writers had been born constituted a foundational motif in the narrative of the nation (2014, 42). More than this, archipelagic thought adds to this firsthand knowledge of the paradigms of the metropolis and brings ambivalence between the idea of national unity and the acknowledgment of diversity among inhabitants of the archipelago, according to Édouard Glissant (1997, 31). The inventors of the nation would therefore have struggled between identification with the metropolis and identification with the different facets of the unstable heterogeneous reality of the Philippines, while looking for international affiliations beyond Spain.[6] The birth of the nation had, therefore, a multifaceted construction that led to the crystallization of the question of what Filipino identity is (Zialcita 2005, 6).

The second circumstance is the development of the archipelago as a hub for the contact of cultures and international trade. Marlon James Sales calls it an "entrepôt," as he links it to the trading tradition in the area (2014, 171), while Irene Villaescusa refers to it as a "Contact Zone," a term borrowed from Mary Louise Pratt (2020, 24).[7] For Villaescusa, Philippine nationalism is rooted in transculturality because of the multiple bonds with other cultures, which transformed the country in the first half of the 20th century (2020, 4). This is partly due to the country's location on the periphery of Asia, between the Indian and Pacific Oceans. This border situation drew Indians, Arabs, Malays, and Chinese to the region before the arrival of the European ships. Later, from 1565 onward, it became a commercial hub between Asia, America, and Europe with the launching of the Manila Galleon route. Cultural contact led to miscegenation, a search for bonds with other regions, diasporic movements, and the blurring of cultural borders, all of which also brings into question the very idea of national literature not just in the Philippines but in different literary traditions around the world.

The concept of national literature was challenged by figures such as Jesús Balmori (1886–1948), an icon of the search for literary and cultural links beyond the nation. Born in the colonial Philippines under Spanish rule, he built most of his career during American rule. He was a deep admirer of Japan until World War II (although his ambivalence still prevailed even during the Japanese occupation of his country [Gasquet 2020, 48–51]), and he developed a special kind of orientalism in his poems, based on the identification of the Philippines with the exotic Orient of the *modernista* poems written by Latin American authors. In 1931, he went to Mexico intending to establish links with poets there—whom he expected to still be *modernistas*—and with the self-imposed mission of giving a public lecture about Japan. However, he was also a nationalist deeply committed to the Philippines' independence, of which he only saw two years. The topics of his poems and the links that he created in his literature and articles with other Asian and Spanish-speaking regions made him a transnational agent (Villaescusa 2020).

Another challenging figure is that of Adelina Gurrea (1896–1970). She was the daughter of Ramona Monasterio Pozo, born in Zamora, Spain, and of Carlos Gurrea Candela, born in the Philippines to a Spanish father and a mestiza mother. In 1921, when she was 25, she traveled to Spain, where she stayed for 37 years (until 1958) and published all her books. Despite the long stay in Spain, she always identified herself as a Filipina.

Besides the challenges made by these and other individual figures, a large array of genres testify to the movements of individuals between nations and again question the isolation of the national culture implied by national literatures. Travel books like that of María Paz Mendoza Guazón (1884–1967) are paradigmatic, but we also sometimes find memoirs or welcome speeches to foreign emissaries that are authentic essays that work on the Philippines' narrative linkage with other cultures. Such is the case of Rosa Sevilla de Alvero's speeches, still unpublished. All this has led to a sense of national identity that is questioned but also developed often in literary works.

In this context, the first objective of this book is to propose a study of Philippine literary production in Spanish stemming from its relationship with other cultures, literature, and arts. In this way, we attempt to break the nation's isolation and show how it is part of, and relevant to, the broad system of literature written in Spanish, but without claiming the ascendence of any country on it. We believe that by showing the connections of Philippine literature with other literatures, the study of Asian and Hispanic traditions will find a space for it within them. This objective is favored by currents alternative to the study of national literatures that are emerging nowadays, connected to the crisis of the nation-state. The "crisis of the nation-state" is a concept that grew popular in the 1990s in the shadow of postmodernism (Berman [1982] 2010) and is linked to the deficiencies of decolonization in the 1960s, globalizing economic alliances and policies, and the technology that has improved traveling and communications. During the tumultuous debate on the validity of the idea of the nation, John Dunn wrote the article titled "Introduction: Crisis of the Nation State?," posed as a question and starting from the idea that nation-states, as they have traditionally been defined, do not exist (1994, 3).[8] The theory behind it had been pinned down from Marxist theory, specifically to the history of Southeast Asia, by Benedict Anderson, who had given an acclaimed definition of the nation as an imagined community (1983).

Departing from this "crisis" situation, Jürgen Habermas proposed scenarios to safeguard democracy in the context of globalization in a book called *The Postnational Constellation* (1998). There, he spelled out the twofold pressure that globalization puts on the nation-state. On the one hand, there is external pressure from commercial and political agreements with other states that affect the self-determination of the nation-state. On the other hand, there is internal pressure created by the influx of foreign people and products manufactured worldwide (84). His political solution was the transnationalization of democracy via higher public participation in the election of representatives within the decision-making institutions of multinational networks. This moves the boundaries of the nation-state so it can become more inclusive, reaching territories further away from its original boundaries and connecting them in a kind of superstate.

Echoing that process, and applying it metaphorically to literature, Bernat Castany Prado proposed the notion of postnational literature as literature that reflects upon and creates dialogue with a worldwide society rather than a national one (2007), while Michel Le Bris put forward the concept of *littérature-monde*, "world literature" (2007). In the case of Philippine literature, these concepts have often been intrinsic to it throughout its history, not just nowadays as Castany suggests. Even if the main topic of Philippine texts written in Spanish was often national identity, as Villaescusa states, this national identity has been constructed by building bridges to other cultures as we have just argued.

Rather than simply thinking about Philippine literature as postnational, we propose taking a postnational approach to it, which in the case of Philippine literature should favor a match between the object of study and the methodology. This approach should overcome the constraints of the stagnant categories imposed by national borders, widening the scope to the relations with other regions, thereby lifting the boundaries between languages and offering a wider representation of other cultural productions not aligned with any blocks. Due to this wider representation of works, it should defy the Eurocentric canon and encourage the presence of decolonializing discourses that expose nationalist and (neo)colonialist actions (such as the Spanish-Portuguese competition for claiming the first circumnavigation). This way of considering Philippine literature converges with at least four emerging fields that have studied Spanish-speaking cultural production in or about the Philippines in a frame of intercultural entanglements: Spanish Asian studies, the Global Hispanophone, Transpacific studies, and Global South studies. They constitute some of the latest attempts to break the dichotomy of Hispanism into Peninsular and Latin American areas of study.

The first of these fields is what has been called "Spanish Asian studies" by Yeon-Soo Kim and Kathleen E. Davies. It was defined in the introduction to a special section that they coordinated in the *Arizona Journal of Hispanic Cultural Studies*, titled "Asia in the Hispanic World: The Other Orientalism." The field addresses "Spain's epistemological construction of Asia" (200). The founding article mentions past works that considered cultural interactions between the Philippines and Spain, namely, those by Robert Richmond Ellis (2012) and Joan Torres-Pou (2013), which mainly dealt with the construction of Spanish colonial discourse and the tensions between the Spanish representatives of colonial power and Filipino society in José Rizal's novels. However, the part related to the Philippines focuses on a center-periphery relationship that is not so obviously present in the other articles from the same volume, which study the epistemological construction of other Asian nations such as Japan and China. The decadence of Spain as an imperial power, and the orientalization to which it was subjected by other European countries, changed how Spain interacted with Asian countries so that it was no longer a center-periphery dynamic. This situation singularizes and problematizes the relationship of Spain with the Philippines and with the Chinese population in the Philippines, as it allows for breaches in the colonial discourse. The Philippine answer to these breaches will be seen in this book in Cristina Guillén Arnáiz's and Rocío Ortuño Casanova's contributions. The American republics, for their part, would also establish cultural ties with the Philippines and acknowledge some parallel situations in their processes of emancipation and identity construction, as is discussed in the chapters by Ernest Rafael Hartwell and Paula C. Park.

The second emerging field is what has been called the "Global Hispanophone." In his work *The Magellan Fallacy*, Adam Lifshey looks at Spanish-language literature from Asia and Africa. To justify the relationship between countries so far apart in the world, he proposes a series of categories that may serve as an umbrella for them: the term "Hispanophone" being useful to describe "literature in Spanish outside the binarism of Spain and Latin America" (2012, 21). "Global literature in Spanish" is the other notion proposed by Lifshey that "points to conceivable remappings of literature in Spanish not only beyond Latin America and Spain but also beyond Asia and Africa" (21). Seven years later, Adolfo Campoy-Cubillo and Benita Sampedro merged both ideas to draw the foundations of the field (and also its limitations) in their introductory article to the special section "Entering the Global Hispanophone" in the *Journal of Spanish Cultural Studies* (2019). To them, the Global Hispanophone "comes to incorporate the cultures and historical experiences of North Africa, Equatorial Guinea, and the Philippines, among other geographic entities: all territories that were once bound by the Spanish Empire, particularly as it existed beyond Latin America, the Caribbean and the Iberian Peninsula itself" (2019, 1). Although the idea of circulation is present in their introduction, it is not their main focus, and the authors cite volumes that consider the cultural output of the single groups included in their definition of Global Hispanophone. Therefore, they include articles that explore the Sahara, Morocco, the Philippines, Equatorial Guinea, and the Sephardic diaspora, both individually and in terms of their relations with the Iberian Peninsula and Mexico. There is again a special emphasis on the relationship of the territories with the Iberian Peninsula, as colonization constitutes their departure point in linguistic matters and determines the language in which the writings are produced.

Transpacific studies, however, mainly considers postcolonial countries "in which interests revolve around efforts by formerly colonized states to achieve cultural, economic, and political sovereignty in their relation to the Pacific region, both as geographical sites and as a series of commercial, military and cultural routes" (Rowe 2014, 134). Although John Carlos Rowe, in the article from which the abovementioned quotation comes, leaves aside the Philippines, its insertion in the Pacific region, albeit liminal, and the relations that it has established with other cultures around the Pacific (starting with Mexico in 1565 with the Manilla Galleon route) make the Asian country an object of study in Transpacific studies.

In the same fashion, Global South studies would also include relations between the Philippines and Latin America beyond the Pacific, as the term refers to the connections between ex-colonial countries, leaving the old metropolises aside to focus on "relations among subaltern groups across national, linguistic, racial and ethnic lines" (Mahler 2017). This volume engages with all four of these fields (which sometimes overlap) but does not completely fit in any of them. We understand that, beyond the idea of literatures in contact and the study of literary relations, there is an inclination to use the idea of the Global Hispanophone to group cultures bound only by their shared former colonial master. This presents two dangers: contriving nonexistent associations and treating possible cultural relations or similarities as praiseworthy contributions made by colonialism.

If the Global Hispanophone provides us with a sufficiently important academic space to prevent the Philippine written production from remaining an academic niche, the book's place in the previous currents is also the result of the relationships that this production establishes with other cultures outside the Hispanic sphere of influence. In addition, we believe that the studies present in this book open up new comparisons and a new vision of other former Spanish colonies. It is for this reason that we have chosen not to fit the book totally into any of the existing emerging fields but rather to talk about it using a postnational frame.

This is justified and concretized in the transcultural contacts studied in this volume. Luis Castellví Laukamp, for instance, in his chapter approaches how missionary chronicles bear witness to the colonial imposition of Christianity on the islands and reflect the encounters between the preacher and the unknown, which were assimilated as supernatural issues. In her chapter, Ana M. Rodríguez-Rodríguez examines the narrative of confrontations with Muslims in the early days of colonization, which are compared with episodes from the so-called Reconquest of Spain from the Muslims (711–1492). The narratives of confrontations with Muslims in the Philippines would link the country to West Asia. This connection was later highlighted by *modernista* poets in the 20th century. The rewritings of the colonial confrontations also took place from the Philippine side, as can be seen in the chapter by Rocío Ortuño Casanova, who examines how the history of the pirate Limahong, a central figure in the Spanish chronicles on the Philippine conquest, was rewritten by Philippine intellectuals in the 19th and 20th centuries, with an eye on the identification of the Philippines with Asia. This identification implied a search for integration into a community of nations different from the Western colonial powers. The need for integration and the search for a supranational identity connect to the communities of nations proposed by Habermas in the essays of *The Postnational Constellation* and are reflected in several works such as José Rizal's letters, where he looked for the origins of the Philippine peoples in Southeast Asia. Claro M. Recto warned of the economic dangers of such an association for the Philippines in the essay *El monroísmo asiático* (1929), in which he foresaw the asymmetrical relationship that might be established in Asia with Japan as a leading power.

Despite the accounts of colonial relationships, the relationships displayed in the texts were not always asymmetrical. This can be seen in the chapters by Park and Hartwell, for instance, which explore contacts with Latin America as a space for decolonializing inspiration and identification. It is true, though, that such contacts often arose as a result of conflict and violence: even the folkloric texts that Isabelo de los Reyes collected at the end of the 19th century, which are examined by Kristina A. Escondo in her chapter, are connected with the violence of the Philippine Exhibition of 1887 and the urgency of making the Philippines known to the Spanish. De los Reyes, however, took advantage of this conflict to to stress the importance of the culture of the native peoples of the archipelago. One of the traits highlighted was an autochthonous, proto-feminist conception of the role of women in society, as opposed to that imposed by Catholicism, which surfaces in the poems written by de los Reyes's mother, Leona Florentino, translated into Spanish from her native Ilocano. Furthermore, out of the violence of colonization and the cultural clash arose particular narrative forms that escape the input provided by each one of the cultures. It is thus that, in the narratives of the Battle of Manila, examined by Sony Coráñez Bolton and David R. George in their chapters, the violence of the confrontation with the Japanese troops is concretized in hybrid forms of original expression, which ultimately connect with genres that also occur in Latin America and do not fit into traditional literary taxonomies.

This connects with the second objective of the book, which consists of questioning the constraints of traditional literary genres to make place for Philippine texts, and other colonial and postcolonial texts, in the category of literature, so that those texts can be taken into consideration in literary studies. This is the case with writings by authors such as Teodoro M. Kálaw (1884–1940) and Rafael Palma (1874–1939), two of the standard figures in 20th-century school anthologies of Philippine literature in Spanish. None of the books that they wrote or edited would incontestably be considered literature. Neither, probably, would those of Jaime de Veyra, Paz Mendoza Guazón, or Epifanio de los Santos[9] or, from the *ilustrado* generation, those of Isabelo de los Reyes or Marcelo Hilario del Pilar, to give some examples. The repertoire of all of these important Philippine authors comprises biographies, letters, essays, opinion columns, studies and compilations of Philippine folklore, and travel books. These are all genres that, in most cases, have been only considered relevant in the fields of history, anthropology, sociology, or political science. For literary studies they are considered "hybrid," not fitting into any literary genre. They are, however, fundamental to reflect the political and social objective of shaping a national identity under colonial occupation, negotiating its position concerning the colonizer and the rest of the world, and spreading these views among a large audience.

In terms of distinction and the sociology of culture, purely creative and literary texts generally hold a higher place in the literary fields of European metropolises than do those containing a message and an intention that are more than purely literary—that is to say, autotelism and the principle of self-referentiality prevail in the literary field (Sapiro 2016, 38). Accordingly, works with political ends are often relegated to an inferior position on the basis that they depart from the description of the "full and fundamental human experience" (Speller 2013, 18), as was noted by Raymond Williams, who in his classic book *Marxism and Literature* advocates literary texts' capacity for ideological expression and an inclusive definition of literature (Speller 2013, 18). The paradox also lies in the fact that extraliterary forces end up intervening in and conditioning internal conflicts in the field "according to ethical, political or economic criteria to which aesthetic stakes are subordinated" (Sapiro 2016, 38). In the case of Philippine literature, these extraliterary forces were related to colonial imposition and to the reaction to it, which even determined the selection of authors included in the Philippine canon. In the section "Philippine Literature" in the *Encyclopedia of the Cultural Center of the Philippines*, a reference work on Philippine arts, we find that of the 54 writers who produced literature in Spanish included in the work, 21 held political positions and 22 held military positions (Ortuño Casanova 2017). This trend can also be confirmed in the case of the authors whom Kálaw and Palma edited, prefaced, and biographized: Apolinario Mabini, Marcelo H. del Pilar, and Mariano Ponce played prominent military roles in the Philippine Revolution, while José Rizal was an ideologue (although opposed to the armed struggle) and martyr of it. This creates the impression of marginalization within the Philippine literary field of authors who did not openly express a nationalist political intention in their works.

Beyond the forces operative in the formation of the canon, extraliterary forces are another element that encourages the development of one genre or another. The Spanish-language Philippine literature that was produced during the US occupation has developed a dimension of resistance against the Americanization of the country. It implies that at that moment they had to answer the situation with genres that fostered resistance and favored particular strategies of national narration and negotiation regarding the positioning of the country and its relations with others. These genres and strategies were in many cases inherited from the anti-colonial resistance to Spain that the previous generation had undertaken. Some of these national and anti-colonial narrative strategies entailed the recovery of a pre-Hispanic textual corpus that was used to define the nation. Others included the previously discussed affiliation with certain regions in geopolitical equilibria, the collection of inspirational data from other countries to build Philippine modernity, the construction of national heroes and national allegories with which the Philippine people could identify, and the testimonies of abuses of colonial power.

The first of those strategies, namely, recovering pre-Hispanic histories of oral tradition, was Isabelo de los Reyes's great undertaking. He compiled, in addition to the two-volume *Historia de Ilocos*, the masterful *El folk-lore filipino* (1889), whose publication coincided with the 1887 Philippine Exhibition in Madrid. The work unveils popular fictional narratives as well as Spanish translations of some of the poetry written by his mother, Leona Florentino.

El folk-lore filipino is difficult to define in terms of genre. Although folk-lorists have links to anthropologists, the compilation contains historical contextualization and works of fiction and poetry. The case of Adelina Gurrea's *Los cuentos de Juana* is somehow clearer. It was also published in Madrid, 55 years after Isabelo de los Reyes's work. *Los cuentos de Juana* is an anthology woven from Philippine folk stories that ultimately, as with the work of de los Reyes, constitutes a pre-Hispanic Philippine mythological catalog, though it is also a fiction anthology. Kristina A. Escondo's chapter in this volume considers both works, those of Gurrea and de los Reyes, and their role in national construction. Shorter and later works, such as *Leyendas filipinas*, written by Araceli Pons and Leonor Agrava and also published in Spain in 1955, pursued a similar goal.

The essay also underwent major development at the time of the American occupation, with volumes such as *La campaña del Kuomintang* (Kalaw 1928) and *El monroísmo asiático* (Recto 1929) but above all with serialized shorter essays published in the press. Essays, opinion articles, and mixtures of both once more proposed models of relationships with other countries and regions, returning us to the idea of a postnational integration of the Philippines. Serialized essays followed the model of the series of articles that were published in *La solidaridad* in the 19th century, such as the series of six articles on Spain and Japan in the Philippines by Marcelo H. del Pilar, which were compiled (after his death and Philippine independence) in the second volume of his *Escritos* (1970).

T. H. Pardo de Tavera (1916; Gasquet 2021), Mendoza Guazón (1930; Villaescusa-Illán 2018), and Jesús Balmori (Gasquet 2020) compiled experiences in their writings—both their own experiences and those of other travelers who had visited similar destinations—to draft a destiny willed for the Philippines. Magazines and newspapers had a broad didactic and disseminating function that gave immediacy to the impact of what was presented but also allowed a certain evolution of the work that was being developed over a longer period. Accordingly, Balmori's travel impressions (considered in Park's chapter), which were published in 1932 in a narrative form (his journey started in May 1931), changed to become a series of poems from the episode covering his arrival in Mexico. In these poems, Balmori contrasted the expectations of Hispanicity with the Mexican reality as seen through the eyes of the Filipino, disappointed at not finding modernist poets in 1931–32, in a more or less humorous way.

Perhaps one of the most original genres discussed in this book is the abovementioned testimony. Sony Coráñez Bolton investigates the expression of trauma after the Battle of Manila in World War II in José Reyes's book *Terrorismo y Redención*, a work that is quite similar in terms of form and theme to Antonio Pérez de Olaguer's *El terror amarillo en Filipinas*, which is considered in David R. George's chapter. It is also close to the short story "Nuestros últimos cinco días bajo el yugo Nipón," written by Paz Zamora Mascuñana, which had been previously studied by Rocío Ortuño (Zamora Mascuñana 1960; Ortuño Casanova 2018). All these works present a narrative of the self that gives a voice to other historical protagonists. José Reyes does so by interspersing excerpts of interviews, lists, original documents, and poems in a work that is akin to a war scrapbook. Coráñez Bolton describes the genre as "Philippine Testimony": short personal narratives about the traumatic event of Manila's destruction, which sometimes contradict the official version—that is, America's version. This narrative simultaneously describes the trauma and negotiates the clash among three cultures: American, Japanese, and Filipino. Interestingly, poetry, a genre entirely recognized as literary, approaches the same topic in a similar way—that is, from the expression of the self in the first person and a very particular narration that combines the chronicle and the fiction. Two examples of the poetic accounts of World War II in Manila are Guillermo Gómez Windham's poem in *Terrorismo y Redención* and the longer poem *Mi bandera: Poema de la victoria* by José Hernández Gavira (1945). This latter work has an epic tone and draws parallels between World Wars I and II, the Philippine Revolution, and the war fought for Philippine independence between 1898 and 1902.

Poetry is, in fact, sometimes also used as an instrument for other political causes already discussed. Poems such as "Oración al dios Apolo" (Recto 1911), "Mi raza" and "El terror de los mares índicos" (Apóstol 1950), and *De Mactán a Tirad* (Zaragoza Cano 1941) fulfill the function of revisiting the Philippines' history and claiming pre-Hispanic mythologies and heroes in a process of rewriting the Hispanic chronicles. Many of the poetic compilations in Spanish also include poems and even whole sections dedicated to the heroes of the revolution: Rizal, Bonifacio, Aguinaldo, and del Pilar (Hilario 1914; Bernabé 1929; Guerrero 1971; Apóstol 1950). The memory of these heroes and the patriotic inspiration that they trigger are also conveyed in the published biographies about them. In this volume, Ortuño Casanova studies the reevaluation of some chronicles—studied as literature by John D. Blanco, Rodríguez, and Castellví Leukamp—including Cecilio Apóstol's poem "El terror de los mares índicos."

Biographies, travel books, and essay collections alike are genres that have been considered hybrid or frictional, and their inclusion as literature depends on how broadly the word "literature" is defined. However, these genres were selected to communicate the needs and concerns of the region. As Brander states, "Genres are both formed by processes of communication and flow into them" (2017, 17). They are structuring elements of discursive interactions, which are in turn structured by them in the search for a literary solution to circumstances different from those of Europe. The taxonomic and closed system of European genres defined in the 18th century expanded across the world via colonialism. At that time, the indigenous literary forms of the colonized territories that did not fit into European taxonomies were declared "oral literature" and occupied a lesser place in the system (Brander 2017), while colonized subjects ended up imitating and subverting these traditional genres to adapt them to their needs. Therefore, in the Philippines, autochthonous literature takes the form of genres such as *komedya, Senákulo*—widely criticized by Spaniards like Vicente Barrantes (1889)—*sarswela*, and *korido*. The latter is an assimilation of Philippine literary forms to the corrido genre (the Mexican version of romance), which expresses heroic legends of characters who often come from the Hispanic tradition in autochthonous languages. Some examples coming from the Hispanic tradition are the stories of the seven Lara princes or Bernardo Carpio, which are syncretized with traditions of their own. Literary syncretism has become fundamental not only in the history of Philippine literature but also in the conception of the Philippine world and movements, as Reynaldo Ileto (1979) theorizes about the popular narrative used for the first time by Gaspar Aquino de Belén in *Pasyon*. This work, which depicts the death and resurrection of Jesus Christ and is sung uninterrupted for days during Lent and Holy Week, originates, according to Fernando Zialcita, from the uninterrupted chanting sessions that were organized around dead datus (2006). The transformation of the ritual through its adaptation to the imposition of Christianity reflects, according to Ileto (1979), the idea that the Philippine masses have of the revolution as a passage from darkness to light, and it explains some of the great political changes in the archipelago's recent history.

Alongside the hybrid genres of the literary production of the late 19th and early 20th centuries sit genres that are no longer considered hybrids, such as the novel.[10] These convey national allegories and follow the model of the previous enlightened generation. Accordingly, we find novels and plays that contain characters and allegorical stories of the nation but also weave, like biographies, essays, and travel books do, subtle intercultural relationships that are not always necessarily marked by the colonial vertical hierarchy and that sometimes reevaluate the relationships established by the colonizers.

It is therefore relevant to speak of all these works as literary, despite their intentions and especially despite the hybridity of their genre, since this hybridity is inherent to Philippine literature in Spanish, as Marlon James Sales explains in his chapter devoted to translation as a language of Philippine literature in Spanish.

The book is divided into five parts. In the first part, "Transnational Grounds of Philippine Literature in Spanish," the authors propose a redefinition of Philippine literature in line with its origins, the language in which it developed, and the affiliations it created. This part also puts forward theoretical questions such as the literary nature of the missionary chronicles, their fit as Philippine literature, the name that this literature should be given, and their role within the so-called *hispanidad*, establishing certain bases that summarize and challenge some previous ideas about the topic scattered in works such as *Hispanofilia filipina* (Fernández Lumba 1981) and *Literatura hispanofilipina actual* (Donoso and Gallo 2011).

The second part, "The (Re)Conquest of History," offers a literary approach to three ethnic groups in the Philippines: Tagalogs, Chinese, and Muslims. This approach involves a twofold perspective: all three chapters have the Spanish chronicles on the Philippines as their departure point. In Ana Rodríguez's chapter, the Spanish chronicles on the conquests of Mindanao and Sulu compare confrontations with Philippine Muslims with other accounts of Christian crusades against Islam, in an attempt to distance the experience of the "Philippine Moors" from the paradigms of Andalusian Muslims and Ottomans. In doing so, the Philippine chronicles propose new ways of approaching Islam.

In their chapters, Luis Castellví Leukamp and Rocío Ortuño Casanova approach texts written by Filipinos in the 19th and the 20th centuries, which reevaluate some chronicles of Spanish confrontations with Tagalogs and Chinese. These texts converge in the intention of *reconquering* history, a process described by Christopher Schmidt-Nowara (2006) in which he includes the annotated edition done by José Rizal of the chronicles on the Philippines, written originally by Antonio de Morga in the 17th century (Morga and Rizal 1890). Both this work and the Philippine texts studied imply processes of negotiation, assimilation, reassessment, and historical updating that suppose an appropriation of Philippine historical accounts written by others.

The third part, "Modernity and Globalization," is based on the passage to modernity and Philippine identity within this modernity. Kristina A. Escondo's work introduces two texts that seek to highlight Philippine folklore in a tumultuous time of change, reaffirming an individuality that in both cases opposes movements demanding the appropriation of the archipelago by the Spanish government. Isabelo de los Reyes's *El folk-lore filipino* was published at the end of the 19th century. At that time, Spain had decided to reevaluate its activities in the Philippines and intended a commercial turn for the colonization. This came together with a propaganda campaign in Spain to spread knowledge of the Asian archipelago. The Philippine Exhibition of 1887 in Madrid, together with the many publications on the Philippines that it spawned, sought to make the territory known to new investors. In the 1940s, when *Cuentos de Juana*, the second text studied by Escondo, was published, the Spanish Fascist Party "Falange" had just been included in Spain's dictatorial regime after the Spanish Civil War (1936–39). Among its claims was the country's "imperial vocation." The problem was that, in reality, most of the regions that the old Spanish Empire comprised were at that time republics opposed to the fascist regime of dictator Francisco Franco, which most of the Philippine Spanish-speaking intelligentsia supported. The need of ties with the old colonies led to a renewed visibility of the Philippines in the Spanish press, literature, and film, partly driven by institutions (Ortuño Casanova 2021). The stories told in those media were used to reinforce the so-called *white legend*, which lauded the beneficial influence that colonialization had had on the archipelago. In the face of both situations and as a reaction to them, the folkloric texts asserted the prevalence of a pre-Hispanic Philippine identity, leading the country outside the Hispanic orbit. The chapter by meLê yamomo, on the other hand, offers the opposite point of view, asserting the metropolitan modernity of the Philippines in the late 20th century, along with the assimilation of colonial sounds.

The fourth part of the book, "Anti-Colonial Writings in the Colonial Language," includes two chapters on writings that use colonial language for an anti-colonial discourse. Cristina Guillén Arnáiz's chapter studies the humorous chronicle of the trip taken by the Filipino Antonio Luna to Madrid, which caricatures the colonial chronicles through subversion of them, and Ernest Rafael Hartwell explores the late 19th-century anti-colonial networks involving the Philippines and the Caribbean from a biopolitical point of view, focusing on common stylistic resources for describing immigrants.

The last part, "Narratives of the Self and World War II," considers two examples of narratives of the self that address, through the overlapping of genres, the trauma of experiencing the Japanese invasion and the Battle of

Manila. David R. George inquires about the life of Antonio Pérez de Olaguer, a Barcelona native of Filipino descent who took multiple trips to the archipelago in search of his origins. Pérez de Olaguer described this process in autobiographical texts such as *Hospital de San Lázaro, Mi vuelta al mundo,* and *El terror amarillo en Filipinas,* the text that narrates the painful experience of the Battle of Manila in World War II. Sony Coráñez Bolton examines the testimony of the same event written by José Reyes in a book that is related to testimonial literature in Latin America, whose location between reality and fiction is still debated.

   In total, this book contains 12 chapters that elaborate on the abovementioned problems surrounding the cultural and identity relations of the Philippines with other regions and the literary nature of Philippine texts. These problems are applicable to other postcolonial nations; therefore, these chapters are key to understanding literature as a fluctuation and negotiation of borders and identity outside the Western (ex-)colonialist powers.

Notes

   1. References to the anniversary of the circumnavigation in the Portuguese press only mention Magellan as head of the expedition. We can find examples on Portuguese official sites such as the Cultural Commission of the Portuguese Marine website, which titles the special reporting of the event "A volta ao mundo de Magalhães" (Comissão Cultural de Marinha 2019), or on the website dedicated to the fifth centennial of the circumnavigation in Portugal, titled "500 years: Magellan's Circumnavigation" (Missão do V Centenário da Primeira Viagem de Circum-Navegação 2019), as well as in the newspapers (Garcia 2020). Meanwhile, official sites in Spain tend to talk about the circumnavigation without mentioning any protagonists, as is the case with their website on the fifth centennial of the circumnavigation (2019) and the exhibition devoted to the event in Seville, which is introduced by a quote from a letter by Juan Sebastián Elcano (https://www.espacioprimeravue ltaalmundo.org/la-primera-vuelta-al-mundo-1519-1522/). Spanish media, however, either includes both names, Elcano and Magellan, in the articles on the ephemerid as initially agreed on by both countries ("El V Centenario de la primera vuelta al mundo, a debate" 2019; Fernández 2019; Astolfi 2021; Alonso 2019) or drops Magellan, just leaving Elcano (Soler Quintana 2021). Neither Portuguese nor Spanish sites mention Henry of Malacca.
   2. Since 2003, Spanish-Filipino Friendship Day has been celebrated every year on June 30, the anniversary of the release of some soldiers who had gotten trapped in a church in Baler during the Philippine revolution of 1898 and who had refused to recognize the end of the war. The cultural products commemorating this event seem to be endless: two films, at least one documentary, a very long list of literary and scholarly books, and a statue devoted to the Spanish soldiers erected in Madrid in 2020 (de la Cruz 2021).
   3. Three events exemplify this dissent against the efforts of European official voices. The first was promoted by the Philippine Embassy in Madrid, which produced a video

based on the illustrated book *First Around the Globe: The Story of Enrique* and organized online debates to explore the idea that the slave was a Filipino (Roxas and Singer 1997; Philippine Embassy in Madrid 2020). The second event was an online conference called "Contacts & Continuities: 500 Years of Asian-Iberian Encounters," organized by Ateneo de Manila University in cooperation with Centro de Humanidades of the Universidade Nova de Lisboa, in Portugal, and the National Historical Commission of the Philippines. Despite the title and description of the conference, which marked a certain continuity with a first meeting organized in Lisbon, the organization subverted its initial image by carefully choosing the participants, who included keynote speakers highly critical of the colonial discourses on the Philippines, such as Vicente Rafael and Ambeth Ocampo. In this way, the talks moved away from the well-worn Eurocentric paths that often conclude with the idea that the European invasion was beneficial for the colonized peoples. At the same time, a virtual festival called the "Henry of Malacca Virtual Festival" was organized. There, planners screened the work *Black Henry* by Luis Francia and exchanged views with filmmakers who had made films about this character, such as Pedro Palma, director of *Henry of Malacca: A Malay and Magellan* (2020); and Kidlat Tahimik, director and protagonist of *Memories of Overdevelopment: A Film Sketch on Henry of Malacca* (1984). Tahimik is also the protagonist of the third event in question, no longer as a filmmaker but as a conceptual artist. In January 2021 he presented his installation "Magellan, Marilyn, Mickey and Friar Damaso: 500 years of RockStar conquerors" at the Crystal Palace of Retiro Park in Madrid (Tahimik 2021). The installation was an ironic criticism of the "civilization" brought by colonialism—a vindication of precolonial culture and, of course, of the figure of Enrique de Malacca, but also the reappropriation of a symbolic space of colonialism: the Crystal Palace had been built in 1887 as the setting for a large colonial exhibition on the Philippines in which native people were exhibited as if in a human zoo.

　　4. As an example, he attributes the arrival of modernism in the Philippines to the visit of the Spanish poet Salvador Rueda to the archipelago in 1915, ignoring the fact that in 1899 poems by Rubén Darío and other Latin American modernists were being published in the magazine *Libertas* of the University of Santo Tomás or that in 1908 there was a modernist literary magazine that detailed the different variants of Latin American *modernismo* called *Domus Aurea*.

　　5. When not using the more neutral "Philippine Literature in Spanish," we follow here Wystan de la Peña's nomenclature (2011), which in Spanish would translate as "Literatura hispanofilipina."

　　6. See the article "Panasiatismo y resistencia al discurso occidental en la literatura filipina en español" for more information on the interest of José Rizal and other Filipino intellectuals in finding connections with other Asian countries (Ortuño Casanova 2021, 12).

　　7. Mary Louise Pratt defines the *contact zone* as "social spaces where cultures meet, clash, and grapple with each other, often in contexts of highly asymmetrical relations of power, such as colonialism, slavery, or their aftermath" (1991, 34).

　　8. The article begins by saying: "Nations consist of those who belong together by birth (genetically, lineally, through familially inherited language and culture). States consist of those who are fully subject to their own sovereign legal authority. A true nation-state, therefore, would consist only of those who belonged to it by birth and of those who were

fully subject to its sovereign legal authority. By this . . . criterion it is unlikely that there is a single nation-state in the world at present, and moderately unlikely that any such state has ever existed" (Dunn 1994, 3).

9. Jaime de Veyra wrote short historical essays like *¿Quién fue Urduja?* (1951) and miscellaneous books like *Efemérides filipinas* (1914), collecting opinion columns, stories, and historical narrative pieces written with Mariano Ponce, and edited other books such as *Pentélicas*, the poem compilation by Cecilio Apóstol (1950). Mendoza Guazón published, besides her travelogue *Notas de viaje* (1930), bilingual essays on the situation of women in the Philippines such as *My Ideal Filipino Girl* (1931) and contributions to newspapers. Epifanio de los Santos, like de Veyra, published a book of miscellany titled *Algo de prosa* (1909), which contained some narratives, poetic prose, and essays, as well as some biographies of relevant Filipino characters.

10. Ottmar Ette recalls that the novel, before becoming consolidated as a literary genre, was considered a hybrid, owing to the mixture of genres and languages that it could contain (2008).

References

Anderson, Benedict. 1997. "First Filipino." In *The Spectre of Comparisons: Nationalism, Southeast Asia and the World*. London: Verso Books.

Apóstol, Cecilio. 1950. *Pentélicas: (poesías)*. Manila: Editorial Hispano-Filipina.

Astolfi, Belén. 2021. "La ruta 'Magallanes-Elcano': La unión de cinco autonomías por los 500 años de la primera vuelta al mundo." *SER*. Radio Bilbao. Economía y negocios. 20 May. https://cadenaser.com/emisora/2021/05/20/radio_bilbao/1621526393_844857.html

Barrantes, Vicente. 1889. *El Teatro Tagalo*. Madrid: Tip. de Manuel G. Hernández.

Beredo, Cheryl. 2011. "Import of the Archive: American Colonial Bureaucracy in the Philippines, 1898–1916." PhD diss., University of Hawai'i at Manoa, Honolulu. http://scholarspace.manoa.hawaii.edu/handle/10125/101724

Beredo, Cheryl. 2013. *Import of the Archive: U.S. Colonial Rule of the Philippines and the Making of American Archival History*. Sacramento: Litwin Books.

Berman, Marshall. [1982] 2010. *All That Is Solid Melts into Air: The Experience of Modernity*. London: Verso Books.

Bernabé, Manuel. 1929. *Cantos del trópico: poesías*. Manila: San Juan Press.

Blair, Emma Helen, and James Alexander Robertson. 1903. *The Philippine Islands, 1493–1898: Explorations by Early Navigators, Descriptions of the Islands and Their Peoples, Their History and Records of the Catholic Missions, as Related in Contemporaneous Books and Manuscripts, Showing the Political, Economic, Commercial and Religious Conditions of Those Islands from Their Earliest Relations with European Nations to the Beginning of the Nineteenth Century*. Cleveland, OH: Arthur H. Clark Company.

Brander, Miriam Lay. 2017. *Genre and Globalization: Transformación de géneros en contextos*. Hildesheim: Olms Georg.

Cabañero, Angelica A., and Filomena Mercado Tann. 1980. "Libraries and Librarianship in the Philippines." *IFLA Journal* 6 (2): 81–95. https://doi.org/10.1177/034003528000600202

Campoy Cubillo, Adolfo, and Benita Sampedro. 2019. "Entering the Global Hispanophone:

An Introduction." *Journal of Spanish Cultural Studies* 20 (1–2): 1–16. https://doi.org /10.1080/14636204.2019.1609212

Cano, Glòria. 2008. "Blair and Robertson's 'The Philippine Islands, 1493–1898': Scholarship or Imperialist Propaganda?" *Philippine Studies* 56 (1): 3–46.

Castany Prado, Bernat. 2007. *Literatura posnacional*. Murcia: Universidad de Murcia.

Caulín Martínez, Antonio. 1993. "Wenceslao E. Retana y la historia de Filipinas." *Espacio Tiempo y Forma. Serie V, Historia Contemporánea*, no. 6. https://doi.org/10.5944/etfv .6.1993.2860

Comissão Cultural de Marinha. 2019. "A volta ao mundo de Magalhães." 5 April. https:// ccm.marinha.pt/pt/multimedia_web/Paginas/a-volta-ao-mundo-de-magalhaes.aspx

Cullinane, Michael. 2003. *Ilustrado Politics: Filipino Elite Responses to American Rule, 1898–1908*. Quezon City: Ateneo University Press.

De la Cruz, Luis. 2020. "Lo que el monumento a los últimos de Filipinas nos cuenta del nuevo nacionalismo español." *El diario*. 24 January. https://www.eldiario.es/madrid /somos/chamberi/monumento-ultimos-filipinas-cuenta-nuevo-nacionalismo-espan ol_1_6407746.html

De la Peña, Wystan. 2011. "Revisiting the Golden Age of Fil-Hispanic Literature (1898–1941)." Pilipinas muna! Филиппины прежде всего! К 80-летию Геннадия Евгеньевича Рачкова. (Pilipinas muna! Filipinas First: Essays in honor of Gennady Paton Rachkova's 80th anniversary), 119–27. Saint Petersburg: MAE (Maklaevsky collection, vol. 4). https://www.kunstkamera.ru/files/lib/978-5-88431-174-9/978-5-884 31-174-9_08.pdf

De los Santos Cristóbal, Epifanio. 1909. *Algo de prosa*. Madrid: Imprenta de Fortanet.

Donoso, Isaac, and Andrea Gallo. 2011. *Literatura hispanofilipina actual*. Madrid: Verbum.

Dunn, John. 1994. "Introduction: Crisis of the Nation State?" *Political Studies* 42 (August 1): 3–15. https://doi.org/10.1111/j.1467-9248.1994.tb00002.x

"El V Centenario de la primera vuelta al mundo, a debate." 2019. El cultural. *El español*. 29 July. https://www.elespanol.com/el-cultural/opinion/dardos/20190729/centenario-pr imera-vuelta-mundo-debate/417459714_0.html

Ellis, Robert Richmond. 2012. *They Need Nothing: Hispanic-Asian Encounters of the Colonial Period*. Toronto: University of Toronto Press.

Ette, Ottmar. 2008. *Literatura en movimiento: Espacio y dinámica de una escritura transgresora de fronteras en Europa y América*. Madrid: Consejo Superior de Investigaciones Científicas.

Fernández, Alba. 2019. "La primera vuelta al mundo." *La vanguardia*. 23 September. https://www.lavanguardia.com/vida/junior-report/20190923/47499876632/primera -vuelta-mundo.html

Fernández Lumba, Enrique. 1981. *Hispanofilia filipina*. S.l.: s.n.

Flores, Roana Marie L. 2020. "Intellectual Jewels of the Nation: An Exploratory Study of Filipiniana Special Materials." *Journal of the Australian Library and Information Association* 69 (3): 375–89. https://doi.org/10.1080/24750158.2020.1782037

Garcia, José Manuel. 2020. "Fernão de Magalhães e o seu legado." *Diário de Tras-os-Montes*. 21 October. https://www.diariodetrasosmontes.com/reportagem/fernao-de -magalhaes-e-o-seu-legado

Gasquet, Axel. 2020. "Filipino Poet Jesús Balmori: Testimonials of His Mexican Journey

Passing through Japan (1932–1934)." In Jie Lu and Martin Camps, eds., *Transpacific Literary and Cultural Connections*, 45–66. Historical and Cultural Interconnections between Latin America and Asia Series. Cham: Palgrave Macmillan. https://doi.org /10.1007/978-3-030-55773-7_3

Gasquet, Axel. 2021. "The Peripheral Spanish World in the Antipodes: The Filipino T. H. Pardo de Tavera in the Centennial Argentina." In Axel Gasquet and Gorica Majstorovic, eds., *Cultural and Literary Dialogues between Asia and Latin America*, 187–207. Historical and Cultural Interconnections between Latin America and Asia Series. Cham: Palgrave Macmillan. https://doi.org/10.1007/978-3-030-52571-2_12

Glissant, Édouard. 1997. *Poetics of Relation*. Translated by Betsy Wing. Ann Arbor: University of Michigan Press.

Gómez Carrillo, Enrique. 1924. *De Marsella á Tokio: sensaciones de Egipto, la India, la China y el Japón*. Paris: Garnier.

Guerrero, Fernando María. 1971. *Aves y Flores, poesias*. Manila: Fil. Hispanas.

Guzmán, Gloria de, and Paulina Pannen. 2004. "The Wonder of Filipiniana." *Jurnal Pendidikan* 5 (2): 120–44.

Habermas, Jürgen. 1998. *The Postnational Constellation*. Edited and translated by Max Pensky. New York: John Wiley & Sons.

Hau, Caroline S. 2017. *Elites and Ilustrados in Philippine Culture*. Quezon City: Ateneo de Manila University Press.

Hernández, Vicente S. 2001. "Trends in Philippine Library History." *Libraries & Culture* 36 (2): 329–44.

Hernández Gavira, J. 1945. *Mi bandera. Poema de la victoria*. Manila: Bureau of Printing.

Hilario, Zoilo J. 1914. *Patria y redencion: poesias*. Manila: Imp. y Lit. de Juan Fajardo.

Ileto, Reynaldo Clemeña. 1979. *Pasyon and Revolution: Popular Movements in the Philippines, 1840–1910*. Quezon City: Ateneo de Manila University Press.

Kalaw, Teodoro M. 1908. *Hacia la tierra del zar: a traves de un viaje rapido. Paisajes e impresiones*. Manila: Libreria "Manila Filatelica."

Kalaw, Teodoro M. 1928. *La Campaña del Kuomintang*. Manila: La Opinion.

Kalaw, Teodoro M. 1930. *Gregorio H. Del Pilar (El Héroe de Tirad)*. Documentos de La Biblioteca Nacional de Filipinas. No. 2. Manila: Bureau of Printing. https://catalog.hat hitrust.org/Record/001871063

Kalaw, Teodoro M. 1932. *Mariano Ponce: Cartas Sobre La Revolución, 1897–1900*. Manila: Bureau of Printing.

Kim, Yeon-Soo, and Kathleen E. Davies. 2014. "Claiming a Space for Spanish Asian Studies." *Arizona Journal of Hispanic Cultural Studies* 18:199–210. https://www.jstor.org /stable/24877957

Le Bris, Michel, Jean Rouaud, and Eva Almassy. 2007. *Pour une littérature-monde*. Paris: Gallimard.

Lifshey, Adam. 2012. *The Magellan Fallacy*. Ann Arbor: University of Michigan Press.

Lifshey, Adam. 2015. *Subversions of the American Century*. Ann Arbor: University of Michigan Press.

Lumbera, Bienvenido, and Cynthia Nograles Lumbera, eds. 1982. *Philippine Literature: A History & Anthology*. Manila: National Book Store.

Mabini, Apolinario. 1930. *Las Cartas Politicas de Apolinario Mabini: Con Prologo y Notas*. Edited by Teodoro M. Kalaw. Manila: Dia Filipino Press.

Mabini, Apolinario. 1931. *La Revolución Filipina (Con Otros Documentos de La Época)*. Edited by Teodoro M. Kalaw. 2 vols. Manila: Bureau of Printing.

Mahler, Anne Garland. 2017. "Global South." In *Literary and Critical Theory*. October 25. Oxford Bibliographies. https://doi.org/10.1093/OBO/9780190221911-0055

Mariñas, Luis. 1974. *La literatura filipina en castellano*. Madrid: Editora Nacional.

Martínez-San Miguel, Yolanda. 2014. *Coloniality of Diasporas: Rethinking Intra-Colonial Migrations in a Pan-Caribbean Context*. New York: Palgrave.

Mendoza Guazón, María Paz. 1930. *Notas de viaje*. Manila: Benipayo Press.

Mendoza Guazón, María Paz. 1931. *My Ideal Filipino Girl*. Manila: College of Medicine.

Missão do V Centenário da Primeira Viagem de Circum-Navegação. 2019. "500 Years: Magellan's Circumnavigation." https://magalhaes500.pt

Mojares, Resil B. 1979. *The Origins and Rise of the Filipino Novel: A Generic Study of the Filipino Novel, until 1940*. Quezon City: University of the Philippines.

Mojares, Resil B. 2006. *Brains of the Nation: Pedro Paterno, T. H. Pardo de Tavera, Isabelo de Los Reyes, and the Production of Modern Knowledge*. Quezon City: Ateneo de Manila University Press.

Mojarro, Jorge. 2019. "'Teodoro Kalaw lee a Gómez Carrillo: *Hacia la tierra del Zar* (1908), un ejemplo de crónica modernista filipina." *UNITAS* 92 (1): 229–55.

Morga, Antonio de, and José Rizal. 1890. *Sucesos de las islas Filipinas por el doctor Antonio de Morga: obra publicada en Méjico el año de 1609*. Paris: Garnier hermanos. http://archive.org/details/ahz9387.0001.001.umich.edu

Nuchera, Patricio Hidalgo, and Félix Muradás García. 2000. "Guía bibliográfica para la historia de las islas Filipinas, 1565–1898." *Anuario de Estudios Americanos* 57 (2): 677–711. https://doi.org/10.3989/aeamer.2000.v57.i2.252

Ortuño Casanova, Rocío. 2017. "Philippine Literature in Spanish: Canon Away from Canon." *Iberoromania*, no. 85: 58–77.

Ortuño Casanova, Rocío. 2018. "Los sonidos de la II Guerra Mundial en Manila: Ruido y autorrepresentación en *Nuestros cinco últimos días bajo el yugo nipón*, de María Paz Zamora Mascuñana." In "Literatura hispanofilipina," edited by Jorge Mojarro, special issue, *Revista de Crítica Literaria Latinoamericana* 44 (88): 291–314.

Ortuño Casanova, Rocío. 2021. "Panasiatismo y resistencia al discurso occidental en la literatura filipina en español: China como 'Asia por antonomasia' a lo largo de dos colonizaciones." *Revista de estudios hispánicos*, no. 55: 1–26.

Palma, Pedro, dir. 2020. *Henry de Malacca: A Malay and Magellan*. Foundation Yayasan DMDI. 1 hr., 7 min.

Palma, Rafael. 1929. *Nuestra Historia*. Manila: Bureau of Printing.

Palma, Rafael. 1931. *Apolinario Mabini (estudio biográfico)*. Manila: Bureau of Printing.

Palma, Rafael. 1949. *Biografía de Rizal*. Documentos de La Oficina de Bibliotecas Públicas, no. 15. Manila: Bureau of Printing. https://catalog.hathitrust.org/Record/001256927

Palma, Rafael. 1968. *Historia de Filipinas*. Quezon City: University of the Philippines Press.

Pardo de Tavera, Trinidad H. 1903. *Biblioteca Filipina ó sea Catálogo razonado de todos los impresos, tanto insulares como extranjeros, relativos a la historia, la etnografía, la lingüística, la botánica, la fauna, la flora, la geología, la hidrografía, la geografía, la legislación . . . , de las islas Filipinas, de Joló y Marinas*. Washington, DC: Library of Congress.

Pardo de Tavera, Trinidad H. 1916. "Recuerdos de Argentina." *Philippine Review/Revista Filipina*, Manila, 1 (2): 42–59.

Park, Paula C. 2022. *Intercolonial Intimacies: Rethinking Latin/o America to the Philippines, 1898–1964*. Pittsburgh: University of Pittsburgh Press.

Philippine Embassy in Madrid. 2020. "Reimagining Enrique de Malacca: Inspiring Historical Fiction Beyond the First Encounter." *Youtube*. Online discussion. Filmed on 31 October. Video, 2:02:36. https://youtu.be/23W69O5PckE

Pilar, Marcelo Hilario del. 1970. *Escritos de Marcelo H. del Pilar*. Edited by Angelita Licunanan de Malones and Jaime Manzano. Vol. 2. Manila: Publicaciones de La Biblioteca Nacional.

Pons, Araceli, and Leonor Agrava. 1955. *Leyendas filipinas*. Madrid: Dosan.

Pratt, Mary Louise. 1991. "Arts of the Contact Zone." *Profession*, 33–40.

Punzalan, Ricardo L. 2006. "Archives of the New Possession: Spanish Colonial Records and the American Creation of a 'National' Archives for the Philippines." *Archival Science* 6 (3): 381–92. https://doi.org/10.1007/s10502-007-9040-z

Rafael, Vicente L. 2016. "Contingency and Comparison: Recalling Benedict Anderson." *Philippine Studies: Historical & Ethnographic Viewpoints* 64 (1): 135–44.

Recto, Claro M. 1911. *Bajo los cocoteros: Almas y panoramas*. Manila: Libreria Manila Filatélica.

Recto, Claro M. 1929. *El monroísmo asiático: (artículos de polémica) y otros ensayos*. Manila: Impr. de Juan Fajardo.

Retana, Wenceslao Emilio. 1895. *Archivo del Bibliófilo Filipino. Recopilación de documentos históricos, científicos, literarios y polítcos, y estudios bibliográficos. tom. 1–5*. Madrid: Minuesa de los Rios.

Rizal, José. 1930. *Epistolario Rizalino*. Documentos de La Biblioteca Nacional de Filipinas. Manila: Bureau of Printing. https://catalog.hathitrust.org/Record/006301766

Roma-Sianturi, Dinah. 2009. "'Pedagogic Invasion': The Thomasites in Occupied Philippines." *Kritika Kultura*, no. 12: 5–26. https://doi.org/10.13185/1487

Rowe, John Carlos. 2014. "Transpacific Studies and the Cultures of U.S. Imperialism." In *Transpacific Studies: Framing an Emerging Field*, edited by Janet Hoskins and Viet Thanh Nguyen. University of Hawai'i Press, 134–50. http://www.jstor.org/stable/j.ct vsrfx0.9

Roxas, Reni, and Marc Singer. 1997. *First Around the Globe: The Story of Enrique*. Makati: Tahanan cop.

Sales, Marlon James. 2014. "Translating 'Asia' in Philippine Missionary-Colonial Texts." *Anais de História de Além-Mar* 15:171–95.

Saniel, Isidoro. 1972. "Forty-Nine Years of the Philippine Library Association." *Journal of Library History (1966–1972)* 7 (4): 301–12.

Sapiro, Gisele. 2016. *La sociología de la literatura*. Translated by Laura Fólica. Buenos Aires: Fondo de Cultura Económica.

Schmidt-Nowara, Christopher. 2006. *The Conquest of History: Spanish Colonialism and National Histories in the Nineteenth Century*. Pittsburgh: University of Pittsburgh Press.

Schumacher, John N. 1973. *The Propaganda Movement 1880–1895*. Manila: Solidaridad.

Soler Quintana, Isabel. 2021. "La vuelta al mundo de Elcano empieza hoy con dos pájaros muertos." *El País*. Cultura. 21 December. https://elpais.com/cultura/2021-12-21/la-vu elta-al-mundo-de-elcano-empieza-hoy-con-dos-pajaros-muertos.html

Speller, John R. W. 2013. "5. Literature and Cultural Politics." In *Bourdieu and Literature*, 131–51. OBP Collection. Cambridge: Open Book Publishers. http://books.openediti on.org/obp/484

Stoler, Ann Laura. 2009. *Along the Archival Grain: Thinking through Colonial Ontologies*. Princeton: Princeton University Press.

Tahimik, Kidlat. 1984. *Memories of Overdevelopment: A Film Sketch on Enrique de Malacca*. Self-funded. 33 min.

Tahimik, Kidlat. 2021. *Magallanes, Marilyn, Mickey y fray Dámaso. 500 años de conquistadores RockStar*. Edited by Museo Nacional de Arte Reina Sofía. Madrid. Exhibition dossier. Accessed 4 March 2022. https://www.museoreinasofia.es/sites/default/files /dossier_kidlat_tahimik_0.pdf

Thomas, Megan Christine. 2012. *Orientalists, Propagandists, and Ilustrados: Filipino Scholarship and the End of Spanish Colonialism*. Minneapolis: University of Minnesota Press.

Torres-Pou, Joan. 2013. *Asia en la España del siglo XIX: Literatos, viajeros, intelectuales y Diplomáticos ante Oriente*. Amsterdam: Rodopi.

Veyra, Jaime C. de. 1914. *Efemérides filipinas*. Manila: Imp. y librería de I. R. Morales.

Veyra, Jaime C. de. 1951. *¿Quién fué Urduja?: Urduja, un ser mitológico, estudio histórico*. Manila: Nueva Era.

Villaescusa-Illán, Irene. 2018. "Un paseo por la modernidad: Reflexiones de Paz Mendoza en sus *Notas de viaje* (1929)." In "Literatura hispanofilipina" edited by Jorge Mojarro, special issue, *Revista de Crítica Literaria Latinoamericana*, 44 (88): 267–290.

Villaescusa-Illán, Irene. 2020. *Transcultural Nationalism in Hispano-Filipino Literature*. Historical and Cultural Interconnections between Latin America and Asia Series. London: Palgrave Macmillan. https://doi.org/10.1007/978-3-030-51599-7

VV.AA. *Encyclopedia of the Cultural Center of the Philippines*. Vol. IX. Manila: CCP.

Wickberg, Edgar B. 1955. "Spanish Records in the Philippine National Archives." *Hispanic American Historical Review* 35 (1): 77–89. https://doi.org/10.2307/2509252

Williams, Raymond. 1977. *Marxism and Literature*. Oxford: Oxford University Press.

Zamora Mascuñana, María Paz. 1960. "Nuestros cinco últimos días bajo el yugo nipón." *Cuentos cortos 1919–1923 y recuerdos de la liberación 1945*. n.p.

Zaragoza Cano, Flavio. 1941. *De Mactán á Tirad (Lapolapo Bañgotbanua y del Pilar): Poema épico histórico*. Manila: Kanlaon Print. Press. http://books.google.com/books ?id=as7RAAAAMAAJ

Zialcita, Fernando N. 2005. *Authentic Though Not Exotic: Essays on Filipino Identity*. Quezon City: Ateneo de Manila University Press.

PART I

Transnational Grounds of Philippine Literature in Spanish

The Prose of Pacification and "Spiritual Conquest" at the Origins of Philippine Literature in Spanish

John D. Blanco

If we were to identify something like the origins of Philippine literature in Spanish, one would need to look no further than the voluminous tomes of self-congratulatory rhetoric written by the missionary orders from the beginning of the 17th century.[1] While depending heavily on the language of theology and Scholastic philosophy, missionary chronicles belong to neither field of knowledge and writing; and, despite the fact that the writings record factual events and testimonies around those events, even later missionaries do not find them useful.[2] Excluded from the canons of theology, philosophy, history, and anthropology, these writings inhabit a kind of discursive netherworld. Is it possible, however, that their blurred outlines perhaps reflect both the fiction and the reality of Spanish colonialism better than any historical study? For in the place of historical fact or philosophical or theological truth, the baroque turns of these chronicles and reports ceaselessly invoke the phantasmagorias of a legal, political, and social order that either never arrived, never finished arriving, or had arrived and stayed for only a short time before leaving. Why do we remain reluctant to recognize these as fictions? And what do their shortcomings and failures tell us about the historical and cultural realities they distort?

Considering further the disavowal and abandonment of these texts by even the orders that were responsible for commissioning them, one might argue that these works remain among the greatest Filipino cultural treasures of the colonial past, bearing witness to the enigmas surrounding the role that the early Spanish colonial past has played in the constitution of the present (see Joaquin 2004, 52). Acknowledging this, however, would entail not only a critical literary study of the symbols, analogies, metaphors, and phantasmagorias that constitute their rhetoric but also a genealogy or counter-history of the events they pretend to describe and narrate (52).[3] This chapter contributes to both tasks by analyzing the discourse of *pacification* and the stakes in promoting a *spiritual conquest* in the Philippines in these texts, both of which not only have had a profound, distorting effect on Philippine historiography but also have exercised a major influence in Philippine Catholicism and religious culture in general.

From Conquest to the Discourse of Pacification

Any study of literary fiction should take into account the historical context in which it was written. But what if the historical context itself remains unknown, contested, or overdetermined by other concerns? In one of his well-known essays on historiography, Philippine historian Reynaldo Ileto exposed the narration of "linear histories" to "a progressivist outlook such as the Judeo-Christian concept of man working out the Divine Plan over time, or the notion of man's perfectibility" (1993, 100). The writing of history, Ileto concluded, "should throw into focus a whole range of phenomena that have been discredited or denied a history. It should have a conception of historical beginnings as lowly, complex, and contingent. It should give equal status to interruptions, repetitions, and reversals, uncovering the subjugations, confrontations, power struggles and resistances that linear history tends to conceal" (125).[4]

The "Judeo-Christian concept of man working out the Divine Plan over time" provides a point of entry into a critical perspective of the missionary chronicles as willful or perhaps wishful histories, whose objectives included the installation and perpetuation of a general fiction: the fiction or myth of the (Spanish) conquest itself. Matthew Restall's *Seven Myths of the Spanish Conquest*, drawing on the historiography of Edmundo O'Gorman and others, exposes the content of this myth in the Americas, highlighting the stakes of explorers, conquistadors, missionaries, and colonial bureaucrats alike in promoting a "myth of completion" through a narrative in which the colonization of the Americas has supposedly taken place (2004, 65–76). This myth portrayed the conquest as both a contract fulfilled between Christopher Columbus and the king, on the one hand, and the manifestation of divine providence under Catholic Spain, on the other.[5] In contrast to this myth, Restall argues:

The Conquest of the core areas of the Andes and Mesoamerica was more *protracted* than Spaniards initially claimed and later believed, and when warfare did end in these areas it was simply displaced out to the ever-widening and never-peaceful frontiers of Spanish America. Conquest violence was also displaced internally, taking on myriad forms of domination and repression, but met continually by an equally diverse set of methods of native resistance. The spiritual and cultural conquests were equally complex and protracted, defying completion to the point of rendering the very concept of completion irrelevant. (75)

Can Restall's thesis serve as a model for understanding early Philippine history? While a full account of the protracted nature of the conquest of the Philippines is only being written today, anecdotal evidence and regional histories all seem to suggest that the constitution of the Philippines as a "frontier" outpost of Spanish rule looked remarkably similar to the frontier zones of northern Mexico and Alta California, the pastoral landscapes of the Southern Cone of Latin America, and even the Amazonian rainforest.[6] As for the immediate aftermath of the conquest, the Philippines experienced depopulation and mortality rates that, while not proportional to the precipitous decline in the Americas (currently estimated at 95 percent, which made up approximately 10 percent of the world population), still amounted to a death toll of about one-third of the pre-Hispanic population overall.[7] Early reports of the conquest by Augustinian priests like Frs. Diego de Herrera, OSA, and Martín de Rada echoed the same atrocities and acts of impunity on the natives that took place in the Americas, as documented by Fr. Bartolomé de Las Casas and others (see Herrera 2006, 34:229–35; Rada 1906, 34:286–94).

On both sides of the Pacific, Spanish conquerors and settlers established themselves in areas where concentrated populations had already settled. Yet outside these cities, the authority of the Crown and the episcopal authority of the Church ceded to the intermediary agency of the religious missionary orders, whose members were called "regular clergy" (from the Latin *regula*, [monastic] "rule") as opposed to the secular or ordinary clergy under the rule of the bishops or ecclesiastical hierarchy. These frontier zones designated the spaces where Spanish authority only existed in a partial, uneven, and fragmentary way, if at all (see Sheridan Prieto 2012). Such areas might be characterized as what James Scott (following Willem van Schendel's work) called "shatter zones": where fugitives of imperial conquest and rule established and sustained alternative societies and cultures alongside the establishment of states and oftentimes in dialogue or negotiation with that state's limits (2009, 7–8).

One of the immediate implications of raising the devastation wrought on native societies in Philippine history during and after the conquest is to show just how overstated the Philippine "difference" regarding the nature and impact of conquest and colonization is with respect to the early histories of New Spain and Peru. Such a theory, promoted by John L. Phelan's famous thesis on the "partial Hispanization" of the Philippines, flies in the face of the massive death, depopulation, and displacement of pre-Hispanic settlements (2010, 158–59). The presumed completion and success of the conquest were thus no less fictional a descriptor for Philippine history after Spanish contact than they had been for Latin American history.

What, then, distinguished the conquest of the Philippines from that of the Americas? One unexamined facet of the problem has less to do with Spanish methods and justifications of violence than with the way(s) in which both the Crown and the Church agreed to *represent* the conquest. Specifically, Philip II's royal Ordinances of 1573 attempt to suppress the history of the conquest in order to pronounce the Spanish Crown's legitimate title over its overseas territories and to enforce the use of the word "pacification" in place of any mention of conquest. According to José Rabasa, the publication of Philip II's royal Ordinances pronounced the official "end" of the conquest by proclaiming "the Crown's monopoly over all expeditions and formulate models for the pacification [*pacificación*] and settlement of new territories" (2000, 89; see also Newson 2009, 6, 254). The Ordinances also laid out the procedures for the Pacification and Laying Out of Towns (Ordenanzas para descubrimientos, nuevas poblaciones y pacificaciones), which made clear that the settlement of lands not already settled would have to take place not under the rights of conquest, as it had under the conquistadors, but rather under *pax hispanica*, Spanish peace: "Los descobrimientos no se den con títulos y nombre de conquista: pues habiéndose de hacer con tanta paz y caridad como deseamos, no queremos quel nombre, dé ocasión ni color para que se pueda hazer fuerza ni agravio a los indios" (*Forbear that any titles and the name of conquest accompany any present and future discoveries:* for insofar as the matter [of colonial settlement] ought to be conducted with all the peace and charity that we desire, we do not want the name [of "Conquest"] to give any occasion or excuse for using force or injury against the Indians) (see Gibson 1995, 126; translation modified by author). The 1624 *Recopilación de las Leyes de Yndias*, which consolidated the various decrees, ordinances, and laws overseas, used even stronger language: "In those agreements in the matter of the discoveries *let the word Conquest be excised*, and the words Pacification and Population be used instead."[8] The 1573 Ordinances also outlined the role of the religious in teaching the Indians how to live in a "civilized manner" (*policía*, lit. polity or civil society) and sternly insisted on the avoidance of conflict and theft of any Indian property on the part of the Spanish settlers (see Nuttall 1921, 743–53; Sheridan Prieto 2012, 61–90).[9] The identification of the Spanish conquest of the Philippines and other Pacific possessions as a *pacification* rather than a *conquest*, then, owes itself primarily to this new principle of Iberian governance under Philip II.[10]

Three aspects of these Ordinances merit analysis. The first is that the discourse of pacification signifies Philip II's effort to complete the near century-long effort of the Crown to claim dominium or legitimate title of the Americas and Philippines, even as rival European powers undertook their own explorations of the New World with ideas of conquest and settlement in mind (see Pagden 1987, 27–108). The year after Columbus ran aground upon the Caribbean islands of the Bahamas, Cuba, and Saint Domingue and believed he had discovered a westward sea route to China, both the Crown and the Church recognized a convergence of interest in providing the legal bases of Iberian exploration, discovery, and settlement (see Schmitt 2006, 108–13; Anghie 1996, 328; Blanco and Valle 2014). This convergence was enshrined by papal bulls like that of Pope Alexander VI in 1493, granting the Spanish kings and their descendants full and free power, as well as authority and jurisdiction, over the lands they "discovered west of the Azores and Cape Verde." The papal bull "Universalis ecclesiae" signed by Pope Julius II in 1508 followed, granting the Spanish Crown the rights of royal patronage (*Real Patronato* or *Patronato Regio*) over the Church overseas. Royal patronage meant the establishment of the king as the vicariate supreme pontiff in the newly discovered lands. Throughout the early decades of the 16th century, the Spanish Crown promised to financially support the establishment and maintenance of the Church overseas, as well as to preside over certain matters of its ecclesiastical organization. In return, Charles V tasked the religious to furnish an argument for Spain's legal title to the Americas over other European powers.

The missionary orders did not make the procurement of this legal title easy. The Dominican preacher Fr. Bartolomé de Las Casas dedicated the first half of the 16th century to not only denouncing the atrocities and abuses of power he witnessed during the decades of the Spanish conquest but also calling into question the legitimacy of Spain's claim to overseas rule.[11] Through the lectures and works of Salamancan jurist Francisco de Vitoria, whom Charles V consulted in the promulgation of the New Laws of the Indies in 1542, missionaries argued that the basis of Spanish legal title to the overseas territories *itself* depended on various conditions and stipulations that had yet to be fulfilled in many areas. These included the proper justification of war (*causa justa*, just war doctrine) but also, of equal significance, the protection and promotion of various universal rights, among which was the right to preach the Christian Gospel freely throughout the world.[12] This point cannot be overemphasized: for to say that the foundation of Spain's title to the territorial possession of the Americas and the Philippines lay primarily in the right of missionaries to preach the Gospel (whether or not the natives were ultimately converted), as well as in the right to seize possession of territory and wealth under the conditions of a "just war," means that members of the Church served as the primary arbiters regarding the legal sanction of the conquest. The conquest's legitimacy, in other words, depended on the evaluation and progress of the mission. Thus, and paradoxically, even as the Church depended on the Crown to promote the task of evangelization overseas, it also rendered the Crown dependent on the Church—particularly the religious orders or regular clergy—in marking the scope and limits of, as well as outlining the preconditions to, the Crown's legitimate title.[13]

The second aspect is that the 1573 Ordinances reiterated the New Laws promulgated by Philip II's father and predecessor, Charles V, in 1542, which decreed one of the responsibilities of the colonial government to be the settlement (called *congregación* in New Spain and *reducción* in the Philippines) of native populations in Spanish towns governed by Spanish laws. This task would begin with missionary labor and culminate either with converted Indians or neophytes freely agreeing to live in Spanish towns or with the official establishment of a town in native settlements proper (see Nuttal 1921, 749). In other words, missionary priests and the mission system would serve as what Herbert Bolton called a "frontier institution," which, along with the military fortress or presidio, would vanquish the unconquered frontier through a combination of Spanish immigration, the conversion of natives to Christianity, and the defense of towns (1917, 42–61). Again, following the words of the 1624 *Laws of the Indies*, "Pacificación y Población" would stand in place of the word "Conquista."[14] Yet, as the Jesuit priest and missionary Fr. José de Acosta made clear in his 1577 treatise on the preaching of the Gospel and Christianization among the barbarians, *Predicación del Evangelio en las Indias* [The

Preaching of the Gospel in the Indies]), Christian conversion and native settlement were inseparable, as the future of one in Spain's overseas territories depended on the other (Acosta 1577, 26). Missionaries, following Acosta, saw themselves as not only preaching conversion but inducing (re)settlement.

Finally, the last aspect of the Ordenanzas (1573) worth mentioning is the date: it indicates that the Ordinaces were to apply to the Philippines from the very beginning, with the catastrophic consequences of the Spanish conquest of the Americas already manifesting themselves in Spanish rapacity and the spread of Old World epidemic diseases. It would be difficult to miss here the Crown's determination to preempt the crisis of authority, genocide, and depredation in the Americas from repeating itself in the Philippines. Spanish jurist Gregorio López's gloss on the word "conquest" in Spain's legal code in 1565—the same year that Admiral Miguel López de Legazpi established the Spanish capital of the Spanish East Indies in Cebu—deserves quoting, as it anticipates the reconception of conquest as an act of pacification during the reign of Philip II: "With regard to such a conquest undertaken not through arms nor terror, as would be the case among wild enemies, good and honest men are to be sent to the people, who would spread conquest by their lives and teachings."[15] Philip II or his secretary (the Marquis Juan de Ovando) certainly had either López's gloss or the royal Ordinances of 1573 in mind when he imparted his instructions to the first official governor of the Philippines, Gómez Pérez das Mariñas (Dasmariñas):

> It is said that there is great need of such *pacification* in the said islands, especially in the very districts where the Spaniards live and travel, for all of the natives are in revolt and unsubdued, because of the lack of soldiers, and of the injuries and annoyances inflicted upon the natives by what soldiers are there. Moreover, as we are informed from there, many provinces of the island of Luçon [Luzon] either have never been subdued, or, if subdued, have revolted—as, for instance, those of Cagayan, Pangasinan, Paya sondan, Cambales, Balente, and others, which are situated among the *pacified* provinces quite near and round about Manila; all the provinces, therefore, are in confusion and disorder. . . . Besides there is the great obligation to endeavor to instruct the many people converted already, who are under my royal protection. These, because of their *lack of the requisite peace and quiet*, live in great hardship and danger; for those who are in revolt and *unpacified* harass them daily, kill and assault them, and burn their crops. Because of this, and because they also kill many Spaniards, not only is there no increase in what has been

gained, but each day that is becoming less. (Blair and Robertson 1906, 7:166, par. 45; italics added)[16]

Philip's instructions revolve around the rhetoric of pacification as pure redundancy: he expresses the need to *pacify* the islands because, well, many of these areas are *unpacified*, which poses a danger to the *pacified* ones, for fear that they may become *unpacified*, and so forth.[17] What is striking about this redundancy here is the way a *prescriptive* term meant to erase the violence of the conquest acquires a *descriptive* dimension, which is precisely how metaphors become naturalized and disappear into the phantasmagorias they have engendered.

Philippine scholars, both before and after (and including) John Phelan, have long characterized the conquest of the Philippines as a relatively bloodless "pacification" (see Phelan 2010, 105). Historians often remark on the admirable restraint and prudence exercised by Ferdinand Magellan and Miguel de Legazpi in their initial encounters with natives in the Visayas and Luzon. Did they realize, however, that colonial officials and missionaries had *from the beginning* set out to preempt the language of conquest through the description of a "bloodless pacification," even as conquistadors like Juan de Salcedo and Martin de Goiti were engaging in the same conquistador practices, reading the same *Requerimiento*, that had been employed in the conquest of the Americas, before pillaging native settlements that would not voluntarily supply Spanish expeditions with provisions?[18]

The Migration of "Conquest" to the Spiritual Realm

The omission and prohibition of the word "conquest" in the official correspondence and memoranda among Crown officials, with words like "pacification" and "population" to be used in its stead, coincided with the curious proliferation of the word "conquest," and of conquest rhetoric more broadly, in missionary chronicles and correspondence. While the early modern period in Europe saw the migration of theological terms and concepts to the secular realm, here we have a case of the opposite. Here, the Spanish Crown rejects conquest as an explicitly acknowledged precondition of law and justice (best captured in the Roman but rather unchristian *vae victis*, to the victor go the spoils), after which the term then migrates to the spiritual realm, where we encounter the missionary prose of *spiritual conquest*.[19] Of course, the migration of concepts and terms from one sphere of life to another is not itself unusual: particularly in the case of Spain, where Counter-Reformation spirituality pervaded every involvement of Spanish arms throughout the 16th and 17th centuries. The metaphorization of missionaries as crusaders or "spiritual warriors," in any case, is well documented. Founder of the Jesuit Order St. Ignatius of Loyola began his career as a soldier: his famous work *Spiritual Exercises* in many ways recalls the training of a military cadet. In the case of the Philippines, one of the early leaders of the Spanish colony in Manila, Jesuit priest Fr. Alonso Sánchez, SJ, led a delegation to Philip II in 1586, requesting not only that the Crown retain the Philippine archipelago as a Spanish possession but also that the colony be granted permission and support to conquer the Middle Kingdom for the greater glory of Spain and Christianity.[20]

Yet if we set aside these individual examples, as well as further abstract speculations linking the religious to medieval conceptions of the Crown and the Church, we see that the rhetoric of "spiritual conquest" responds to a series of specific circumstances associated with the expansion of pacification discourse in the late 16th century. On the one hand, the prose of spiritual conquest underlined the specifically *political* task the Crown would assign to the missionary orders: to effectively complete a truncated conquest by not only preaching and teaching the Christian religion but also persuading (or coercing) native populations to live in concentrated settlements.[21] On the other hand, in the hands of the missionaries the spiritual conquest represented this political task in religious terms: as a constant battle with the Devil or devils (*demonios*) for the "conquest" of souls and their disabusal (*desengaño*) of the Devil's deceptions regarding not only the presumed abuses and superstitions of their pagan traditions but also the danger and folly of becoming Christian.

The introduction and rapid spread of demonology among missionaries in the New World preceded the late 16th century. Fernando Cervantes traces its emergence—with accompanying campaigns promoting the extirpation of idolatry and Christian phantasmagoria around the Devil's agency in the New World—to a Franciscan-inspired nominalist streak that pit the corruptibility of nature with God's saving grace in terms of a stark opposition (1994, 5–39). While this Manichean streak is oftentimes most associated with the radical separation of nature and grace in Protestant doctrines, Cervantes demonstrates its prevailing influence among missionaries, particularly as the 16th century wore on and it appeared evident that the apparent success of Christian conversion belied the proliferation of syncretisms and hybrid forma-

Fig. 1. Detail of a painting attributed to José Dans (19th c.) hanging in the St. James
the Apostle Church in Paete, Laguna (Philippines). The central panel depicts the
Creation as the basis for understanding Universal History, flanked on both sides
by a fleet of Christian martyrs and saints (*on the left*) and a fleet of demons (*on the
right*). Photograph courtesy of author.

tions.[22] Padre Acosta's words in 1588 capture well this spirit of Manichaeism
in the missionary endeavor: "El demonio, enemigo del linaje humano, ator-
mentado de acerbísima envidia, procura con todas sus fuerzas y artificio
que en la conversión de los gentiles a la fe la obra de Dios no prospere; y
así levanta innumerables impedimentos para, arrebatar el fruto de la divina
semilla de los corazones de los oyentes" (The Devil, enemy of the human race,
tormented by the most acerbic envy, labors with all his might and artifice for
the conversion of gentiles to the faith [as] the work of God not to prosper;
and thus he erects innumerable barriers to arrest the flowering of the divine
seed in the hearts of those who hear it) (Acosta 1577, 64). In Acosta's eyes,
any recourse to the natural theology of his predecessor Fr. Bartolomé de las
Casas, OP, or even Acosta's own fellow Jesuit and young contemporary Mat-
teo Ricci, SJ, remained suspect.[23]

   Examples of spiritual warfare against the Devil and his deceptions in the
Philippines abound. In 1598, Fr. Marcelo de Ribandeira, OFM, describes the
necessity of certain friars to maintain their contemplative lives in isolation,
while others lead "la Guerra espiritual que con los príncipes de las tinieblas
tienen los religiosos que se ejercitan en la conversión de los infieles sacán-
doles de la esclavonia del demonio" (the spiritual war that the religious who
are engaged with the conversion of the unfaithful have with the princes of

darkness, rescuing the former from the devil's enslavement) (1970, 57). This theme of the Devil as a predatory slave owner is echoed by the Dominican preacher Fr. Francisco Blancas de San José, OP, who describes the Devil's reign over the world as follows: "Nangangahas siyang magbansag na siya ang hari sa sanglibutang; at di man gaua niya manga tauo, ay quinacaniyang alipin, at quinacaniyang holi, at quinacaniyang bihag" (He dares to call himself the king of the world; and moreover makes people his slaves [alipin], his prey, his captives) ([1614] 1994, 105; see also Rodriguez [1614] 1994, 363).

The slide from spiritual war to spiritual *conquest*, however, seems to coincide with the self-identification and self-recognition of the missionaries as the sole arbiters of "pacification" during the Catholic kings' expansion to Asia. The anonymous Jesuit play (presented in the form of a colloquy) *Coloquio de la conquista espiritual del Japón hecha por San Francisco Javier* (Colloquy of the spiritual conquest of Japan accomplished by St. Francis Xavier), written around 1622, seems to be an early example of the phrase "spiritual conquest" in circulation.[24] This work commemorates the arrival of the Jesuit priest St. Francis Xavier to Japan and his successful conversion of a Japanese *daimyo* (mistakenly identified as a "king"), despite the efforts of the Devil and his lieutenants to frustrate his journey. Around the same time, Franciscan friar Fr. Paolo da Trinidade wrote *Conquista Espiritual do Oriente* (Spiritual conquest of the Orient) in Goa between 1630 and 1636; and in 1639 Jesuit priest Fr. Antonio Ruiz de Montoya wrote *La conquista espiritual: Hecha por los religiosos de la Compañía de Jesús, en las provincias del Paraguay, Parana, Uruguay y Tape* (The spiritual conquest: Achieved under the religious belonging to the Jesuit Order in the provinces of Paraguay, Paraná, Uruguay and Tape). In the Philippines, Augustinian priest Fr. Gaspar de San Agustín, OSA, titled his history of the Augustinian mission *Conquistas de las Islas Filipinas: La temporal por las armas del señor don Felipe II el prudente; y la espiritual por los religiosos del orden del nuestro Padre San Agustín y progresos de la Provincia del Santísimo nombre de Jesús* (Conquests of the Philippine Islands: The temporal conquest under the arms of Lord King Philip II the Prudent; and the spiritual conquest under the religious belonging to the Order of our Father Saint Augustine and the advancements made by the Province of His Most Holy Name of Jesus) in 1698. What these examples all seem to have in common is the anticipation, prefiguration, or supplementary relationship of the mission and the missionary orders to an Iberian conquest under erasure, *after* the term "conquest" had been prohibited from official correspondence.

The ambiguity of whether these and other writers were speaking of a purely metaphorical war or an actual one, however, is difficult to determine. Cecilia Sheridan Prieto, in her insightful work on Mexico's northern frontier, demonstrates how religious chronicles often slid from metaphor into arguments about legal jurisdiction. Missionaries like Fr. Guillermo de Santa María, OSA, and Fr. Andrés de Pérez Ribas, SJ, begin to invoke the persistence of an actual state of war that continued even after the stated goals of "population, pacification, and conversion" had been ostensibly met—*una guerra viva* on the frontier of northern Mexico and Sonora—and which rendered the establishment of garrisons and churches, as well as the promotion of military violence and religious indoctrination, indistinguishable (Sheridan Prieto 2012, 63–64).[25] In 1665, Philippine Dominican Fr. Hector Polanco, OP, echoes this frontier rhetoric in invoking the "ongoing spiritual conquest" in the Philippines as a main reason that missionaries should not be subject to the authority of the king's royal patronage:

> No se siguen en el Perú y México en donde los Yndios ha muchos años que están reducidos a la Fe y obediencia de Vuestra Magestad y los ministros en quieta y pacífica posesión de las Christianidades. En Filipinas están los ministros *en viva conquista espiritual*, enarboladas las banderas de la Fe y Religión Christiana . . . [y] *si no se tratara de reducir estos con humildad, paciencia, buen tratamiento, ejemplo y doctrina no se contuviera la ferocidad de su natural, y costumbres, y destruyeran a las Christianidades que ya están formadas.*

> (One cannot follow [the model of replacing missions with secular parishes] that obtains in Peru or Mexico, where for many years the Indians have been reduced to the Faith and in obedience to Your Majesty and the ministers in the tranquil and pacific possession of these Christian lands. In the Philippines the religious remain in a state of an ongoing [*viva*] spiritual conquest, hoisting high the banners of the Faith and Christian religion . . . *and unless one attempts to settle [reducir] these Indians in towns with humility, patience, good temperament, example, and orthodoxy, the ferocity of their nature and customs will not be held in check, and they will destroy the Christian kingdoms already fashioned*). (cited in Colin and Pastells 1663, 734–35; italics added; translation mine)

As if to emphasize his meaning, Polanco catalogs the many revolts and uprisings that, in his opinion, have left the islands in a *state of total ruin.*[26]

The migration of the language of "conquest" and its missionary "soldiers"

from a political to spiritual realm was employed by Friar Polanco and his contemporaries to argue for and justify a self-contradictory order on the colonial
borderlands: one that called on Crown resources and support for the constantly threatened mission towns or *doctrinas*, while prohibiting the direct
interference of royal authority in the work of native resettlement led by these
missions (739 passim). In this way, the "viva conquista espiritual," ongoing
spiritual conquest, paradoxically prolonged the conquest in the name of com-
pleting it, leaving the mission as frontier institution and legal limbo fruitlessly
trying to corral and coerce ostensibly "Christianized" populations into settlements, while also defending the Church's autonomy to administer its mission
parishes or *doctrinas* outside the sphere of both civil and canon law.

Fr. Juan Francisco de San Antonio, OFM, in his 18th-century chronicle
of the Franciscan Province, went as far as to suggest that the main obstacle
to the spiritual conquest was the natives themselves and that the only way
to arrest the violence of their essential nature would have to be through the
violence of spiritual conquest. "Tan perenne es el genio de estos Naturales,"
he wrote, "que es necesaria violencia, para que tomen alguna robustez sus
raíces" (So unchanging is the genius of these natives that violence is necessary, so that their roots gain strength to take hold) (San Antonio 1738, 371).
The author characterized the natural "perversions" of the natives as so deeply
ingrained that without the constant presence of the missionary and his power
to wield violence over his flock of parishioners, they would inevitably return
to their pagan idolatry and devil worship. "Por esta experimentada beleydad
[*sic*] propusieron los Religiosos," he added, "que se estuviese cada Ministro
perpetuamente residente en el Partido, que le tocase, sin vagar de lugar en
lugar, para conquistar mas Tierras, y mas Gentes" (Given this proven fickle-
ness the Religious Fathers proposed . . . that each Minister remain a *permanent* resident in play, where it pertains to him, without wandering from place
to place in order to conquer more Lands and Peoples) (371; italics added).
This argument authorized not only the exercise of violence by missionaries
on their native flocks of neophytes but also the permanent establishment of
missions and missionaries against the institution of the official Church and
ordained priests.

The persistence of the frontier, with the mission as both frontier institution and agency of frontierization, bore testament to the unfinished conquest. Throughout the provinces where the movement of both Crown and
Church officials alike was severely restricted, the presumed "natural perversity" of Christian neophytes mirrored the *legal perversion* of a permanent

exception to the law: a perpetual deferral of episcopal and Crown authority in favor of the entrenchment of the contingent authority and "legal impunity" (*immunitas*) of the religious orders.

Missionary Writings as a Form of Literature

It may be said that Philippine national martyr José Rizal first exposed the missionary chronicles as imaginative literature when he denounced the fiction of pacification in Antonio de Morga's 1603 *Sucesos de las Islas Filipinas* (Historical events of the Philippine Islands) with the following statement: "Acaso el verbo *pacificar* significase entonces *meter la guerra*" (Maybe the verb *to pacify* thus means *to wage war*). By serving as a euphemism and smokescreen for continual recourse to war and conquest, the fictions of a completed conquest and ensuing pacification foreclose a proper historical evaluation of Spain's precarious presence in the Philippines outside the capital city Intramuros. Under the prose of spiritual conquest, the catastrophe of depopulation and displacement was effaced, not to mention the constant irruption of uprising and rebellion throughout the colonial period. In their place, we see the gradual, progressive, and planned expansion of "pacified" settlements, whose completion was destined from the time of the prophecies of Isaiah. Pacification discourse masked the coercion involved in acts of conquest with a juridical discourse that the subjection of the natives was free and unforced. Once in place, ideology rewrites its origins: it is through this erasure that official histories and documents of the conquest take on the opacity of what William Henry Scott (1982) has called a "parchment curtain."

A second consequence pertaining to the migration of "conquest" to the spiritual realm has to do with the productive confusion between legal and theological meanings of the word on the missionary frontier. Through the prose of spiritual conquest, missionaries obscured the absence of civil and ecclesiastical law outside Manila with an imaginary matrix of Christian phantasmagorias—divine punishments; miracles of faith and devotion; apparitions of the Virgin Mary; the charade of enchantment, disenchantment, and re-enchantment; and holy amulets protecting the faithful (or superstitious) from demons (see Aguilar 1998, 38–44). Serge Gruzinski (borrowing a term from Lacanian psychoanalysis) called this matrix a Christian *imaginaire*, which provided a field of signification that ceaselessly called for interpretation, verification, and demystification—in a word, the law—even as these acts generated a proliferation of other symbols, signs, and images whose instructions lay outside it (2006, 147–59).

A third consequence of regarding missionary chronicles as a form of literature would be the urgency of going beyond a critical history of the conquest of the Philippines and its aftermath; to arrive at a more coherent and comprehensive understanding of Spain's presence or absence in the Philippines. Specifically, the literature of spiritual conquest should inspire readers to further connect the dots in the patchwork of fragmented histories, legends, fables, and bits of folklore that hint at the genealogies or counter-histories of Philippine culture, which is what transforms a historical narrative of the past into a memory screen or allows it to interface with the present (see Gruzinski 2006; Ileto 1999).[27] The fictions of contemporary Philippine novelists have attuned us to the way that historical experience is encoded in the colloquial expressions, customary habits, cultural artifacts, and even dreams as wish fulfillments that populate our every day. Would this not also hold true for the dreams, hallucinations, and hauntings that missionaries reported among natives struggling to reconcile the erosion of their former ways of life while simultaneously accommodating a new order that never managed to arrive? Or for the gods and monsters that populated the colonial frontier, where the experience of native displacement and disorientation turned familiar landscapes into netherworlds and living hells?

Notes

1. Isaac Donoso (2016, 26–28) and Jorge Mojarro (2016) have both considered these works as a form of Philippine baroque literature.

2. Consider, for instance, the introduction to the history of the Philippines by Augustinian priest Fr. Joaquín Martínez de Zuñiga, OSA: "Las historias de Philipinas se componen de volúmenes grandes, y tomos en folio mayores. . . . Para llenar estos libros ha sido preciso a nuestros Historiadores, que por lo común son Regulares, tratar muy por extenso . . . noticias poco interesantes al resto de los hombres. . . . Para no caer en este error, he suprimido varias reflexiones, que se debieran hacer; arreglándose á las Leyes de la Historia, he callado otras, por que no se debe decir todo lo que se sabe, dejándolas de intento, para que el Lector imparcial las haga por sí mismo." Zuñiga 1803, iii–v passim. Historian Gloria Cano has further illustrated the degree to which US pro-imperialist officials reinforced the view that missionary chronicles ought to be treated with suspicion. See Cano 2008, 31–34.

3. For an explanation of this distinction, see Foucault 1977, 146; Blanco, 2019, 131–40.

4. On the relationship of this "literary pastoralism" in the theme of divine providence to a "pastoral politics," see Blanco (2005) 2008: 68–87.

5. See also O'Gorman 1998, 1–9; Moffitt-Watts 1985, 73–102; Zamora 1993.

6. An early pioneer of this opinion was Renato Constantino, whose two-volume his-

tory of the Philippines describes this explicitly (1975); see also James Scott 2009; Lessing 1962; Majul 1999.

7. For the Americas, see Diamond 1997, 78; for the relationship of the estimated population in the Americas to world population, see https://www.pri.org/stories/2019-01-31 /european-colonization-americas-killed-10-percent-world-population-and-caused.   For population estimates of the early modern Philippines, see Corpuz 1999, 62–127, 598–668; Newson 2009, 9–24.

8. "En las capitulaciones de descubrimientos se excuse la palabra *Conquista*, y se use de las de *Pacificacion, y Poblacion*" (ley 6. Tit. I. Lib. 4; italics added). Cited in *Recopilacion de leyes de los reynos de las Indias, mandadas imprimir y publicar por la Magestad Católica del Rey Don Carlos II . . . : va dividida en tres tomos, con el índice general, y al principio de cada tomo el índice especial de los títulos que contiene : tomo tercero. por la viuda de D. Joaquin Ibarra* 1791, 79.

9. "It is clear," Newson writes, "that the Ordinances of 1573, aimed at bringing about the peaceful subjugation of newly discovered territories, had little impact on the course of conquest in the Philippines" (2009, 254).

10. For an incisive contrast between the changing role of the missionaries in the New World versus the Philippines, see Elizalde and Huetz de Lemps 2015, 185–220.

11. Las Casas's famous work *Brevíssima relación de la destrucción de las Indias* was published in 1542 and is today considered the foundational text in Spain's "black legend" of genocide and depredation in the Americas. For a history of these debates, see Pagden 1987, 57–145.

12. "The papal missionary mandate," Carl Schmitt writes, "was the true legal title to the *conquista*. . . . The Dominican order, to which Vitoria belonged, and the other orders engaged in converting the Indians were guardians and executors of the missionary mandate from which the *jure gentium* of legitimate title for a secular *conquista* could be developed. These orders also were agencies of the pope and of the church as an authority in the international law of the *respublica Christiana*" (2006, 112). See also Anghie 1996, 321–36.

13. This did not always happen: in Peru, for instance, friars went so far as to claim that "the supervision of the indigenous people should be reserved entirely to them, and they saw themselves as their only lords. . . . It was also asserted that the religious wanted to put the government of the natives directly under the pope with themselves as his representatives" (Poole 2004, 103–4).

14. Native communities that refused either baptism or (re)settlement were de facto allowed to maintain their own "uses and customs" (*usos y costumbres*), provided these did not openly conflict with Spanish laws. The resulting political organization of the colony would be split between those administered by Spanish law (*república de españoles*) and those administered by native customs and laws (*república de indios*) (see Deardorff 2018, 166–67; Graubart 2006, 1–29).

15. "Iin hac conquesta, non ab armis neque à terroribus, velut contra hostes fieri solet, incipiendum. Sed mittendi sunt ad eos boni & probi viri, qui vita & doctrina polleant." Gloss on ley 2 of the second (of seven) divisions of law or *Partidas*, title 23; cited in Gibson 1995, 127. The *Siete Partidas* was the code of Spanish law originally drafted under the direction of Alfonso X "the Wise" of Castile around 1265.

16. Unfortunately, I have not been able to consult the original document in the Archivo General de Indias: see "Instrucciones de gobierno a Gómez Pérez das Mariñas" (AGI Filipinas, 339, L. 1, F.365V–389R).

17. For an insightful analysis of the semiotic of redundancy in the interpretation of law, see Deleuze and Guattari 1982, 111–48.

18. See, for example, the account by Fr. Martín de Rada, OSA, of Juan de Salcedo's expedition into northern Luzon: "All those villages were entered in the same way, by first summoning them to submit peacefully, and to pay tribute unless they wished war. They replied that they would first prove those to whom they were told to pay tribute, and consequently, the Spaniards would attack them, making an entrance among them by force of arms and the village was overthrown and whatever was found was pillaged" (in Blair and Robertson 1906, 34:286–87; also cited in Keesing 1962, 15).

19. For the "reoccupation" of theological terms in early modern Europe, see Blumenberg 1985, 64–65, 103–24. Robert Ricard's classic work *Conquête Spirituelle du Mexique* (1933) (English translation: *The Spiritual Conquest of Mexico*, 1982) documents the foundation and spread of Christianity by the mendicant and missionary friar religious orders (Franciscans, Dominicans, and Augustinians) in New Spain between 1523 and 1572. More than any other work in recent memory, it popularized the term "spiritual conquest" (*conquête spirituelle*) as a shorthand way to describe both the complementarity and the tension that has always existed between the religious and worldly or "temporal" goals of Spain's overseas conquests. The precise origins of this phrase, if such exist, remain undocumented by Ricard and later scholars who have employed it.

20. Interestingly, Fr. Sánchez's ambitions were discouraged and blunted by his confessor and superior, who was none other than Fr. José de Acosta, SJ. See Ollé 2000, 136–49.

21. See Mingo 1985, 83–101. The author writes: "Los once capítulos finales de las ordenanzas, referidos a las «pacificaciones», suponen el definitivo esfuerzo por parte de la Corona para concluir la guerra indiana. A fin de conseguirlo proponen una serie de actuaciones, cuyas piezas claves serán los misioneros, y cuya finalidad es realizar la penetración y el contacto con los indios de forma pacífica, lo que supondría su voluntaria integración en la dinámica de los repartimientos" (92).

22. See Blumenberg 1985, 145–80. Blumenberg identifies the influence of Manichaeism as a fault line within divergent interpretations of Christianity from its very origins.

23. As Cervantes writes, "By denying paganism any natural means towards a supernatural end—unless, of course, both the means and the ends could be classified as diabolic—Acosta effectively equated paganism with idolatry" (1994, 29).

24. See García Valdés 2007, 35–57. Her estimation of the date of publication appears on p. 12.

25. On the violence of "spiritual conquest" in northern Mexico, see Hausberger 1993, 27–54; Rozt Dupeyron 2015, 76–108.

26. "Aquellas Christiandades . . . necesitan de soldados espirituales que trabajen sin descanso en ellas para assegurarlas para Dios y Vuestra Magestad" (These Christian kingdoms . . . need spiritual soldiers who will work without rest to assure their fealty to God and Your Majesty) (cited in Colin and Pastells 1663, 737).

27. Two of the more insightful reflections on the interface of culture as history and

history as culture are Neferti Tadiar, *Things Fall Away: Philippine Historical Experience and the Making of Globalization* (2009), and Caroline Hau, *Necessary Fictions: Philippine Literature and the Nation, 1946–1980* (2001).

References

Acosta, Fr. José de, SJ. 1577. *Predicación del evangelio en las Indias.* Biblioteca Virtual Miguel de Cervantes. http://www.cervantesvirtual.com/obra-visor/predicacion-del -evangelio-en-las-indias--0/html/fee5d58a-82b1-11df-acc7-002185ce6064_117.html

Aguilar, Filomeno V., Jr. 1998 *Clash of Spirits: The History of Power and Sugar Planter Hegemony on a Visayan Island.* Honolulu: University of Hawai'i Press.

Anghie, Anthony. 1996. "Francisco de Vitoria and the Origins of International Law." *Social & Legal Studies* 5:321–36. https://doi.org/10.1177/096466399600500303

Blair, Emma, and James Robertson, eds. 1903–1909. *The Philippine Islands, 1493–1898.* 52 volumes. Cleveland: Arthur H. Clark Company.

Blancas de San José, Fr. Francisco, OP. (1614) 1994. *Sermones.* Ed. José Mario C. Francisco, SJ. Quezon City: PULONG Sources for Philippine Studies, Ateneo de Manila University.

Blanco, John D. (2005) 2008. "The Pastoral Theme in Colonial Politics and Literature." *Diliman Review* 52, no. 1. Reprinted in *Philippine Studies: Have We Gone Beyond St. Louis?*, ed. Priscelina Patajo Legasto, 68–87. Quezon City: University of the Philippines Press.

Blanco, John D. 2019. "From Colonial History to Colonial Genealogies." Special issue, "Capitalism-Colonialism-Catholicism," ed. Daniel Nemser. *Journal of Early Modern Cultural Studies* 19, no. 2 (spring): 131–40.

Blanco, John D., and Ivonne del Valle. 2014. "Reorienting Schmitt's *Nomos*: Political Theology, and Colonial (and Other) Exceptions in the Creation of Modern and Global Worlds." *Política Común* 5. https://doi.org/10.3998/pc.12322227.0005.001

Blumenberg, Hans. 1985. *The Legitimacy of the Modern Age.* Trans. Robert M. Wallace. Cambridge: MIT Press, 1985.

Bolton, Herbert. 1917. "The Mission as a Frontier Institution in the Spanish-American Colonies." *American Historical Review* 23, no. 1 (October): 42–61.

Cano, Gloria. 2008. "Blair and Robertson's 'The Philippine Islands, 1493–1898': Scholarship or Imperialist Propaganda?" Special issue on Blair and Robertson. *Philippine Studies* 56, no. 1 (March): 3–46.

Casas, Fr. Bartolomé de las. (1542) 2006. *Breuíssima relación de la destruyción de las Indias / colegida por el Obispo do[n] fray Bartolomé de las Casas.* Fundación Biblioteca Virtual Miguel de Cervantes y Universidad de Alicante. http://www.cervantesvirtual.com /obra/breuissima-relacion-de-la-destruycion-de-las-indias--colegida-por-el-obispo -don-fray-bartolome-de-las-casas-o-casaus-/

Cervantes, Fernando. 1994. *The Devil in the New World: The Impact of Diabolism in New Spain.* New Haven: Yale University Press.

Colin, Fr. Francisco, SJ, and Pablo Pastells, SJ. 1663. *Labor Evangélica, ministerios apostólicos de los Obreros de la Compañía de Iesvs, fundación, y progresos de su Provincia en las Islas Filipinas.* 3 volumes. Madrid: Ioseph Fernández de Buendía.

Constantino, Renato. 1975. *The Philippines Pt. 1: A Past Revisited*. Quezon City: copyright Renato Constantino.

Corpuz, O. D. 1999. *Roots of the Filipino Nation*. Quezon City: Aklahi Books.

Deardorff, Max. 2018. "Republics, Their Customs, and the Law of the King." *Rechtgeschichte Legal History* 26 (September): 162–99.

Deleuze, Gilles, and Félix Guattari. 1982. *A Thousand Plateaus: Capitalism and Schizophrenia*. Trans. Brian Massumi. Minneapolis: University of Minnesota Press.

Diamond, Jared. 1997. *Guns, Germs, and Steel: The Fates of Human Societies*. New York: Norton.

Donoso, Isaac. 2016. "La literatura filipina en español durante la era barroca." *Humanities Diliman* 13, no. 1 (January–June): 23–61.

Elizalde, María Dolores, and Xavier Huetz de Lemps. 2015. "Un singular modelo colonizador: El papel de llas Órdenes religiosas en la administración española de Filipinas, siglos XVI al XIX." *Illes Imperis* 17, no. 3: 185–220.

Foucault, Michel. 1977. "Nietzsche, Genealogy, History." In *Language, Counter-Memory, Practice: Selected Essays and Interviews*, trans. Donald F. Bouchard and Sherry Simon, 139–64. Ithaca: Cornell University Press.

García Valdés, Celsa Carmen. 2007. "La Conquista Espiritual del Japón, comedia Jesuítica Javeriana, y la perspectiva Paulina de la evangelización." In Ignacio Arellano Ayuso, Alejandro González Acosta, and Arnulfo Herrera, eds., *San Francisco Javier entre dos continentes*, 35–57. Madrid: Iberoamericana Vervuert. https://dialnet.unirioja.es/serv let/libro?codigo=290503

Gibson, Charles. 1995. "Arrival and Conflict: Conquest and So-Called Conquest in Spain and Spanish America." In Lamb 1995.

Graubart, Karen. 2016. "Competing Spanish and Indigenous Jurisdictions in Early Colonial Lima." In Kenneth Mills, ed., *Oxford Research Encyclopedia in Latin American and Caribbean History*. New York: Oxford University Press. https://doi.org/10.1093/acref ore/9780199366439.013.365

Hau, Caroline. 2001. *Necessary Fictions: Philippine Literature and the Nation, 1946–1980*. Quezon City: Ateneo de Manila University Press.

Hausberger, Bernd. 1993. "La violencia en la conquista espiritual: Las misiones jesuitas de Sonora." *Jahrbuch für Geschichte Lteinamerikas / Anuario de Historia de América Latina* 30, no. 1 (December): 27–54. https://doi.org/10.7788/jbla-1993-0104

Herrera, Fr. Diego de, OSA. 1906. "Letter to Felipe II." In Blair and Robertson 1906, 34:229–35.

Ileto, Reynaldo. 1979. *Pasyon and Revolution: Popular Movements in the Philippines, 1840–1910*. Quezon City: Ateneo de Manila University Press.

Ileto, Reynaldo. 1993. "Outlines of a Non-Linear Emplotment of Philippine History." In Lisa Lowe and David Lloyd, eds., *The Politics of Culture in the Shadow of Capital*, 98–131. Durham: Duke University Press.

Ileto, Reynaldo. 1999. "Rizal and the Underside of Philippine History." In *Filipinos and Their Revolution: Event, Discourse, and Historiography*, 29–78. Quezon City: Ateneo de Manila University Press.

Joaquin, Nick. 2004. *Culture and History: Occasional Notes on Filipino Becoming*. Pasig City, Manila: Anvil Publishing.

Keesing, Felix Maxwell. 1962. *The Ethnohistory of Northern Luzon*. Stanford: Stanford University Press.

Lamb, Ursula, ed. 1995. *The Globe Encircled and the World Revealed*. Aldershot, UK: Variorum.

Lessing, Felix. 1962. *The Ethnohistory of Northern Luzon*. Berkeley: University of California Press.

Majul, Cesar Adib. 1999. *The Muslims of the Philippines*. Quezon City: University of the Philippines Press.

Mingo, Marta Milagros del Vas. 1985. "Las Ordenanzas de 1573, sus antecedents y consecuencias." *Quinto Centenario* 8:83–101.

Moffitt-Watts, Pauline. 1985. "Prophecy and Discovery: On the Spiritual Origins of Christopher Columbus's 'Enterprise of the Indies.'" *American Historical Review* 90, no. 1:73–102.

Mojarro, Jorge. 2016. "Crónicas de las Indias Orientales: Orígenes de la literatura hispanofilipina." PhD diss., Universidad de Salamanca. https://www.academia.edu/33185219 /TESIS_DOCTORAL_CR%C3%93NICAS_DE_LAS_INDIAS_ORIENTALES_Or %C3%ADgenes_de_la_literatura_hispanofilipina

Newson, Linda. 2009. *Conquest and Pestilence in the Early Spanish Philippines*. Honolulu: University of Hawai'i Press.

Nuttall, Zelia. 1921. "Royal Ordinances Concerning the Laying Out of New Towns." *Hispanic American Historical Review* 4, no. 4 (November): 743–53.

O'Gorman, Edmundo. 1998. *El proceso de la invención de América*. México: Fondo de Cultura Económica.

Ollé, Manel. 2000. *La invención de China. Percepciones y estrategias filipinas respecto a China durante el siglo XVI*. Wisbaden: Harrassowitz Verlag.

Owensby, Brian. 2008. *Empire of Law and Indian Justice in Colonial Mexico*. Stanford: Stanford University Press.

Pagden, Anthony. 1987. *The Fall of Natural Man: The American Indian and the Origins of Comparative Ethnology*. Cambridge: Cambridge University Press.

Phelan, John L. 2010. *The Hispanization of the Philippines: Spanish Aims and Filipino Responses 1565–1700*. Madison: University of Wisconsin Press.

Poole, Stafford. 2004. *Juan de Ovando: Governing the Spanish Empire in the Reign of Philip II*. Tulsa: University of Oklahoma Press.

Rabasa, José. 2000. *Writing Violence on the Northern Frontier: The Historiography of Sixteenth-Century New Mexico and Florida and the Legacy of Conquest*. Durham: Duke University Press.

Rada, Fr. Martín de. 1906. "Letter to the Viceroy of Nueva España, Martin Enriquez." In Blair and Robertson 1906, 34:286–94.

Recopilacion de leyes de los reynos de las Indias, mandadas imprimir y publicar por la Magestad Católica del Rey Don Carlos II . . . : va dividida en tres tomos, con el indice general, y al principio de cada tomo el índice especial de los títulos que contiene : tomo tercero. por la viuda de D. Joaquin Ibarra. 1791.

Restall, Matthew. 2004. *Seven Myths of the Spanish Conquest*. Oxford: Oxford University Press.

Ribandeira, Fr. Marcelo de (OFM). 1970. *Historia del Archipiélago y otros Reinos / History of the Archipelago and Other Kingdoms*. Trans. Pacita Guevara Fernandez. Manila: Historical Conservation Society.

Ricard, Robert. 1982. *The Spiritual Conquest of Mexico*. Trans. Lesley Byrd Simpson. Berkeley: University of California Press. First published in 1966.

Rodriguez, Agustín Martín G. (1614) 1994. "Diskurso at Sermon: Ang Sinabi at Sinasabi sa *Sermones* ni P. Blancas de San José." In Blancas de San José (1614) 1994, 353–69.

Rozt Dupeyron, Guy. 2015. "Reflexiones personales sobre la conquista espiritual y consolidación temprana de la colonización hispana en el Septentrión novohispano." *Revista de Ciencias Sociales y Humanidades* 24 (July–December): 76–108.

San Antonio, Juan Francisco de, OFM. 1738. *Chronicas de la apostólica Provincia de S. Gregorio de Religosos Descalzos N.S.P.S. Francisco en las Islas Philipinas, China, Japón &c.* . . . Sampaloc. https://archive.org/details/chronicasdelaapo00sana/page/n4/mode/2up

Schmitt, Carl. 2006. *Nomos of the Earth in the International Law of Jus Publicum Europaeum*. Trans. G. L. Ulmen. London: Telos Press.

Scott, James. 2009. *The Art of Not Being Governed: An Anarchist History of Upland Southeast Asia*. New Haven: Yale University Press.

Scott, William Henry. 1982. *Cracks in the Parchment Curtain and Other Essays in Philippine History*. Quezon City (Manila): New Day.

Scott, William Henry. 1994. *The Discovery of the Igorots*. Quezon City: New Day.

Serge Gruzinski. 2006. *La guerra de las imágenes: De Cristóbal Colón a "Blade Runner" (1492–2019)*. Trans. Juan Jose Utrilla. Mexico: Fondo de Cultura Económica.

Sheridan Prieto, Cecilia. 2012. *Fronterización del espacio hacia el norte de la Nueva España*. Zacatecas: Instituto Mora.

Tadiar, Neferti. 2009. *Things Fall Away: Philippine Historical Experience and the Making of Globalization*. Durham: Duke University Press.

Zamora, Margarita. 1993. *Reading Columbus*. Berkeley: University of California Press.

Zuñiga, Fr. Joaquín Martínez de. 1803. *Historia de las Philipinas*. Sampaloc.

Translation Is a Language of Hispanofilipino Literature

Marlon James Sales

The invisibility of what has been called in Spanish *literatura hispanofilipina,* *literatura hispano-filipina, literatura filipino-hispana, literatura fil-hispana,* and *literatura filipina en español* partly emanates from the connotations elicited by these labels. Although on the surface there appears to be a tacit understanding of what this literary tradition looks like, the scholarly literature written to date shows divergences as to what its nature and scope should be. For example, in a special edition of the journal *Transmodernity* on the Spanish Philippines, Álvarez Tardío (2014) asserts:

> Denominamos a la literatura filipina escrita en español con la etiqueta de "literatura hispanofilipina," un vocablo que permite identificar claramente su filiación filipina, dejando ver igualmente su componente hispano.

> (We refer to Philippine literature written in Spanish with the label "literatura hispanofilipina," a word that allows for a clear identification of its Filipino affiliation, while at the same time letting its Hispanic component shine through.) (41)[1]

On the other hand, Donoso (2014) avers in that same edition that the term "'literatura filipina en español' hace referencia a una literatura escrita en Filipinas en lengua española" ("Filipino literature in Spanish" refers to a literature written in the Philippines in the Spanish language) (9). These definitions allude to two different points of reference, with the former underscoring the racial aspects of authorship and the latter the geopolitics of literary production.

The debates further expand when we examine which descriptor should take precedence in the label. Ofilada (2014, 55–56) insists on using the term *literatura filhispana* to highlight the Philippines' belongingness to the Hispanic world. The phrase circumvents what he views as a reduction of the universality of Hispanism within the limiting boundaries of Filipinoness, which the term *literatura hispanofilipina* purportedly evokes. A similar argument had been made by Alinea (1964, xiii–xiv) and Farolán (1980, i). Both recommended, somewhat flippantly, that the term *filipino* be mentioned first because the literature in question was written by Filipinos and Spaniards who considered themselves Filipinos. In contrast, Donoso (2014, 10) argues that *fil-hispano* panders to an elitist Hispanophilia among Spanish-speaking Filipinos. The term, Donoso continues, implies pushing this literature to the margins of the national canon in a bid to dissociate it from the masses who do not know Spanish. To be sure, other peripheral Spanish-language traditions in Asia and Africa, which together with the Spanish Philippines constitute the recently coined category of the Global Hispanophone, are subject to an analogous scrutiny (Kim and Davis 2014; Ndongo-Bidyogo 2015). Their uncomfortable positioning as minor literatures—or, more precisely, as *minoritized* literatures—with respect to their canon's more representative texts makes cultural hybridity a key issue for their identification and survival (Lomas López 2015, 271–75; Tauchnitz 2018, 122–25).

As fraught as it already is, this literary tradition becomes even more complicated once it gets enmeshed with the issues pervading English-language scholarship. Pivoting to English proves unavoidable because of its status as the co-official language of the Philippines, which in turn contributes to the further minoritization of Spanish. Within the field of Hispanic studies itself, only a few investigations have been written by Filipino scholars in either Spanish or a Philippine vernacular, with English usually standing in as a linguistic recourse. But with English comes another dispute: That the adjective *filipino/a* in Spanish lends itself to at least two different concepts in English requires that it be analyzed semantically in light of the evolving research paradigms on the Philippines (cf. Campomanes 2003). Although employed invariably in the Spanish-language texts to describe anything related to the Philippines and the Filipinos, *filipino/a* may be taken to mean "Philippine," which puts emphasis on the Philippines as a site, either physical or imagined. It may also be interpreted as "Filipino," a more pliable identitarian descriptor that can be adapted to fluxes created by new nationalisms. So which is it? Is it "Philippine literature in Spanish" or "Filipino literature in Spanish"? Is it *Panitikan sa Pilipinas sa Wikang Kastila* or *Panitikang Filipino sa Wikang*

Kastila? Can we describe this literature as "Philippine" when portions of its canon are taken from the works of Filipino authors in the diaspora like Edmundo Farolán, Elizabeth Medina, and Edwin Lozada? Alternatively, can we say this literature is "Filipino" if we include authors like Manuel Blanco, Wenceslao Retana, and José Felipe del Pan, who did not identify as Filipinos but wrote extensively about the Philippines?

Questions like these are symptomatic of a bigger ontological crisis saddling the field. The Philippine/Filipino literary tradition in Spanish suffers from an unfortunate reputation of being neither Asian nor Hispanic enough to merit the attention it deserves from either tradition. This resonates with the Filipinos' vague self-referencing as the Latinos of Asia, which oversimplifies the intricacies of a national identity forged by successive waves of human displacements (Ocampo 2016, 77–86). The Philippines remains alien to many Hispanists, who are inclined to lump it together with the vast expanse of sites collectively known as Latin America (Fradera 2001, 99; Morillo-Alicea 2013, 27). This happens even if the peculiarity of the Filipino experience readily distinguishes it from its American counterparts (Ney 2012, 397). On the other hand, it is almost impossible to conceive of Asian studies with Spanish as a tool despite the wealth of Spanish-language resources written on Asia, particularly on the Philippines (Kim and Davis 2014, 200; Lifshey 2016, 7–8). What this does is erase many counternarratives from a history long dominated by Anglo-American perspectives (Buschmann, Slack, and Tueller 2014, 15). Privileging other voices that have elected to express themselves in languages other than English has the potential of recuperating these counternarratives. This privileging is especially relevant for the Philippines, where Spanish's colonialist overtones were co-opted into an *ilustrado* aspiration for nationhood before finally bowing down to a new colonial language (Peña 2001).

The discontents of Philippine/Filipino literature in Spanish also draw on the supposed isolation of the language in which it should be written and read. The assumption, it would appear, was that Spanish should always and exclusively be the language of this literary tradition and that this language stood in opposition to other languages that were the actual linguae francae of the Philippines. But if this literary tradition has both Hispanic and Filipino roots, it should follow that its singularity did not stem from any one medium of creative expression. Rather, it must have arisen from intricate creative processes fusing the indigenous with the colonial (Ofilada 2014, 57). The very possibility of compounding two adjectives together to describe this tradition and debating which of them should be placed first marks a conceptual synthesis that cannot be fully reckoned in one language.

In this chapter, I contend that translation is a language of what I will refer to as Hispanofilipino literature. I am not claiming that Spanish is not the main language of the texts we are studying. It is, in fact, a feature that establishes the membership of texts in this corpus. I do claim, however, that Spanish is not the only language of this literature. Hispanofilipino literature should admit other iterations embodying the translational realities of a multilingual Filipino nation. To set the scope of this corpus, I am adopting Peralta-Imson's definition of "Philippine literature in Spanish," which includes "the writings in this language—whether utilitarian, artistic or creative—written by Spaniards, *mestizos* or native Filipinos" (1997, 1; italics in original). I am dropping the hyphen in "Hispanofilipino" to scale down the entitlement commonly ascribed to hyphenated Filipino identities (Tuason et al. 2007), thus democratizing a literature whose minoritization is brought about by its association with a lettered elite. The term also highlights the diversity of Filipino identities, among whose permutations the ability to write in Spanish can be had. In choosing Hispanofilipino, I am applying an informed strategy myself that directly transposes the adjective from Spanish into English. My strategy foregrounds the conceptual incommensurability between the descriptor and its English-language translations, as well as the task of proposing a translation solution gesturing to the identitarian ambiguities at the heart of this literary tradition.

The Language of Translation

Developments in cultural theory have come to regard translation as a language. Kenyan academic Ngũgĩ wa Thiong'o (2012) calls translation "the language of languages [that] opens the gates of national and linguistic prisons" (61). Meanwhile, the Nobel laureate Octavio Paz (1971) maintains that no text can completely be original because language itself is a translation. Elevating translation to the status of a language is an ethical and political response to its invisibility. As in Anglophone literatures (Venuti 1995), translation continues to be dismissed in Spanish-language literatures as a second-rate practice of textual creation. A distinction is still made between literature and translated literature on the pretext that, notwithstanding the tautology, anything translated is secondary to anything "created." Indeed, the literary histories of Alinea (1964), Soriano (1965), Mariñas (1974), Farolán (1980), and Donoso and Gallo (2011) made light of translation and its place in the canon. References to translations were treated, if at all, as afterthoughts to a more committed discussion about what was implicitly regarded as the main body of work of Hispanofilipino authors.

The first step in subverting the hierarchy between literature and translated literature is to consider language and translation as coeval. As Paz points out, if language is translation, it must also be true that "cada traducción . . . constituye un texto único" (each translation . . . constitutes a unique text) (9). Translated literature has been examined increasingly from a perspective of primacy, and more so in minority-language cultures, which are "translation cultures *par excellence*" (Cronin 2003, 139; italics in original). Along these lines, originality can no longer be treated as an intrinsic property of literature and should instead be regarded as a function of translation. This is so because a text becomes an original only when a translation of it has been created (Niranjana 1992, 3). In other words, while an original text precedes a translation sequentially, it is actually translation that gives the text its originality.

Translation has historically aroused suspicion in the Philippines. The degree to which a translation could faithfully reveal the intended meaning of a text was a concern even at the outset of colonial rule (Rafael 1993). Later Filipino writers echoed this concern. In an 1886 letter, Paciano Rizal criticized his brother José for his translation of the Swiss folktale of William Tell. José's translation, Paciano wrote, left much to be desired because "se ha separado algún tanto . . . del especial giro del tagalo" (it has been somewhat detached . . . from the special idiom of Tagalog) (Kalaw 1930, 217). For his part, Rafael Palma wrote about a translation of the municipal code by his contemporary Pedro Paterno that had been rejected by the censors (1914, vii–viii). Paterno's translation, Palma surmised, allegedly contained dubious commentaries that rendered it unfaithful to its source. Many years after, León Ma. Guerrero expressed his dissatisfaction with the existing translations of the *Noli me tángere* (Touch me not), or *Noli* hereafter, in the preface of his own English-language translation of the novel. He complained that the translations by non-Filipinos lacked an understanding of the national situation, while those by Filipinos suffered from an "exaggerated reverence for the original text" (in Rizal 1961, xvi). Such was the anxiety over translations of Hispanofilipino texts that in a speech he would have delivered in Madrid if it were not for his sudden demise in Rome, the Hispanist and politician Claro M. Recto ([1960] 1990, 726) recorded his reservations against substituting Spanish-language texts with "traducciones bastardas" (bastard translations).

Despite the apparent reticence, there was a certain awareness among Hispanofilipino authors that it was through translation that literature could remain relevant to Filipinos. Unconvinced with his Spanish-language version of Francisco Balagtas's opus *Florante at Laura*, Rafael Palma concluded that "quien no ha nacido poeta no sirve para traducir a un poeta" (he who is not born a poet is useless in translating a poet) (1914, 190). He then called on poets to translate Balagtas from Tagalog into Spanish "para bien de la literatura patria" (for the good of national literature). Palma's call was answered upon the publication of Epifanio de los Santos's translation in 1916. Seven decades later, Federico Espino Licsi (1980) offered a spirited defense of translation in a speech he delivered in Spanish, Tagalog, and English. He criticized the selective memory of some Filipino Hispanists who were lobbying for the obligatory teaching of Spanish in the Philippines without problematizing how this campaign advanced colonialism in a nation that no longer spoke the language.[2] Palma and Espino Licsi approached translation from different angles. Palma advocated for its practice to curb the decline of Spanish, while Espino Licsi thought of it as an alternative mode of access for those who did not speak the language. Palma wrote about translating *into* Spanish, while Espino Licsi talked about translating *from* it. Both, however, espoused the view that Spanish was a patrimony of the Philippines whose preservation in the national consciousness could be attained by embedding it in translations.

Hispanofilipino literature is indeed incomplete if we refuse to admit that it has been conversing with us all along in diverse ways through languages other than Spanish, with translation underpinning all the attendant exchanges. It has to be stated clearly that the claim that translation is a language of Hispanofilipino literature comes with the presupposition that translating is more than imitation. Like any other language, translation is a purposive enunciation of ideas to a speech community that relies on its network of shared meanings and discursive repertoires. In what follows, we shall see examples of such exchanges in two broad applications. First, we will examine translation as a product of a textual transfer that takes the form of a publication or a section thereof. We will then proceed to analyze translation's more immanent metalinguistic role in the interpretation of literature against the ever-changing linguistic landscape of the Philippines.

Translation as Literary Publications

The scholarly discussions on translation and Hispanofilipino literature over-whelmingly focus on the writings of Rizal, particularly his *Noli* and its sequel, *El filibusterismo* (Subversion), or *Fili* hereafter, published in 1887 and 1891, respectively. For many Filipinos, the experience of reading Hispanofilipino literature is limited to these novels, which became obligatory in Philippine schools through Republic Act No. 1425, or the so-called Rizal Law of 1956. While the law has authorized reading a translation as an alternative to the unexpurgated originals in Spanish, no translation is considered "official." Schools are free to choose which *Noli* and *Fili* to teach to their students from an array of translations into English and, more commonly, Filipino.[3] Here lies the problem. Many translations printed by local commercial publishers are abridgements that have effaced important cultural references and have dimin-ished the tenor of the discourse. The more highbrow translations, like Guerre-ro's influential English-language version from which several translations into Filipino were derived, have their own artistic, ideological, and pedagogical biases (Anderson 1998, 238–47). An uncritical reliance on these translations thus runs counter to the intention of the Rizal Law, which envisioned Rizal's novels as materials for inculcating nationalism among Filipino students.

It would be imprecise to conclude that the *Noli* and *Fili* were the only specimens of translation in the canon. The history of Hispanofilipino liter-ature is dotted with translations, even though many of them remain under-circulated. The first known books published in the Philippines in 1593 were translations into Tagalog and Chinese of the Christian doctrine (Sanz 1958). Other translated materials in the form of catecheses, sacramentaries, and devotional texts were produced by Spanish missionaries thereafter. The *Ver-dad nada amarga* (An unbitter truth), a Spanish-language translation by the Dominican Baltazar de Santa Cruz of the medieval tale of Barlaam and Josaphat, came out in 1692, the first time a novel was ever published in the Philippines (Cañizares 2000, 263). Santa Cruz's translation was derived from a 16th-century Latin version by the French Jesuit Jacques de Billy of St. John Damascene's hagiography in Greek. A Tagalog version by the Jesuit Anto-nio de Borja, addressed to "mga kapatid kong Tagalog" (my Tagalog brothers and sisters), would come out in 1712 (Blanco 2020, 318; his translation). This translation was a turning point in the localization of literature from a for-eign source, a forerunner of the Filipino novel as we know the genre today (Mojares 1976, 46; Veyra 1961, 16).

Indigenous writers also had a hand in producing translations, the most famous of whom was the Batangas-born Gaspar Aquino de Belén, whose translation into Tagalog of Fr. Tomás Villacastin's prayers of commendation for the dead was produced around 1703. The second part of this work contained Aquino de Belén's most celebrated masterpiece, the *pasyon*, a narration in verse of Christ's passion, death, and resurrection. When nationalist fervor surged toward the end of the 19th century, the local intelligentsia deployed translation as a weapon against the colonial establishment, as in the *Dasalan at Tocsohan* (Prayer and mockery), a satirical rewriting of Catholic prayers by Marcelo del Pilar, Pedro Serrano, and Rafael Enríquez that ridiculed friars and their abuses (Mojares 2006, 455). The title capitalized on the double entendre of the word "tocsohan," which in the Tagalog of the period may also refer to a kind of doctrinal instruction in a question-and-answer format.

Translation accompanied the political transition from one colonial regime to another when the Philippines came under US control in 1898. The growing fascination for Rizal during this period prompted many translations of his writings, including the first versions of the *Noli* and *Fili* into English, which was imposed as the new official language by the Americans, and the local vernaculars (Craig 1927, 216–21). Translating literatures from other European languages with Spanish as relay became fashionable (Jurilla 2010, 97–101): *Les mystères de Paris* by the French author Eugène Sue was translated into Tagalog in 1912 as *Ang mga Hiwaga ng Paris* (The mysteries of Paris) by Francisco Sugui; *Quo vadis* by the Polish Henryk Sienkiewicz was translated in 1915 as *Saan ka Paparoon?* (Where are you heading?) by Aurelio Tolentino; and *Het yzeren graf* by the Flemish Hendrik Conscience was translated in 1917 as *Ang Libingang Bakal* (The iron grave) by Rosendo Ignacio. All three were extracted from existing Spanish-language translations.

Translation also thrived in the newspapers. Isabelo de los Reyes's *El Ilocano*, regarded as the first Philippine newspaper in an indigenous language (Taylor 1927, 26), was in reality a bilingual publication in Spanish and Ilokano, the lingua franca of the northern Philippines. Other periodicals such as *El Renacimiento*, *El Ideal*, *La Vanguardia*, and *El Debate* were printed alongside *Muling Pagsilang* (Rebirth), *Ang Mithi* (The ideal), *Taliba* (Sentinel), and *Pagkakaisa* (Unity), their Tagalog-language editions (43). Translated literature was serialized in some of these newspapers. Enrique Segovia Rocaberti's play *El voto de castidad* was adapted in Tagalog by Julián Cruz Balmaceda as *Sa Pinto ng Langit* (At heaven's gates) and was published in *Ang Mithi* between August and November 1917. Francisco Laksamana's *Dugo sa Dugo* (Blood against blood), a translation of Mary Elizabeth Braddon's *The Octoroon* based on its Spanish-language translation *Lucha de razas* (Struggle of races), was published in *Taliba* between February and May 1921 (Jurilla 2010, 108–9).

Some Hispanofilipino authors complemented their publications with translations. Among the poems in Fernando Ma. Guerrero's posthumous anthology *Aves y flores* (Birds and flowers) was *Salmo de la vida* (1971, 348–49), his take on Henry W. Longfellow's *A Psalm of Life*. In *Mi copa bohemia* (My Bohemian cup), José Hernández Gavira featured his translations into Spanish of two poems by a certain Rady Joven Rodríguez, a poetess from Bulacan (1937, 176–79). Although the source texts are no longer available, we know of the existence of these poems, entitled *Preguntas* (Questions) and *Muñeca del cabaret* (originally, Madonna of the dancing hill), because of Hernández Gavira's translations.

Even Manuel Bernabé, widely acclaimed at that time as the national poet (Alinea 1964, 139; Veyra 1961, 77), did his share of translations. Some of them, like the Spanish-language version of Marcelo del Pilar's *Ang Kadakilaan [ng] Dios* (God's greatness) and Hermenegildo Flores's *Hibik ng Filipinas sa Inang España* (The Philippines' lament to Mother Spain), appeared in the monthly bilingual magazine the *Philippine Review/Revista Filipina* (Licuanan de Malones and Manzano 1970, 331–33, 347–55). More remarkably, translation was what earned Bernabé in 1924 his first Premio Zóbel, the most prestigious literary prize in Hispanofilipino literature (Brillantes 2006, 62). He received the prize for his translation into Spanish of Omar Khayyam's *Rubaiyat*, based on Edward Fitzgerald's famous English-language translation. First published in *La Vanguardia* (Mariñas 1974, 63), the translation was included subsequently in Bernabé's poetry anthology *Cantos del trópico* (Songs of the tropics). The anthology contained two other translations: *A Celia* (To Celia), from the dedicatory prologue of the *Florante at Laura* (289–92), and *La creación* (The creation), from Thomas Lidley's libretto for Franz Joseph Haydn's oratorio *Die Schöpfung* (311–22).

Translating Hispanofilipino literature persisted after Spanish lost its status as an official language of the Philippines in the 1973 Constitution and was reduced finally to an optional language in 1987.[4] Many parallel translations were produced from this point on. Pilar E. Mariño published a selection of Jesús Balmori's short stories in Spanish and English in 1987 and a compendium of Hispanofilipino short stories in 1989. Some of the stories from Mariño's compendium were republished in Spanish and Filipino by Magdalena C. Sayas about a decade later. Hilario Ziálcita's poetry collection was published in 2004 with an English-language translation by Sor Caritas de St. Paul de Sevilla and Caridad Ziálcita-Sevilla. Edmundo Farolán published a bilingual collection of poems in 2006. Three years later, he collaborated with Paulina Constancia in a compilation of short stories. Isabelo de los Reyes's *El folk-lore filipino* (Filipino folklore) was published with an English-language translation by Salud C. Dizon and María Elinora Peralta-Imson in 1994 and reprinted in 2010. The poetry collection of José Palma, launched posthumously as *Melancólicas* (Melancholies) by his brothers Manuel and Rafael in 1912, was published anew in 2010 with a translation into English by Alfredo S. Veloso. Veloso was a prolific translator who had under his belt several parallel translations in Spanish and English, including Recto's *Bajo los cocoteros*, published under the title *Beneath Coconut Palms* (1963), and *Poética*, an anthology of Hispanofilipino poetry (1966). The novel *La oveja de Nathán*, which won its author, Antonio Abad, the 1929 Premio Zóbel, was reprinted under the title *Nathan's Sheep* with a parallel translation by Lourdes Brillantes. It was published in 2013 by Georgina Padilla, granddaughter of the founder of the prize.

There were also translations published without an appended source text. Veloso's English-language translation of the biography of Doña Gliceria Marella (2011), originally written by Francisco Zaragoza, was published by Veloso's widow and the Knights of Rizal more than four decades after the translator's passing. The *Efemérides filipinas* (Philippine events) of Jaime de Veyra and Mariano Ponce was translated into Filipino in 1998 by Edgardo Tiamson, Teresita Alcántara, and Erwin Bautista. The Tagalog translation of Pedro Paterno's *Nínay* by Román G. Reyes, with editions from 1908 and 1909, was reprinted in 2002 by the De La Salle University Press. For their *Tesoro literario de Filipinas* (Philippine literary treasures), Lourdes Brillantes, Salvador Malig, and Renán Prado translated short stories into Spanish that were authored by some of the most revered names in Filipino fiction in English. Among them were Nick Joaquin, N. V. M. Gonzalez, and F. Sionil José, all of whom had been proclaimed National Artists by the Philippine government. Also mentionable are the writings by Spanish authors about the Philippines that have been translated by Filipinos. Some notable titles include *Cuentos filipinos* (Philippine stories) by José Montero y Vidal, translated by Renán Prado, Evelyn Soriano, Heide Aquino, and Shirley Torres (2004); and Trinidad Regala's *Terror in Manila* (2005), a translation of Antonio Pérez de Olaguer's memoirs of the Japanese invasion of the Philippines.

The foregoing list, though not exhaustive, maps out the itinerary of Hispanofilipino literature in relation to its languages. Translation moved to different directions, with Spanish operating either as its source, relay, or target language. A collaborative network of actors transgressing linguistic, racial, chronological, and geographical lines has intervened continuously in the creation, circulation, and recovery of Hispanofilipino literature. Such intersectional crossings show that no single group of people could claim this literary tradition as exclusively their own doing. They also indicate that Hispanofilipino literature has assigned various positionalities to Filipinos, who, aside from being originators of the texts, have become their mediators, receptors, onlookers, and subjects.

Translation as Metalanguage

Translation usually entails the transformation of a preexisting text into another language, typology, or form. Whether the product is published bilingually or not, there is always an identifiable source text located outside the translation that preceded it in the order of production. Rizal's *Noli* in Spanish preceded León M. Guerrero's translation into English. Fitzgerald's English-language translation of the *Rubaiyat*, a translation from an earlier text in Persian, preceded Bernabé's Spanish version. The story of Barlaam and Josaphat went from Greek to Latin before ending up in Santa Cruz's Spanish and Borja's Tagalog. But there have also been cases in Hispanofilipino literature where translation co-occurs with other authorial processes in constituting texts in their first composition. Translation acts in these cases as a literary metalanguage that informs the reading of the texts. It does so by enunciating, exemplifying, and expounding on their culturally hybridized content through an enactment of linguistic multiplicity in writing.

Consider the example of the *Librong pagaaaralan nang mga Tagalog nang uicang Castila* (The book with which the Tagalogs will learn the Castilian language) ([1610] 2011). Written by Tomás Pinpín, a Tagalog printer, this first grammar of Spanish in the Philippines was a veritable repository of translations. While its more famous bilingual poem was exhortatory in nature, directed at the indigenes who wished to learn Spanish so that they would not be "brutos salva[j]es" (brute savages) (5), it likewise contained poems for teaching vocabulary:

> Ang cambing, la cabra, / ang aso, el perro, / ang maya,y, gorion, / ang ouac, el
> cuervo, / ang bahay, la casa, / silid, aposento, / ang dingding, pared, / ang bob-

ongan, techo, / ang tangsó, laton / ang bacal, el hierro, / ang loual, ay, fuerza, / ang loob, ay dentro. (32–33)

At first glance, translation in this stanza was nothing more than a correlation between Tagalog words and their possible Castilian equivalents. But translation was also what made this poem compositionally possible. The choice of words and their corresponding translations were assembled in a manner that the rhyme and meter of Tagalog poetry were replicated. The language of this verse was neither Tagalog nor Spanish; it was the co-occurrence of these two languages that caused the words to constitute a poem. Should we remove any of the two, all we would be left with is a lexical enumeration in one language without any notional continuity (i.e., goat, dog, sparrow, raven, house, chamber, wall, roof, brass, steel, force, inside).

This metalinguistic property of translation is profitable for annotating *costumbrista* literature. In the 1800s a literary movement called *costumbrismo*, which showcased idealized portrayals of the colonies, swept across the Spanish-speaking world. *Costumbrista* writings on the Philippines made use of indigenous cultures to portray the peripheries for the colonial center. For instance, in Pedro Paterno's *Nínay* (1885), the first novel written by a Filipino, the funerary practices of local mestizos are framed using the *pasiám*, the Hispanofilipino term for the Catholic prayer recited on nine successive days following the death of a loved one. *Nínay* is embellished with hyperexoticized snippets of colonial life, made even more striking with the addition of some words in the baybayin, the ancient Tagalog writing system, as a visual device (165). Words from Indian languages also crop up in an outlandish excursus that transports the story briefly to an unnamed island (264–71).

Translation in *Nínay* appears overtly in the footnotes. It can go anywhere from a simple word-for-word transfer, like the word "perezosa" (31), translated intralinguistically as a "meridiana o sofá de siesta" (divan or lounge sofa), to longer explicitations, like the Tagalog "bonga" (62), laymanized in Spanish as a species of palm, and then translated into its scientific nomenclature *Areca catechu*. At one point, the phrase "caimán convertido en piedra," a reference to a legend about a crocodile that was turned into stone by St. Nicholas of Tolentino to save a Chinese boater in the Pasig River, is discussed in untranslated French in a four-page footnote (66–69). The second edition of Paul de la Gironière's *Aventures d'un gentilhomme breton aux Îsles Philippines* (Adventures of a Breton gentleman in the Philippine Islands) (1857, 97–100) is cited as the source of this information, although with a slight error in the page numbers.

Strategies like these provoke an uncomfortable tug-of-war between familiarity and remoteness. By gratuitously implementing zero translation (i.e., retaining content words from a foreign language in the main body of the text), Paterno introduces his readers to unknown worlds teeming with strange surroundings, rituals, and sensations. The barrage of untranslated toponyms, flora, fauna, household objects, and other similar context-bound referents keeps readers at a distance, converting the reading process into a spectatorship of the bizarre. But as the readers gaze at this strangeness from afar, Paterno begins annotating the narrative with the familiar images of the everyday, simultaneously conjuring "a voyeuristic pleasure in the quaint and local [and] a universalizing impulse that connects the local to cultural phenomena elsewhere in the world" (Mojares 2006, 44). The colonies, deliberately made distant through a profusion of ethnological terminologies in languages other than Spanish, are refamiliarized for the readers with Paterno acting as an all-knowing interpreter and guide.

Postcolonial literature, Bandia (2010) contends, is a form of translation because through it "the language of colonization is bent, twisted or plied to capture and convey the sociocultural reality or worldview of an alien dominated language culture" (265). Hispanofilipino literature is no exception. From Rizal's enumeration of local fish species in the *Noli* (1887, 123) to the colorful descriptions of mythological creatures in Adelina Gurrea's *Cuentos de Juana* (Juana's tales; 1943), Hispanofilipino texts are replete with culture-specific realia that signal the difficulties of displacing ideas between languages by resisting translation. Untranslated words do not necessarily have exoticizing ends—or, at least, they do not always come across as willful attempts at estrangement. In many Hispanofilipino texts, realia are primarily signposts of a world where a narrative transpires, a fictionalized vision of the Philippines that camouflages colonialism as a seamless and even idyllic encounter of cultures.

But translation can also unfurl the tensions of colonialism by simulating its violence in very unsettling ways. Jesús Balmori's poem *La letra con sangre entra* (literally, "the letter enters with blood"), from his anthology *El libro de mis vidas manileñas* (The book of my Manila lives) (1928), is a stinging reproach of the language policy of the American colonial rule. It recounts the story of a certain Lucio Rosales, a customer at a local post office, who is informed by an employee, Román Iturralde, that all transactions are conducted in English:

—Ako'y si Dr. Lucio Rosales.—¿Wariu wont? / —Kukunin ko ang sulat na nasa aking ngalan. / —Ay kent get wariu sey. You betar espik inglis. / —Bakit, ano ka ba, ¿amerikano negro?.

(—I am Dr. Lucio Rosales.—¿What do you want? / —I will retrieve a letter under my name. / —I can't get what you are saying. You better speak English. / —Why, who do you think you are? ¿A black American?) (64)

The story unfolds as a translational exchange between Rosales, who insists on speaking Tagalog, and Iturralde, who struggles to speak English, as evidenced by Balmori's accommodation of English sounds to Tagalog phonology. In an anthology mostly written in Spanish, this poem stands out for restaging the frictions of the US language policy in the Philippines. It invents a translatese, a mock language inflected by English, Spanish, and Tagalog, to recreate the strains of speaking multiple languages all at once. Calquing the inverted question mark of Spanish in Tagalized English amplifies the dissonance, which is further troubled at the end of the stanza by a racialized conflation between linguistic prestige and skin color.

Balmori's translatese is incorporated in other poems of his anthology. The resulting babel of tongues in these poems can be read as a criticism of the colonial condition, particularly its incursions into language. Through these poems, Balmori shows that the intelligibility of colonial speakers is contingent upon how well they can participate in an unending cycle of translation, instantiated in several instances in a composite of fragmentary languages. The immediate effects may be jarring, as in the poem *Miusic to Mister Rait* (Music to Mr. Wright) (7), cryptic song lyrics written entirely in translatese. The evocations are hardly ever commensurate, as in *No, no es lo mismo* (No, it's not the same) (31–32), a poem with lines from Tagalog, Ilokano, Kapampangan, Ilonggo, and Spanish about the burdens of reproducing meanings across languages. But as in *Salute, oh de Pinedo!* (Hail to de Pinedo!) (243), which memorializes the Manila leg of the 1925 intercontinental flight by the Neapolitan aviator Francesco de Pinedo, it is only through this compositeness that we could read a text as a coherent whole and allow ourselves momentarily to suspend disbelief and speak a foreign language (Italian in this case) after tweaking a few Spanish words.

The translatese in Balmori's poems calls to mind other linguistic hybrids that have found their way to Hispanofilipino literature, such as the Spanish-

Chinese pidgin spoken by the diasporic Chinese communities in Manila and the nearby provinces, whose earliest surviving account dates back to 1718 (Fernández 2018, 152). Literary approximations of this pidgin were recorded in Montero y Vidal's story *El payo de Chang-Chuy* (1876, 225–63), among others.[5] Montero y Vidal identified two of its distinguishing features, namely, the substitution of the /r/ with the /l/ and the addition of /e/ or /o/ at the end of Spanish infinitives, which according to the writer add a comical effect to the text (227–28).[6] When the story was translated as *Chang-Chuy's Umbrella* in 2004, the pidgin remained intact in the English-language version but with the addition of bracketed annotations as a reading aid (Montero y Vidal 2004, 205). This strategy suggests that the translators were aware that the goal of the translation was not simply a matter of making the readers understand the conversation; it was likewise a matter of performing a linguistic hybrid in written discourse and conveying the message that that performance was an underlying theme in the story.

Such examples offer us a more nuanced concept of translation. While translation is customarily thought of as a product emerging from the afterlife of a text, the preceding examples demonstrate that it can also happen at a primordial locus of origination where literatures are birthed. Translation is as much a literary prelife as it is an afterlife. Hispanofilipino writers authored their works in translation, straddling as they did the various languages they had at their disposal. As a literary metalanguage, translation addresses colonial difference in multiple, and even contrary, ways. On the one hand, it can homogenize the particularities of colonial life by associating them with the cultural commonplaces that a readership recognizes more easily. But on the other, it can expose the problematic equivalences that colonialism sought to impose by disfiguring a colonial language and uncovering its limitations as a medium of expression (cf. Rafael 2015).

Some Concluding Points

The study of Hispanofilipino literature has generally downplayed the role of translation in the production, circulation, and reception of its texts. As such, it has not been unusual to conceptualize Hispanofilipino literature as a collection of texts entirely written in Spanish and seemingly unaffected by the translational exchanges that, in the first place, have made texts in a colonial language a conceivable fixture of a multilingual Filipino society. But as this chapter has shown, Hispanofilipino literature has turned to translation throughout its history to come to being and survive. Various authors have participated in its conduct and have acknowledged its relevance in perpetuating a legacy that was already on the wane. It is this chapter's contention, therefore, that translation is one of the languages of Hispanofilipino literature.

Literary theorist Pascale Casanova (2004) writes that translation establishes the value of literature (21). "The most closeted literary spaces," she adds, "are characterized by an absence of translation" (107). The problem we think we have in Hispanofilipino literature may not be so much about having to access it through a language most Filipinos no longer know. Our problem lies instead in the presumption that creating Hispanofilipino literature stops at that moment it is first written down or that it ceases to exist if no Filipino readers can enjoy it in the original Spanish. By approaching translation as a language, we are emancipating Hispanofilipino literature from an unnecessary hermetism that restricts its development to a single language, thus remapping its achievements and potentials in a constellation of multiple tongues.

Notes

1. Unless otherwise specified, all translations in this chapter are mine. Archaic orthographical conventions are retained in the citations as long as they do not hamper readability.

2. I am indebted to Paula C. Park for forwarding a copy of Espino Licsi's text. Espino Licsi was an accomplished translingual writer who wrote in at least four languages: Spanish, Tagalog, English, and Ilokano.

3. "Filipino," the name of the Tagalog-based Philippine national language, was coined only in 1973. For older texts, the term "Tagalog" is preferred. Before the recent reforms in Philippine basic education, the *Noli* and *Fili* were the main literature component of a subject called "Filipino" in the third and fourth years of high school.

4. Presidential Decree No. 155, issued that same year, maintained Spanish's official status for certain purposes on a temporary basis (Fernández 2013, 372).

5. Montero y Vidal was unable to capture the final velar sound /ŋ/ here. The spelling in Tagalog should have been "payong."

6. Fernández (2018, 139) warns us that the Spanish-Chinese pidgin should not be confused with Chabacano, the Spanish-based creole of the Philippines. In fact, in Montero y Vidal's story, Chang-Chuy was conversing in pidgin with a cigarette vendor, who in turn was speaking in Chabacano. Chabacano is a full-fledged literary language in its own right. I am unable to include a lengthier discussion of Chabacano literature here because of space constraints, but readers may want to consult Romanillos (2006) for a comprehensive introduction to the subject.

References

Alinea, Estanislao B. 1964. *Historia analítica de la literatura filipinohispana (desde 1566 hasta mediados de 1964)*. Manila: Imprenta Los Filipinos.

Álvarez Tardío, Beatriz. 2014. "El privilegio de subvertir: La literatura hispanofilipina." *Transmodernity* 4 (1): 41–53.

Anderson, Benedict. 1998. *Spectres of Comparison: Nationalism, Southeast Asia and the World*. London: Verso.

Balmori, Jesús. 1928. *El libro de mis vidas manileñas*. Manila: Manila Gráfica.

Bandia, Paul F. 2010. "Post-colonial Literatures and Translation." In *Handbook of Translation Studies*, edited by Yves Gambier and Luc Van Doorslaer, 264–69. Amsterdam: John Benjamins.

Bernabé, Manuel. 1929. *Cantos del trópico*. Manila: San Juan Press.

Blanco, Jody. 2020. "*Barlaam and Josaphat* in Early Modern Spain and the Colonial Philippines: Spiritual Exercises of Freedom at the Center and Periphery." In *Iberian Empires and the Roots of Globalization*, edited by Ivonne del Valle, Anna More, and Rachel Sarah O'Toole, 303–29. Nashville: Vanderbilt University Press.

Braddon, Mary Elizabeth. 1921. *Dugo sa Dugo*. Translated by Francisco Laksamana. Manila: Vanguardia Print.

Brillantes, Lourdes Castrillo. 2006. *81 Years of Premio Zóbel: A Legacy of Philippine Literature in Spanish*. Makati: Georgina Padilla y Zóbel and the Filipinas Heritage Library.

Brillantes, Lourdes Castrillo, Salvador B. Malig, and René Ángelo Prado, trans. 2009. *Tesoro literario de Filipinas*. Quezon City: BMP Publications.

Buschmann, Rainer F., Edward R. Slack Jr., and James B. Tueller. 2014. *Navigating the Spanish Lake: The Pacific in the Iberian World, 1521–1898*. Honolulu: University of Hawai'i Press.

Campomanes, Oscar V. 2003. "The Vernacular/Local, the National, and the Global in Filipino Studies." *Kritika Kultura* 3:5–16. https://doi.org/10.13185/1566

Cañizares, Patricia. 2000. "La *Historia de los dos soldados de Cristo, Barlaan y Josafat* traducida por Juan de Arce Solorzeno (Madrid 1608)." *Cuaderno de Filología Clásica. Estudios Latinos* 19:259–71.

Casanova, Pascale. 2004. *The World Republic of Letters*. Translated by M. B. DeBevoise. Cambridge, MA: Harvard University Press.

Craig, Austin. 1927. *Rizal's Life and Minor Writings*. Manila: Philippine Education.

Cronin, Michael. 2003. *Translation and Globalization*. London: Routledge.

Donoso, Isaac. 2014. "Ensayo historiográfico de las letras en Filipinas." *Transmodernity* 4 (1): 7–23.

Donoso, Isaac, and Andrea Gallo. 2011. *Literatura hispanofilipina actual*. Madrid: Verbum.

Espino Licsi, Federico. 1980. "Filipinas, el idioma español y el tercer mundo." In *Punto y Coma*, 18–23. Quezon City: Department of European Languages, University of the Philippines.

Farolán, Edmundo. 1980. *Literatura filipino-hispana*. Manila: Versman.

Farolán, Edmundo. 2006. *Itinerancias (Comings and Goings)*. San Francisco: Carayan Press.

Farolán, Edmundo, and Paulina Constancia. 2009. *Cuentos hispanofilipinos*. Quezon City: Central Book Supply.

Fernández, Mauro. 2013. "The Representation of Spanish in the Philippine Islands." In *A Political History of Spanish: The Making of a Language*, edited by José del Valle, 364–79. Cambridge: Cambridge University Press.

Fernández, Mauro. 2018. "El pidgin chino-español de Manila a principios del siglo XVIII." *Zeitschrift für romanische Philologie* 134 (1): 137–70. https://doi.org/10.1515/zrp-2018-0006

Fradera, Josep M. 2001. "La formación de una colonia. Objetivos metropolitanos y transacciones locales." In *Imperios y naciones en el Pacífico—La formación de una colonia: Filipinas*, edited by María Dolores Elizalde, Josep M. Fradera, and Luis Alonso, 83–103. Madrid: CSIC.

Gironière, Paul de la. 1857. *Aventures d'un gentilhomme breton aux Îsles Philippines.* 2nd ed. Paris: Firmin Didot Frères, Fils et Cie.

Guerrero, Fernando Ma. 1971. *Aves y flores.* Manila: s.n.

Hernández Gavira, José. 1937. *Mi copa bohemia: poesías.* Manila: s.n.

Jurilla, Patricia May B. 2010. *Bibliography of Filipino Novels, 1901–2000.* Quezon City: University of the Philippines Press.

Kalaw, Teodoro M., ed. 1930. *Epistolario Rizalino.* Vol. 1. Manila: Bureau of Printing.

Kim, Yeon-Soo, and Kathleen E. Davis. 2014. "Claiming a Space for Spanish Asian Studies." *Arizona Journal of Hispanic Cultural Studies* 18 (1): 199–210.

Licuanan de Malones, Angelita, and Jaime J. Manzano, hijo, eds. 1970. *Escritos de Marcelo H. del Pilar.* Vol. 2. Manila: National Library.

Lifshey, Adam. 2016. *Subversions of the American Century: Filipino Literature in Spanish and the Transpacific Transformation of the United States.* Ann Arbor: University of Michigan Press.

Lomas López, Enrique. 2015. "Sergio Barce, una literatura entre Marruecos y España." In *Literaturas hispanoafricanas: Realidades y contextos*, edited by Inmaculada Díaz Narbona, 271–92. Madrid: Editorial Verbum.

Mariñas, Luis. 1974. *La literatura filipina en castellano.* Madrid: Editora Nacional.

Mariño, Pilar E., trans. 1987. *Cuentos de Balmori.* Quezon City: National Bookstore.

Mariño, Pilar E., trans. 1989. *Philippine Short Stories in Spanish, 1900–1941.* Quezon City: Office of Research Coordination, University of the Philippines.

Mojares, Resil B. 1976. "Barlaan, Urbana at Basio: Three Philippine Proto-Novels." *Philippine Quarterly of Culture and Society* 4 (1): 46–54.

Mojares, Resil B. 2006. *Brains of the Nation: Pedro Paterno, T. H. Pardo de Tavera, Isabelo de los Reyes and the Production of Modern Knowledge.* Quezon City: Ateneo de Manila University Press.

Montero y Vidal, José. 1876. *Cuentos filipinos.* Madrid: Imprenta Ariban y C^{a}.

Montero y Vidal, José. 2004. *Cuentos filipinos.* Translated by René Ángelo Prado, Evelyn Soriano, Heide Aquino, and Shirley Torres. Quezon City: Ateneo de Manila University.

Morillo-Alicea, Javier. 2013. "Uncharted Landscapes of 'Latin America': The Philippines in the Spanish Imperial Archipelago." In *Interpreting Spanish Colonialism: Empires, Nations, and Legends*, edited by Christopher Schmidt-Nieto and John M. Nieto-Phillips, 25–53. Albuquerque: University of New Mexico Press.

Ndongo-Bidyogo, Donato. 2015. "De la inexistencia conceptual a la visibilización de las otras literaturas hispánicas." In *Literaturas hispanoafricanas: Realidades y contextos*, edited by Inmaculada Díaz Narbona, 11–17. Madrid: Editorial Verbum.

Ney, Stephen. 2012. "Asia's Christian-Latin Nation?—Postcolonial Reconfigurations in the Literature of the Philippines." *Cross/Cultures*, no. 145: 393–408.

Niranjana, Tejaswini. 1992. *Siting Translation: History, Post-Structuralism, and the Colonial Context*. Berkeley: University of California Press.

Ocampo, Anthony C. 2016. *The Latinos of Asia: How Filipino Americans Break the Rules of Race*. Stanford: Stanford University Press.

Ofilada, Macario. 2014. "La singularidad de la literatura filhispana." *Transmodernity* 4 (1): 54–66.

Palma, José. 2010. *Melancholies*. Translated by Alfredo S. Veloso. Manila: Old Gold Publication.

Palma, Rafael. 1914. *Voces de aliento: Colección de artículos literarios*. Manila: Imprenta Cultura Filipina.

Paterno, Pedro. 1885. *Nínay (costumbres filipinas)*. Madrid: Imprenta de Fortanet.

Paterno, Pedro. 2002. *Nínay (Ugali nang Catagalugan)*. Translated by Roman G. Reyes. 3rd ed. Manila: De La Salle University Press.

Paz, Octavio. 1971. *Traducción: Literatura y literalidad*. Barcelona: Editorial Tusquets.

Peña, Wystan de la. 2001. "The Spanish-English Language War." *Linguae et Litterae* 4–5:6–28.

Peralta-Imson, María Elinora. 1997. "Philippine Literature: Spanish Evolving a National Literature." *Linguae et Litterae* 2:1–19.

Pérez de Olaguer, Antonio. 2005. *Terror in Manila: February 1945*. Translated by Trinidad O. Regala. Manila: Memorare Manila 1945 Foundation.

Pinpin, Tomas. [1610] 2011. *Librong pagaaralan nang manga Tagalog nang uicang Castila*. Edited by Damon L. Woods. Manila: UST Publishing House.

Ponce, Mariano, and Jaime C. de Veyra. 1998. *Efemérides filipinas*. Translated by Edgardo M. Tiamson, Teresita A. Alcántara, and Erwin L. Bautista. Quezon City: University of the Philippines.

Rafael, Vicente L. 1993. *Contracting Colonialism: Translation and Christian Conversion in Tagalog Society under Early Spanish Rule*. Durham: Duke University Press.

Rafael, Vicente L. 2015. "The War of Translation: Colonial Education, American English, and Tagalog Slang in the Philippines." *Journal of Asian Studies* 74 (2): 283–302. https://doi.org/10.1017/S0021911814002241

Recto, Claro M. [1960] 1990. "La cruzada por el español en Filipinas." In *The Complete Works Claro M. Recto*, edited by Isagani R. Medina and Myrna S. Feliciano, 714–26. Pasay: Claro M. Recto Memorial Foundation.

Recto, Claro M. 1963. *Bajo los cocoteros / Beneath Coconut Palms*. Translated by Alfredo S. Veloso. Quezon City: Asvel.

Reyes, Isabelo de los. 2010. *El folk-lore filipino*. Translated by Salud C. Dizon and María Elinora Peralta-Imson. 2nd ed. Quezon City: University of the Philippines Press.

Rizal, José. 1887. *Noli me tángere: Novela tagala*. 1st ed. Berlin: Berliner Buchdruckerei-Actien-Gesellschaft.

Rizal, José. 1961. *The Lost Eden (Noli me tangere)*. Translated by León Ma. Guerrero. Bloomington: Indiana University Press.

Romanillos, Emmanuel Luis A. 2006. *Chabacano Studies: Essays on Cavite's Chabacano Language and Literature.* Cavite: Cavite Historical Society.

Santos, Epifanio de los. 1916. *Florante: Versión castellana del poema Tagalo con un ensayo crítico.* Manila: Philippine Review.

Sanz, Carlos. 1958. *Primitivas relaciones de España con Asia y Oceanía.* Madrid: Librería General de Victoriano Suárez.

Sayas, Magdalena C., trans. 1997. *Cuento/ Kuwento.* Manila: De La Salle University Press.

Segovia Rocaberti, Enrique. 1922. *Sa Pinto ng Langit.* Translated by Julián Cruz Balmaceda. Manila: Limbagang Paredes.

Soriano, Rosa Reyes. 1965. *Cultura hispano-filipina: Breve historia de la literatura hispano filipina.* Manila: Nueva Era Press.

Tauchnitz, Juliane. 2018. "Límites poscoloniales–límites de lo poscolonial: 'La higuera (o El ocaso del patriarca)' del escritor hispanomarroquí Ahmed El Gamoun." In *Transafrohispanismos: Puentes culturales críticos entre África, Latinoamérica y España,* edited by Dorothy Odartey-Wellington, 120–36. Leiden: Brill.

Taylor, Carson. 1927. *History of the Philippine Press.* Manila: s.n.

Tuason, Ma Teresa G., Amethyst Reyes Taylor, Laura Rollings, Temma Harris, and Carling Martin. 2007. "On Both Sides of the Hyphen: Exploring the Filipino-American Identity." *Journal of Counseling Psychology* 54 (4): 362–72. https://doi.org/10.1037/0022-0 167.54.4.362

Veloso, Alfredo S., trans. 1966. *Poética: Antología de poetas filipinos / Poetry: Anthology of Filipino Poets.* 9th rev. ed. Quezon City: Asvel.

Venuti, Lawrence. 1995. *The Translator's Invisibility: A History of Translation.* London: Routledge.

Veyra, Jaime C. de 1961. *La hispanidad en Filipinas.* Madrid: Publicaciones del Círculo Filipino.

Villacastín, Tomás de. 1760. *Mañga panalañging pagtatagobilin sa caloloua nang tauong naghihingalo.* Translated by Gaspar Aquino de Belén. 5th ed. Manila: Imprenta de la Companía de Jesús.

Wa Thiong'o, Ngũgĩ. 2012. *Globalectics: Theory and the Politics of Knowing.* New York: Columbia University Press.

Zaragoza, Francisco C. 2011. *Doña Gliceria Marella: Angel of the Revolution.* Translated by Alfredo S. Veloso. Paranaque: Old Gold Publishing and the Order of the Knights of Rizal.

Ziálcita y Legarda, Hilario. 2004. *La nao de Manila y demás poesías / The Manila Galleon and Other Poems.* Translated by Caritas de St. Paul Sevilla and Caridad Sevilla. Manila: Caridad Sevilla.

Transpacific *Tornaviajes*

Toward a Filipino-Mexican Redefinition of Hispanidad

Paula C. Park

Affirming that the Spanish term *hispanidad* or the related term "Hispanic" in English carries negative connotations related to some form or residue of imperial hegemony is nothing new. While each term takes its baggage from different historical moments and contexts, it could be said that they partake in the legacy of the 19th-century discursive clash between the so-called Anglo-Saxon race and the so-called Latin race or perhaps that of the centuries-old Spanish Black Legend.[1] Yet the more specific origins of the ideologically charged connotations of *hispanidad* can be largely traced back to an article published in 1926 in which Spanish priest Zacarías de Vizcarra, then serving as a chaplain in Buenos Aires, proposed that the Royal Spanish Academy distinguish the meaning of the term, which was until then being employed to refer to a mode of speech in the Spanish language, that is, as a synonym for *hispanismo*. *Hispanidad*, Vizcarra suggested, should mean "el conjunto de todos los pueblos de cultura y origen hispánico diseminados por Europa, América, África y Oceanía" (the set of all peoples of Hispanic culture and origin spread across Europe, America, Africa and Oceania) and "el conjunto de cualidades que distinguen del resto de las naciones del mundo a los pueblos de estirpe y cultura hispánica" (the set of all the qualities that distinguish the peoples of Hispanic origin and culture from the rest of the nations of the world) (quoted in Tateishi 2004, 6).[2] This renewed approach to Hispanic-ness was further advanced by Spanish ideologue Ramiro de Maeztu, who had befriended Vizcarra during his years as Spanish ambassador in Argentina. In *Defensa de la hispanidad* (Defense of Hispanicity) (1934), Maeztu reaffirms Spain's cultural legacy in the world by defining *hispánicos* as "todos los pueblos que deben la civilización o el ser a los pueblos hispanos de la península" (all the peoples who owe civilization or their being to the Hispanic people in the peninsula) (1998, 84).[3] In Maeztu's view, peoples from the former colonies of the Spanish Empire had an enormous debt to Spain. In lieu of paying this debt, all ex–Spanish colonies had to remain spiritually united to the former metropole, he argued, on the basis of a common language, culture, and, most of all, religion. This ideology began to be officially promoted in 1940 as the Franco regime created the Consejo de la Hispanidad (Council of Hispanicity), an institution that sought to strengthen Spain's relations with the former colonies of the Spanish Empire by reasserting Spain's global cultural authority—an effective use of soft power.

Hispanism, which I broadly define, for the moment, as the study and appreciation of cultural productions from the Spanish-speaking world, has had to deal with these and other extremist takes on the discourse of Hispanidad that help to perpetuate the Spanish Black Legend. As observed by Brad Epps, "In international Hispanism, particularly in the United States, Spain does not enjoy the position of dominance that many once considered its due" (2005, 234).[4] In the Philippines, the usages of the term "Hispanic" vary, but its overall resonance is not so different from that in the Americas. It tends to be associated with Spain, colonialism, and the host of meanings that come with that. Yet, over the past few years, various scholarly works on Hispanic/Filipino cultural productions have been published, resulting in a delinking from the neo-imperial or neo-colonialist frameworks to which they have been relegated. For example, the first volume of *More Hispanic Than We Admit*, published by the Manila-based Vibal Foundation, looks into diverse transcultural Hispanic productions in the Philippines. As articulated by Isaac Donoso Jiménez, editor of the volume, "'Hispanic' does not refer to Spain, but rather to the specific Philippine adaptation of Hispanic culture" (2008, x).[5] This seemingly superfluous definition alerts us to the trajectories of all things Hispanic in the Philippines. Following Glòria Cano, editor of the second volume of *More Hispanic Than We Admit*, the United States played a key role in the lamentable detours of Hispanism in the Philippines. The US administration, Cano argues, deliberately cast Hispanic culture in a detrimental light by "shaping the notion of a dark age of Spanish rule, described as anachronistic, despotic, tyrannical, medieval and halting" (2015, xiv).[6] Another significant collaborative approach to Hispanophone Filipino literature is the 2014 special issue of *Transmodernity: Journal of Peripheral Cultural Production of the Luso-Hispanic World*, edited by Andrea Gallo, for whom the study of these literary works must be placed within a framework of plurilingualism

(2014). More recently, Jorge Mojarro edited two special issues for the journals *Revista de Crítica Literaria Latinoamericana* (2018) and *UNITAS* (2019), both of which invite Latin Americanist literary critics and scholars of Philippine literature to dialogue with each other.

This chapter seeks to further the effort to rethink Hispanism in the Philippines and to do so transpacifically, by way of presenting two case studies from the 20th century wherein the Manila-Acapulco galleon trade, a commercial link that was made possible after Spanish friar and navigator Andrés de Urdaneta's *tornaviaje* (return voyage) from the Philippines to New Spain in 1565, was ardently evoked. First, I examine the work of Hispanophone Filipino writer Jesús Balmori (1887–1948), who has as of late garnered significant attention.[7] Extending the work of various Balmori critics, I focus on a trip the Filipino author made across the Pacific and his consequent stay in Mexico in the early 1930s. Balmori does not employ the term *tornaviaje*; however, he alludes to it in a series of articles and poems, suggestively titled "De Manila a México" (From Manila to Mexico), which he published upon his return to the Philippines. The second part of this chapter analyzes a series of lectures delivered by Filipino scholars in Mexico in 1964 as part of the commemoration of the fourth centenary of the 1564 expedition that resulted in Urdaneta's successful completion of the return voyage from the Philippines to New Spain. My objective is not to set aside the ideologically motivated attempts to recover and celebrate all Hispanic/Filipino productions but to explore alternative perspectives and usages of the discourse of pan-Hispanism inherent in the controversial concept of Hispanidad.

"De Manila a México": On Balmori's Dream of Literary Conquest

At the turn of the 20th century, Spanish-language newspapers, journals, and book publications flourished in the Philippines. However, partly due to the rise of Filipino writers of English, Tagalog, and other languages of the Philippines, the reception of Hispanophone Filipino works within and beyond the Philippines remained minimal. In this context, Balmori's 10-month trip to Mexico in 1931 and 1932 acquires symbolic dimensions. Fortunately, we know about Balmori's voyage because upon his return to Manila in May 1932, Balmori published "De Manila a México" in the Philippine cultural journal *Excelsior*. The series of travel chronicles and poems ran from June 1932 to February 1934.

At the beginning of "De Manila a México," Balmori refers to his trip as a "peregrinaje" (pilgrimage) and Mexico as the "país que me propongo visitar en un sueño de conquista literaria" (country that I resolve to visit in a dream of literary conquest) (Balmori 1932a, 12). This rather ambitious aspiration—to "literarily" conquer Mexico—reminds us of Nicaraguan writer Rubén Darío's voyage to Spain in 1892, a trip that contemporaneous Venezuelan *modernista* writer Manuel Díaz Rodríguez referred to as an "inverted conquest" of Spain. By 1892, the year Darío went to Spain for the fourth centenary of Christopher Columbus's "discovery" of the Americas, it was evident that Hispanic American *modernismo* had managed to reverse the until then uneven flow of literary works across the Atlantic. The circulation of literary models from Europe to the Americas had been "inverted," as young Spanish writers were fervently reading and trying to emulate *modernista* authors from Hispanic America, most of all Darío.[8] By going to Mexico in 1931, it is as if Balmori, an avid reader of Darío and other *modernista* authors, envisioned further altering the transoceanic flow of cultural products in the Spanish-speaking world.[9] To this effect, upon his return to the Philippines, Balmori made sure he reported that he had been welcomed with "full honors" in Mexico, a recognition that critic Axel Gasquet finds "by all means exaggerated" (2020, 47).

In the first half of "De Manila a México," Balmori presents his experience in different moments across the Pacific with a mixture of admiration, sense of familiarity, and disenchantment. On his way to Mexico, he made stops in Hong Kong, Moji, Kobe, Osaka, Yokohoma, Honolulu, and Los Angeles, which encouraged him to reflect on his Filipino identity. As discussed by Axel Gasquet, in Japan, Balmori was alarmed by the Western modernization of Japanese society (2020, 51–53). But in Hawaii, Balmori unexpectedly experienced the luring potential of US rule as he marveled at "American influence and power, [reflected] in everything, from its surprising constructions to its marvelous Aquarium" (la influencia y poderío americanos se reflejan en todo, desde sus construcciones sorprendentes a su maravilloso *Acuarium*). Yet, one aspect that reconfirms Balmori's ambivalent attitude toward the United States is that throughout the voyage, he was in constant tension with US passengers on board. He narrates, for instance, one confrontation with a woman who tells him that he is not Filipino. Her logic is that the Filipinos she knows look much more like Chinese and Japanese people than Balmori. In addition, she insists that he must be Spanish. For someone who fervently admired and praised Spain and Spanish culture, being identified as Spanish might have been a compliment. Yet, on this occasion, and throughout his life in fact, he sought to maintain the distinctiveness of Filipinos or, as put by Isaac Donoso

Jiménez, "una estética filipina" (a Filipino aesthetic) (2010, xxvi). After a long argument in which other Americans on the ship intervene, it is settled that Balmori is Filipino, but with a caveat: that Filipinos are "un tipo disparejo al de los asiáticos" (a type that is dissimilar to that of Asians) (Balmori 1932b, 14). Further interrogating Balmori, another woman from the United States asks him whether Filipinos still live in bamboo houses and whether they had successfully prohibited them from eating dog meat. In other words, this woman, a teacher, no less, wonders whether the US administration had managed to "civilize" Filipinos, to teach them not only how to govern themselves but to let go of at last their wild and unruly customs.[10] "¡No sea usted bárbaro!" (Don't be savage!), another teacher intervenes in the conversation addressing Balmori, and then adds, "¡Coma usted gallina!" (Eat chicken!) (1932b, 14). Instead of being offended by these rebukes, Balmori reports that he resolved the quarrel by telling them that instead of living in bamboo houses, Filipinos now lived in caves and that although the government had successfully eradicated the consumption of dog meat, they allowed Filipinos to eat cats. He effectively manages to minimize the force of these insults, which are articulated as cultural concerns, by mocking the sense of superiority of these US passengers and ultimately revealing their "supina ignorancia acerca de nuestro pueblo" (profound ignorance about our peoples) (1932b, 14).

Counterpointing the tension with the US passengers, Balmori befriends two South American diplomats on board: a Peruvian consul in Japan named Manuel Martínez and a Chilean diplomat named Carlos Dávila Espinoza, who had just finished his tenure as ambassador of his country to the United States. Making clear the spontaneous affection they develop, Balmori writes, "Huelga decir que desde el primer día, queda establecida la alianza entre Perú, Chile y Filipinas" (Needless to say, from the first day, the alliance between Peru, Chile, and the Philippines is established) (Balmori 1932b, 13). In this manner, Balmori reaffirms the Philippines' right to find and form their own allies, without having to seek the approval or supervision of the United States. This intimacy with the South American diplomats, moreover, prepares the way for a reevaluation of the Philippines' Hispanicness.

When Balmori reaches the United States, specifically the city of Los Angeles, one would expect his fresh experiences with the Americans on the ship to influence his impression of all things American. However, he is fascinated by the women and enticed by the landscape and architecture, as when he was in Hawaii. He exclaims: "¡Oh, los Angeles! Paraíso de mujeres y flores, que semeja una corte oriental fastuosa y gentil. Tiene el sello de España en sus calles, sus edificios, sus vergeles, sus templos, hasta en sus monumentos nacionales, y nos recuerda a Filipinas por su cielo azul, lleno de sol, que nos obliga a quitarnos la chaqueta y andar en mangas de camisa, borrachos de calor" (Oh, Los Angeles! Paradise of women and flowers that resembles a lavish and gentle Oriental royal court. It bears the seal of Spain on its streets, its buildings, its gardens, its temples, even in its national monuments, and it reminds us of the Philippines with its blue sky, full of sunshine, that forces us to take off our jackets and walk around in short sleeves, drunk from the heat) (Balmori 1932c, 25). The Californian city produces an overwhelming sense of the familiar for Balmori. It represents the possibility of conflating Asia, the United States, and Spain; and this confluence is what reminds him of the Philippines. Thus, the transpacific voyage invites Balmori to ponder about what it means to be Filipino, while reflecting on the intersections of umbrella categories like "Asian," "American," and "Hispanic."

While Balmori's short stops in Los Angeles and, prior to that, Hawaii seem to have left an unexpectedly positive impression of the United States on him, Mexico did the opposite. In the Latin American country, Balmori's first and constant impression was disillusionment. Mexico was nothing like what he had imagined from reading Salvador Díaz Mirón, Juan de Dios Peza, and Amado Nervo—three Mexican poets Balmori strongly admired and who are evoked in the second part of "De Manila a México" (Balmori 1933b, 25; 1934c, 15). Instead, the Filipino was faced with heavily armed military personnel: "doscientos, o trescientos, o cuatrocientos Generales," he recalls in a hyperbolic manner, "héroes de mil batallas en mil revoluciones" (two hundred, three hundred, or four hundred generals . . . heroes of one thousand battles in one thousand revolutions) (1933a, 13; 1934a, 34). In other poems Balmori mocks the plethora of terms and expressions employed in Mexican speech. For instance, he says he does not understand the excessive use of diminutives or how his own first name, Jesús, could morph to "Chucho" (1933a, 13). Yet when it comes to literary and cultural achievements, Balmori cannot help but continue praising Mexico: "Hablan muy mal el castellano," he concludes, "pero escribiendo, hasta los niños nos pueden dar sendas lecciones de la mejor literatura" (They speak Spanish very badly, but in writing even their children could give us some lessons on the best literature) (1933b, 25).

The way many of the poems in the second half of "De Manila a México" portray Mexico and Mexicans reveals Balmori's elitist attitude toward culture and the Spanish language, an attitude that was prevalent in Hispanophone Filipino circles (Rodao 2012, 290). In an interview with Filipino writer Manuel

Bernabé, Balmori assures him that Filipino Spanish was "purer, cleaner, more Castilian" than Mexican Spanish (quoted in Gasquet 2020, 50). Through this interview we find out that Balmori was gravely disappointed with his Mexican experience. However, Mexican newspaper reports on Balmori's activities while he was there tell a remarkably different story. Through these we find out that Balmori was an incessant organizer of a variety of cultural events, such as poetry recitals, lectures on the Philippines, and a Japanese film series, and that he held Mexico in very high regard. For instance, a short article in *El Nacional* mentions that at a festival in homage to the Escuela del Estudiante Indígena, Balmori had recited a poem suggestively titled "Saludo a la raza" (Greeting to the race), which according to the article resonated with Amado Nervo's "La raza de bronce" (The bronze race). After reciting this poem, Balmori turned to the Mexican audience, which received him with "cálidos aplausos" (warm applause), to thank Mexico for defending the Philippines' autonomy and territorial integrity. In doing so, he called Mexico "la avanzada de la América Latina" (the advanced one of Latin America) ("El poeta filipino" 1931, 5).

This same attitude of gratitude toward Mexico is what we perceive in one of the last poems of "De Manila a México," titled "Acapulco." This poem evokes, at last, the Manila-Acapulco galleon trade. It reads as follows:

> En los primeros años de la conquista ibérica
> Fue Acapulco el granero, la tienda y el Tesoro del pueblo filipino.
> De ahí nuestra identidad en la fauna y la flora,
> En la flor y la espiga que nuestros campos dora,
> En música y en bailes, en todo lo exterior;
> Nos ligaron a México, y a México debemos
> En grandes proporciones mil cosas que tenemos
> En el arte y la ciencia, en el son y el color.

> (In the early years of the Iberian conquest,
> Acapulco was the barn, the shop and the treasure of the Filipino people.
> Thus, our identity in fauna and flora,
> in the flowers and the wheat that tans our fields,
> in music and dance, in everything around us,
> we were linked to Mexico, and to Mexico we owe,
> in great proportion thousands of things that we have,
> in art, science, in sound and color.)
> (Balmori 1934b, 15)

According to Balmori, Filipinos were indeed culturally indebted—but to Mexico, not Spain. This diverges, quite significantly, from the ideology that was being promoted at around the same time the poem was published: that all Hispanic peoples—let us recall Maeztu's words—were indebted to Spain. Moreover, the cultural debt to Mexico is not expressed with a sentiment of inferiority or resentment toward a foreign power. Instead, it is articulated within a framework of familiarity, consumed by a sense of nostalgia for a former unity. Hence, Balmori claims that the galleons served as "palpitante puente / entre tu hermoso pueblo y mi patria querida!" (a palpitating bridge / between your beautiful nation and my beloved homeland) (1934b, 15).

Nonetheless, "Acalpulco" ends with all Hispanic American nations bowing to Spain. Undoing the image of an exclusive Mexican-Filipino unity presented in the lines quoted above, the poetic voice remarks: "Cuando España salía de su gloriosa casa, / Y al pasear su bandera por los pueblos del mundo, / Los pueblos, que eran suyos, rendían sus banderas" (When Spain left her glorious house / And waved her flag before the peoples of the world, / these peoples, who were hers, surrendered their flags) (1934b, 15). The ending of the poem not only clouds Balmori's appreciation for Mexico and his longing for a "palpitating bridge" between the Philippines and Mexico but also prefigures how throughout the second half of the 1930s the discourse of Hispanidad in the Philippines would become increasingly conservative, turn more Spain centered, and lean toward Francoism. As historian Florentino Rodao convincingly demonstrates, during the Spanish Civil War, Spanish Falangists in the Philippines dominated not only the political but also the cultural discourse of the Spanish-speaking community. Throughout the war, cultural journals such as *Excelsior*, the *Philippine Free Press*, and *Pro-Cervantes* clearly and openly supported Franco (Rodao 2012, 35, 65). In this context, it is thus not surprising to find a poem by Balmori, published in *Excelsior* in July 1939, titled "Poema de la Nueva España" (Poem of New Spain). While at first sight the title of the poem suggests a possible allusion to New Spain (meaning colonial Mexico), there is none of that. Instead, the poetic voice praises not only Spain but, in a more focused manner, Franco's rise to power: "Nuevo cauce imperial grandioso y necesario, / Fuerte rumbo divino, nueva siembra en la entraña; / Que en el final balance, con Dios como notario, / Se liquidó la cuenta y Franco gana España" (New grandiose and necessary imperial channel, / powerful divine route, new sowing in the belly; / which in the final balance, / with God as a notary, / liquidated the account and Franco wins Spain). Balmori goes on to characterize Franco as a sacred Christlike figure, and the poem, indicating that the Filipino poet might have visited Spain and witnessed Franco's rise to power in 1939, morphs into a farewell: "Te saludo al dejarte, seo de hispanidad / En cuyo altar, alzando tu propio corazón, / Se consagró tu cuerpo, pan de la Humanidad; / Se malogró tu sangre, vino de Redención" (I greet you as I leave you, cathedral of Hispanicity, / On whose altar, raising your own heart, / Your body was consecrated, bread of Humanity; / Your blood was spoiled, Redemption's wine) (1939, 16).[11] By praising Franco and calling him later "la centella que está alumbrando al mundo" (the spark illuminating the world), Balmori promotes a vision of Hispanidad that is centered, without question, on the former Spanish metropole. "Copa de oro que se hace pedazos ya no es copa" (A cup of gold broken apart is no longer a cup), he affirms in this sense at the end of the poem: "Pero es oro, y ansina te rompas en pedazos / Más que nunca eres patria, y más que nunca España" (But it is gold, and this way, torn apart / more than ever you are fatherland, and more than ever Spain) (16).[12] Without a doubt, by the late 1930s Balmori fully adhered to the ideology of Hispanidad, as it was embraced and would be promoted during the Franco regime.

Balmori was certainly not alone in the Philippines in his praise of Francoism in the late 1930s and onward. Lorenzo Pérez Tuells (1898–1956), for example, has an ode to Franco in his *La vuelta de Don Quijote* (The Return of Don Quijote), which was posthumously published in 1973, while Manuel Bernabé (1890–1960) was a regular contributor to journals that openly supported Franco.[13] One could say that it is unfair to focus on these works of Balmori instead of others in which it is quite evident that he defended a sense of Filipinidad that was delinked from a Francoist Spain. For instance, in his novel *Los pájaros de fuego* (Fire birds), which was written during the Japanese occupation of the Philippines and the devastating destruction of Manila in 1945, we find Balmori's definitive distrust of civilizational discourses, militarism, and fascist regimes (2010). One could add that during the late 1930s there were also other Filipino authors who sought to reflect on the Philippines' Hispanidad in much less ideologically compromised works. For example, *La hispanidad en Filipinas*, an essay by Filipino literary critic Jaime C. de Veyra that was finished in 1940 but not published until later, gives an overview of Philippine literature in Spanish from the colonial period until the first decades of the 20th century, and not once does he praise Spain or Franco's regime. Nonetheless, a poem like Balmori's "Poema de la Nueva España" is worth quoting and remembering, as it is indicative of the highly politicized trajectory that overshadowed the boom of Hispanophone literary and cultural productions before 1936. It helps us to see, as demonstrated by Rodao, how the Falangist discourse that seeped into Hispanophone Filipino literary circles during the Spanish Civil War radically changed the course of Hispanism in the Philippines. To quote Rodao, "Fue el punto de no retorno: en apenas tres años desaparecieron muchos de los esfuerzos realizados durante tres siglos" (It was the point of no return: in just three years many of the efforts carried out during three centuries disappeared) (2012, 309). While I largely agree with this statement, in the next section I examine how another transpacific endeavor, the 1964 celebrations of the fourth centenary of the expedition that led to the discovery of the *tornaviaje* from the Philippines to the Americas, presented the possibility of redirecting this trend. As idealistic as the remembrance of the beginning of the transpacific galleon trade was, we will see how it offered a chance to actualize Balmori's "palpitating bridge" and to reconsider the course and function of Hispanidad both in Mexico and in the Philippines.

Tornaviaje as Concept

Many and varied were the highly anticipated events of 1964, or the "Year of Mexican-Philippine Friendship," as it was denominated. One of the culminating points was the simultaneous inauguration of two identical marble structures on both sides of the Pacific on November 21, 1964: one in Barra de Navidad and the other in Manila. The first was the port from which the expedition led by Spanish explorer Miguel López de Legazpi had set sail on November 21, 1564, and the second, the capital city on the other side of the ocean that Legazpi founded, following a conquest led by his grandson, the New Spain–born Juan de Salcedo, six years after the expedition's arrival in present-day Cebu. Filipino writer and diplomat León María Guerrero III (1915–82), who was at that time serving as ambassador to the Philippines in Spain, was chosen to speak at the inauguration in Barra de Navidad. "Aquí," he began, "hace precisamente cuatrocientos años, levantaros velas las naos 'San Pedro' y 'San Pablo' y los pataches 'San Luchas' y 'San Juan de Letrán', y se hicieron a la mar Miguel López de Legazpi, el adelantado, con el gobernador de la armada, Andrés de Urdaneta, y cuatrocientos mexicanos" (Here, exactly four hundred years ago, the 'San Pedro' and 'San Pablo' galleons and the 'San Lucas' and 'San Juan de Letrán' pataches set sail, under the command of Miguel López de Legazpi, the adelantado, with the governor of the armada,

Andrés de Urdaneta, and four hundred Mexicans) (Roces 1965, 28). Ample credit was given, as one would expect in a diplomatic festivity like this, to the commander of the expedition, Legazpi. However, Guerrero was much more inclined to praise Urdaneta, the one who plotted a safe route back from the Philippines to New Spain.[14] According to Guerrero,

> Nadie antes de Urdaneta había conseguido descifrar el enigma del tornaviaje en el Pacífico. Hombres audaces, pilotos clarividentes, como Magallanes, Juan Sebastián Elcano, Carrión, Loaysa, y Villalobos, cruzan el Mar Océano, rumbo al Poniente, pero no consiguen volver, y para regresar a Europa, tienen que dar la vuelta al mundo.
>
> Volver a América es hazaña de Urdaneta. Legazpi es el Ejército, y se mete tierra adentro. Urdaneta es la Armada, y este gran marino mexicano, casi inmediatamente después de establecido el fuerte Santísimo Nombre de Jesús en Cebú, y aún antes del sitio de Maynilad, leva anclas otra vez para buscar los vientos y las estrellas del tornaviaje, que ha de hacer posible el enlace secular entre virreinato de Nueva España y la capitanía general de Nueva Castilla, es decir, entre México y las Filipinas.

> (Nobody before Urdaneta had managed to decipher the enigma of the return voyage in the Pacific. Bold men, clever pilots, like Magellan, Juan Sebastián Elcano, Carrión, Loaysa, and Villalobos, head west across the Oceans, but they do not manage to return; to return to Europe, they must circumnavigate the world.
>
> The return to America is Urdaneta's feat. Legazpi is the Army and moves inland. Urdaneta is the Navy, and this great Mexican sailor, almost immediately after the strong [Archdiocese of] Most Holy Name of Jesus was established in Cebu and even before the siege of Maynilad, weighs anchor again in search of the winds and the stars of the return voyage [tornaviaje], which will establish the secular link between the viceroyalty of New Spain and the general captaincy of New Castile, that is, between Mexico and the Philippines.) (Roces 1965, 29)

Before Urdaneta completed the tornaviaje, before the establishment of the Manila-Acapulco galleon trade, Europe served as mediator between Asia and the Americas. Spain was conceptually and literally at the center of the Spanish Empire, while the Americas, the Pacific, and the archipelago that Magellan had "discovered" in 1521 were relegated to the margins. Instead of being imposed, this center-margin structure was largely unavoidable. Urdaneta's *tornaviaje* therefore marked the beginning of a permanent shift in the conceptualization of the world, or at the very least the so-called Hispanic world. This conceptualization is furthered by the fact that as merchants and other key figures from New Spain and the Philippines began to take matters into their own hands, to make their negotiations with each other, the Manila-Acapulco galleon trade gradually developed a life of its own.[15] The reciprocal nature of the commercial network helped make it possible first to ignore and then eventually to question the authority of the Spanish Crown. "El tornaviaje," León María Guerrero declares in this regard during his Barra de Navidad speech, "palabra evocadora, concepto sugeridor de lo que va a ser la historia del Pacífico, pues las relaciones entre América y el Asia siempre ya serán recíprocas" (Tornaviaje, an evocative word, a concept indicative of what the history of the Pacific will be, as the relations between the Americas and Asia will from now on always be reciprocal) (Roces 1965, 29). There is not much room for Spain or Europe in the concept of the *tornaviaje*.

Guerrero's characterizations of Legazpi's crew as "four hundred *Mexicans*" and of Urdaneta as a "great *Mexican* sailor" are provocative and yet anachronistic, imprecise. Despite being ideologically motivated (they clearly elevate the Mexican state), they do pose a fair question: when did subjects from the colonies begin to develop consciousness of a new identity, an identity distinct from one dictated by law, that is, imposed by the Spanish metropole? To be sure, Guerrero was not the only one to "Mexicanize" historical moments and actors from the Spanish colonial past during the 1964 celebrations. Other diplomats and scholars, both Filipino and Mexican, were similarly tempted—or perhaps expected—to do so. For instance, during a lecture delivered in Mexico City, Filipino historian Carlos Quirino (1910–99) referred to Juan de Salcedo, Legazpi's grandson, who led the conquest of Manila in 1571, as "the first Mexican" (1964). Arguably inspired by Quirino, Mexican author and diplomat Rafael Bernal (1915–72), who was commissioned to write a monograph for the 1964 celebrations, gives his work a suggestive title: *México en Filipinas: Estudio de una transculturación* (Mexico in the Philippines: Study of a transculturation) (1965). In it, Bernal clearly regards Legazpi's 1564 enterprise as a Mexican endeavor.[16] For this, he turns our attention to one of the first documented uses of the expression "Mexican" that dates to this time period: an anonymous letter sent from Seville to Valencia in 1566, which announces Urdaneta's successful return from Manila to Acapulco and credits this feat to the "Mexicans."[17]

Beyond the inauguration of monuments, statues, and historical sites, a crucial part of the 1964 celebrations consisted in exchanging cultural production and knowledge. Filipinos and Mexicans gifted each other archives and facsimile copies of important Mexican and Filipino literary works. Four fellowships were offered to Filipino scholars to go to Mexico to study methodologies for the teaching of Spanish, and two Filipino historians, Quirino and Abraham Laygo, were invited to Mexico's Archivo General de la Nación to make copies of documents that were considered relevant to the historiography of the Philippines.[18] Moreover, a number of Filipino intellectuals and two Filipino ballet companies went to Mexico to give presentations and performances, while a group of Mexican scholars and artists traveled to the Philippines. Presentations on the part of Filipinos focused more on scientific and social fields, such as linguistics, the educational system, and health in the Philippines, while Mexican lectures were geared more toward literature and culture.[19] Some of the lectures centered specifically on the understudied exchanges of cultural influences between Mexico and the Philippines. For instance, José Villa Panganiban, director of the Institute of National Language in the Philippines, gave a lecture on the presence of Nahuatl terms in Tagalog.[20] Sharing research and cultural perspectives in such wide-ranging fields signaled an epistemological shift: the production of knowledge and culture was no longer assumed to sprout from Spain, Europe, or the United States but to grow in and across the Pacific. It is here that we are reminded of Balmori's poem "Acapulco." It is here where we see the possibility not only to remember the "palpitating bridge" between Mexico and the Philippines but also to rebuild it and cross it back and forth.

Conclusion: Rerouting Hispanism

Balmori's "De Manila a México" and the 1964 diplomatic celebrations for the expedition that resulted in the discovery of the *tornaviaje* from the Philippines to Mexico guide us to think of other Hispanisms that do not place the former metropole at the center. While in Balmori's writings Mexico has an ambiguous position, the diplomatic festivities of 1964 successfully demonstrated that the approaches to being Filipino and Hispanic did not have to emanate from Spain but could very well come from Mexico as well as *between* Mexico and the Philippines. "It was on the Manila Galleon," Filipino author Nick Joaquin would write in this respect years later, "that we began to become the Philippines" (1990, 36). Throughout the 1930s, however, Hispanophone Filipino authors were lured by the promise of remaining linked to "Mother" Spain. Many of them, Balmori being one example, could not help but veer into a pro-Franco Hispanist discourse with a markedly conservative edge that tended to emphasize the ties between language and Christian militarization. To an extent, this discourse was reactionary, fueled by the ongoing competing US-centric ideology of Sajonismo. Yet there is no reason to adopt an apologetic attitude for the exaltation of Francoist Spain. To borrow and adapt an observation made by critic Angel Loureiro in regard to Spanish intellectuals at the turn of the 20th century, it would be irresponsible to link all Filipino writers' appreciation of Spain and Hispanic culture after 1939 to Franco's regime, but it would be equally imprudent not to reflect on the connection between the two or to simply turn a blind eye to these trajectories.[21]

To be clear, the weight of the connections between the Franco regime and Hispanidad is impossible to be undone. Yet we should recall them alongside efforts within and beyond the Philippines wherein the residues of the Spanish Empire have taken different forms and not necessarily in Spanish. In fact, quoting Anglophone Filipino writer Nick Joaquin above enables me to suggest a different definition of Hispanism.[22] If earlier in this chapter I defined Hispanism as the study of Spanish-language cultural productions, I now end by contending that Hispanism in the Philippines and the rest of the world does not and should not hope that the Spanish language stays "on course," its unifying force preserved. Hispanism is composed of many cores that do not revolve around one center, Spain. I rely, in this sense, on recent conceptualizations of the Global Hispanophone as a "centrifugal force" (Campoy-Cubillo and Sampedro Vizcaya 2019, 5).

A centrifugal Hispanism entails, I further argue, the migratory routes and experiences of subjects from former colonies of the former Spanish Empire. We could look, for this, into the numerous times in which Filipino writer Carlos Bulosan (1913–56) mentions the contact and solidarity among Filipino and Mexican migrants in the United States in his semiautobiographical novel *America Is in the Heart* (1946). Most of these mentions regard minor social encounters; they involve Filipino men who mingle or have intimacy with Mexican women they meet at Mexican cafés and bars, on the street, or at work in the fields. But from time to time, they refer to the concrete united action of Filipino and Mexican farm labor activists: from meetings to demonstrations and labor movement publications. Toward the end of the novel, the ailing first-person narrator expressly identifies with Mexican migrants. "I began to feel like the Mexicans," he says when he is denied access to a sanitarium, "who thought the doctors were killing them off because there were too many of them" (Bulosan 1973, 253). On another occasion, he commiserates with a starving Mexican boy, who reminds him of his own younger self, and wonders: "Would he grow up to revolt against his environment? Would he strike at his world? Would he escape?" (302). These instances reveal that the "palpitating bridge" between Mexico and the Philippines that Balmori evoked at around the same time Bulosan was writing *America Is in the Heart* is not limited to historical archives or controlled by official diplomatic discourses. Bridges can also be built from below; they can, moreover, be built between diasporic Filipinos and Mexicans.

As Rudy P. Guevarra Jr. has observed, the Manila galleon trade brought an exchange of commercial goods, but most of all people: "Filipino and Mexican *indios* and *mestizos* were key actors in the human and cultural exchanges that took place and forged centuries of racial and cultural blending" (2012, 9). Even after the galleon trade came to an end in 1815, the cultural bond between Mexicans and Filipinos remained, ready to be renewed. Hispanicness can be, and has been, redefined by Filipinos as much as it has been readapted by Mexicans and many others in the Americas. In the end, Hispanism in the Philippines and the rest of the world does not—and should not—center on the Spanish language. It should not continue to operate on the basis of an illusory hope that it stays on course, that its imagined purity be preserved. Instead, it should take into consideration the many familiar as well as unfamiliar and unexpected *viajes* and *tornaviajes* that bearers of Hispanic cultures have taken and continue to take not only across the Atlantic and the Americas but also across the Pacific.

Notes

1. The bibliography for the "Latin race" debate is ample. For an introduction on how it played out in Hispanic America, see Gobat 2013. For a study on the vilification of Spain in the literary and cultural imaginary of the United States toward the end of the 19th century and the beginning of the 20th century, see DeGuzmán 2005.

2. A few years later, Vizcarra attempted to justify, from a religious perspective, the commemoration of October 12 and advised that it be renamed *Fiesta de la Hispanidad*. This proposal would be developed at length in *La vocación de América* (America's vocation) (1933). For an analysis of Vizcarra's ideologies, see Tateishi 2004. All translations from Spanish, unless otherwise noted, are mine.

3. Prior to being published as a book in 1934, the essays in *Defensa de la hispanidad* were initially featured as articles in 1931 and 1932, in the journal *Acción Española*.

4. It is worthwhile to add that within the United States, there is a more recent history that contributes to tainting the reputation of all things Spanish or Hispanic. Although "Hispanic" is in many contexts used interchangeably with "Latino/a/x," some people associate the former with the administration of Richard Nixon (1969–74); they interpret the term as a top-down effort to categorize (or catalogue) peoples of various Latin American descent. On the officialization of this term during Nixon's regime, see Leeman 2013.

5. It should be noted that the "We" in the title of these volumes is not a decision of Donoso and Cano but part of a book series from Vibal Foundation. In the effort to explore the Philippines' transnational and multiethnic composition, they have been publishing a number of books that are titled following the same format, namely, *More Pinay Than We Admit: The Social Construction of the Filipina* (2010, ed. Maria Luisa T. Camagay); *More Tsinoy Than We Admit: Chinese-Filipino Interactions Over the Centuries* (2015, ed. Richard T. Chu); *More American Than We Admit: America's Cultural Influence on the Philippines* (2015, ed. Julian Go); and *More Islamic Than We Admit* (2017, ed. Isaac Donoso and Samuel K. Tan).

6. Cano reminds us of a fervent debate that predominated in Hispanophone Filipino circles throughout the first decades of the 20th century: whether Filipinos should embrace "Sajonismo" or "Hispanismo." For an analysis on this debate, see Ortuño Casanova 2019.

7. Recent studies about Balmori's novels and poetry include Park 2014; Lifshey 2016, chap. 5; Arighi 2016; Villaescusa Illán 2020, chap. 5; Gasquet 2020; and López-Calvo 2020. Without a doubt, many of these are the result of the publication of Balmori's third novel, *Los pájaros de fuego* (2010), edited by Isaac Donoso Jiménez, who provides a comprehensive introduction to Balmori's life and works.

8. Consult González 2010 for an excellent introduction to Hispanic American *modernismo*, which differs from *modernismo* in Brazil as well as in the Anglophone world. For more on Díaz Rodríguez's take on the symbolism of Darío's 1892 visit to Spain, see Mejías-López 2009, 116–24.

9. For an excellent overview of the impact of *modernismo* in the Philippines, see Feria 2018.

10. On the civilizatory discourse adopted by the US administration in the Philippines, see Rafael 2000, chap. 2.

11. These lines indicate that Balmori might have visited Spain at around the time he wrote this poem. So far, I have not been able to confirm that Balmori was in Spain in 1939. I am only aware of a visit he made in 1924 (Feria 2018, 262).

12. It is worthwhile noting that with these second and third to last lines of the poem, Balmori was rewriting two verses from the Peruvian José Santos Chocano that read, "Un anillo de oro hecho pedazos, / ya no es anillo, pero siempre es oro" (A ring of gold broken to pieces / is no longer a ring, but it is gold), two lines that are inserted in an earlier poem by Balmori, titled "Canto a España" (Martín de la Cámara 1923, 51).

13. I thank Rocío Ortuño-Casanova for pointing out these references to me.

14. It is fairly acknowledged that another member in Legazpi's 1564 expedition, Alonso de Arellano, had completed the *tornaviaje* before Urdaneta. Arellano was in charge of the San Lucas patache, which had been considered lost since December 1, 1564, just a few days after Legazpi's expedition had begun. Arellano completed the *tornaviaje*, with Martín de

Ayamontes as pilot, on August 9, 1565. Nonetheless, Urdaneta and Felipe de Salcedo, who was captain of one of the ships that completed the *tornaviaje* led by Urdaneta, adamantly contested the veracity of Arellano's feat, and therefore Urdaneta is amply credited as being the "discoverer" of the *tornaviaje*. For a summary of Arellano's accounts of his travels across the Pacific and Urdaneta's reaction to them, see Bernal 1965, 52–57; 2012, 182–90.

15. Historian Carmen Yuste López examines how throughout the 18th century merchants from New Spain continued to make negotiations with merchants in Manila for the import of textiles, spices, and other goods. "El eje transpacífico no fue en efecto," she maintains, "un 'Pacífico de los ibéricos'. Fue, sin lugar a dudas, un Pacífico intercolonial, un océano de intercambios en el que filipinos y novohispanos sacaron el mayor provecho" (The transpacific axis was not in effect a 'Pacific of the Iberians', but an intercolonial Pacific, an ocean of exchanges wherein Filipinos and New Spaniards were able to get the most out) (Yuste López 2007, 22).

16. See Bernal 1965, chap. 4.

17. The anonymous letter reads, "Los continuos fracasos y desastres no iban a arredrar a los españoles de la Nueva España, a los novohispanos, es decir, a los mexicanos" (The continuous failures and disasters would not intimidate the Spaniards of New Spain, the New Spaniards, that is, the Mexicans), and ends with the following statement: "Ello es cosa grande, y de mucha importancia: y los de México están muy ufanos con su descubrimiento, que tienen entendido que serán ellos el corazón del mundo" (This is a great feat of great importance: and the ones of Mexico are satisfied with their discovery, which they believe will make them the center of the world) ("Copia de una carta" 1975). Bernal quotes this line multiple times (1965, 45; 2012, 182).

18. Quirino and Laygo's bibliographic work was published in Manila in 1965 under the title *Regésto, guión catálogo de los documentos existentes en México sobre Filipinas*.

19. For instance, León María Guerrero gave a presentation on the state of the Spanish language in the Philippines, Pura Santillán Castrense on the educational system of the Philippines, and José Rodríguez on leprosy. The lectures can be found in the conference proceedings published in Manila in 1965 (Roces 1965). Silvio Zavala presented on Mexican history, Agustín Yañez on Mexican literature, Mario Ojeda Gómez on international politics in Mexico, León Portilla on Mexico's indigenous literature, Luis Villoro on contemporary Mexican culture, Luis González on the Mexican Revolution, and María Eugenia Revueltas on Mexican music. For a more complete list and institutional affiliations of the Mexican presenters, see Zea 1964.

20. The title of Villa Panganiban's talk was "Influencias lingüísticas mexicanas en el lenguaje tagalo" (Roces 1965).

21. Loureiro writes: "It could be rash, and perhaps even irresponsible, to thread a narrative line with the Spanish constructions of Spanish America leading from Menéndez Pelayo to Maeztu and to the Francoist regime, with precursors and variations such as Castelar, Valera, Galdós, Altamira and Unamuno among many others. But it would be equally irresponsible not to question the preparatory role that nineteenth century Spanish constructions of Latin American, both liberal and conservative, had in the later development of the ideological and political program in defense of the concept of *Hispanidad* used by Francoism and developed around the notion of a spiritual legacy that Spain bequeathed to its former American possessions" (2003, 73–74).

22. It is worthwhile to mention that Nick Joaquin traveled to Mexico from the United States in 1957, with a fellowship from Harper Publishing Company. The result, *The Woman Who Had Two Navels* (1961), hints at this portion of the trip at the end as Joaquin indicates that the novel was written in "Madrid-Mallorca-Manhattan-Mexico-Manila."

References

"Copia de una carta venida de Sevilla a Miguel Salvador de Valencia." 1975. In *Viaje y tornaviaje a Filipinas, 1564*, edited by Andrés Henestrosa. Mexico City: Novaro.

Arighi, William. 2016. "Gender, Modernity, and the End of the Fil-Hispanic World." *Comparative Literature Studies* 53 (1): 57–77.

Balmori, Jesús. 1932a. "De Manila a México: Capítulo I." *Excelsior*, no. 938: 12–13.

Balmori, Jesús. 1932b. "De Manila a México: Capítulo VI." *Excelsior*, no. 943: 13–14.

Balmori, Jesús. 1932c. "De Manila a México: Capítulo VII." *Excelsior*, no. 956: 12–13.

Balmori, Jesús. 1933a. "De Manila a México: Atrio." *Excelsior*, no. 981: 7–8.

Balmori, Jesús. 1933b. "De Manila a México: Barbarismos idiomáticos." *Excelsior*, no. 982: 25.

Balmori, Jesús. 1934a. "De Manila a México: México aristócrata." *Excelsior*, no. 986: 34.

Balmori, Jesús. 1934b. "De Manila a México: Acapulco." *Excelsior*, no. 988: 15.

Balmori, Jesús. 1934c. "De Manila a México: Artes y Letras." *Excelsior*, no. 988: 15.

Balmori, Jesús. 1939. "Poema de la Nueva España." *Excelsior*, no. 1072 (July): 12–16.

Balmori, Jesús. 2010. *Los pájaros de fuego: Novela filipina de la guerra*. Edited by Isaac Donoso Jiménez. Manila: Instituto Cervantes en Manila.

Bernal, Rafael. 1965. *México en Filipinas: Estudio de una transculturación*. Mexico City: Universidad Nacional Autónoma de México.

Bernal, Rafael. 2012. *El Gran Océano*. Mexico City: Fondo de Cultura Económica.

Bulosan, Carlos. [1946] 1973. *America Is in the Heart: A Personal History*. Seattle: University of Washington Press.

Campoy-Cubillo, Adolfo, and Benita Sampedro Vizcaya. 2019. "Entering the Global Hispanophone: An Introduction." *Journal of Spanish Cultural Studies* 20 (1–2): 1–16.

Cano, Glòria. 2015. "Introduction." In *More Hispanic Than We Admit: Insights into Philippine Cultural History 2*, edited by Glòria Cano, xi–xxviii. Quezon City: Vibal Foundation.

DeGuzmán, María. 2005. *Spain's Long Shadow: The Black Legend, Off-whiteness, and Anglo-American Empire*. Minneapolis: University of Minnesota Press.

Donoso Jiménez, Isaac. 2008. "Preface." In *More Hispanic Than We Admit: Insights into Philippine Cultural History*, edited by Isaac Donoso Jiménez, ix–xiv. Quezon City: Vibal Foundation.

"El poeta filipino J. Balmori en un festival." *El Nacional*, October 10, 1931, 5.

Epps, Brad. 2005. "Keeping Things Opaque: On the Reluctant Personalism of a Certain Mode of Critique." In *Ideologies of Hispanism*, edited by Mabel Moraña, 230–66. Nashville: Vanderbilt University Press.

Feria, Miguel Ángel. 2018. "El modernismo hispanofilipino ante la critica española (1904–1924)." *Revista de Crítica Literaria Latinoamericana* 44 (88): 241–66.

Gallo, Andrea, ed. 2014. "Philippines." Special issue, *Transmodernity: Journal of Peripheral Cultural Production of the Luso-Hispanic World* 4 (1).

Gasquet, Axel. 2020. "Filipino Poet Jesús Balmori: Testimonials of His Mexican Journey Passing through Japan (1932–1934)." In *Transpacific Literary and Cultural Connections: Latin American Influence in Asia*, edited by Jie Lu and Martín Camps, 45–66. New York: Palgrave Macmillan.

Gobat, Michel. 2013. "The Invention of Latin America: A Transnational History of Anti-Imperialism, Democracy, and Race." *American Historical Review* 118 (5): 1345–75.

Guevarra, Rudy P., Jr. 2012. *Becoming Mexipino: Multiethnic Identities and Communities in San Diego*. New Brunswick, NJ: Rutgers University Press.

Joaquin, Nick. [1961] 1972. *The Woman Who Had Two Navels*. Manila: Solidaridad.

Leeman, Jennifer. 2013. "Categorizing Latinos in the History of the US Census: The Official Racialization of Spanish." In *A Political History of Spanish*, edited by José Del Valle, 305–23. New York: Cambridge University Press.

Lifshey, Adam. 2016. *Subversions of the American Century: Filipino Literature in Spanish and the Transpacific Transformation of the United States*. Ann Arbor: University of Michigan Press.

López-Calvo, Ignacio. 2020. "A Peripheral, South-South Literary Exchange: Balmori and the Reception of Latin American Modernismo in the Philippines." In *Transpacific Literary and Cultural Connections: Latin American Influence in Asia*, edited by Jie Lu and Martín Camps, 45–66. New York: Palgrave Macmillan.

Loureiro, Angel G. 2003. "Spanish Nationalism and the Ghost of Empire." *Journal of Spanish Cultural Studies* 4 (1): 65–76.

Maeztu, Ramiro de. 1998. *Defensa de la Hispanidad*. Madrid: Ediciones Rialp.

Martín de la Cámara, Eduardo, ed. 1922. *Parnaso filipino: Antología de poetas del archipiélago magallánico*. Barcelona: Casa Editorial Maucci.

Mejías-López, Alejandro. 2009. *The Inverted Conquest: The Myth of Modernity and the Transatlantic Onset of Modernism*. Nashville: Vanderbilt University Press.

Mojarro, Jorge, ed. 2018. "Literatura hispanofilipina." Special issue, *Revista de crítica literaria latinoamericana* 88 (2).

Mojarro, Jorge, ed. 2019. "Transpacific Connections of Philippine Literature in Spanish." Special issue, *UNITAS* 92 (1): 1–402.

Ortuño Casanova, Rocío. 2019. "Quijote-Sancho y Ariel-Calibán: La introducción de Filipinas en la corriente hispanoamericanista por oposición al ocupador yankee." *UNITAS* 92 (1): 256–87.

Park, Paula C. 2014. "Jesús Balmori, la radio y la crítica al jazz en los años 30." *Revista Filipina* 2 (1).

Quirino, Carlos. 1964. "El primer mexicano en Filipinas." *Historia Mexicana* 14 (2): 250–60.

Rafael, Vicente. 2000. *White Love and Other Events in Filipino History*. Durham: Duke University Press.

Roces, Alejandro R., ed. 1965. *Filipinas y México: Colección de discursos y conferencias pronunciados con ocasión de la celebración del Año de la Amistad México-Filipina en el cuarto centenario de la llegada de la expedición mexicana en Filipinas, Año de Amistad Filipino Mexicana*. Manila: Comité del Año de Amistad Filipino-Mexicana.

Rodao, Florentino. 2012. *Franquistas sin Franco: Una historia alternativa de la Guerra Civil Española desde Filipinas*. Granada: Editorial Comares.

Tateishi, Hirotaka. 2004. "Zacarías de Vizcarra y *La vocación de América*: Apuntes sobre la Hispanidad y el nacional-catolicismo." *Mediterranean World*, no. 17: 41–53.

Veyra, Jaime C. de. 1962. *La hispanidad en Filipinas*. Madrid: Publicaciones del Círculo Filipino.

Villaescusa Illán, Irene. *Transcultural Nationalism in Hispano-Filipino Literature*. Cham: Springer International, 2020.

Yuste López, Carmen. 2007. *Emporios transpacíficos: Comerciantes mexicanos en Manila, 1710–1815*. Mexico City: Universidad Nacional Autónoma de México.

Zea, Leopoldo. 1964. "Año de la Amistad Mexicano-Filipina." *El Porvenir*, 2 December.

PART II

The (Re)Conquest of History

Moros and Spaniards in the Philippines

Negotiating Colonial Identity in the
Margins of the Spanish Empire

Ana M. Rodríguez-Rodríguez

Three main factors contribute to the particularities of the Spanish-Muslim encounter in the Philippines: the colony's geographical and economic marginality, the previous colonial experience in America, and, of course, the prolonged direct contact that colonizers had with Islam for centuries in multiple contexts. In the Philippines, Spaniards are in an ex-centric location, far away from the political, economic, and cultural center, in a hostile environment where there is a real threat of literal and symbolic disintegration. Nevertheless, Spaniards hold in the Philippines an authoritative position, especially once they conquer most of the archipelago with the small but significant exception of the southern islands (Mindanao and Sulu mainly). The Philippines constitutes a mixed, ambiguous, and ambivalent space where a variety of ideological elements come into play, in a strange and complex colonial site, due to the presence of human groups that are unknown but seem familiar.

The writings about this issue in the 16th and 17th centuries use a variety of strategies to represent the encounter with new realities and characters. By analyzing them, we can inquire about the complex negotiation processes of an identity in conflict with itself in a marginal environment. The analysis of the contacts between the Spanish monarchy and Islam in the Philippines widens our knowledge of colonial procedures in the Spanish Empire. It also contributes to our understanding of the relations with Islam, the most salient element of Otherness in the Spanish collective consciousness of these centuries, in an often-problematic colony due to its lack of independent financial productivity and to the difficulty to control all human groups inhabiting the islands.

Islam arrived first to the Sulu archipelago with merchants who established several Muslim communities at the end of the 13th century, which were reinforced with missionaries and Malayans who started settling in the islands at the beginning of the 15th century. Toward the middle of this century, a sultanate was established under Sharif ul-Hashim, and in the 16th century the constant contacts, both political and commercial, with other Muslim areas in Malaysia transformed Sulu into an integral part of the expanding Malayan *dar ul-Islam*. Between the end of the 16th and the beginning of the 17th centuries, political alliances with Muslim principalities that had organized to confront the colonizing Western powers, in addition to the permanent work of missionaries, consolidated the Islamic presence in Sulu. In Mindanao, Muslim missionaries, probably of Arab descent, arrived on the island in the 15th century. In the first quarter of the 16th century, the Muslim population grew through migrations and conversions encouraged by an acceleration of the Islamization process through marriage alliances with neighboring communities. At the beginning of the 17th century, the colonizing and evangelizing efforts by the Spaniards reinforced attitudes favoring the establishment of Islam, as it caused a general consciousness of belonging to a wide Islamic community, especially during Sultan Qudarat's reign (1619–71).

Mindanao and Sulu, the Philippine territories where Islam had time to settle more strongly, constantly defied Spain's colonial power. The southern area would resist all occupation attempts for three centuries. This is undoubtedly the longest and hardest resistance encountered by Spain in all its colonial enterprises. Between 1565 and 1663, four distinct stages can be identified:

1. The first stage, until 1578, was marked by fights between Spaniards and Borneans, who, allied with Suluans, were trying to increase their political, economic, and religious influence on the archipelago.
2. During a second period, for around two decades, Spaniards tried to reduce the inhabitants of Mindanao and Sulu to vassalage, while they introduced Christian missionaries and attempted to avoid the influence of Muslim neighboring communities. However, all efforts to establish colonies in the Muslim lands failed miserably.
3. Between 1599 and 1635, Maguindanaos actively rebelled against Spanish power, attacking or intimidating the indigenous populations who participated in the colonial enterprise. Simultaneously, they tried to consolidate their power in preparation for future confrontations.
4. In 1635 the Zamboanga fort was established in Mindanao. The Spanish

victories in Maguindanao in 1637 and 1638 led to the establishment of missions and some conversions, but especially among the non-Muslim populations in these areas. Muslim resistance increased while Spaniards tried to depopulate Muslim-controlled areas by destroying their plantations. But threatened by a possible Dutch attack in Manila and exhausted by the ineffectiveness of their efforts, they established peace treaties with Muslim mandataries that were not maintained for a long time. Finally, Spaniards abandoned Zamboanga and all the nearby forts in 1663 when they faced a possible Chinese attack in Manila, and for the next 50 years there were no significant attacks from either side. (Majul 1999, 155–56)

Outside of the main Muslim-Spanish conflict areas, geographical difficulties and the scarcity of the Spanish population suggested that Spaniards never had real control over the Philippines. Areas like Manila, which were apparently secured, were isolated and dangerously vulnerable to possible attacks by nearby powers and to the possibility of rebellion by the indigenous and immigrant populations who disproportionately outnumbered those of Spanish origin. As late as 1637, after about 80 years of colonization, Manila only had 150 houses inhabited by Spaniards, while the population grew with the continuous arrival of Chinese immigrants, the increase of mestizo populations, and the surge of liberated Black slaves (Kamen 2003, 208–9).

From a financial perspective, the Philippines did not have a central role in the organization of the empire. The value of the archipelago did not rest on its economic productivity, since it had few exploitable resources and lacked the abundance and variety of spices of other nearby areas (Kamen 2003, 205). During these two centuries the Philippines was a strategic territory in the Pacific Ocean, valued not so much for its intrinsic qualities but as a bridge for the Christianization of Asia and as a gate to commercial activities between New Spain and China's southern ports and the Spice islands, a context where the Manila galleon played a pivotal part. However, even more important than the economic and commercial value of the islands, the evangelization of the Philippines was a priority sublimated by many protagonists of the conquest's early years, since they perceived it as the first step toward the Christianization of all Asia (233). The strong theocratic component of Spanish colonialism manifested itself particularly in the Philippines, and many times the missionaries were the only visible representatives of the metropolis, which gave them enormous prestige and power. The power of religious orders in the Philippines was immense during the three centuries of Spanish presence in the islands. It was they who learned the indigenous languages, which gave them control of the channels of communication between conquerors and indigenous populations. The Jesuit Alejandro López, for example, was Spain's ambassador on many occasions on the island of Mindanao, and Father Francisco de Combes underlines in his book *Historia de Mindanao y Joló* López's pivotal role in the relations with Sultan Qudarat (Rodríguez-Rodríguez 2013, 152–53).

This situation provoked serious confrontations between the religious orders and the civil authorities, especially in relation to such a polemic issue as the conquest and colonization of Muslim territories in the southern islands. The Jesuit Alonso Sánchez wrote in a letter dated June 18, 1583, that Spaniards entered the new lands behaving like thieves, damaging the honor and lives of indigenous peoples, and therefore the latter had the right to expel them as if they were pirates or tyrants (Colín 1900, 312). There were complex discussions for decades about the best way for Jesuits to manage their interlocutory work with the native populations, and they were often accused of wanting to monopolize this role by refusing, for example, to teach them Spanish and therefore ensuring their role as intermediaries.[1] However, the main discussions revolved around the legitimacy of conquest in the islands, the conditions for a just war, the appropriate way to preach the Gospel, and the collection of tributes. The fact that some of the indigenous populations were Muslim hindered the application of the legal protection and respect that, at least in theory, Spaniards intended to apply to the rest of human groups, which increased the tensions between civil and religious representatives. The conquest of America had laid the groundwork for colonization methods, but for many governors, judges, and so forth, those methods were not fully valid to confront the reencounter with the *moro* in this colonial context. Therefore, because of the presence of Islam in the islands, this confrontation incorporated cultural and religious elements that were not present in the American scenario. For example, while civil conquerors like Melchor de Ávalos (first *oidor* of the Audiencia de Manila) asked the king for permission to enslave Filipino Muslims based on their refusal to accept the preaching of the Gospel, many priests like Father Combes denied this alleged refusal to receive information about the Catholic faith and emphasized the slight implantation of Islamic practices in order to defend the possibility of conversion. Melchor de Ávalos in a letter to the king[2] positions himself clearly in the conflict between civil and religious authorities: "the Bishop Don Domingo de Salazar has attacked the conquerors many times" (Ávalos 1584, 90). The religious orders argued that the conquerors' only motivation was to increase their personal wealth and that priests were moved by the goal to extend the Gospel all across the Orient and therefore had the obligation to condemn the abuses of power they witnessed so often. While conquerors begged the king to steal from Muslims and enslave them for being *moros* and rejecting conversion, priests responded by denying refusals to convert (Gayo 1950, 27). Father Herrera, in a letter sent to Philip II on July 25, 1570, explains that families with a Muslim husband and pagan wife presented their children to the priests to make them Christian. He also argues that many of them were only *moros* by name and that they ate pork. He recognized that other Muslims, like those in Borneo, were better Muslims, although recently converted, and even after being injured by Spaniards they were friends with them and gave them food, clothes, and gold in exchange for Spanish silver. He concludes this letter sharply confirming that the only reason why Spaniards tried to steal from them was because they were Moors and that this was not a legitimate reason (Blair and Robertson 1903–9, 34:232–33). Father Ortega also wrote to the viceroy in 1573 denouncing the attitude of civil authorities:

> En estas invasiones y exploraciones la ley de Mahoma es preferida a la de Dios . . . y no hay cuidado en seguir su ley y las instrucciones cristianas. . . . En lugar de engendrar en sus pechos y almas amor y buena voluntad, crean y engendran odio y aborrecimiento contra nosotros y contra el nombre de Jesucristo crucificado, a quien ellos deben enseñar y predicar a los nativos.

> (In these invasions and explorations the law of Mohammed is preferred to the law of God . . . and there is no care in following His law and Christian instructions. . . . Instead of generating in their chests and souls love and good will, they create and generate hatred and abhorrence against us and against the name of Jesus Christ crucified, about whom they should teach and preach to the natives.) (quoted in Gayo 1950, 29; also in Blair and Robertson 1903–9, 34:260)[3]

The separation between *indios* and *moros* created by the Spaniards to classify the inhabitants of the Philippines responded only to religious criteria, as shown by the fact that at the beginning of their presence in the islands they used the term *moros* to refer to all Filipinos, since they detected Muslim practices in a greater or lesser degree. Later, the application of the word *moros* decreased since Spaniards perceived that Islam was not widespread in the islands, as we can read in this report sent from Manila:

> The natives of this island of Luzon, whom we Spaniards commonly call moros, are not so; for the truth is that they do not know or understand the law of Mahoma—only in some of the villages on the seacoast they do not eat pork, and . . . have had dealings with the moros of Burney, who have preached to them a little of the teaching of Mahoma. (Kroeger 1988, 621–24; see also Blair and Robertson 3: 1903–9, 141–42)

In the Philippines there was a clear separation between Muslim and non-Muslim populations (Mastura 1976, 100–101) that segregated a part of the population inside a lower subcategory whose perception was established by prejudiced information from previous experiences. Ethan Hawkley explains that when "Spanish soldiers invoked Santiago's name at the battles of Manila and Maguindanao, they were not only calling upon the powers of heaven, but also calling upon the powers of history—their history" (2014, 285). I would add that this situation creates an anxiety in the writing process that arises from the difficulty to reorganize perceptions when that history feels inadequate to fully grasp the new context and its variations. These texts transpire all the elements that characterized Spanish-Muslim relations in this area in the 16th and 17th centuries: instability, disorientation when trying to interpret the presence of Muslims in this new context, fluidity and confusion of racial and religious categories, reimagination of the role of Christian Spain against its oldest enemies, and, of course, the urgency to represent all this complexity and adapt it to the expectations of the readers in Spain.

There is a greater complexity in texts written by priests for several reasons, mainly because they had more real contact with Muslims in the Philippines. Francisco de Combes wrote *Historia de Mindanao y Joló* (1667) as a reaction to the mandatory abandonment of the Zamboanga fort, an important strategic point for the colonization of the island of Mindanao. Combes arrived in Manila in 1643 as a result of the petition made by Father Marcelo Mastrilli in a letter to Philip IV asking for 40 Jesuit missionaries to evangelize the island as part of the colonizing efforts in Mindanao. He was sent to Zamboanga in 1645 under the orders of Father Alejandro López, and his role as translator and ambassador was crucial on many occasions (Combes 1897, 12).

We do not have a lot of information about how the *Historia de Mindanao y Joló* was conceived and written. We can only confirm that it had to be finished before the death of Combes, in December 1665, and that he deals with information he witnessed directly or that was provided by witnesses' testimonies. The last event he narrates is the Spanish departure from the Zamboanga post and the handing over of the fort to Don Alonso Macombon in 1662. We do not take a great risk concluding that Combes started writing sometime between 1649 and 1656 and that he finished between 1662 (the abandonment of Zamboanga) and 1665 (the author's death). The book arrived in Madrid in February 1665 (Retana 1897, xix) and was printed in 1667. Wenceslao Retana considers this book the first written history of Mindanao and Sulu. It narrates events that happened between the arrival of Magellan in 1521 and the Spanish departure from Zamboanga. It introduces hundreds of characters and events related to Mindanao and Sulu during this wide time frame, which Combes portrays to facilitate a wider knowledge of this marginal corner of the empire, practically unknown outside the Philippines, and to influence with his opinions the politics that should be applied to the colony. The book is a long and ambitious historical treaty with the intention of rescuing Mindanao and its surroundings from the margins of the imperial enterprise:

Campaña de nuestra Espiritual conquista en estas Islas, es la mas celebrada en este Archipielago, haziendola famosa las armas, é Ilustre el valor, que a pesar de los inaccesibles montes que la defienden de las malezas que la cierran; cienagas, y lagunajos que la siruen de vallados, y fosos incontrastables; abrió a porfia del esfuerço inmenso campo a tan ilustres victorias.

(Campaign of our spiritual conquest in these islands, [Mindanao] is the most celebrated in this archipelago, making it famous by the arms, and illustrious by the courage, which in spite of the inaccessible mountains defending it, the weeds enclosing it; swamps and lagoons that work as fences, and unconquerable pits; opened to stubbornness of an immense effort the field to such illustrious victories.) (Combes 1897, 1)

After this first presentation, Combes offers a complete portrait of Mindanao, Sulu, and the surrounding territories by distributing this content in eight books thematically organized. Not only was he in direct contact with some of the narrated events, as I mentioned earlier, but he also had a chance to consult very important texts directly related to the events he presented. He sometimes reproduces these texts literally, as is the case with the peace treaties signed with kings of Mindanao and Sulu and the letters exchanged between the corsair Coseng and Governor Manrique de Lara (Combes 1897, 430–33, 444–47, 614–18). These materials were easy to access in Zamboanga, headquarters of Spanish operations in Mindanao and Sulu, especially if we take into account that Combes was an assistant to Father Alejandro López, the main ambassador of Spanish authorities with the Mindanao sultan, and one of the main experts of Spanish-Muslim relations in the area.

When Combes arrived in Zamboanga, Spaniards had already been in the city for 10 years. The victories of 1637 and 1638 in Maguindanao against sultan Qudarat and in Sulu against sultan Muwallil Wasit (also named Rajá Bongsu), under the direction of Governor Hurtado de Corcuera, were an important injection of optimism into the project, and they led to the establishment of missions by the Jesuits. The main goal was extirpating Islam from the south of the Philippines. Copies of the Koran and other Arab manuscripts were destroyed, along with several tombs of sultans and Muslim missionaries. Earlier, during an expedition to Sulu in 1628, soldiers under the governor's orders had destroyed, among others, the tomb of the sultan's father (Blair and Robertson 1903–9, 22:209). Combes writes about a similar occurrence in the same years (Combes 1897, 45). The purpose of this type of action was to eliminate the pilgrimage rites that made Sulu "la Metropoli de la falsa Religion, y la Meca deste Archipielago" (the metropolis of the false religion, and the Mecca of this archipelago) (44) in order to strip Muslims away from everything that united them in their resistance against the Spaniards, precluding their conversion. Missionary activities had to slow down during these years because of the continuous Muslim resistance and the complication of the conflict with the Dutch presence in the area. There was a constant danger of Muslim-Dutch association, which would have had fatal consequences for the Spaniards. Spain's intention was to enforce an aggressive approach consisting of the destruction of their ways of life: plantations and cattle farms. After the failure of several peace agreements, Qudarat declared a jihad against the Spaniards and called on the sultans of Sulu, Ternate, and Makkasar to help with the expulsion of the invaders of Muslim territories, which started a very violent but indecisive war. The situation had a radical spin with the abandonment of Zamboanga in 1663, which brought a period of relative peace and the end of important Muslim incursions into Spanish-dominated territories. Spaniards had failed in their attempts to conquer Mindanao and the Sulu archipelago.

Combes narrates a resounding failure with a variety of causes. Numerical inferiority is one of them, but not the only one or even the most decisive.

Tactical advantages, like the use of horses and weapons, which should have given Spaniards an advantage, were disabled many times by the geographical characteristics of the islands, such as the mountainous terrain or the difficult weather. The presence of multiple simultaneous enemies during the conflict, like the Dutch ships or Chinese corsairs, contributed to a dispersion of forces. Manrique de Lara, governor of the Philippines between 1653 and 1663, had to deal with a horrible economy, the isolation derived from only having the Manila galleon as a means of communication outside the Philippines, continuous harassment from the Dutch, shortage of troops and resources, and constant rebellions by indigenous groups (October 1660, December 1660, December 1661) and the Chinese (May 1662).[4] But above all, it was the peculiar resistance of Muslim populations that mainly unbalanced Spanish efforts:

> What made the Moros unconquerable was the sound balance in their political-military organization between pre-Muslim decentralization and Muslim-sponsored centralization. Given their acceptance of certain features of Muslim culture, resistance became meaningful to the moros. (Phelan 1959, 143)

Given the characteristics of Spain's expansion during the early modern period, it would have been inconceivable for them to implement a colonial methodology that would distinguish between adopting Catholicism and accepting political control, and it was not until the middle of the 19th century that both elements started to be separated in the colonial policies applied to the Philippines. Conquest and evangelization traveled hand in hand in the island territories occupied by the Spaniards.

On November 8, 1662, orders were received to close and abandon the Zamboanga fort and to redirect all available troops to Manila. The orders' execution was delayed until January 1663 after Christian Filipinos accused Spaniards of abandoning them in front of the great danger they faced from Muslims in the area. But, finally, over 6,000 Christians were left behind in Zamboanga when the Spanish left (Combes 1897, 639; Majul 1999, 164). Most of them went to Muslim-dominated territories, where they returned to their original religions. Majul mentions a Dutch report dated June 15, 1663, declaring that approximately two-thirds of the Christian population had converted to Islam by then (Van der Chijs 1891, 242; Majul 1999, 165). The Jesuits' worst predictions became real, and the fears expressed by Father Combes when he tried to appeal to Governor Manrique de Lara were confirmed: "La salud de las Islas, solamente consistia en tener guarnecido el puesto de Samboangan, porque con solamente residir alli los Españoles . . . se le quitaua al Mindanao, y Ioló la mitad del poder. . . . Dios nuestro Señor los confunda, y defienda a estos pobres Naturales, tan destituidos de amparo humano" (The health of the islands only consisted of having the post of Zamboanga inhabited, because only with Spaniards living there . . . Mindanao and Jolo lost half their power. . . . Have Our Lord confound them, and defend these poor natives, so unprovided of human protection) (Combes 1897, 619–31).

In chapter 12 of book 1, titled "Sectas y supersticiones de estas islas" (Sects and superstitions of these islands), Combes offers his first judgment about Islam in the islands, where he shows his ambivalence toward Islam very early in his book, trying to demonize it while simultaneously downplaying its impact:

> No obstantes tantas mentiras, . . . son pocos los que hazen aprecio dél, y lo general es ser todos Ateistas . . . porque de moros, fuera de no comer puerco, y el circuncidarse, y la multitud de mugeres, no saben otra cosa. . . . Corralat . . . tiene su mezquita, y haze acudir á ella; pero en saliendo de su pueblo, cada qual viue como quiere, menos algunos principales, que a exemplo del Rey, han hecho punto de honra, el parecer moros. . . . El que con la fineza de la Morisma, junta la excelencia de valiente hechizero, es el Rey Corralat . . . si Dios no sepulta en los abismos su cuerpo, la han de adorar los Mindanaos, y fundar otra casa de Meca.

> (Despite so many lies, . . . few appreciate it, and in general all are Atheists . . . because they do not know anything about being Moors, outside of not eating pork, getting circumcised, and having multiple wives. . . . Corralat . . . has his mosque, and makes them go there; but once they leave his village, everyone lives as he pleases, with the exception of some leaders who, following the king's example, have made a matter of honor, acting like Moors. . . . The one who brings together the finesse of being Moor, along with the excellence of brave magician, is king Corralat . . . if God does not bury his body in the Abyss, Mindanaos will adore him, and will fund another house of Mecca.) (Combes 1897, 46–48)

The perception of Islam in the Philippines is slippery and polyhedral. Other episodes in the *Historia* also show a spectrum of complex situations, characters, and opinions that move around quicksand and slide between life views that are apparently far distant ideologically but come closer to each other in frontier characters and scenes that enter a side of reality without completely abandoning its opposite. The ambivalence characterizes the text's protagonists (and their representation by Combes). Before converting to Christianity, Orancaya Vgbu, "despues de muchos debates, pedia por partido ser moro, y christiano" (after many debates, asked . . . to be Moor and Christian) (Combes 1897, 523); a married couple with a Christian wife and Muslim husband help Father Francisco Ángel when he escapes captivity (276–79); Linao, "indio . . . muy fauorecido nuestro, y muy querido hijo el Padre Alexandro Lopez, que lo crio desde niño" (an Indian . . . very favored by us, and very dear to Father Alexandro Lopez, who raised him since he was a child), betrays the fathers for greed (584–85). In *Historia de Mindanao y Joló* nothing is simple or univocal. Ambiguity and oscillation are at the center of this particular portrait of the Philippines by Father Francisco de Combes. He does not hide scabrous or uncomfortable episodes, including some that involve Spanish soldiers in cases of abuse of indigenous girls, like the daughter of their ally Molobolo, who stops aiding the Spaniards after this episode: "Que diria el viejo Molobolo, quando su hija le contasse su infamia, con circunstancias tan feas, que dizen la amarró de pies, y manos para conseguirla" (What would the old Molobolo say, when his daughter told him her infamy, with such horrible circumstances, because they say he tied her by the feet and hands to rape her) (196). Gaspar de Morales, governor of Joló, also betrays the trust of Salibansa, chief of Tandum, sexually abusing his daughter, a 10- or 12-year-old girl, who Morales "mandó lleuar a su casa, haziendo escandalosa a los moros nuestra Santa Fé, é infame el trato Español" (ordered to bring to his house, making our Holy Faith scandalous to the Moors, and infamous having to treat with Spaniards) (403). He also explains how Gaspar de Morales was killed by the *joloans*, an act that in Combes's opinion was God's punishment caused by "la impiedad de Morales, en no querer lleuar Padre" (Morales's impiety, not wanting to bring a father) to his mission, proving that "el fin que Dios dá triste, é inglorioso a los despreciadores de sus Sieruos" ("God gives a sad and inglorious end to those who despise His servants (412).[5]

For Combes, the abandonment of the southern islands is a failure for Spain and its representatives, and the anxiety derived from this failure and the desperate effort to avoid its fulfillment are the starting points of Combes's *Historia de Mindanao y Joló*. He tries to discursively appropriate a world that is beginning to slide between his fingers. The evangelizing enterprise, which justifies in Combes's view the Spanish presence in the islands, and the need to offer a propagandistic weapon to this end, is the origin of the manipulation that the *moro* suffers in this book. The Jesuits, more than any other religious order in the Philippines, had the goal of converting as many indigenous individuals as possible, both Muslims and non-Muslims.[6] For Combes and the Jesuits, conversion justifies their presence in the islands and the colonizing efforts, especially when trying to convert the infidel *moro*:

> The Spanish race appeared to them as God's new Chosen People, destined to execute the plans of Providence. Spain's mission was to forge the spiritual unity of all mankind by crushing the Protestants in the Old World, defending Christendom against the onslaughts of the Turks, and spreading the gospel among the infidels of America and Asia. . . . With the conversion of the peoples of Asia all the races of mankind would be brought into the fold of Christianity. (Phelan 1959, 4–5)

After Hurtado de Corcuera's great victory against Mindanao, it is ordered that "saliesse triunfante en el carro triunfal de su Amor el Santissimo Sacramento, para que hecho notorio, y reconocido entre aquellas Naciones el Autor de nuestras vitorias, y Capitan de nuestras armas, y Dios de nuestras batallas, se les hizieran mas terribles" (the Holy Sacrament is displayed triumphant in a triumphal car of His love, so that being noted, and recognized by those Nations who the Author of our victories is, and Captain of our armaments, and God of our battles, they were more terrible to them) (Combes 1897, 260). For don Pedro de Almonte's entry on May 26, 1649, in Zamboanga after his victory against Buhayen, a solemn procession followed and a mass and sermon were organized, with very active participation of the soldiers in the religious celebrations (302). The religious aspects of the conflict are emphasized, and they tint the fight with qualities of a crusade against Islam, transcending the elements of a local fight to be reframed in the global and historic fight against Muslims, who sometimes are portrayed as the quintessential enemies of Catholicism and therefore of the Spanish monarchy. The celebrations in Manila reinforced these aspects, and they included processions with rescued captives (Barrantes 1878, 304–5), imitating those that took place in Spain after prisoners from Algiers and other Mediterranean locations returned home, presided by images of Christ and Saint Francis Xavier, "el primer apóstol de Mindanao" (the first apostle of Mindanao), who "puso los cimientos de nuestra Santa Fé en aquella isla, que hay quien juzgue ser una de las celebradas islas del moro" (set the pillars of our Holy Faith in that island, which is thought to be one of the most celebrated by the Moor) (316). Texts written around these years keep returning to this aspect of the confrontation with the peoples of Mindanao and Sulu. These texts distinguish very clearly and emphatically between Christian and Muslim Filipinos, while at the same time they magnify the narration of the long and complex conversion process:

> Costó mucho su reducion a la Fé, porfiando á los principios en defender obstinadamente su perfidia. . . . Diósele a entender, y quan enemiga es la luz de nuestra Santa Fé de las tinieblas de la Morisma, y al fin, rendido a la continua bateria del zeloso Ministro, abaxó su dura ceruiz al yugo suaue de Iesu Christo . . . y festejóse el bautismo con las mayores demostraciones de regozijo, y aparato, que pudo hazer el gusto, que todos recibieron de tan ilustre triunfo.

> (It was difficult to reduce him to the faith, arguing stubbornly in the beginning to defend their perfidy. . . . It was explained to him how much the light of our Holy faith is enemy to the shadows of the Moor, and finally, surrendered his stubbornness to the constant insistence of the zealous Minister, he surrendered to Jesus Christ's soft yoke . . . and the baptism was celebrated with the largest demonstration of happiness, and pomp, which caused the pleasure that everyone received of this illustrious triumph.) (Combes 1897, 469)

Conversions of higher-ranked individuals are more relevant, especially when they were previously Muslims, as is the case of Libot, father-in-law of the feared corsair Dato Achen. Libot converts to Catholicism and, in his last minutes of life, rejects threats coming from the king of Burney, who warned him that if he did not die as an honorable member of Islam, he would deprive him of his possessions, punish his daughter by enslaving her, and, finally, feed the animals with his body, leaving it unburied in the fields. Libot not only keeps his Catholic faith but also asks his daughter to be buried as a Christian "sin las ceremonias, y labatorios supersticiosos de los moros" (without the ceremonies and superstitious ablution rites of the Moors) (Combes 1897, 519). She, who was still a Muslim, was the object of an aggressive conversion campaign by the governor and the Jesuits, who tried to convince her with threats of the outrageous burial they would give her, throwing her in a garbage dump after publicly dragging her body along the streets (521–22). Finally, the *mora* Vley converted to Christianity, adopting the new name of Catalina and giving a big victory to Christians that would be used as a propagandistic tool in texts such as Combes's.

Combes constantly tries to reinforce that Muslims in the Philippines were an edulcorated version of Islam, and therefore they could not be included in the same group as Ottomans or Mediterranean Moors. He tries to separate them from any negative association that could introduce in his text the idea of an unavoidable failure for the Jesuit-sponsored Christianization enterprise in the southern islands, which was not always supported by civil authorities in Manila, New Spain, or Madrid. But Combes also shows an incapacity to fully disengage from preconceived ideas that strongly influenced the representation of Muslims and produced images tainted with negativity, rejection, and hatred. At the end of the 17th century, the idea of an Asian empire, which was actually never taken seriously in Madrid, was abandoned. And the missionaries had already discarded the possibility of a fast conversion of the Asian continent around the same years (Kamen 2003, 227). *Historia de Mindanao y Joló* is a complex and polyphonic text, characterized by its ambivalence in its constant search for a solution to the Spanish-Muslim clash in the Philippines. Combes writes this book with an obvious immediate goal: to try to convince authorities of the need to keep the Zamboanga fort active. With this in mind, he tries to strip away the most disturbing elements from his representation of Muslims, while he simultaneously demonizes them as the main obstacle to achieving the colonizers' objectives in the archipelago. Islam and its representatives are ideological instruments that are manipulated to achieve some ends: defending Spanish presence in Muslim-controlled territories, glorifying Jesuits' work in the islands, and criticizing colonial policies, especially at the local level. Ultimately, this book is a desperate attempt to dominate an unknown world where a long-known Other cannot be fully understood without a paradigm change. Without the development of this new interpretive paradigm, what we find in the writings analyzed here are paradoxical and ambivalent texts where the writing subject reveals an urgency to rethink his contact with a new form of alterity. These texts are very different, and they were produced under a variety of personal and historical circumstances, but they share a questioning of traditional categories and also the possibility of new ways to approach Islam. The contact with Muslims in the Philippines in the first centuries of Spanish colonization and the writings produced during these times offer new paths to reconsider the relations of Spain and Islam. With this reconsideration, we will be able to fully understand this complex, polyhedral, and often confusing relation, which is pivotal to also comprehend the fluctuations of the Hispanic subject during Early Modernity and beyond.

Notes

1. As soon as they arrived in the Philippines, Jesuits spent the first few months in the islands learning languages they would need in the evangelizing work ("se dedicaban al estudio de los idiomas que necesitarían para evangelizar") (Prieto Lucena 1993, 57).

2. The original manuscript is in the Archive of the Indies in Seville (Filipinas, leg. 18). It has been published by Hanke, *Cuerpo de documentos del siglo XVI sobre los derechos de España en las Indias y las Filipinas* (1943, 67–97). My quotes come from Hanke's edition, and all translations are mine.

3. Translations of sources originally in Spanish are mine, unless otherwise noted.

4. Prieto Lucena (1984) analyzed this period in great depth employing important documents where the governor's complaints about the islands' difficult situation are constant.

5. Gaspar de Morales (governor of Joló), Francisco de Atienza (governor of Zamboanga), and Diego Fajardo (governor of the Philippines) are examples of civil and military authorities denigrated by Combes for their bad government and for hindering the Jesuits' efforts in the islands. Combes (1897) denounces harassment by these authorities in many occasions (see 376, 453, 485, 490, 492 and chapters IX, X, XI, and XII of Book 8).

6. For more information about Jesuit writings on the Philippines in the 16th through 18th centuries, see Descalzo 2016, 117–48.

References

Ávalos, Melchor de. 1584. *Carta de Melchor de Ávalos a Felipe II*. Acapulco, March 3. Filipinas: Archivo General de Indias.

Barrantes, Vicente. 1878. *Guerras piráticas de Filipinas contra mindanaos y joloanos*. Madrid: M. G. Fernández.

Blair, Emma Helen, and James Alexander Robertson. 1903–9. *The Philippine Islands, 1493–1803*. 55 vols. Cleveland: A. H. Clark Company.

Colín, Francisco (SJ). 1900. *Labor evangélica, ministerios apostólicos de los obreros de la Compañía de Jesús, fundación, y progresos de su provincial en las islas Filipinas*. Edited by Pablo Pastells (SJ). Barcelona: Henrich.

Combes, Francisco de. 1897. *Historia de Mindanao y Joló*. Edited by W. E. Retana. Madrid: Viuda de M. Minuesa de los Ríos.

Descalzo, Eduardo. 2016. "Las crónicas oficiales de la Compañía de Jesús en Filipinas (1581–1768)." *Nuevas de Indias. Anuario del CEAD* 1:117–48.

Gayo y Aragón, Jesús. 1950. *Ideas jurídico-teológicas de los religiosos de Filipinas en el siglo XVI sobre la conquista de las islas*. Manila: Universidad de Santo Tomás.

Hanke, Lewis. 1943. *Cuerpo de documentos del siglo XVI sobre los derechos de España en las Indias y las Filipinas*. México D. F.: Fondo de Cultura Económica.

Hawkley, Ethan. 2014. "Reviving the Reconquista in Southeast Asia: Moros and the Making of the Philippines, 1565–1662." *Journal of World History* 25, no. 2/3 (June/September): 285–310.

Kamen, Henry. 2003. *Empire: How Spain Became a World Power, 1492–1763*. New York: Harper Collins.

Kroeger, James H. 1988. "Muslims in the Philippines." *Boletín eclesiástico de Filipinas* 64:621–24.

Majul, Cesar Adib. 1999. *Muslims in the Philippines.* Quezon City: University of the Philippines Press.

Mastura, Michael O. 1976. "Administrative Policies Towards the Muslims in the Philippines: A Study in Historical Continuity and Trends." *Mindanao Journal* 3 (1): 98–115.

Phelan, John Leddy. 1959. *The Hispanization of the Philippines: Spanish Aims and Filipino Responses, 1565–1700.* Madison: University of Wisconsin Press.

Prieto Lucena, Ana María. 1984. *Filipinas durante el gobierno de Manrique de Lara, 1653–1663.* Sevilla: Escuela de Estudios Hispano-Americanos.

Prieto Lucena, Ana María. 1993. *El contacto hispano-indígena en Filipinas según la historiografía de los siglos XVI y XVII.* Córdoba: Universidad de Córdoba.

Retana, Wenceslao E. 1897. "Prólogo." In *Historia de Mindanao y Joló*, i–cxliv. Madrid: Viuda de M. Minuesa de los Ríos.

Rodríguez-Rodríguez, Ana M. 2013. "Old Enemies, New Contexts: Early Modern Spanish (Re)-Writing of Islam in the Philippines." In *Coloniality, Religion, and the Law in the Early Iberian World*, edited by Santa Arias and Raúl Marrero, 137–57. Nashville: Vanderbilt University Press.

Rodríguez-Rodríguez, Ana M. 2018. "Mapping Islam in the Philippines: Moro Anxieties of the Spanish Empire in the Pacific." In *The Dialectics of Orientalism in Early Modern Europe, 1492–1700*, edited by Javier Irigoyen-García and Marcus Keller, 85–99. London: Palgrave MacMillan.

Van der Chijs, J. A. 1891. *Dagh-register gehouden int Casteel Batavia vant passerende daer ter plaetse als over geheel Nederlandts-India. Anno 1663.* Batavia: G. Kolff.

Pedro Chirino's Philippines beyond the 17th Century

Luis Castellví Laukamp

For all its relevance, the Hispanic-Philippine corpus is often ignored in scholarship on the *crónicas de Indias* (chronicles of the Indies). Nonetheless, the word "Indias" encompassed the Philippines, which were even described as "adjacent" to the Americas (see Grau y Monfalcón 1640, 2ʳ). Indeed, the Indies were deemed a trans-Pacific region (Padrón 2015, 6). Although the Philippines had their own governor-general from 1565 onward (Legazpi), they came under the viceroy of New Spain. The Manila galleon connected this city with Acapulco. In fact, most settlers/missionaries in the archipelago were either Spaniards who had previously lived in New Spain or Mexican Creoles (Crewe 2017, 24).

From a jurisdictional or administrative viewpoint, the Philippines were part of Latin America until Mexico's independence in 1821. Subsequently, the archipelago remained a (partially) Hispanic country for decades. For this reason, we should approach the terms "colonial" and "Latin American" as concepts that stretch much further in time and space than is currently the norm.[1] Moreover, given the Philippines' belated exit from the Spanish Empire in 1898, the archipelago presents the interesting phenomenon of late colonial-era writers such as José Rizal (1861–96) and Isabelo de los Reyes (1864–1938) writing in Spanish on earlier colonial authors like Pedro Chirino (1557–1635).[2]

This Jesuit missionary authored the *Relación de las islas Filipinas* (Account of the Philippine Islands) (Rome, 1604), which was commissioned by Claudio Acquaviva—the fifth superior general of the Society of Jesus—and became the first chronicle entirely devoted to the archipelago. Chirino also wrote a much longer *Historia de la provincia de Filipinas de la Compañía de Jesús* (History of the Philippine province of the Society of Jesus), which was published for the first time in 2000 (see Chirino 2000). Both works have historical and literary interest. The first section of this chapter will focus on the *Relación*, although references to the *Historia* will be made when appropriate. The second section will explore the uses to which Chirino's chronicle was put in the 19th century. One of my objectives is to build bridges between early modern and modern scholarship working on Philippine literature in Spanish. The chapter will address not so much the continuity as the dissonances that various utopia-related themes present in the *Relación* when read under the lens of 19th-century Filipino nationalism.

There are several reasons why Chirino's works (and, more broadly, Spanish Philippine chronicles) are worth exploring. First, major Filipino intellectuals of Rizal's generation (not only Reyes but also Pedro Paterno and Trinidad Pardo de Tavera) read, and indeed cited, these chronicles. Thus, this corpus helps understand the worldview of the Spanish-speaking Filipino elite known as the *ilustrados*, who had an acute historical awareness and a determination to rewrite the history of the Philippines. In fact, the influence of the chronicles continues even beyond the 19th century, as key 20th-century Filipino novelists (such as Antonio Abad) and poets (such as Flavio Zaragoza Cano) drew on them when they recreated the Spanish colonial times in their fiction.

Second, due to the paradoxical status of the chronicles—canonical as forerunners to Filipino literature in Spanish yet marginal inasmuch as their readership has been limited—this corpus transcends conventional demarcations between "center" and "periphery." European ventures in Asia were contemporary to the colonization of the Americas. Cortés conquered Tenochtitlan in 1521, the same year as Magellan's death on the Philippine island of Mactan. Half a century later, in 1571, Legazpi (re)founded Manila on an indigenous settlement. The city became an important link in the series of commercial, political, and military enterprises that characterized the emergence of a planetary consciousness in the 16th century (Gruzinski 2012, 262; Irving 2010, 8).

However, the rise of a global, modern mentality evidenced by the chronicles coexists with vestiges of the Middle Ages. This tension is already present in Antonio Pigafetta (ca. 1480–ca. 1534), an Italian survivor of the Magellan-Elcano circumnavigation (1519–22) and author of one of the first European reports that mentions the Philippines. Pigafetta combines Renaissance scientific curiosity with an uncritical acceptance of fantastic rumors. As a result, his chronicle established pervasive myths and nowadays is read as an early modern precursor of the orientalist discourse (see Pigafetta 2007, xxxiii; Rubiés 2003, 418).

Chirino (2000, 48), who read Pigafetta in Rome and quoted him in his *Historia*, has a similar approach to writing history. Both authors illustrate the tension between history as a record of facts and history as a creative form based on—but not bound by—facts.

Just as the Orientalists—following Said (2003, 40)—"created" the Orient, early modern Europeans "created" the Philippines: indeed, the territorial cohesion of the archipelago would only crystallize with the Spanish colonial administration (Górriz 2010, 14). Centuries before Rizal, Pigafetta laid the first stone that led to the "invention" of an *imagined community*—to borrow Anderson's title (2006)—that was named the Philippines (1543) after Philip II of Spain. Later authors—Chirino but also Bartolomé Leonardo de Argensola (1609)—exploited the reputation of Pigafetta's 1521 report to authorize the focus on imaginative elements in their own chronicles.

Unlike Argensola, Chirino was not an armchair historian. In fact, he had spent twelve years in the Philippines (1590–1602) and traveled widely within the islands before he wrote his *Relación*. Nevertheless, firsthand knowledge does not guarantee accuracy or objectivity. While inspiring vocations of future missionaries was his primary, self-confessed goal (see Chirino 1604, 196), his penchant for digressions (e.g., folklore, miracles, cautionary tales) converted the chronicle into a text where the real and the fantastic intermingle. Moreover, the literariness of Chirino's sources—previous chronicles, letters by other Jesuits, "cordel" literature[3]—nurtured his imagination.

In this sense, the Jesuit idealizes the Philippines in three key aspects: territory, natives, and missionaries. Chirino's archipelago is extremely rich in natural and mineral resources. Indeed, his *Relación* satisfies not only the missionary's thirst for conversions but also the conquistador's thirst for wealth. Moreover, like other religious chronicles, the *Relación* devotes even more pages to the "spiritual conquest" of native Filipinos than to descriptions of the natural setting. In this sense, we will examine hyperbolic cases of docility, ease of conversion, and fervor among the indigenous populations. Finally, the missionaries constitute the third element of the process of idealization. Chirino offers a hagiography of his own religious order. The Jesuits are not only unimpeachable but also capable of reviving the thaumaturgy of ancient Christianity in the Philippines. As we shall see, this is one of the aspects of his chronicle that most irritated the *ilustrados*.

This was to be expected, as Chirino's worldview was light-years away from 19th-century secularism. Like other Baroque chroniclers, he was aware of the persuasive, mnemonic usefulness of what I shall call the *marvelous*

Christian, a combination of (1) wonderment at an idealized reality, with (2) abundant miracles. For instance, Chirino begins his chronicle in awe with the "golfo grande de infinitas islas" (vast gulf of innumerable islands) known as the Pacific Ocean, to paraphrase the court historian Herrera y Tordesillas (1601, 5:72).

Chirino's Idealized Philippines

At the outset of the *Relación*, Chirino (1604, 2) shares his wonderment at the fact that the Portuguese, "habiendo . . . descubierto, navegado y poblado al Maluco y la China y Japón, que son como los extremos, y circunferencia, no tuviesen noticia del medio o centro, que son las Filipinas" (having . . . discovered, sailed and populated the Moluccas, China and Japan, which are, so to speak, the perimeter or circumference, had no news of its middle or center, which are the Philippines). Geography is, therefore, the first element used by the author to idealize the setting of his chronicle. The *Relación* emphasizes the centrality of the Philippines, given their strategic location, to evangelize the rest of Asia.

In addition, Chirino describes the archipelago as exceptional for its natural and mineral resources. Chapter 4 of the *Relación* surveys the Philippines with admiration: wealth and abundance are its leitmotivs. In this sense, it should be noted that the frontispieces of the Philippine chronicles by Morga (1609) and Argensola (1609), respectively entitled *Sucesos de las islas Filipinas* (Historical events of the Philippine Islands) and *Conquista de las islas Malucas* (Conquest of the Moluccas), portray women holding cornucopias, the Baroque symbol of plenitude. Indeed, as pointed out by Padrón (2015, 4), the archipelago represented an almost inexhaustible cornucopia of riches and wonders.

However, the early modern Philippines offered few mineral resources (particularly little gold). In fact, some islands did not even have enough supplies for the Spanish colonizers. Compare the cornucopia with this letter from the missionary Martín de Rada (1577, 44^r): "En la villa de Cebú los más aún no alcanzan a sustentarse con arroz y pescado. . . . Los más de los que están en las islas reniegan del que los trajo a tierra donde no pueden ganar de comer" (Most Spaniards in Cebu still cannot sustain themselves with rice and fish. . . . Most settlers in the Philippines regret having come to this land where they cannot make enough living to feed themselves). The situation was somewhat better in Manila, but even there, food was not abundant. Rada adds that many Spaniards would accept with "suma felicidad" (great joy) the opportunity to leave the Philippines and return to New Spain (44^r).

Thus, the historical reality was far from the idealized Philippines of the *Relación*. Descalzo (2016, 11) points out that many missionaries perceived the archipelago as "el confín del mundo no solo en un sentido geográfico" (the end of the world not only in a geographical sense). His article even describes the Philippines as a *desterradero*, that is, a godforsaken place where inconvenient characters from New Spain or even Spain were exiled as a punishment. Of course, none of this appears in the published chronicles. Distance from Europe gave much room for maneuver to Chirino, who maintained illusions of wealth and prosperity about the Philippines that hark back to Pigafetta.

Thus far I have argued that Chirino presents an idealized archipelago. Some authors have used the term "Eden" (Descalzo 2011, 36–37). Perhaps the word "utopia" is more appropriate, given its projection toward the future. The idealization of heretofore unknown islands opens the way to the configuration of better worlds by means of religious conversion. According to Rodríguez Torres (2007, 222), early modernity was prone to utopian thinking. This is confirmed by the *Relación*, read in the light of the *Historia*.

For instance, let us examine the description of the Philippine island of Bohol. The *Relación* contains the above-mentioned *topoi* of abundance (see Chirino 1604, 74). But the *Historia* adds a twist: "La Fe divina, que en tan breve ha dado tanto ser a nuestros Boholanos, podrá ennoblecerlos tanto, andando el tiempo, que hagan lo mismo en su Loboc, y con él, su isla otro paraíso" (The divine Faith, which in such a short period of time has given so much new life to our Boholanos, will be able to ennoble them to such an extent that, as time goes by, the same will happen in Loboc, and thereby, their island will become another paradise) (Chirino 2000, 262). In other words, by means of conversion, the Spaniards were helping native Filipinos toward the construction of a Philippine paradise.[4]

Another remarkable feature of the quotation is Chirino's emphasis on faith's ennobling nature. The Jesuits went to the Indies to "save" the souls of natives from the devil (cf. Valcárcel 1997, 307). For this reason, after each digression, the chronicle returns to the main narration with expressions such as "volvamos a nuestra ocupación de las almas" (let us return to our task concerning souls) (Chirino 1604, 41). A great part of the *Relación* consists of descriptions of native Filipino societies. The desire to understand their idiosyncrasies does not only stem from ethnological curiosity. Rather, such knowledge is deemed indispensable for the undertaking of missionary activities (Górriz 2000, 32). Thus, like many religious chroniclers, Chirino is more interested in the indigenous world than in nature.

Chirino wants to convey this message: the docile, intelligent nature of native Filipinos renders the Philippines an ideal location for settlement. Thus, the Jesuit constantly sings their praises, for instance, by highlighting their trade skills. He also lauds the Tagalog language and, in fact, introduced its alphabet for the first time to a European audience. Moreover, he admires the speed at which the natives learned Spanish (see Chirino 1604, 7, 35, 41). The *Relación* is full of such praise.

But the main reason for these compliments is the natives' predisposition to receive the Gospel (cf. Descalzo 2012, 978). The Jesuit portrays them converting after little missionary effort. In fact, the word "fervor" appears in the titles of three chapters (45, 63, and 81), always referring to catechumens or converts. Furthermore, Chirino (1604, 191) describes mass conversions as "llamas de aquel celestial incendio . . . del cual hasta los niños pequeños son inflamados" (flames of that heavenly fire . . . which sets even little children alight).

The image of fire is plethoric. Unfortunately, the flames of the conquest were not only metaphorical but also literal. I am referring to the military enterprise that Spanish sources, following the 1573 ordinances that discouraged the use of the term "conquest," describe as *"pacificación"* (pacification) (see Newson 2009, 6).[5] Despite its euphemisms, the *Relación* offers evidence of the violence between the Spaniards and native Filipinos. In fact, when Chirino (1604, 6) arrives at the archipelago, he encounters recent wounds: "En la pacificación de estas islas hubo harta resistencia y muertes de algunos de los nuestros" (During the pacification of these islands there was much resistance and some of our people died).

Rizal (2012, 201) wrote about the consequences of this clash in his famous essay *Filipinas dentro de cien años* (The Philippines a century hence) (1889), in which he stated that "las ambiciones conquistadoras del pueblo español" (the conquering ambitions of the Spanish people) depopulated the archipelago shortly after its incorporation into the Crown of Castile. Recent research shows that he was not exaggerating (see Newson 2009; Blanco 2019).

Unfortunately, we do not have early modern indigenous sources to know the vision of the defeated. Chirino gives little information about it for obvious reasons. However, other Spanish texts offer a counterpoint to his idealization. Philippine historiography of the 17th century begins with Chirino's *Relación*

(1604) and ends with Gaspar de San Agustín's *Conquistas de las islas Filipinas* (Conquests of the Philippine Islands) (1698). This friar also wrote a letter to a Spanish friend who asked for information about native Filipinos:

> Es cosa digna de admirar que hasta sus perros se visten de otra naturaleza, y tienen particular ojeriza con los españoles, y en sintiéndoles se deshacen a ladrar: como los niños, viendo al Padre, que luego lloran, y así desde la cuna comienzan a tener horror, a toda cara blanca.

> (It is something worthy of admiration that even their dogs have a different nature, and a particular animosity toward Spaniards, and thus they start barking as soon as they sense their presence; likewise, their children cry when they see the Father, and thus from the cradle they begin to be afraid of all white faces.) (San Agustín 1720, 20r)[6]

I am aware of the time lapse between Chirino and Gaspar de San Agustín. However, the gap does not seem insurmountable when it comes to studying the shock of colonization. In fact, this mental state must have been even more acute at Chirino's time than in the 18th century, given the temporal proximity of the conquest. According to Rafael (1988, 59), "The shock of colonization never fully disappeared." The fact that this phenomenon is conspicuous by its absence in the *Relación* is yet another example of its idealization of both the spiritual conquest and native Filipinos.

Unlike other chroniclers such as Argensola, who at least acknowledges that religious conversion often went hand in hand with "la avaricia y otros excesos de nuestros capitanes y soldados" (greed and other excesses of our captains and soldiers), Chirino does not recognize the excesses of the Spaniards. Ethnography is often buried under the hagiography of the Society of Jesus (Rubiés 2003, 442). For example, the Jesuits of the *Relación* apparently learn new languages in just a few months: "Parece don del cielo la facilidad" (Such easiness seems a gift from heaven). The chronicler himself claims to speak "la lengua china además de las lenguas bisaya y tagala" (Chinese, Bisaya, and Tagalog) (Chirino 1604, 34, 62).

Certainly, there is much (printed) evidence of Spanish friars learning local languages, particularly Tagalog and Hokkien. However, Chirino exaggerates. Jesuits also resorted to interpreters, whose presence he never acknowledges.[7] Centuries later, Rizal's *Noli me tangere* (1887) would mock the Spanish friars who thought they could speak Tagalog: "El P. Dámaso improvisaba en este idioma. . . . Es fama que ninguno de los presentes comprendió el conjunto del sermón" (Father Dámaso improvised in Tagalog. . . . It is notorious that no one in the audience understood his sermon in its entirety) (2011, 343).[8]

Such exaggeration is even more blatant when it comes to the *marvelous Christian*. Chirino's *Relación* contains 78 divine interventions (punishments, miraculous healings, prevention of shipwrecks, etc.). Thus, on average, one supernatural episode occurs every two and a half pages. Although the miracles distort the image that the reader forms of native Filipino cultures and of the Spanish colonization, they contribute to extolling the Society of Jesus.

In light of the above, it is unsurprising that the *Relación* was well received by later Jesuits such as Francisco Colin (1663), Chirino's continuator. On the other hand, posterity has been unkind to this chronicle. This was particularly the case in the archipelago it described, where 19th-century nationalism saw Chirino as the epitome of the problems caused by Spanish rule.

Chirino and 1898

Chirino's worldview is infused with spirituality. Given the double mechanism of the *marvelous Christian* (idealization and miracles), the Jesuit's approach distances his work from history and brings it closer to literature. It is thus little wonder that the *Relación* was a problematic yet important source for Filipino writers of the 19th and 20th centuries.

For example, the novelist Antonio Abad (1894–1970) longed for times before occupation by the United States. For this reason, *La oveja de Nathán* (Nathan's sheep) (1929), a plea against American imperialism, describes with enthusiasm the Spanish expeditions narrated by Morga (see Abad 2013, chap. 2).[9] The novel, which otherwise is set in the early 20th-century Philippines, also describes a miracle that seems reminiscent of Chirino's *Relación*: "La Virgen . . . había salvado a los pasajeros de la lancha, gracias al fervor con que una vieja pueblerina, llegada de muy lejos, había invocado su santo nombre" (The Virgin . . . had saved the passengers in the boat, thanks to the fervor with which an old lady from a remote village had invoked her holy name) (308).

Moreover, before the political shift of 1898, Filipinos used the chronicles to denounce Spanish colonialism. The resurgence of interest in this corpus coincided with the rise of the Philippine nationalist movement known as Propaganda. The decade began with the reedition of Chirino's *Relación* (Manila, 1890) and Morga's *Sucesos* (1890, by Rizal). Shortly afterward, a new edition of

Argensola's *Conquista* (1891) appeared in Zaragoza. The reissue of Chirino is the least ambitious of the three, as it merely reproduces the chronicle without adding any paratext. However, it is the only one published in the Philippines. Among 19th-century readers of the *Relación*, two *ilustrados* stand out. First, the aforementioned Rizal, who in a letter in German (September 17, 1888) to his friend Ferdinand Blumentritt reveals he had already read the text before its 1890 reedition: "Ich finde Chirino zu priestlich und man-chmal kindlich: er erzählt Märchen, glaubend dass die Religion mit solchen Unpässlichkeiten besser und mächtiger sein würde" (I find Chirino too priestly and sometimes childish; he tells fairy tales because he believes that religion would be better and stronger with these stories that are entirely out of place) (see Kalaw 1938, 5:308).

Events that in the 17th century could pass for miracles would hardly do so after the Enlightenment. In this sense, Rizal's later letter (April 4, 1893) to the Jesuit Pablo Pastells is revealing. After reproaching him for the "puerilidades que santifican en milagros" (trivialities that Catholics sanctify by means of miracles), Rizal explains the phenomenon by resorting to auto-suggestion: "Todo se explica cuando se desea y todo se acepta cuando se quiere. La volun-tad tiene un poder enorme sobre la imaginación, y viceversa" (Everything can be explained when there is desire and everything becomes acceptable when there is a will. Will has enormous power over imagination, and vice versa) (see Kalaw 1936, 4:122).

Moreover, his *Noli me tangere* does not quote Chirino but alludes to the racist disciplinary measures defended by the friar Gaspar de San Agustín (see Rizal 2011, 109). In addition, several chapters of his novel reveal Rizal's famil-iarity with the chronicles. For instance, there are three episodes that satirize *milagrería* (fake miracles) (see Rizal 2011, 59, 287, 361). See also this speech by Elías, the protagonist's doppelgänger: "¿Llamáis fe a esas prácticas exteriores, religión a ese comercio de correas y escapularios, verdad a esos milagros y cuentos que oímos todos los días? . . . Para esto no necesitaba un Dios dejarse crucificar" (Do you call "faith" these external practices, "religion" this trade in cinctures and scapularies, "truth" these miracles and tales that we hear every day? . . . God did not need to let himself be crucified for the sake of this) (Rizal 2011, 541).

After the publication of the novel and the subsequent ecclesial (over)reac-tion, Rizal affirmed he had lost his religious faith (Retana 1907, 140). In a draft letter (March 5, 1887) in French contained in his notebook *Clínica médica* (Medical clinic), he claimed to have written the *Noli me tangere* in order to rebut the "calomnies que pendant des siècles on a entassées sur nous et notre pays" (slander that for centuries has been piled on our country and us) (see Castellví Laukamp 2017).

It is worth taking a step back in order to assess the meaning of this quotation. In his book *The Wretched of the Earth*, Fanon (2004, 149) emphasizes that colonialism is not just about controlling the present and future of a dominated country. As a matter of fact, colonialism also "turns its attention to the past of the colonized people and distorts it, disfigures it, and destroys it." This results in the cultural alienation of the natives, who are told that without the colonizer they would regress to barbarism—hence, the efforts of colonized intellectuals to remind their people of the great chapters of precontact history. The past is a source not of shame but of dignity, and thus an inspiration for anticolonial nationalism.

Rizal's prologue "A los filipinos" (To the Filipinos) in his edition of Morga (1890, vi) illustrates this point: "Si el libro logra despertar en vosotros la conciencia de nuestro pasado, borrado de la memoria, y rectificar lo que se ha falseado y calumniado, entonces no habré trabajado en balde" (If the book succeeds in awakening in you the awareness of our past, which has been erased from our memory, and in rectifying what has been falsified and slandered, then I will not have worked in vain). Although Rizal cited Chirino frequently, he included him among the authors who had misrepresented Filipino history. In fact, his first footnote to Morga affirmed that the *Relación* "más es historia de misiones que de Filipinas" (is more devoted to the history of the missions than to the Philippines) (Morga 1890, xxix).

Rizal's reaction to Chirino is comparable to Said's (2003) criticism of the Orientalists. Indeed, Rizal used his footnotes to Morga to articulate a counterdiscourse that uncovered the errors, misrepresentations, and omissions of the chroniclers (see Schmidt-Nowara 2006, 182). In his opinion, authors such as Chirino downplayed the role of the natives in the construction of their own country. For this reason, it was necessary for Filipinos to rewrite Philippine history, which had been reduced by religious chroniclers to a succession of "milagros y cuentos" (miracles and tales), to borrow an expression from the *Noli me tangere* (Rizal 2011, 541). In fact, Rizal's Morga (1890) portrayed the pre-Hispanic Philippines as a paradise lost. His *Noli me tangere* denounced Spanish colonization as a "cáncer social" (social cancer) (see Rizal 2011, 3). Rizal did not frame the problems caused by colonialism as bad contemporary governance but rather as endemic to Spanish control since early modernity (see Castellví Laukamp 2017). In this respect, Chirino's chronicle and Rizal's oeuvre are poles apart.

Isabelo de los Reyes would have agreed with Rizal. Although their respective anticolonial nationalisms were different,[10] they shared common ground in their criticisms of Spanish historiography. See Reyes's *Historia de Filipinas* (History of the Philippines) (1889a, vi): "Los primeros cronistas bebieron en tradiciones orales y escasísimos escritos. . . . Después vinieron los analistas del siglo XVII a completar esos datos, aumentando a su vez considerablemente los errores y la confusión con sus detalles imaginarios" (The first chroniclers drew on oral traditions and very few texts. . . . Then, the 17th-century analysts came to complete these data, thereby greatly multiplying the mistakes and confusion with their imaginary details). On the same page, Reyes denounces the "miopía" (short-sightedness) of religious chroniclers who only wrote about events that concerned their order.

Such was Spain's discredit that the *ilustrados* denounced not only its 19th-century colonial policies but also the methodology of its historians. In this sense, the Creole elite of Puerto Rico followed a similar path. Reyes's quotation could be compared with this statement by Alejandro Tapia y Rivera (1854, 4–5) about the Caribbean chronicles of the Spanish clergy: "escritos que en estilo incorrecto, llevan el sello pueril de candidez y credulidad rústica propia de los tiempos" (texts written in an incorrect style that have the childish marks of naivety and rustic credulity of their time). This author also decries the chroniclers' lack of interest in Borinquen (pre-Hispanic Puerto Rico), an indigenous world of which there is barely "escasas y vagas noticias" (scarce, imprecise news). But Puerto Rican and Philippine criticism coexisted with a certain affection for Spain, especially in the case of Rizal.

Nevertheless, a new collapse of the waning Spanish Empire was looming on the horizon. Toward the end of the 19th century, other nations represented modernity: the United Kingdom, France, and Germany in Europe; the United States in the Americas; and Japan in Asia. In a new age marked by science, technology, and capitalism, the Spanish *frailocracia* (friarocracy, given the power of religious orders) in the archipelago was a vestige of former times (see Reyes 2014, 53).

In works such as *El diablo en Filipinas; según rezan las crónicas* (The devil in the Philippines; according to the chronicles) (included in Reyes 1887, 115–38) and *El folk-lore filipino* (Filipino folklore) (1889b), Reyes used his knowledge of ethnography to examine stories that had passed for truths throughout centuries—for example, the tale of the demon who admitted to being afraid of Christians, which Colin (1663, 387) took from Chirino (1604, 67) and then expanded.[11] Reyes (1887, 129) discusses it with humor: "a veces el demonio teme a los cristianos, solo por serlo" (sometimes the devil is afraid of Christians, just because they are Christians).

In his description of the Taytay region, Chirino (1604, 112) had proudly stated: "Las supersticiones e idolatrías se han arrancado, de manera, que apenas hay rastro de ellas, ni cosa que a ellas parezca" (Superstitions and idolatries have been uprooted, so that there is hardly a trace of them, or anything that resembles them). In this sense, the *Relación* is a constant lament about the "idolatría y supersticiones de los filipinos" (idolatry and superstitions of the Filipinos) that were to be eradicated (see chap. 21). Conversely, Reyes argues that the Spaniards merely replaced local idolatries with Catholic superstitions. See how he explains the purpose of his satire *El diablo en Filipinas* (Reyes 1899, 100):

> En este folleto, entre empalagosos e irónicos elogios a los frailes, se dejaban deslizar pruebas históricas de que ellos, en vez de enseñar la verdadera religión cristiana a los filipinos, son los que les hicieron creer ese gran cúmulo de supersticiones y patrañas sobre seres sobrenaturales, apariciones de difuntos, etc.

> (In this booklet, amid cloying and ironic praise of the friars, I introduced historical evidence suggesting that, instead of teaching true Christian religion to the Filipinos, they made them believe in a heap of superstitions and lies about supernatural beings, apparitions of the deceased, etc.)

In short, superstition persisted under different guises.[12] Instead of *diguatas* (local idols) and spirits of their ancestors, Filipinos had come to believe in the devil, demons, witches, mermaids, and elves. Hence, *El diablo en Filipinas* can also be read as a counterpoint to Chirino's *Relación*. For its part, *El Folk-lore filipino* offers a lesson in cultural relativism by putting Catholic imagery on the level of native paganism (see Reyes 2014, 9). In his opinion, folklore—be it from Europe or the Philippines—should be studied as such.

The *ilustrados*—starting with Rizal and Reyes—understood that, in a colony dominated by religious orders, satire on the *marvelous Christian* in the Spanish chronicles could help emancipate the minds of the Filipinos. Literature and historiography were two sister weapons in the struggle for the intellectual freedom of the archipelago and the dignity of its native inhabitants. A paradox of history: chronicles such as Chirino's *Relación* would end up serving the ends in the antipodes—literally and metaphorically speaking—of those who commissioned them.

Notes

I would like to thank Professor Adam Lifshey for his comments on an earlier version and Dr. Rosemary Clark and Dr. Parker Lawson for their proofreading.

1. The category of the Global Hispanophone, which incorporates all of the territories that were once bound by the Spanish Empire, would be of help. See Campoy-Cubillo and Sampedro Vizcay (2019, 5): "The historical connections underlying the roots of the Global Hispanophone can arguably be traced as far back as . . . the sixteenth century in the case of the Philippines."

2. For a comparable intra-colonial experience, see Cuba and Puerto Rico. José Martí (1853–95) began his famous essay "Nuestra América" (Our Americas) (2012, 157) by mentioning the poet-chronicler Juan de Castellanos (1522–1607). Castellanos also appears among the sources of the *Historia geográfica, civil y natural de la isla de San Juan Bautista de Puerto Rico* (Geographical, civil and natural history of Puerto Rico) by Íñigo Abbad y Lasierra (1788), which was republished in the 19th century (see Abbad y Lasierra 1866).

3. I refer to Castellví Laukamp (2020) for a study of this popular genre, which was mostly composed of anonymous broadsides of low literary quality, and its impact on Chirino's representation of miracles.

4. In the 19th century, Spanish intellectuals such as Miguel de Unamuno and W. E. Retana would modernize/secularize this discourse without challenging the vision of imperial Spain as a positive agent of civilization (see Schmidt-Nowara 2006, 162–63).

5. See John D. Blanco's chapter, in this volume, for a detailed analysis of the 1573 ordinances and, more broadly, the Spanish rhetoric of pacification.

6. In the 19th century, there was still a need to refute Gaspar de San Agustín: "En cuanto al horror a las caras blancas es cuando menos exagerado: nada tiene de extraño que un niño llore al presentársele un objeto que no tiene siempre a su alrededor. A muchos niños he visto yo prorrumpir en llanto al mirar mis anteojos. Cierto es que algunos tratan con nosotros lo menos posible o por despego, o por embarazo, o por antipatía, pero hay infinitos que nos profesan cariño" (As for the fear of white faces, it is at least an exaggeration: there is nothing strange about a child crying when presented with an object with which he is not familiar. I have seen many children burst into tears when they see my glasses. It is true that some Filipinos have as little contact with Spaniards as possible, either out of disregard, embarrassment, or antipathy. However, countless Filipinos profess affection for us) (Mas 1842, 1:118).

7. Conversely, see González de Mendoza (1586, 15): "Este libro se trajo a la ciudad de Manila, estampado en la misma China, y se tradujo en nuestra lengua por intérpretes que son chinos de nación" (This book, which had been printed in China, was brought to Manila, where Chinese translators rendered it into Spanish).

8. Father Dámaso delivers the first part of his sermon in Spanish and the second in Tagalog. Rafael (1988, 1–3) analyzed the former, which is incomprehensible due to the friar's bombastic, inaccessible Spanish. Thus, Father Dámaso overdoes his Spanish and neglects his Tagalog. Both actions reflect his contempt for native Filipinos, and, more broadly, the colonizer's self-proclaimed superiority vis-à-vis the colonized.

9. Cf. the epic poem *De Mactán a Tirad* (From Mactan to Tirad), which includes in its glossary an entry on Pigafetta, the source of its first part: "Sabio historiador y cronista español [*sic*] y uno de los compañeros de Magallanes al desembarcar en Cebú" (Wise Span-

ish [*sic*] historian and chronicler and one of Magellan's companions when he disembarked in Cebu) (Zaragoza Cano 1941, 233).

10. Reyes's strong Ilocano identity coexisted in tension with the notion of a broader Filipino nationhood. Conversely, Rizal could unproblematically merge his Tagalog and Filipino identities (Mojares 2006, 349–50). Rizal's letter to Marcelo H. del Pilar (February 4, 1889) is illustrative in this respect: "Tengo sin embargo que lamentar su demasiado *ilocanismo*, que como V. sospecha puede un día troncharnos, como un argumento en contra nuestra" (Nevertheless, I must decry Reyes' excessive *Ilocanism*, which as you suspect, might one day cut us off, as an argument against us) (Kalaw 1931, 2:116–17).

11. See Paterno 1894, 152: "Así, una idea emitida por el P. Chirino es tomada a ciegas por los demás cronistas posteriores, y si es un error de apreciación personal, ahora se le repite y consagra como dogma, por la confirmación de tantos testimonios uniformes, sin parar mientes en que son todos copistas, y ninguno original" (Later chroniclers follow blindly Father Chirino, and if he makes a mistake in a subjective assessment, it is then repeated and consecrated as dogma, and thus confirmed by so many uniform testimonies, without realizing that they are all copying each other, and none of them is original). Cf. Said 2003, 62.

12. Cf. Pardo de Tavera 1920, 58: "Cuando los misioneros predicaron su religión, condenaron las antiguas supersticiones paganas, pero enseñaron otra nueva superstición más poderosa que la primitiva" (When the missionaries preached their religion, they condemned the ancient pagan superstitions, but they taught a new superstition that was more powerful than the former, primitive one).

References

Abad, Antonio M. 2013. *La oveja de Nathán*. Edited by Lourdes Castrillo Brillantes. Makati City: Georgina Padilla y Zóbel, Filipinas Heritage Library y Ayala Foundation.

Abbad y Lasierra, Íñigo. 1866. *Historia geográfica, civil y natural de la isla de San Juan Bautista de Puerto Rico*. Edited by José Julián Acosta y Calvo. Puerto Rico: Imprenta y librería de Acosta.

Anderson, Benedict. 2006. *Imagined Communities: Reflections on the Origin and Spread of Nationalism*. London: Verso.

Argensola, Bartolomé Leonardo de. 1609. *Conquista de las islas Malucas*. Madrid: Alonso Martín.

Argensola, Bartolomé Leonardo de. 1891. *Conquista de las islas Malucas*. Edited by Miguel Mir. Zaragoza: Imprenta del hospicio provincial.

Blanco, John D. 2019. "Traditions, Customs, and Law in the Colonial World." Unpublished paper, Far Eastern University.

Campoy-Cubillo, Adolfo, and Benita Sampedro Vizcaya. 2019. "Entering the Global Hispanophone: An Introduction." *Journal of Spanish Cultural Studies* 20:1–16.

Castellví Laukamp, Luis. 2017. "Rizal before 'Rizal': Lessons from His Notebook." *Newberry Library* (blog). 8 December. https://www.newberry.org/rizal-rizal-lessons-his -notebook

Castellví Laukamp, Luis. 2020. "Los milagros en la *Relación de las islas Filipinas* (1604) de Pedro Chirino." *Colonial Latin American Review* 29:177–94.

Chirino, Pedro. 1604. *Relación de las islas Filipinas*. Roma: E. Paulino.

Chirino, Pedro. 1890. *Relación de las islas Filipinas*. Manila: Imprenta de D. Esteban Balbás.

Chirino, Pedro. 2000. *Història de la província de Filipines de la Companyia de Jesús, 1581–1606*. Edited by Miquel Batllori and Jaume Górriz. Barcelona: Pòrtic.

Colín, Francisco. 1663. *Labor evangélica*. Madrid: José Fernández de Buendía.

Crewe, Ryan Dominic. 2017. "Connecting the Indies: The Hispano-Asian Pacific World in Early Modern Global History." *Estudos Históricos Rio de Janeiro* 30:17–34.

Descalzo, Eduardo. 2011. "La historia natural y moral de Filipinas en la obra de Pedro Chirino, S.I. (1557–1635)." In *Ciencia y cultura entre dos mundos. Segundo simposio. Fuentes documentales y sus diversas interpretaciones*, edited by José L. Montesinos and Sergio Toledo, 25–47. La Orotava, Tenerife: Fundación canaria Orotava de historia de la ciencia.

Descalzo, Eduardo. 2012. "La implantación de la Compañía de Jesús en Filipinas a través de la obra del P. Pedro Chirino, S.I." In *Actas de la XI reunión científica de la Fundación española de historia moderna, el Estado absoluto y la monarquía*, edited by Antonio Jiménez Estrella and Julián J. Lozano, 1:973–83. Granada: Universidad de Granada.

Descalzo, Eduardo. 2016. "*Las misiones más trabajosas, y difíciles, que tiene la universal Compañía*: Dificultades de la labor misional de la Compañía de Jesús en Filipinas (1581–1768)." *Revista Estudios* 32:467–95.

Fanon, Frantz. 2004. *The Wretched of the Earth*. Translated by Richard Philcox. New York: Grove Press.

González de Mendoza, Juan. 1586. *Historia de las cosas más notables, ritos y costumbres del gran reino de la China*. Barcelona: Juan Pablo Manescal.

Górriz, Jaume. 2000. "Introducción." In *Història de la província de Filipines de la Companyia de Jesús, 1581–1606 de Pedro Chirino*, edited by Miquel Batllori and Jaume Górriz, 27–38. Barcelona: Pòrtic.

Górriz, Jaume. 2010. *Filipinas antes de Filipinas. El archipiélago de San Lázaro en el siglo XVI*. Madrid: Polifemo.

Grau y Monfalcón, Juan. 1640. *Justificación de la conservación, y comercio de las islas Filipinas*. Madrid: s.n.

Gruzinski, Serge. 2012. *L'aigle et le dragon: Démesure européenne et mondialisation au XVIe siècle*. Paris: Fayard.

Herrera y Tordesillas, Antonio de. 1601. *Historia general de los hechos de los castellanos en las islas y tierra firme del mar océano*. Vol. 5. Madrid: Imprenta Real.

Irving, D. R. M. 2010. *Colonial Counterpoint: Music in Early Modern Manila*. Oxford: Oxford University Press.

Kalaw, Teodoro, ed. 1931. *Epistolario rizalino*. Vol. 2, *Tomo Segundo, 1887–1890*. Manila: Bureau of Printing.

Kalaw, Teodoro, ed. 1936. *Epistolario rizalino*. Vol. 4, *Tomo cuarto, 1892–1896*. Manila: Bureau of Printing.

Kalaw, Teodoro, ed. 1938. *Epistolario rizalino*. Vol. 5, *Tomo quinto. Primera parte. Cartas de Rizal a Blumentritt en alemán, 1886–1888*. Manila: Bureau of Printing.

Martí, José. 2012. *Ensayos y crónicas*. Edited by José Olivio Jiménez. Madrid: Cátedra.

Mas, Sinibaldo de. 1842. *Informe sobre el estado de las islas Filipinas*. Vol. 1. Madrid: s.n.

Mojares, Resil B. 2006. *Brains of the Nation: Pedro Paterno, T. H. Pardo de Tavera, Isabelo de Los Reyes, and the Production of Modern Knowledge*. Quezon City: Ateneo de Manila University Press.

Morga, Antonio de. 1609. *Sucesos de las islas Filipinas*. México: Gerónimo Balli.

Morga, Antonio de. 1890. *Sucesos de las islas Filipinas*. Edited by José Rizal. Paris: Garnier hermanos.

Newson, Linda. 2009. *Conquest and Pestilence in the Early Spanish Philippines*. Honolulu: University of Hawai'i Press.

Padrón, Ricardo. 2015. "Las Indias olvidadas. Filipinas y América en la cartografía imperial española." *Terra Brasilis (Nova Série)* 4:1–13.

Pardo de Tavera, Trinidad. 1920. *El legado del ignorantismo. Conferencia dada el 23 de abril de 1920 ante la Asamblea de Maestros en Baguio*. Manila: Bureau of Printing.

Paterno, Pedro. 1894. *Los tagalog*. Madrid: Tipografía de los sucesores de Cuesta.

Pigafetta, Antonio. 2007. *The First Voyage around the World, 1519–1522: An Account of Magellan's Expedition*. Edited by Theodore J. Cachey. Toronto: University of Toronto Press.

Rada, Martín de. 1577. "Letter: Manila, to Father Alonso de la Vera Cruz." Ayer MS 1943. Newberry Library.

Rafael, Vicente L. 1988. *Contracting Colonialism: Translation and Christian Conversion in Tagalog Society under Early Spanish Rule*. Quezon City: Ateneo de Manila University Press.

Retana, W. E. 1907. *Vida y escritos del Dr. José Rizal*. Madrid: V. Suárez.

Reyes, Isabelo de los. 1887. *Filipinas: Artículos varios sobre etnografía, historia y costumbres del país*. Manila: J. A. Ramos.

Reyes, Isabelo de los. 1889a. *Historia de Filipinas*. Manila: Imprenta de D. Esteban Balbás.

Reyes, Isabelo de los. 1889b. *El Folk-lore filipino*. Manila: Imprenta de Santa Cruz.

Reyes, Isabelo de los. 1899. *La sensacional memoria sobre la revolución de 1896–97*. Madrid: Tip. Lit. de J. Corrales.

Reyes, Isabelo de los. 2014. *Ang diablo sa Filipinas ayon sa nasasabi sa mga casulatan luma sa Kastila / The Devil in the Philippines*. Edited by Benedict Anderson, Carlos Galache, and Ramon Guillermo. Mandaluyong City, Philippines: Anvil Publishing.

Rizal, José. 2011. *Noli Me Tangere*. Edited by Isaac Donoso. Quezon City: Vibal Foundation.

Rizal, José. 2012. *Prosa selecta, narraciones y ensayos*. Edited by Isaac Donoso. Madrid: Verbum.

Rodríguez Torres, Adriana. 2007. "Utopía y crónicas de Indias: una construcción recíproca." In *Narración y reflexión: Las crónicas de Indias y la teoría historiográfica*, edited by Karl Kohut, 219–42. México, D.F: El Colegio de México.

Rubiés, Joan-Pau. 2003. "The Spanish Contribution to the Ethnology of Asia in the Sixteenth and Seventeenth Centuries." *Renaissance Studies* 17:418–48.

Said, Edward. 2003. *Orientalism*. London: Penguin.

San Agustín, Gaspar de. 1698. *Conquistas de las Islas Filipinas*. Madrid: Imprenta de Manuel Ruiz de Murga.

San Agustín, Gaspar de. 1720. "Carta de Fr. Gaspar de San Agustín a un amigo suyo en España, que le pregunta [por] el natural ingenio de los indios naturales de estas Islas Filipinas." Ayer MS 1429. Newberry Library.

Schmidt-Nowara, Christopher. 2006. *The Conquest of History: Spanish Colonialism and National Histories in the Nineteenth Century*. Pittsburgh: University of Pittsburgh Press.

Tapia y Rivera, Alejandro. 1854. *Biblioteca histórica de Puerto Rico*. Puerto Rico: Imprenta de Márquez.

Valcárcel, Simón. 1997. *Las crónicas de Indias como expresión y configuración de la mentalidad renacentista*. Granada: Diputación Provincial de Granada.

Zaragoza Cano, Flavio. 1941. *De Mactán á Tirad (Lapolapo, Bañgotbanua y Del Pilar). Poema épico histórico*. Intramuros, Manila: Kanlaón Printing Press.

China Was No Longer the Enemy

The Reassessment of Limahong in
Philippine Literature in Spanish

Rocío Ortuño Casanova

In their book *The Empire Writes Back*, Bill Ashcroft, Gareth Griffiths, and Helen Tiffin concluded that, for them, postcolonial literature was any literature "affected by the imperial process from the moment of colonization to the present day," since "there is a continuity of preoccupations throughout the historical process initiated by European imperial aggression" (2005, 2). They focused on how postcolonial cultures appropriated writing, which used to be an agent of marginalization of the colonial subject, to redefine their own culture. In this way, postcolonial cultures managed to put the periphery to which they belonged at the center of the discourse (36).

In the Philippines, postcolonial literature actually started already during the Spanish colonial era, when the so-called Filipino *ilustrados* envisioned a free Philippines and took up the pen at the end of the 19th century to write it, while also reacting to Spanish writings on the archipelago.[1] In *The Conquest of History*, Christopher Schmidt-Nowara proposed the case of José Rizal's edition of Antonio de Morga's *Sucesos de las Islas filipinas* as an example of appropriating the writing of the colonizer in postcolonial literature, in a similar fashion to that proposed by Ashcroft, Griffiths, and Tiffin (Schmidt-Nowara 2006; Morga and Rizal 1890). According to Schmidt-Nowara, this edition of the Spanish chronicles, commentated by a Filipino nationalist, responded to a revision of the past with the purpose of forging a new national future, a process that was also taking place in Puerto Rico and Cuba (2006, 42). Rizal himself expressed this necessity of reevaluating his prior understanding of Filipino history at the beginning of the work. He said that he was producing that edition because of the "necesidad de dar primero á conocer el pasado, á fin de poder juzgar mejor el presente y medir el camino recorrido durante tres siglos" (necessity of first revealing the past, in order to be able to better judge the present and measure the path traversed over three centuries) (Morga and Rizal 1890, v). This is probably the most famous case of the reexamination of the Spanish chronicles by Filipino nationalists in order to reassess their own history, which had previously reached them exclusively through the voices of the colonizers. There are, however, other cases of rewriting Filipino history during the last decades of the 19th century, departing from the chronicles to create their own narrative. These include *The History of the Philippines* and the *History of Ilocos*, published by Isabelo de los Reyes (Reyes y Florentino 1889, 1890; Thomas 2013, 19).

In this chapter, I explore three Filipino narratives on the Chinese pirate Limahong and his interactions with the Philippines. Two of these narratives were written at the end of the 19th century: "Expedición de Li-Mahong contra Filipinas en 1574" by Isabelo de los Reyes (1882) and the poem "El terror de los mares Índicos" by Cecilio Apóstol (1894); and one was written in the 1960s: *La aventura de Limahong* by Antonio Abad (1963). The two texts written at the end of the 19th century reacted to the Spanish discourses about China that were circulating at that time and suggested a different idea on the relation between the Philippines and China to that which was being encouraged by Spain. Indeed, all three of these writings proposed a revision of the 16th- and 17th-century chronicles and subverted them by offering an incipient decolonial view, portrayed in the Romantic stereotype of the pirate as the epitome of freedom. The aim of the chapter is to show how these three narratives, interwoven by the ongoing process of building a national identity (Zialcita 2006), challenge this process by simultaneously advocating for connections with other nations, in a move similar to those of postnational times. The process of nation-state building that paradoxically originated in a global context with Romanticism began with acknowledging the necessity of creating alliances with other nation-states. This awareness influenced the narratives about the Philippines until the independence period, to which the third text to be examined, *La aventura de Limahong*, belongs. The narratives that I examine here propose ties specifically with China, suggesting that *ilustrados* and later generations distanced themselves from and reacted to the generalized Western bias against China embedded in the original chronicles and Spanish texts that were subverted in the Filipino writings. To highlight this departure from the Western discourses on China, which served as a catalyst for decolonial discourse, I will describe how Limahong and his deeds were depicted in the Spanish chronicles. This will provide context for understanding the subversion of these portrayals in Filipino writings.

Eighty-one years passed between the 1882[2] publication of "Expedición de Li-Mahong contra Filipinas en 1574" by Isabelo de los Reyes (1864–1938) in *Diario de Manila*, and 1963, when Antonio Mercado Abad (1894–1970) finished what is perhaps the last novel among the classic writers of Philippine literature in Spanish, *La aventura de Limahong*.[3] Between these two dates, in 1894, Cecilio Apóstol (1877–1934) published his first poem, "El terror de los mares Índicos," in *El comercio*.[4] All three texts belong to different genres, which in the cases of de los Reyes's and Abad's works are actually hybrid genres. This may cause doubts about their classification or even their labeling as literature according to the Western categorizations.[5] In Isabelo de los Reyes's text, despite being an essay, elements of epic storytelling appear throughout the story, making it at times as thrilling as a book of adventure. For example, at the end of the second part, we read:

> Habiendo navegado un día los portadores de la noticia, lograron alcanzar a los piratas; más, cuando intentaban ganar la delantera á fuerza de remos, 20 botes chinos volvieron contra ellos, disparando la artillería. En tan crítica situación, los españoles procuraron huir á la playa. Li-Ma-Hong mandó sacar los abastos y la vela de la embarcación abandonada, y acto seguido continuó su derrota, dejando nuestra nave.

> (Having sailed one day, the bearers of the news managed to reach the pirates; however, when they tried to gain the lead by force of oars, 20 Chinese boats turned against them, firing artillery. In such a critical situation, the Spaniards tried to flee to the beach. Li-Ma-Hong ordered the supplies and the sail to be removed from the abandoned vessel, and immediately continued on his way, leaving our ship behind.) (Reyes y Florentino 1887, 47)

The involvement of the narrator in the adventure and the detail with which the succession of events is recounted, replacing the details absent in the historical data with details invented or extracted from popular tradition, arouse the reader's interest and bring the chronicle closer to literature. Despite this, de los Reyes already advanced in this youthful work the national vindication that he would further develop in later works.

De los Reyes belonged to the first generation of *ilustrados* who were descendants of wealthy native Filipino and mestizo families, whose children traveled to Europe in the 1880s to complete their studies. These educated and wealthy young people adopted "liberal" ideas in the sense of "progresista, reformista or reformador, librepensador" (progressive, reformist, or freethinker) (Thomas 2013, x). Later on, they reoriented their ideas toward protesting Spain's exercise of colonial power in the Philippines. They distinguished themselves and were called *ilustrados* due to their erudition and their desire to investigate and transmit the history and traditions of their nation. In doing so, they contributed to laying its foundations during the Spanish colonial period.

There is, however, what could be considered a second generation of *ilustrados*, whose members were born around the time of the revolution in 1896. They published most of their works during the American occupation of the Philippines. However, their objectives were different from those of the first generation, as were their social and political contexts: their writings were still combative and had decolonial intentions, but while in the first generation Spanish language was used to make their demands understandable for the invader, during the second generation they used Spanish to resist the new invader and to approximate themselves culturally to the community of Spanish-speaking countries constituted by the Latin American republics.[6] Due to the prolific output of writings by this second generation, they were considered to constitute a "golden age of Philippine literature," and this included Cecilio Apóstol.

The first poem written by Apóstol was published in a stage prior to the Philippine revolution, although the rest of his work would be produced during that so-called golden age, which spanned from 1902 to 1946, coinciding with the American occupation. For this reason, the poem reflected situations that were typical of the Spanish occupation period, such as the rejection of the Chinese community and the lack of freedom under colonial power. However, these situations persisted during the American occupation and even during democracy. Thus, the consideration of the Chinese community in the country, and the opposition to the oppressive regime established, continued to appear in Apóstol's poetry throughout his work. In this way, his first poem, which romantically idealized an "outlaw" such as the pirate as a symbol of freedom, laid the foundation for recurring themes in his body of work.

Regarding the connections to Latin America, they were brought about in this case not just by the use of the Spanish language but also by the shared aspiration for freedom and independence and by the use of the pirate character as a remembrance of the country's history in a foundational narrative for the nation. Pirates, indeed, also made up part of the Latin American past and were revered as an important character of the narratives at the time of the Latin American nation-states' construction. As Nina Gerassi-Navarro states, in the last decades of the 19th century, piratical narratives emerged in Latin America as part of a generalized attempt by writers to "create national legends and myths in the hope of defining their heritage and formulating a unified vision of their past" (1999, 3). However, the intention of the piratical narratives is conflictive: in America, the pirate was not idealized, for he represented the historical difficulties that the new nations had gone through in their construction. Nevertheless, as Gerassi-Navarro also explains, the image of the pirate was indeed used to articulate ideas of nationhood while historical events were being resignified, as happened in Filipino literature (4). Therefore, the Latin American–Philippine connection via the pirate figure contributed to integrate Philippine literature into a pan-Hispanic literary tradition, in accordance with the aspirations of some writers of the golden age of Fil-Hispanic literature.

The difference between the stories of pirates in Latin America as linked to the narratives on the nation and the narratives around Limahong lies in the fact that Latin American pirates were actually Europeans who had looted the colonial territories. They were, therefore, Europeans attacking the European colonizers. This posed a challenge to the Latin American perspective on pirates, as while the pirates attacked the colonial institution, they also belonged to the colonial power. In the case of the Chinese pirates in the Philippines, the attack on the colonial power came from outside the European sphere of power itself, and even from outside China's sphere of power, since Limahong was an outlaw in his own country. Therefore, the idealization of his rebellion against the colonial power is more justified than in the case of the Latin American narratives. This idealization also connected with the "turn to Asia" of the first generation of the Enlightenment, which looked up to this continent while searching for their origins and a distinctive identity outside the sphere of Western influence (Ortuño Casanova 2021).

Antonio Abad's latest text appeared during a period that Isaac Donoso has called the "Silver Age of Spanish-Filipino literature" (2020). This period comprises literary texts written from 1946 onward. Abad's previous novels *El Campeón* (written in 1939 and published in 2012) and *La oveja de Nathan* (from 1928) already approached the origins and foundations of the Philippine homeland and the resistance to its present by means of two national allegories that entailed a recovery of an idealized past (Villaescusa-Illán 2020, 197, 204). In the case of *La aventura de Limahong,* the author himself defined it as "half fiction, half historical" on the title page, attesting the hybridity of genres. This extensive 245-page manuscript brought the classical Philippine literature in Spanish to an end, after less than 100 years of history.

Limahong in the Spanish Colonial Chronicles of the 16th and 17th Centuries

The story of how Limahong stormed the shores of Luzon and was contained—though not defeated—by Juan de Salcedo, a Spanish conquistador and grandson of Miguel de Legazpi, in 1574 began to be told in the first Spanish accounts of the Philippines. Only one year after the episode took place, the governor of the Philippines himself, Guido de Lavezares according to Juan Francisco Maura, apparently wrote the text *La relación del suceso de la venida del tirano chino* (1575), in which, according to the editor, "there is no fiction," although he may have exaggerated the number of enemy soldiers, unlike in other texts by the same author (Maura 2004, 2). The basis for asserting whether or not there is fiction involved is tenuous when the introductory text mainly relies on sources that postdate the events described. The fact is that this chronicle and the account of Martín de Rada, an Augustinian who witnessed the events and who in 1575 would join the Spanish expedition to China, inspired several missionaries throughout the 17th century to narrate what was considered to be a crucial episode in the history of the conquest of the Philippines.

Among these later chronicles, Marcelo Ribadeneira in 1599 reported that "llegó por mar un gran corsario Chino, llamado Limaon[7] que puso en gran peligro toda aquella tierra haciendo con los suyos mucho daño cuando llegó a Manila" (a great Chinese corsair called Limaon arrived by sea and put the whole land in great danger, causing much damage with his men when he reached Manila) (Ribadeneira 1601, 12–13). Faced with the cruelty of the corsair, who, according to Ribadeneira, destroyed the well-being of the islands and the good relationship between the Spaniards and the Chinese peoples and who mercilessly slit the throats of defenseless soldiers, Captain Salcedo arrived as God's envoy in an attack in which, according to Ribadeneira, "favoreció el Señor a los nuestros" (13) (the Lord favored our people). Christianity played a significant role in this narrative, and was used as an argument to justify the conquest of the Philippines. Throughout the story, there are multiple examples in which the Spanish characters of the story win battles by invoking God, the Virgin Mary, or the saints. Ribadeneira recalled how the Spanish soldiers resisted the pirates by entrusting themselves to the apostle St. Andrew. This resistance, according to Ribadeneira's account, impressed Limahong so much that he was forced to withdraw his attack (13). In an attempt to show the bravery of the Spaniards, who in the end failed to defeat Limahong, Ribadeneira insisted on Limahong's admiration for them, portraying the pirate, by contrast, as a cunning coward, for he escaped being killed. Pedro Chirino added savagism to the characterization of Limahong by noting that he caulked his ships with his own blood (1604, 5). Francisco Colin, for his part, agreed that Limahong caulked his ships with human blood, without specifying whose blood it was (1663, 132). In any case, both versions contributed to the bloodthirsty legend of the sailor. Limahong's reputation for cowardice and savagery is further marred by the cardinal sin of pride, attributed to him by the Augustinian Juan de Medina, and caused, according to the friar, by the robberies that the pirate had committed both in the Philippines and in China (1893, 91). In this way Juan de Medina highlighted the fact that the pirate also caused damage in China, putting Limahong's perversity beyond the conflict between nations, as a personal initiative.

While Antonio de Morga maintained the most canonical version of the story in his chronicle in a synoptic way (Morga and Rizal 1890, 13–14), Francisco Colin attempted a more historicist perspective, going back for the first time to the sources on the origin of the legend and of Limahong himself. This is a resource that we can also see in Antonio Abad's novel; however, in the case of the Filipino text, the account of the pirate's childhood will be used to justify his wickedness or, rather, his errors. Francisco Colin adduced an alleged noble origin of the pirate, which is a classic characteristic of the hero in many mythologies. However, Colin was wary of this connection being made with the hero and asserted that the Chinese was a "natural evil-doer." The friar justified the fact, considered paradoxical at the time, that the pirate had noble origins but evil instincts by equating Limahong with Lucius Catiline, saying of Limahong that he "*nobili genere natus, sed ingenio malo, prauoque fuit,*" paraphrasing what Sallustus had said about Catiline (Colin 1663, 130). Antonio Abad diametrically opposed this premise when recounting Limahong's childhood and ancestry. He highlighted that both Limahong's father and Limahong's preceptor were educated in the precepts of Confucius and Mencius. The former advocated for ethics and gentleness in relationships with other people, while the latter a theorist who emphasized the innate goodness of people. In addition, Limahong's father even instructed his tutor to educate him in the precepts of Confucius, Mencius, and Lao-Tse, who was known for being an active opponent of violence.

In Colin's erudite account, the arrival of Juan de Salcedo was again marked by the divine design, which supported his triumph despite carrying only 70 men in the face of the thousands of Chinese corsairs ravaging Manila. The opposition between Salcedo and Limahong is enhanced in this account by portraying Salcedo as a giver of life (1663, 131) and comparing the pirate to Piro and Hannibal in his capacity for destruction. Hence, in the 17th century, and despite the incredible enterprise of confronting two empires, Limahong was only characterized as a counterpoint to Salcedo, the real hero. The antagonism between the two characters was inserted in the secular struggle between good and evil proper to the Christian imaginary, initiated in Genesis and developed throughout the different crusades, that of Jerusalem, the Iberian reconquest, the conquest of America, and the conquest of the Philippines. The purpose of the repetition of the Limahong legend was therefore to justify that the Spaniards had divine favor in their self-imposed mission to conquer Asian lands and to reaffirm the protective role that the Spaniards had also attributed to themselves in the Philippines.

This account is interestingly challenged by a short annotation by José Rizal in the Filipino edition of Morga's chronicle, in which Rizal redirects the reader to the text by Isabelo de los Reyes in order to find a counterpoint for Morga's account, which essentially aligns with all the abovementioned points in the description of Limahong (Morga and Rizal 1890, 14). This brief note discreetly questioned the Spanish version by suggesting a comparison with the version written by a Filipino who, as we shall see, attempted a divergent point of view from the aforementioned chronicles, focusing on the actions and motivations of the Chinese rather than on the feats of the Spaniards. This new point of view did not rely on new accounts of the same facts: rather, it placed the focus on underlying parts of the story that might have not been interpreted positively by the Spaniards but that gained new significance at the end of the 19th century. One line to pull, for instance, is the account of Father Colin, who, delving into the actions of Limahong, told how he tried to "further draw the natives away from the obedience of the Spaniards" in such a way that "he promised them great comforts and a reduction in tribute" (1660, 132). The benefit "to the natives" did not go unnoticed: something that was considered a betrayal to the Spanish nation, to the Chinese, and to God became for the founders of the Philippine nation a benefaction to the people.

No written Philippine versions of the story of Limahong from the 16th century have survived; however, as alternative versions, we have Chinese texts on Limahong's piratical exploits, which seem to differ from the Spanish ones. According to the Chinese, the motivation for the Spaniards to fight Limahong was not their bravery or a command from God: it was Captain Wang Wanggao from China, who was sent by the Fujian government and the Ming dynasty to Luzon to persuade the Spaniards to attack the pirate (Min-gu 2019). This also creates an alternative perspective on who attacked whom, as Limahong may not have been the provoking actor in the confrontation. The Spanish chronicles depicted the origin as an unexpected encounter between Francisco de Bazán and the Chinese pirate in the middle of the sea. Instead, it is likely that the true motive behind the confrontation was the Spanish interest in trading with China. In addition, the Chinese texts attribute the defeat of Limahong to Wanggao, giving closure to the episode which, due to the fact that Guido de Lavezares's account was incomplete, was absent from the Spanish versions. The Chinese texts omit any Spanish contribution to the pirate's defeat. Despite this omission, the episode also implies an attempt by the Spanish Empire to cooperate with the Ming empire (Shutz 2019). In any case, the cooperation was short-lived according to Phillip B. Guingona, as from this episode onward the Spanish perspective toward the Chinese changed: in his own words, it was the beginning of a "haunting" idea about the Chinese that implied a constant fear of the supposed threat of a Chinese invasion. This fear, according to Guingona, "led to reactionary pogroms and a schizophrenic Spanish-Chinese policy" (2017).

Limahong in the 19th Century

Publications on Limahong were revitalized in the 19th century coinciding with the rise of the concept known as the *yellow peril*, which was spreading throughout Europe. This referred to the supposed threat of world invasion and the potential destruction of Western values to be carried out by the Chinese, as promulgated around the mid-19th century in the American press and from the 1890s onward throughout Europe. As John Dower stated, the threat did not start from any concrete evidence but from a "vague and ominous sense of the vast, faceless, nameless yellow horde: the rising tide, indeed of color" (1993, 156).

In the Philippines, a series of books and articles began to be published about the threat posed by the Chinese to the Spanish interests in the territory. In 1886, a debate was opened in the Spanish-language Philippine press on the issue of Chinese immigration, after a surge of 60,000 Chinese arrivals in 10 years (Jordana y Morera 1888, 3). The detractors of Chinese immigration were the newspapers *Boletín de avisos, Diario de Manila*, and *La Oceanía española* (Jordana y Morera 1888, 1). The latter even published a special volume compiling the articles that it had devoted to the detraction of the Chinese presence, titled *Los Chinos en Filipinas: Males que se experimentan actualmente y peligros de esa creciente inmigración* (Pan 1886). This was followed by other volumes and pamphlets criticizing this aspect and others, such as the persistence of the Chinese in maintaining their own habits without integrating into Philippine society, even if they had remained in the country for a long time. The works exposing these problems were, among others, *La Inmigración china y japonesa en Filipinas* (1892) and *La inmigración china en Filipinas* (Jordana y Morera 1888), both published in Madrid, and Rafael Comenge's book published in Manila, *Cuestiones filipinas 1ª parte, Los chinos* (1894). All of them concurred with the prevalent Western discourse that demonized the Chinese, and at the same time, they favored a revision of Limahong's legend. This revision is evident in Vicente Barrantes's work on the wars against the Muslim pirates in the southern Philippines, in which the author attributes the triumph of the Chinese corsair to the secret help of the Portuguese (1878, 396). In this way, he underestimated the possibilities of the Chinese. But above all, this revision of the legend appears in the volume *El ataque de Li Ma Hong a Manila en 1574* by Juan Caro y Mora (1894). Caro y Mora focused on extolling the efforts of Legazpi, his successor Gido de Lavezares, Martin de Goiti, and Juan de Salcedo to take possession of, organize, and "when necessary" submit the inhabitants of the islands and on lauding the heroism and inflexibility of these protagonist characters (Caro y Mora 1894, 2). His account certainly has literary overtones, leaving rhetorical questions as cliffhangers at the end of the chapters, with the aim to create intrigue about the motives and destinies of the protagonists.

The 94 pages following the first chapter were devoted to collecting and comparing the chronicles of the 17th-century Limahong invasion. The author did a thorough job of analyzing the sources, although without critically examining some of their points, such as the claims that the Chinese corsairs surprised Bazán at sea, that there were many more Chinese than Spaniards, that the Spanish soldiers resisted heroically until their inevitable deaths, and that some of the indigenous individuals sought protection from the *encomenderos*. He only deviated from the original sources to put the heroism of the Spaniards in historical perspective. See, for example, how he portrayed Juan de Salcedo:

Por las venas del joven militar, admiración de su época, recuerdo glorioso de
España en esta centuria é indeleble memoria del heroísmo y arrojo de nues-
tros soldados en todos los siglos, corría la sangre castellana que dio vida á
Isabel la Católica y al cardenal Cisneros, á D. Juan de Austria y á Hernán
Cortés y á tantos más.

Through the veins of the young soldier, admiration of his time, the glorious
memory of Spain in this century and the indelible memory of the heroism
and courage of our soldiers in all centuries, ran the Castilian blood that gave
life to Isabella the Catholic and Cardinal Cisneros, to D. Juan de Austria and
Hernán Cortés and so many others. (Caro y Mora 1894, 10)

The search for heroic antecedents in such illustrious sagas in the history of
Spain at a time of faltering imperial self-conception dignified Salcedo's actions
in the process of turning him into a hero. Fernando Savater, in his classic
work *La tarea del héroe* (The hero's task), adopted a structuralist approach to
look for common elements in the hero's construction in different myths and
to reflect on the ethical implications of the hero (1981, 136–67). According
to Savater, the hero is characterized by his exercise of virtue and action, the
independence and freedom of his own being, the search for his origins, and
the fact that he is always fiction, being the imaginary realization of a desire.
All this implies that he is exemplary, that his heroism is based in the future
rather than the past (because of the implications of his acts that will serve for
the future good), and that his nature is utopian.

In the case of Salcedo in Caro y Mora's account, the search for the hero's
origins is a task undertaken by the narrator, who employs a historical perspective to examine events that had happened three centuries earlier. This
same omniscient narrator extols Salcedo's virtue by silencing the affronts
of his superiors and succoring them when necessary to highlight his com-
mitment to the patriotic cause. Salcedo was not driven by low passions or
quarrels; he was courageous and self-sacrificing even though he had been
wronged in the past. In addition, the historical perspective contributed to
enhance the transcendence that his actions had for the following generations.

However, despite the desire to universalize the figure of the hero, aspects
such as the exemplary role, the notion of freedom and independence, and
even the idea of virtue are closely related to the ethics of the culture in which
he emerges. Caro y Mora's account was published in 1897, in the midst of the
war between Spain and the Philippines. Hence, the depiction of Salcedo as a

hero who had inherited heroism through his Castilian lineage can be seen as a model for the Spanish soldiers fighting at that moment in the Philippines and as a hope for the nation in the belief that they would overcome this mishap as they had overcome Limahong centuries ago.

As for the approach to the Chinese in Caro y Mora's account, we can distinguish two opposing views: on the one hand, that of the followers of Limahong, who were mainly from Fokien[8] and Kuantung; on the other hand, that of the emperor, who is alluded to as the "Hijo del Cielo" (Son of Heaven) and depicted as a fair person. He was aggrieved by Limahong's plundering actions and commanded him to be imprisoned with a price on his head (Caro y Mora 1894, 16). This duality in the view of the Chinese, embodied in the dishonesty of those who come into contact with the Philippines (pirates) and the idealized faraway empire, matches the perception of the Chinese in the Philippines that María Dolores Elizalde Pérez-Grueso has described. According to Elizalde, in the 19th century China was to the Spaniards a great imperial nation, an object of admiration and mystery. However, the Chinese population in the Philippines, usually originating from Fokien, were perceived in relation to their activities in the colony and not so highly considered, as it was with the pirates of the account (2008, 101).

Change of Perspective: The Filipinos

Of the three Filipino texts I propose, the one by Cecilio Apóstol and the one by Isabelo de los Reyes are contemporary to the 19th-century sinophobic campaign undertaken by the West, related to the *yellow peril*. The third account, that of Antonio Abad, appeared after independence, just before the beginning of martial law in the Philippines. The new image of Limahong that is offered in these three accounts therefore takes three different forms, according to their moment of publication. Isabelo de los Reyes's account was published in a moment of initial identity search, and as a result, Limahong was considered to be part of the Filipino essence, and the account added arguments to the intellectual currents headed by Rizal or Mariano Ponce, who fought for a reunion of the Philippines with its Asian essence to overcome colonial identity conflicts.[9] Cecilio Apóstol also contributed to the romantic exaltation of the pirate as a hero who opposed the imposed social order and the empire. Finally, Abad humanized the pirate by emphasizing his childhood and his motives, presenting him as a person with whom the Filipino public could identify.

Lord Raglan distinguished between the mythical and the historical hero in his classic work *The Hero: A Study in Tradition, Myth, and Drama*. Raglan stated that the historical hero incorporated values, ideas, myths, and concerns of the society to which he belonged (1936, 214). Just as Salcedo was configured in the narrative of Caro y Mora as a Spanish hero who gathered in himself the ancestry of previous heroic Spanish historical figures, Limahong came to embody for the Filipinos the preeminence of Asia over the West and the impetus for questioning the colonizers. This situation was remembered and thus interpreted at a time when Filipinos were searching for their roots and their own heroes. In fact, other indigenous heroes from different parts of the Philippines gained renewed attention at the time, such as Lakandula, the Tondo leader who made a pact with Legazpi for the occupation of Manila and then rose up against the colonial power. Isabelo de los Reyes included the story of Lakandula in the same volume in which Limahong's story was published in Spain (Reyes y Florentino 1887, 87–108). This can be explained by the self-orientalizing movement among the Filipino *ilustrados*, described by John D. Blanco in his article "Oriental Enlightenment and the Colonial World: A Derivative Discourse?" This movement, patent in the late 19th century, constituted an emerging discourse of Filipino racial consciousness that implied that "the inhabitants of the archipelago shared a consciousness that was rooted in a precolonial sense of national or perhaps even pan-(Southeast) Asian belonging" (Blanco 2016, 61). In fact, in the article "Panasiatismo y resistencia al discurso occidental en la literatura filipina en español," I argue that since the late 19th century there has been a search for an association or affiliation with China and Japan, vis-à-vis the Western colonizers, that was reflected in literature in the two generations of *ilustrados* (Ortuño Casanova 2021). Those two generations were spearheaded by Mariano Ponce and Teodoro Kálaw, respectively. The text by Isabelo de los Reyes is framed in this concern to understand the origin of the Filipinos in a search for identification with something other than the Western colonizer. It is from this impulse for identity and within the framework of the rise of orientalism and ethnography that Filipinos would explore and appropriate Asian discourses and heroes for their own purposes, based on international studies and indigenous knowledge (Thomas 2013, 17) and that de los Reyes wrote his first article in the press.

An energetic, erratic, and heterodox intellectual, as described by Resil Mojares (2006, 255), de los Reyes was originally from Ilocos Norte. He did a commendable job in the search for a historical and ethnographic point of view dissident from what could be learned in the seminary of Vigan or the

Colegio de San Juan de Letran but in accordance with his political concerns. His article on Limahong is only the first in a series of articles that sought to recuperate and put value on characters and traditions of his region and his country by studying and questioning Spanish historiographical sources side by side with autochthonous materials. Maybe the most outstanding feature of his account on Limahong is that it pioneers in telling, in Spanish, a part of the story from the perspective of the Chinese pirate rather than purely from the perspective of the Spaniards. De los Reyes detached his narration from Spanish chronicle sources in the first lines, although he would return to them later. Moreover, he no longer labeled the encounter with Limahong as an attack, a noun that implies an unjustified action against a legitimate and stable regime; rather, he described the confrontation as a war over a territory that did not belong to any of the opposing parties, as we see in the first lines of the text (Reyes y Florentino 1887, 7).

On the other hand, Limahong's biography, his childhood and how he became who he was, does not constitute a parenthesis in the narration of the attack, as it does in the chronicles. After the initial digression to explain the sources of information, de los Reyes built a chronological narration in which he portrayed the evolution of the character step by step. He took up the mythical idea present in Colin's chronicle of the pirate's noble roots and highlighted the idea that he was from "a good family" (1887, 7). De los Reyes then traced back Limahong's arrogance to his desire to win the games that he used to play as a child. The beginning of his piratical adventures was recounted as just a bunch of youthful adventures, noting that he was only 19 years old when he began working for another Chinese pirate (7). He was not quite a hero yet, though: during his early adventures, Limahong was compared to Attila. De los Reyes referred to Limahong's plundering and his cruelty to other pirates and to the Spaniards.

De los Reyes even puts the blame for Limahong's confrontation with the Chinese emperor on a ruse that the emperor himself perpetrated to deceive Limahong and that Limahong himself uncovered (1887, 44). Bazán and other Spanish characters were devoid of the heroism that they had been presented with in the chronicles, as de los Reyes highlighted their mistakes. For instance, they thought at the beginning of the war against Limahong that the attackers were *undominated* indigenous people instead of Chinese pirates, and when looking at the boats approaching the coast in Ilocos, they thought that they were Portuguese squadrons. After focusing on the mistakes committed by the Spaniards, the narration returned to Limahong's perspective and actions.

By doing so, de los Reyes laid the groundwork for the romantic portrait of the pirate that would later be consolidated by Cecilio Apóstol's poem, in which he also depicts the pirate as a dreamer (46). De los Reyes reviewed the Spanish sources in a pioneering way: he reassessed the number of soldiers that appeared in these sources and provided alternative explanations for the contradictions that he observed in the official accounts (47, 64). Thus, although he did not completely detach himself from the colonial perspective in the sense of identifying himself with the Spanish soldiers, which he called "ours" (50), and of emphasizing Limahong's outrages as opposed to the defenselessness of the Spaniards (56), the resistance of the Spaniards to the attack was not depicted as a deed full of heroism, as it had been in the chronicles of the 17th century.

Furthermore, de los Reyes described Limahong's kingdom in Pangasinan in a positive way:

Los naturales de aquella provincia retiraron su adhesión a España y proclamaron a Li-Ma-Hong por Rey de Pangasinan. Con esto el pirata tomó posesión de aquel pueblo y comenzó a gobernarlo, siendo en todo obedecido por sus nuevos súbditos. En el referido islote fundó un bonito pueblo, rodeado de una estacada de cinco varas de alto, y en el centro fabricó un fuerte denominado de *oro*, en el cual cabían buenamente 600 hombres con sus ranchos, y en medio de esta segunda muralla construyó un hermoso palacio adornado con muy ricas preseas que trajo en su escuadra; edificó una pagoda hermoseada por muchas lámparas y preseas de plata.

The natives of that province withdrew their adherence to Spain and proclaimed Li-Ma-Hong King of Pangasinan. With this, the pirate took possession of that town and began to govern it, being obeyed in everything by his new subjects. On the aforementioned islet he founded a beautiful town, surrounded by a wall five rods high, and in the center he built a fort called of gold, in which 600 men with their ranches could fit, and in the middle of this second wall he built a beautiful palace adorned with very rich treasures that he brought in his squadron; he built a pagoda adorned with many lamps and silver treasures. (Reyes y Florentino 1887, 58)

The reaction of the inhabitants seems ambivalent according to this account. While some of them accepted the new regime with gratitude, others supported the Spaniards in their attacks because of what the narrator called the ominous yoke of Li-Ma-Hong (60).

De los Reyes himself also maintained an ambivalence in his discourse about Limahong: while he did not position himself on the side of the Chinese, he seemed to appreciate and acknowledge their exploits and especially succeeded in giving some voice to the antagonist, the Chinese pirate. By doing so, he set the stage for the next two works that we are going to consider here. He used his text to question and contrast the sources found on Limahong, initiating a trend based on the need to understand and challenge the past that also guided Rizal's abovementioned work on Antonio de Morga's chronicle. In this way, de los Reyes explored alternative forms of identity outside of the monolithic colonial discourse, from which, as I said, he does not totally detach himself, although he managed to incipiently challenge the coloniality of power.

The appeal of the pirate as an outlaw on the margins of the empire who challenged the rules of capitalism made him the perfect 19th-century romantic hero as opposed to the by then obsolete former stereotypical protagonist figure of the shepherd (Arlandis and Reyes 2018, 180). Poems such as "La canción del pirata" by José de Espronceda and *The Corsair* by Lord Byron contributed to whitewash the character of the pirate, who had been formerly considered a villain. Cecilio Apóstol's text followed Espronceda's and Byron's tradition and depicted Limahong as a rebellious, fierce, proud, and dreamy pirate, a symbol of patent freedom, according to Apóstol's words, "en su vista feroz, dominadora, / en su actitud soberbia, aterradora, / que del genio algo tiene y del gigante" (in his fierce, dominating sight, / in his proud, terrifying attitude, / which has something of the genius and of the giant) (1950, 14). The Filipino author drew his pirate like Espronceda's, looking at infinity from the prow of his ship: "De pie en el puente, en actitud de acecho, / con los brazos cruzados sobre el pecho, / fija la vista en el confín distante, / como si algo buscara tras la bruma" (Standing on the bridge, in a stalking attitude, / with his arms crossed over his chest, / he fixes his eyes on the distant border, / as if he were looking for something behind the mist) (13). There are multiple parallels with the song that Espronceda devotes to a pirate, including collocations such as the "blando movimiento" (soft movement) of the waves (Apóstol 1950, 16; Espronceda 1870, 58) or references to the peoples who "le rinden vasallaje" (render him vassalage) (Apóstol 1950, 15), reminiscent of the nations that "han rendido / sus pendones" (have rendered / their banners) (Espronceda 1870, 59), as well as the change of the poetic voice from the third to the first person, emulating the words of the pirate himself.

Despite these European connections, we cannot forget the Philippine antecedents for this. Besides de los Reyes's account, it is interesting to remember that Jose Rizal's second novel was titled *El filibusterismo*. While the word has acquired various meanings throughout history (it was also the name of the Cuban independence party in Spanish colonial times), according to the Real Academia Española dictionary, *filibustero* comes from the Dutch *vrij*, free, and *buiter*, plunderer, and is usually translated as "corsair"— also understood in the colonial context as "subversive." Let us remember that the novel was published in Ghent, so the Dutch-speaking origins of the term acquire a relevant meaning, especially knowing that Rizal could also speak Dutch. Taking this into account and knowing the literary and social impact of Rizal in the Philippines and Spain, even before his death,[10] we cannot disregard the relationship between the piratical theme and the criticism of the established system made by the Filipino hero in his novel in the case of Cecilio Apóstol's poem.

The poem "La canción del pirata," which was published for the first time in 1835 in the magazine *El Artista*, represented the beginning of a new poetics in the trajectory of its author, José de Espronceda, which was marked by the influence of Lord Byron (Kirkpatrick 2005, 372). According to Sergio Arlandis and Agustín Reyes Torres, the change was produced by a rebellious and hostile attitude toward the limited and constraining values of society in Espronceda's time, his rejection of said society's morals, and the lack of answers to new concerns in human thought (2018, 180). This led to a poetics characterized by the simplicity of language and not so deeply marked by rhetorical pomposity (despite not freeing itself from a grandiloquent tone) (180).

In the case of the young poet Cecilio Apóstol, a well-educated, knowledgeable person and a great admirer of *ilustrados* like Isabelo de los Reyes and José Rizal, he used his writing to support rebellion against the dominance of the colonial power. In his text, Apóstol depicted Limahong valiantly in charge of his ship, dreaming of the "Promised Land" that could be found in the Philippines (1950, 13). He equated the pirate with Moses, extending the metaphor of the search of the promised land as in the way to the Philippines, "la Perla del Oriente / que allá en el horizonte alza su frente" (the Pearl of the Orient / that there on the horizon raises its brow) (15). The comparison to Moses is connected to the idea of rebellion: Moses rebelled against the order established by the Pharaoh to free his people and lead them to the place designated by God. The oppressed people were for Limahong the pirates in his charge, fleeing from the Chinese emperor, who had also made a pact with the Spaniards. In stanzas 31–33, Limahong takes the floor to tell in first person how the emperor tried to deceive him out of envy:

Mi augusto nombre saturó el espacio.
Del gran Emperador llegó al palacio,
Lo mismo que al tugurio del mendigo.
El Hijo de los cielos, envidioso
de mi renombre, astuto y receloso,
me hablo de paces, me llamó su amigo.

(My august name saturated the space.
From the great Emperor came to the palace,
The same as to the beggar's hovel.
The Son of the heavens, envious
Of my renown, cunning and suspicious,
spoke to me of peace, called me his friend.)
(Apóstol 1950, 21)

The episode was resolved when Limahong discovered the emperor's trap. At that moment, Limahong equated himself to the emperor by proclaiming himself sovereign "del índico Océano / más inmenso, más grande todavía" (21) (of the Indian Ocean / more immense, greater still). The poem then goes on to justify the attraction that the Philippines exerted on the pirate, who is then humanized to recognize his "nostalgic desire for land" despite his great power over the sea (21). Hence, he sets out for Luzon. The poem concludes with an ode to the Philippines along the lines of the previous poem in the same collection, "Patria" (7–11). In the last four stanzas, Limahong takes the poetic voice to sing of the beauty of the Philippines. It is an exoticized Philippines, and in its depiction, he alludes to the victory over colonialism:

Yo crucé por tus selvas perfumadas
y en la espuma miré de tus cascadas
jugar tus ninfas en alegre bando.
Yo vi tus valles, tus enhiestos montes,
y trasponer el sol tus horizontes
las nubes de Occidente arrebolando.

(I crossed through your perfumed jungles
and in the foam I watched your waterfalls,
your nymphs play in a joyful party.
I saw your valleys, your towering mountains,

and the sun pierced your horizons
and the clouds of the West shimmering.)
(Apóstol 1950, 22)

The symbolism of the sun overcoming the Western clouds alluded to tropes that were already present in the famous poem "Mi último adiós" by José Rizal (1896) and in "Tierra adorada" by José Palma, published in his *Melancólicas* of 1912, a volume that was prefaced by Cecilio Apóstol but that in reality had been composed years earlier. This poem served as lyrics for the anthem of the Philippine Republic. We find ourselves, therefore, faced with a series of tropes extended in Romantic Philippine literature in Spanish of the time that contain a subversive message. Limahong became a part of those patriotic clichés along with a series of national characters and heroes that were emerging at the turn of the century, to the point that the legend of his reign in Ilocos, and the hypothesis that the Ilocanos were descendants of the pirates who followed him and settled in that region of Luzon, passed into academic and political texts (Tan 1986, 143). Ferdinand Marcos, coming from Ilocos, even called himself a descendant of the pirate (White 2014, 16).

The release of Abad's book coincided with Ferdinand Marcos's first year as president of the senate, before he was elected president of the nation in 1965 and subsequently became a dictator in the Philippines. On September 21, 1972, after a reelection in 1969 surrounded by controversy (Molina 1984, 723–24; McCallus 1989, 129), Marcos imposed martial law throughout the country and repealed the Constitution of 1935. According to McCallus (1989, 129), martial law initially achieved certain social approval thanks to the propagandistic spread of cultural myths, which provided Marcos's regime with some political legitimacy. Actually, this was done by making use of the propagandistic movement developed by *ilustrados* in Spain at the end of the 20th century. Marcos reapplied some old ideas and based his regime on a supposed defense of what was truly Filipino: traditional values, a strong leader, and the heroes, ideas, and images of the independence revolution of 1896 (130). Those ideas were already present in the social turmoil of the 1960s and are matched by Abad's book. Limahong, as a character, had all the ingredients needed to become an admired figure at that time: it had been vindicated by the *ilustrados* that he had fought the Spaniards back, and he was supposedly the ancestor of northern Filipinos and Filipinas, including Ferdinand Marcos.

Indeed, Abad's book contained a clear societal concern from the very first pages. The book is presented as partly fictional (and is actually mostly fictional) and tells the story of the power struggles in the China Sea that left in their midst a mob of victims ignored by their leaders. The play began with the plundering and quarrels between the three authorities in force in the 16th century in the China Sea: namely, the emperor of China; the Portuguese governor of Amboina (or the Spice Islands, as Abad also calls them; the Molucca Islands); and Chang Hsi-Lao, a great pirate who confronted both the Chinese and the Portuguese empires. The situation reported is the abandonment of the cities and peoples of the Asian coast, which "languished in poverty" (Abad 1963, 1), while China and Portugal fought over Macao, strategically using the booms and busts of Chang Hsi-Lao. In this account, Limahong appeared as a victim of this circumstance: his father's town was razed to the ground by Chang Hsi-Lao three days after his birth. His mother died in the labor, and his early childhood is narrated with dramatic overtones: fed with dissolved honey, with a noble and rich father who had to rebuild his fortune after the attacks, he was brought up together with Sio Kho, a Japanese boy somewhat older than Limahong himself, who had been abandoned to his fate by some fishermen on an island and had then been taken in by Limahong's father. This boy would later be known as Homoco, Limahong's second-in-command, who appeared in the Spanish chronicles as his faithful ally in the attack on Luzon.

Sio Kho turned out to have a corrupting influence on Limahong, who, according to Abad's account, had he not gotten to know the other, was destined to inherit his father's business and be a good boy. In Abad's story, the Japanese are innately treacherous and cruel, different in essence from the Chinese. In the narrator's words, "Su innata crueldad, su disimulo, su insensibilidad al dolor físico, su sonrisa de lacayo, su árido egoísmo, ¿no pregonaban bastante que sus progenitores no eran chinos?" (Abad 1963, 24) (His innate cruelty, his dissimulation, his insensitivity to physical pain, his lackey's smile, his arid selfishness, did they not fairly trumpet that his progenitors were not Chinese?). This description of the Japanese character is not in vain: it is allegorical of the recent history of Japan in the Philippines. We should bear in mind that in 1963, the memory of the Japanese invasion of 1943 and the 1945 Battle of Manila, in which the Philippine capital was ravaged by Japanese fire and American bombing raids, was still fresh. Limahong was driven by the Japanese Sio Kho to repeat the history of those who had victimized his family and raze villages himself.

The novel is an allegory of the successive rotations of power and oppressions imposed on the Asian people. This idea would reappear in the Philippine literary tradition during the Marcos period, when several writers and playwrights staged scenes of oppression that actually happened during the colonial occupation of the Philippines, to protest the violence and oppression of the Marcos dictatorship itself without being retaliated against (Ortuño Casanova 2017). This idea, reminiscent of a historical dialectic, detracts from the responsibility of Limahong, who is caught up in this system of recurrence of history. The character is much more humanized than in the previous stories and is determined to assume his fate as a hero of freedom but also as an antihero. The message of the fatalism of destiny that takes shape, since Limahong's tutor warned that the sea would be his empire but also his tomb, prevails (Abad 1963, 16).

At the end of the story, Limahong was a character who had achieved everything by escaping from multiple enemies—Chinese, Muslims, Japanese, and Spaniards—and who had mastered the art of escape as his best weapon (Abad 1963, 241). The end is left open, as are the ends of the chroniclers' accounts. Limahong returned to the sea, where he felt free again, but the omens that came to his mind and the storm that broke out while he sailed in a small boat foretold a dark end for the pirate. He concluded by anticipating that that might be his ending, saying, "Yo he nacido en el mar. El mar es mi elemento y el mar fue mi imperio. La única tumba digna de un emperador es el mar" (I was born in the sea. The sea is my element, and the sea was my empire. The only tomb worthy of an emperor is the sea).

Conclusion

Despite the efforts of the different colonial chronicles to extol Spanish heroism in the face of the pirate's perfidy and to underline the divine support that the Spanish colonization was supposed to have, we see in these chronicles the seed of what would become the Philippine narratives on the episode. Filipino writers reviewed the chronicles to build their own narratives, focusing on aspects that also appeared in the 16th and 17th century accounts: Limahong's noble origin, his rebellion against the Chinese empire—which in the 19th century was already an enemy of both Spain and the Philippines—and even the assumption of the pirate's point of view, which can also be seen in the chronicle by Gaspar de San Agustín, *Conquistas temporal y spiritual.* The Augustinian friar dedicated 10 chapters of his second book to the story of Limahong (1698, 2:275–330) and therein transcribed a letter from the pirate, telling of his fears and plans in the face of the Spanish threat. In the 16th century, Limahong represented the danger to the established order, and so it was portrayed in the chronicles, written by Spanish missionaries who were, with their work, both sustaining the empire and justifying it with the work of evangelization. This all came to be questioned as the Filipino intellectuals changed their attitude toward the Spanish colonization and the Chinese presence in the archipelago, while establishing the foundations of identification and nation building. The reconsideration of colonial texts, the "writing back" discussed at the beginning of this chapter in terms of appropriating a colonial literary corpus after the colony, actually occurred at odd moments. The rewriting of Philippine history took place many years before the end of the colony, constituting an early case of self-reflection with the de los Reyes and Apostol texts and a late one with Abad. Limahong was not completely idealized by the Filipinos as a classical hero, as is Salcedo in the Castilian texts. However, the nuances of his figure, his liberationist aspirations, his humanity, and his tragic fate took on the trappings of a myth with which readers could identify. Limahong was an outlaw, an antihero who achieved great things but who also knew nostalgia, hope, fear, and defeat.

Notes

1. Regarding *ilustrado* writings that react to Spanish colonialist texts, see Cristina Guillén Arnáiz's chapter, this volume, on Antonio Luna's *Impresiones*.

2. Three more editions of the story were published, the fourth one as a self-standing book in the *Biblioteca del Diario de Manila* in 1888 (De los Reyes y Florentino 1888).

3. It was never published. The references to it are taken from the manuscript kept at the main library of the University of the Philippines Diliman. A bilingual edition is being prepared by Ignacio López-Calvo and Rocío Ortuño Casanova and will be released from the Vibal Foundation in 2024.

4. It was republished in his complete works *Pentélicas* (Apóstol 1950).

5. For further explanation on the controversy about what constitutes literature and how Philippine genres fit into that definition, see the introduction to this volume.

6. This idea is developed in Paula C. Park's chapter, "Transpacific *Tornaviajes:* Toward a Filipino-Mexican Redefinition of Hispanidad," this volume, as well as in the pages of the special issue of the journal *UNITAS* coordinated by Jorge Mojarro in May 2019, "Transpacific Connections of Philippine Literature in Spanish" (*UNITAS* 92, no. 1).

7. The spelling of the pirate's name is not consistent. Limaon, Li-Ma-Hong, or Li Feng are some common names for the same corsair. I do not standardize it in the quotes, but I will refer to him with the currently accepted Western spelling: Limahong.

8. Also called Hokkien in the Philippines; today, Fujian.

9. Megan Thomas delves into the rise of ethnography and folklore within the Enlightenment in the late 19th century, starting from European Orientalist ethnography and relying—in the absence of precolonial indigenous texts—on 17th-century chronicles that they skeptically review (2013, 34–35).

10. Beyond the legal consequences of his novels and the demand for them in the Philippine archipelago, where they were banned by censors, there were literary responses to them: two years after the publication of *El filibusterismo*, Ventura F. López published *El filibustero*, a short novel that tries to caricature the novels of Rizal (Fernández López 1893). Likewise, in 1907, a representation was announced in Valencia's Princesa theater of a Philippine historical drama in three acts and with original prose by the Philippine "general José María Balmori"—a work entitled *Los filibusteros*, which promised to change the perspective of the Spaniards on the causes for the independence of the Philippines ("Teatros" 1907).

References

Abad, Antonio. 1963. *La aventura de Li Ma-Hong*. Unpublished.

Apóstol, Cecilio. 1950. *Pentélicas: (poesías)*. Manila: Editorial Hispano-Filipina.

Ashcroft, Bill, Gareth Griffiths, and Helen Tiffin. 2005. *The Empire Writes Back: Theory and Practice in Post-Colonial Literatures*. New York: Routledge.

Barrantes, Vicente. 1878. *Guerras Piráticas de Filipinas Contra Mindanaos y Joloanos*. Madrid: M. G. Hernández. http://hdl.handle.net/2027/ucl.b4517581

Blanco, John. 2016. "Oriental Enlightenment and the Colonial World: A Derivative Discourse?" In *Filipino Studies: Palimpsests of Nation and Diaspora*, edited by Martin F. Manalansan and Augusto F. Espiritu, 56–84. New York: NYU Press. www.jstor.org/stable/j.ctt18040v1.7

Caro y Mora, Juan. 1894. *Ataque de Li-ma-hong á Manila en 1574; reseña histórica de aquella memorable jornada*. Manila: Amigos del Pais. http://archive.org/details/ataquedelimahong00caro

Chirino, Pedro. 1604. *Relacion de las islas filipinas, i de lo que en ellas an trabaido los padres de la Compannia de Jesus*. Roma: Estevan Paulino.

Colin, Francisco. 1663. *Labor Evangelica, Ministerios Apostolicos De Los Obreros De La Compania De Jesus, Fundacion, Y Progressos De Su Provincia En Las Islas Filipinas*. Madrid: Joseph Fernandez de Buendia.

Comenge, Rafael. 1894. *Cuestiones Filipinas 1ª Parte, Los Chinos: (Estudio Social y Político)*. Manila: Imp-Litogr. de Chofré y Compañía.

Donoso, Isaac. 2020. "La Edad de Plata de la literatura hispanofilipina (1946–1987)." *Dicenda. Estudios de lengua y literatura españolas* 38 (September): 119–37. https://doi.org/10.5209/dice.70155

Dower, John W. 1993. *War without Mercy: Race and Power in the Pacific War*. New York: Pantheon.

Elizalde Pérez-Grueso, María Dolores. 2008. "China—España—Filipinas: Percepciones españolas de China—y de los chinos—en el siglo XIX." *Huarte de San Juan. Geografía e historia*, no. 15: 101–11.

Gerassi-Navarro, Nina. 1999. *Pirate Novels: Fictions of Nation Building in Spanish America*. Durham: Duke University Press.

Guingona (顧恒), Phillip B. 2017. "A Ghost and His Apparition Roam the South China Sea: Limahong and the Dream of a Hokkien Nation (南中國海上陰魂不散的鬼魅及其幻影：林鳳和一個閩南民族的夢)." *Translocal Chinese: East Asian Perspectives* 11 (1): 90–124. https://doi.org/10.1163/24522015-01101006

Jordana y Morera, Ramón. 1888. *La Inmigración China En Filipinas*. Madrid: Tip. de Manuel G. Hernández.

La Inmigración China y Japonesa En Filipinas: Documentos. 1892. Madrid: Imp. Luis Aguado.

Lavezares, Guido de. [1575] 2004. "Relación Del Suceso de La Venida Del Tirano Chino." Edited by Juan Francisco Maura. *Anexos de la Revista Lemir*. Parnaseo, Universitat de València. http://parnaseo.uv.es/lemir/textos/maura/index.htm

Maura, Juan Francisco. 2004. "Introducción a Relación Del Suceso de La Venida Del Tirano Chino Sobre Este Campo." *Revista Lemir* 8 (Anexo): 2–14.

Medina, Juan de. [1630]1893. *Historia de Los Sucesos de La Orden de N. Gran P. S. Agustin de Estas Islas Filipinas: Desde que se descubrieron y se poblaron por los españoles, con las noticias memorables.* Manila: Litografía de Chofré y Compañía.

Min-gu, Nam. 2019. "만력연간(萬曆年間), 려송(呂宋)의 입공(入貢) 요청(要請)과 명조(明朝)의 대응(對應) — 복건(福建)당국의 역할을 중심으로 —." 명청사연구 52:181–215.

Mojares, Resil B. 2006. *Brains of the Nation: Pedro Paterno, T. H. Pardo de Tavera, Isabelo de Los Reyes, and the Production of Modern Knowledge*. Quezon City: Ateneo de Manila University Press.

Morga, Antonio de, and José Rizal. 1890. *Sucesos de las islas Filipinas por el doctor Antonio de Morga, obra publicada en Méjico el año de 1609.* Paris: Garnier hermanos. http://archive.org/details/ahz9387.0001.001.umich.edu

Ortuño Casanova, Rocío. 2021. "Panasiatismo y resistencia al discurso occidental en la Literatura filipina en español: China como 'Asia por antonomasia' a lo largo de dos colonizaciones." *Revista de Estudios Hispánicos* 55 (2).

Pan, José Felipe del. 1886. *Los Chinos En Filipinas*. Manila: La Oceanía Española.

Raglan, Lord. 1936. *The Hero: A Study in Tradition, Myth, and Drama*. London: Watts. http://archive.org/details/in.ernet.dli.2015.101509

Reyes y Florentino, Isabelo de los. 1887. *Filipinas Articulos Varios: De Isabelo de Los Reyes y Florentino Sobre Etnografia, Historia y Costumbres Del Pais; Con Un Prólogo Critico de d. Cesareo Blanco y Sierra.* Manila: J. A. Ramos. http://name.umdl.umich.edu/aqq0195.0001.001

Reyes y Florentino, Isabelo de los. 1888. *Expedición de Li-Mahong contra Filipinas en 1574, por Isabelo de Los Reyes y Florentino.* [4a edición]. Manila: est. tip. de Ramirez.

Reyes y Florentino, Isabelo de los. 1889. *Historia de Filipinas.* 2nd ed. Manila: Balbás.

Reyes y Florentino, Isabelo de los. 1890. *Historia de Ilocos.* Manila: La Opinón.

Ribadeneira, Marcelo de. 1601. *Historia de las islas del archipielago y reynos de la gran China, Tartaria, Cuchinchina, Malaca, Sian, Camboxa y Iappon, y de los sucedido en ellos a los religiosos descalços.* Barcelona: Imprenta de Gabriel Graells y Giraldo Dotil.

San Agustín, Gaspar de. 1698. *Conquistas de Las Islas Philipinas: La Temporal Por . . . Don Phelipe Segundo El Prudente; y La Espiritual, Por Los Religiosos Del Orden de . . . San*

Agustin... Parte Primera... Edited by Nicoló Billy and Manuel Ruiz de Murga. Vol. 2. Madrid: en la Imprenta de Manuel Ruiz de Murga.

Savater, Fernando. 1981. *La tarea del héroe: Elementos para una ética trágica.* Madrid: Taurus. https://dialnet.unirioja.es/servlet/libro?codigo=54993

Schmidt-Nowara, Christopher. 2006. *The Conquest of History: Spanish Colonialism and National Histories in the Nineteenth Century.* Pittsburgh: University of Pittsburgh Press.

Shutz, J. Travis. 2019. "Limahong's Pirates, Ming Mariners, and Early Sino–Spanish Relations: The Pangasinan Campaign of 1575 and Global History from Below." *Philippine Studies: Historical and Ethnographic Viewpoints* 67 (3–4): 315–42.

"Teatros." 1907. *El Pueblo. Diario republican de Valencia* (2 November): 2.

Thomas, Megan. 2013. *Orientalists, Propagandists, and Ilustrados.* Quezon City: Ateneo University Press.

Villaescusa-Illán, Irene. 2020. *Transcultural Nationalism in Hispano-Filipino Literature.* Historical and Cultural Interconnections between Latin America and Asia series. London: Palgrave Macmillan. https://doi.org/10.1007/978-3-030-51599-7

White, Lynn T., III. 2014. *Philippine Politics: Possibilities and Problems in a Localist Democracy.* London: Routledge.

Zialcita, Fernando Nakpil. 2006. *Authentic Though Not Exotic: Essays on Filipino Identity.* Quezon City: Ateneo de Manila University Press.

PART III

Modernity and Globalization

Finding, Framing, and Forging Filipino Identities in Isabelo de los Reyes's *El folk-lore filipino* and Adelina Gurrea's *Cuentos de Juana*

Kristina A. Escondo

In 1887, budding journalist Isabelo de los Reyes won the silver medal at the Exposición Filipina in Madrid for his work *El folk-lore filipino*. Intent on reviving histories from pre-Hispanic Philippines, de los Reyes collected folkloric material from Ilocos Sur, Zambales, and Malabon. A little over a half century later, in 1943, writer Adelina Gurrea published *Cuentos de Juana: Narraciones malayas de las Islas Filipinas*. Through Gurrea's childhood memories, the titular narrator Juana recounts stories about beings central to the folklore and "saber popular" (popular knowledge) of Negros Occidental in the region of Visayas.

In the time between the publications of these two works, the Philippines saw the archipelago transferred from the fallen empire of Spain to the rising one of the United States. It would not be a surprise, then, to imagine that both Isabelo de los Reyes's and Adelina Gurrea's texts might shed light on political, social, and economic problems in their country. Both reference the nation as the driving force behind their works, highlighting the relationship between folklore and patria. In citing "el patriotismo" as his motivation for writing *El folk-lore filipino*, de los Reyes explains, "Cada uno sirva á su pueblo según su manera de pensar, y yo con el *Folk-Lore ilocano* creo contribuir á esclarecer el pasado del mio" (Each one serves his village according to the way one thinks, and with *El folklore Ilocano*, I believe I can contribute in clarifying the past of my own)[1] (1889, 18). Likewise, Gurrea dedicates *Cuentos de Juana* "a la memoria de mi padre, que fue tan amante de los libros y de su Patria" (to the memory of my father, who was such a lover of books and of his Fatherland)[2] (2009, 45).

But why the focus on folklore, specifically? What *is* folklore? Even as Isabelo de los Reyes was collecting material for his text in the 19th century, the word was a slippery one to define. When the term "folklore"—translated by de los Reyes as *saber popular*—was introduced by Englishman William Thoms in 1846, it generally encompassed the study of a people's "traditional," vernacular stories, customs, superstitions, and beliefs. In studying these cultural artifacts in comparison with those from other regions, one might be able to deduce information regarding a population's prehistoric ancestry (de los Reyes 1889, 8). However, as de los Reyes developed his working definition of the term—in contrast to mythology, for example, which focuses on the sacred—his first question was "si es ciencia o no" (if it is a science or not) (19). After summarizing some of the major currents of thought surrounding the matter, he settles on the following definition: "La ocupación del pensamiento humano, que tiene por objeto recoger todos los datos que la gente no ilustrada conozca y tenga, que aun no hayan sido estudiados" (The occupation of human thought, whose objective is to gather all of the data that the unlearned people know and have that still have not been studied) (22). Throughout the text, he emphasizes his impartial objectivity and formal, systematic collection of work: "Si esta colección de mis artículos folk-lóricos tiene algun mérito, que no encuentro, consistirá únicamente en la fidelidad y buena fé en la descripción . . . y tanta es mi imparcialidad, que he sacrificado á la ciencia el cariño de los ilocanos" (If this collection of my folkloric articles has some merit that I do not find, it may only be in the fidelity and good faith of description . . . and such is my impartiality, that I have sacrificed the Ilocanos' affections to science) (17). However, as other scholars have also noted, he liberally inserts his own comments and clarifications throughout the text when it serves to establish his authority.

Adelina Gurrea, on the other hand, did not provide any sort of definition of folklore or speculation thereof—only stating in her dedication that the book was "escrito con aromas folklóricos de nuestra tierra" (written with the folkloric aromas of our land) (2009, 46). In contrast to de los Reyes, her objective was not to carry out a formal study of folklore—these were local stories told to her as a child by her nanny, Juana. Yet, gesturing to the formal, systematic method of collecting folkloric material, she desired to preserve these stories in the way that they were told to her: "Yo lo relato como Juana me lo narró, sin poner ni quitar nada y sin obligar a nadie que crea las explicaciones de aquellas personas que lo comentaron" (I tell it as Juana narrated it to me, without adding or leaving anything out and without obliging anyone to believe the explanations of those people that brought it up) (55). Born in La Carlota in the Philippine province of Negros Occidental in 1896, Gurrea and her family moved to Spain in 1921, where she spent most of the rest of her life until her death in 1971. While her family was primarily of Spanish origin, she remained devoted to the Philippines, expressing her nostalgia for her childhood memories there and a desire to preserve Philippine culture (Álvarez Tardío 2009, 8). Yet, she also infused these stories with a critical eye that questioned the conduct of both Spanish and American colonizers—a critique that is particularly salient considering *Cuentos de Juana* was published just a few years after the end of the Spanish Civil War and an indication that these narratives were likewise inextricable from one's contemporary sociopolitical atmosphere. For Gurrea, then, folklore was a repository for these memories and a way to preserve stories—and sociopolitical critiques—shared by a local community.

When thinking about Isabelo de los Reyes's and Adelina Gurrea's stories and their references to the Philippines as their inspiration, folklore studies can be useful in looking at how these knowledges were grounded and used under conditions of colonial domination and exploitation. It can also help in considering the way they viewed, made sense of, and constructed the very complicated notion of Filipino identity. Because de los Reyes, the "father of Filipino folklore," wrote during Spanish colonization, and Gurrea, Zobel award winner in 1956, wrote during American occupation of the Philippines (and, importantly, during Francisco Franco's dictatorship in Spain), it makes sense to study the two in tandem to affirm the historical continuity of the Philippines' evolving political, social, and cultural trajectories and contexts under empire, as well as to consider the complex framing and defining of a unifying Filipino national identity.

Bearing these themes in mind, this chapter first outlines some common analytical trends when looking at how Isabelo de los Reyes's *El folk-lore filipino* attempted to find and frame Filipino identity under the colonizing influence of Spain. The scholars studied here examine de los Reyes's use of folklore to recover a shared, pre-Hispanic cultural heritage to claim and conceive of a united Filipino identity under Spanish colonialism; to link his use of this collective knowledge with nationalism and anti-colonial struggles; and to analyze how he used folklore to reflect on and engage with the political landscape as Spanish colonialism neared its end. Next, I look at how Adelina Gurrea's *Cuentos de Juana*, written during the imperial regime of the United States, carried on the folkloric tradition set by de los Reyes to reflect on the meaning

of a Filipino identity. Her work, which acknowledged the Philippines' indigenous folklore, bridges the gap between these autochthonous traditions and
the modern, hybrid narratives that affirm the continuity of the archipelago's
history. At the same time, *Cuentos* likewise criticizes the oppression and suffering wrought by both Spain's and the United States' imperial designs. Notably, both writers used Spanish—a language whose status changed as the Philippines changed hands from Spain to the United States—in their recounting
of these tales and, by extension, in their thinking about what it means to
be Filipino. Therefore, by exploring the tensions between the dueling Hispanic and Filipino influences in their works, I argue that the fluidity of folklore allowed each author to continuously configure and reconfigure a Filipino
identity that, even within the tangles of empire, attempted to find its home in
local knowledges.

The Social Bases of Folklore

By the end of the 19th century, folklorists began making connections to processes of nation building by calling attention to a country's distinctive origins
and affirming the continuity of a nation's history. We can see how, taken further, the genre had developed as a tool of resistance by colonized or otherwise dominated peoples, raising a unifying consciousness based on a shared
identity in anti-colonial struggles. In contemporary studies, folklore broadens
its scope by looking at creative expression and how it reflects and informs a
community's reality, value systems, and interactions. Thus, the relationship
between folklore and its commentary on the sociopolitical changes of the late
19th and early 20th centuries does not come as a surprise.

  Dorothy Noyes, in her study on the social bases of folklore, opens with a
brief discussion about the term and then posits the following key questions
for the discipline: "What commonplace relationships exist between bodies
of knowledge and groups of people? What relationship should scholars posit
between cultural forms and social structures?" (2012, 13). As she situates her
analysis, Noyes remarks on how these linkages hold enormous value—for
example, among politicians and the territories they govern; for industries,
such as tourism, restaurants, and decor; and as both an empirical and theoretical object of study. In an overview of the Philippine context, Erlinda K.
Alburo likewise underscores the gains of folklore study as part of national
development, especially in folk media, pedagogy, and tourism (1992, 213). For
Alburo, Philippine folklore studies includes

protest songs, jokes, new dance forms, speech patterns and other aspects of popular culture which are current not only among the supposedly backward rural folk but also circulating among the lowland urbanized and marginal people like women, laborers, preadolescents, and the unlettered. What is studied is not just the final product but also the doing, and the experiences and symbols involved, which are deemed equally important. (213)

Both Noyes and Alburo recognize the ways folklore interacts not only with literature and history but also with politics, policymaking, economics, and societal development. Noyes further highlights folklorists' self-awareness of their own role in creating this area of study and comments on how "nationalist, populist, revolutionary, and colonialist scholars around the world have continued to produce cultural objects in the hope of modeling social futures" (2012, 14).

From here, both Noyes and Alburo draw from Richard Bauman's work, most notably his contributions in the book *Toward New Perspectives in Folklore* (1972) and *Verbal Art as Performance* (1977), among others. Alburo focuses on his concept of folklore as "artistic action in social life," whereas Noyes looks at Bauman's exploration of the "social base" of folklore, which is where I turn my focus (Alburo 1992, 213; Noyes 2012, 14). Noyes underlines Bauman's argument that people were connected to folklore not through tradition but through performance—folklore, while it often emphasized communal identity, did not tend to express a preexistent identity among insiders; rather, "it more often constructed one, aggressively or humorously, at social boundaries" (2012, 14). However, communicating this distinct identity required a common code. For Noyes, the shared forms that were generated in ongoing social interaction—rather than a common identity—were the necessary conditions for folklore (14). From here, Noyes traces the interlocking development of three main approaches: the first views folklore as the "cultural forms proper to the deepest stratum of social life, flattened and superseded by the historical, hierarchical, or institutional overlay of modernity"; the second sees it as the "expressive bonds of community, which assert or maintain its differential being against external pressures"; and the third turns to performance, finding "the social base of folklore in the contingencies of a situation it seeks to transform" (14–15).

While I do not intend to debate various approaches to folklore studies or to define the term, I do draw from Alburo's broadened definition of what might be considered folklore and from Noyes's concept of the social base of folklore[3] in examining the relationships between cultural forms, social structures, and the respective colonial contexts in de los Reyes's and Gurrea's works. In analyzing the relationships between people and various bodies of knowledge, folklore provides an equalizing, performative method that explores how humans create identities, develop strategies of control or resistance, view the world, and reflect on it. During Spanish colonization and American occupation, the genre's reminders of one's roots, community, and future promise serve as the perfect medium for reflecting on and constructing a Filipino national identity.

Isabelo de los Reyes and *El folk-lore filipino*

Many scholars have written about Isabelo de los Reyes's use of folklore to trace the pre-Hispanic origins of Philippine peoples, to frame this heritage as a shared Filipino identity, and to promote these identities to affirm *ilustrado* nationalism and anti-colonial struggle.[4] During the 19th century, a *filipino* described a creole who was born on the archipelago but was of peninsular Spanish descent (Anderson 2000, 52). Consequently, in *El folk-lore filipino*, de los Reyes did not describe himself as *filipino*—rather, he described himself in other ways, often highlighting his identity as an Ilocano and signaling the regionalism prevalent during his time. Nonetheless, he sought out a common heritage among the major Philippine populations. De los Reyes writes in his introduction:

> ¿Quién puede asegurar de fijo cuales fueron los aborígenes de este Archip-iélago? En un principio yo opinaba que los ilocanos eran de raza distinta que los tagalos, en razón á que existen algunas diferencias, tanto que muchas veces distingo á primera vista por su solo aspecto el uno del otro. Pero después de haber yo estudiado detenidamente las costumbres, supersticiones y tradiciones de uno y otro pueblo, me mudé de parecer.

> (Who can say with certainty who were the aborigines of this archipelago? At first, I would say that the Ilocanos were of a distinct race from the Tag-alogs because there existed some differences, such that often I could easily distinguish one from another at first glance. But after carefully studying the customs, superstitions and traditions of different towns, I changed my mind.) (1889, 11)

Filomeno V. Aguilar Jr. examines this text—among others by the *ilustrados*, de los Reyes's contemporaries—and how it problematizes the search for origins and its relationship with constructing Filipino identity. His article importantly traces the contradictory relationship between racial science discourses and nationalism in the *ilustrados'* development of this identity. As he does so, Aguilar maps out the evolution of the term *filipino* from referring to a peninsular creole to its modern-day iteration as a national-ethnic descriptor. As the *ilustrados* began to imagine the nation and who belonged to it, Aguilar mentions that their contemporary conceptualizations of race initially served to produce a counter-discourse to the "unscientific" claims of Spanish colonial friars and authorities (2005, 610). The search for origins aimed to highlight an ancient civilization—which in some ways might have been superior to Europe—of which one could be proud: "The glories of the preconquest age of *our* [Philippine] ancestors underscored the failure and injustices of Spanish colonialism. The friars were faulted for the colony's backwardness" (611). However, he also argues that, while this counter-discourse debunked charges of the Philippine peoples' inferiority to Europeans, it influenced the development of an emerging Filipino identity that—to varying degrees—included some and excluded others:

> On the one hand were "the civilized Filipinos" [*los Filipinos civilizados*], who did not resist conversion to Catholicism; on the other were "the mountain tribes" [*las tribus montañesas*], who resisted and therefore were not civilized. . . . The ancestors were to be identified partially on the basis of "race"—Malayness—and partially on "civilization," principally acceptance of Spanish culture. (612)[5]

The 1887 Exposición Filipina in Madrid, for example, exemplifies this divide between assimilation and exclusion: it simultaneously awarded de los Reyes a silver medal for *El folk-lore filipino* and put on display "mountain tribes" to represent the Philippines. For the *ilustrados*, this was distasteful and offensive: "In addition to the affront to basic human dignity, the exposition was unacceptable precisely because 'savages' embodied the Philippines" (614).

Yet, in the introduction to *El folk-lore filipino*, de los Reyes defined himself as "hermano de los selváticos, aetas, igorrotes y tinguianes y nacido en esta apartada colonial española" (brother of the forest dwellers, the Aetas, the Igorots and the Tinguians born of this remote Spanish colony) (1889, 19), for which he received ample criticism. Benedict Anderson points out that these so-called primitive peoples lived (and continue to live) in the cordillera along the coastal plain of Ilocos and that de los Reyes would have seen them coming down from the forests to the lowlands for commercial trade (2000, 17). Anderson emphasizes that, in de los Reyes's day, no one would have spoken of the forest dwellers in these terms; however, "one begins to see how it was possible for him to think of his province as a big *pueblo* and a *patria adorada*, since in the most concrete way it linked as brothers the 'wild' pagans of the mountains and a man who won prizes in Madrid" (17). Megan C. Thomas concurs in her study referencing de los Reyes's ethnological work: "De los Reyes was unworried about the potential liabilities of associating the civilized Ilocanos with their 'savage' ancestors and brethren. . . . What struck de los Reyes was the possibility—perhaps inevitability—of cultural change, a change that occurred not through racial mixture but through civilizational contact" (2012, 90–91). While some of de los Reyes's characterizations were not unproblematic, his general belief that people could be—and should be—educated to the ends of developing a "civilized" society demonstrates a more racially inclusive vision of a Filipino national identity.

Anderson likewise notes that de los Reyes's participation in developing a "ciencia nueva" (new science) emphasized the intellectual inertia of his peninsular counterparts in a colonial regime that was being left behind as the rest of the Western world turned to modernity. In de los Reyes's quest to collect folkloric material from various Philippine regions, he aimed to establish the archipelago's shared cultural heritage, one whose origins did not rely on coloniality. For example, he meticulously pointed out the ways supernatural beings existed as an originally Philippine belief, distinct from the worldview brought by the Spanish. The *mangmangkik*, for example, are not devils, "según la idea que los católicos tienen de los demonios, ni sombras ó espectros, ni cafres" (according to the idea that Catholics had about demons, nor are they shadows nor ghosts nor barbarians) (de los Reyes 1889, 32). Rather, de los Reyes emphasized, they were old *anitos* of the trees, a type of demigod of Ilocos—the *mangmangkik* absolutely did not come from a European construct. The text also included short descriptions of various supernatural beings, as well as flora, fauna, traditions, and the like. These descriptions, peppered with de los Reyes's own interjections about the material, highlighted his own knowledge as one that Spanish folklorists lacked. With this in mind, Aguilar interprets de los Reyes's identification with the "forest dwellers" as tongue-in-cheek—by claiming brotherhood with them, de los Reyes accentuated that Spanish folklorists were behind the times (2005, 615).

In analyzing folklore's link to anti-colonial struggles and the ways in which it engages with the sociopolitical landscape, Ma. Diosa Labiste underscores the relationship between de los Reyes's scholarly folkloric work and what she terms "insurgent journalism." De los Reyes's journalism, according to Labiste, can be labeled as insurgent due to the existence of a "dominant and legitimate authority that . . . is threatened by the rebellion of its colonial subjects" and also "acknowledges the constraints of coercion and hegemony in the space in which it operates" but simultaneously seeks out resistance within this space (2016, 35). Folklore, on the other hand, as stories about people, "is capable of constituting a public" (40). Therefore, she argues, journalism and folklore work in tandem as a memory device that allows one to reflect on the political landscape of the time and opens up avenues for critiquing politics and anti-colonial expression (42).

Labiste sensibly focuses on de los Reyes's adaption of folklore as a journalistic style that highlighted folklore's relevance to the present in its critique of colonial society. However, I would like to note that the opposite—that is, considering the adaptation of journalism as a *folkloric* style—may have likewise served de los Reyes as a performative device that reworked folklore's association with the "mythic" to one that situates journalism as its modernized aesthetic. In doing so, de los Reyes refreshes the authority and progressiveness of folklore on a historical continuum, emphasizing that stories exploring societal transformation and their fluid interpretations of public opinion have always been embedded in Philippine practice. De los Reyes's reflections on the transformative possibilities through folklore-journalism situate political and anti-colonial critique as a traditional, ongoing, shared form.

This critique can be seen in the only short story in the first volume categorized as "¿Folk-lore administrativo?" (Administrative folklore?). De los Reyes recounts the story of Isio, a young man who had to leave his studies in Manila due to the death of his parents. After toiling away at what little land he has—and eventually restoring his family's property to its prior splendor—he is appointed *cabeza de barangay* of his province, a leadership position he does not want but is obliged to accept. Unfortunately, this subjects him to a corrupt political and highly bureaucratic system in which he must either maintain his principles but fall into financial ruin or live comfortably, if not lavishly, through the exploitations of his fellow citizens.

As a result, Isio is driven by the corruption to flee to the mountains. There, he tricks the native Igorots with "magic" to become their leader, claiming to have been sent by the *anitos* to help them change their ways else they be punished. He takes on the role of a missionary, "lifting them up" with his own civilizing mission:

La religión que enseñaba era la Anitería malaya, ó sea, la misma que se conservaba en aquellos bosques, pero perfeccionada y reducida á racional sistema. Combatía Isio el catolicismo con los argumentos de los herejes y atacaba la sociabilidad, ó sea la idea de reducir á la vida civilizada á los igorrotes con las objeciones del católico contra el socialismo exagerado, por supuesto, todo presentado en formas sofísticas que alucinaban no sólo á aquellos monteses, sino que logró además adeptos aún entre los ilocanos.

(The religion [Isio] taught them was Malay Anitism, that is, the same religion that was preserved in those mountains, but perfected and reduced to a rational system. Isio fought Catholicism using the heretics' own arguments, and attacked sociability, that is, the idea of reducing the Igorots to a civilized life with the Catholic's objections against exaggerated socialism, of course, all presented in sophisticated ways that not only captivated those mountain people, but further gained him followers even among the Ilocanos.) (de los Reyes 1889, 334–35)

As noted above, the "primitive" description of the Igorots, the tension between Malay *anitería* and Spanish Catholicism, and the characterization of the indigenous belief system as "perfected" by a "rational" system of thought suggest that de los Reyes—like the other *ilustrados* of his day—grappled with the back-and-forth between assimilation and exclusionary politics. On the one hand, he critiqued the oppressive nature of Spanish bureaucracy and the hypocrisy of Catholicism; on the other, the indigenous *anitería* needed to be "improved." Again, while Anderson's analysis focuses on de los Reyes's consideration of them and other groups as his Filipino "brothers," Aguilar's analysis highlights how the *ilustrados* were "molded by the nomenclature and reach of the Spanish colonial state" in which Filipino nationalism was "also entangled with the appropriation and internalization of a high-minded imperialist agenda" (Aguilar 2005, 621).

This entanglement is especially salient when considering de los Reyes's use of Spanish to write *El folk-lore filipino* rather than his native Ilocano or any of the Philippine languages. Initially, one may be tempted to view his use of Spanish as a further assimilatory act—like José Rizal and the other *ilustrados'* Spanish-language writings, it could be interpreted that de los Reyes viewed the European language as more cosmopolitan. While this may not entirely be untrue, Anderson also points out that, in contrast to almost all of Latin America, Spanish was not imposed on the archipelago—around 3 percent of the population spoke it, and perhaps only 1 percent of Ilocanos could follow (2000, 59). Therefore, "it was an 'international language' more than it was a colonial one" (61).

Thinking back to Dorothy Noyes's and Richard Bauman's discussion on folklore, de los Reyes's imagined Filipino identity was not *entirely* defined by a shared, pre-Hispanic heritage, although it sought to be rooted in it. Though de los Reyes viewed folklore as evidence of a tradition that existed before Spanish colonization, he likewise acknowledged the inextricability of colonizing influences on the Philippines's cultures. He therefore constructed a Filipino identity at the social boundaries of this shared colonial experience—one that is Malay and "civilized." Still, he attempted to articulate a vision of an alternative world—one that found its roots in the multiplicity of Philippine traditions but that did not shy away from incorporating practices from other regions or even from the Spanish colonial powers—in a distinctly Filipino way. Through the systematized study of folklore, de los Reyes utilized colonial methodologies to bring together diverse stories from Ilocos, Zambales, and Malabón to configure these stories under the common experience of colonialism and reconfigure Filipino identity as one with a plurality of origins.

Adelina Gurrea and *Cuentos de Juana*

In contrast to the numerous studies on Isabelo de los Reyes's *El folk-lore filipino*, scholarship on Adelina Gurrea and her short story collection, *Cuentos de Juana: Narraciones malayas de las Islas Filipinas* (1943), is comparatively sparse. As mentioned earlier, Gurrea was born and grew up in La Carlota, Negros Occidental (Visayas), in 1896, just a month after the Cry of Biak-na-Bato that commenced the Philippine revolution against Spain. However, her claim to Filipino identity differs from that of Isabelo de los Reyes. Unlike de los Reyes, Gurrea mostly had Spanish heritage (her paternal grandmother was a Tagalog mestiza; her paternal grandfather and maternal grandparents were Spanish) and spent most of her adult life in Madrid. Rosario Cruz-Lucero, in her necessary analysis of the historical and literary traditions that contextualize *Cuentos de Juana*, points out that Gurrea's Spanish background may be one reason (among others) for her exclusion from the Philippine literary canon and that one might expect that she would have produced colonialist fiction, written with the bias of the colonizer (2013, 100). However, Cruz-Lucero notes, "Gurrea is not to be so easily pinned down to this category" (100).

Thinking back to Filomeno V. Aguilar and Isabelo de los Reyes, "the ilustrados' mixed heritage would . . . cloud the borders of Filipinoness" by finding an affinity with the "progressive" Malay populations and by fostering an ambiguous relationship with Spanish colonialism that gave the *ilustrados* access to European civilization and modernity (Aguilar 2005, 612). Following this tradition, Gurrea's broad claim to a Filipino identity may likewise be based on an orientalist nostalgia. However, Beatriz Álvarez Tardío rightly points out the importance of the Spanish Civil War, the ensuing Francoist dictatorship, and its effects on women's societal roles on influencing Gurrea's work and identity, nuancing this claim even further (2009, 10, 17).[6] Considering *Cuentos de Juana* was published a mere four years after the end of the Spanish Civil War, it would be remiss not to consider this context in understanding, examining, and appreciating the complexities of how Gurrea frames Filipino identity in this collection.[7] Similar to de los Reyes's *El Folk-lore filipino*, Gurrea's text simultaneously preserves memories of her childhood home and culture and denounces Spain's oppressive conduct, both as a former colonizer in the Philippines and, in her adulthood, as a repressive, fascist regime in its own land.

While Gurrea likely never read Isabelo de los Reyes's work,[8] I show how she carried on his folkloric tradition to reflect on the evolving meaning of a Filipino identity during the American occupation of the Philippines and simultaneously to critique Spain for its past and present conduct. Beatriz Álvarez Tardío's authoritative text *Writing Athwart: Adelina Gurrea's Life and Works* (2009) provides biographical and historical context for this section and is complemented by excellent analyses of *Cuentos de Juana* by Rosario Cruz-Lucero and Irene Villaescusa Illán. Cruz-Lucero argues that these stories "may be read as a palimpsest of the whole of Philippine history, with its indigenous system of thought and knowledge refusing to be erased or overwritten but instead, actively engaging with its colonial history" (2013, 100). Similarly, Villaescusa Illán explores how *Cuentos de Juana* emphasizes a "double cosmovision" of the Philippines that incorporates both Spanish colonizer and indigenous Filipino perspectives in relating the processes of transculturation during Spanish colonialism (2020, 97). Tying this back to Dorothy Noyes's study on the social bases of folklore, Gurrea's engagement with the relationship between Philippine cultural forms and social structures, complicated by Spain's colonial presence and the United States' imperial one, may serve to reflect on her own "expressive bonds" with the culture of her childhood in the archipelago in the midst of the more complicated culture of her adulthood.

Gurrea opens the book by immediately telling the reader, "Juana me contó estos cuentos" (Juana told me these stories) (2009, 47), emphasizing that these were local stories of the island of Negros. She mentions Juana as having the nickname *Baltimore*, referencing a large American battleship that had destroyed a Spanish fleet in Cavite's harbor in 1898. Gurrea then describes Juana's dark skin, flat nose, small eyes, and large mouth. Much like de los Reyes, Gurrea is acutely aware of visible racial differences between the indigenous Filipinos and the Spanish colonizers. In contrast to de los Reyes, Gurrea does not seek to recover a pre-Hispanic cultural heritage to claim Filipino identity; rather, her vision—while at times contradictory and problematic—attempts to be a more inclusive one. On the one hand, she situates Juana as the teller of these stories who, as an indigenous Filipino, authenticates them. This suggests that Gurrea, primarily of Spanish descent, did not view herself as having this authority and, therefore, was excluded from having an "authentic" Filipino identity; Villaescusa Illán rightly points out the distinct characterizations of "natives" versus nonnative Filipinos in the *Cuentos*.

On the other hand, telling these stories from her childhood speaks to Gurrea's perception of herself as an extension of Juana and, therefore, suggests that Filipino identity could also include Spanish creoles like herself. Villaescusa Illán also argues that the ensuing transcultural orientalism in the text imagines and remembers the Philippines "as the oriental homeland in a mode of reflective nostalgia" (2020, 112). Further, she explores the tensions underlying Gurrea's desire to remain "objective" in this framing of her childhood memories as simply being faithful to Juana's storytelling and her unease with the uneven colonial power relations, conflicting religious beliefs, and cultural conflicts that were then embedded into her everyday life (100–101). Taken together, I read the nostalgic, blurred lines between Juana's and Gurrea's voices as echoing folklore's social bases: its communal bonds; its assertion of difference (for Gurrea, against Francoist Spain); and its capacity to reflect on its contemporary situation to construct national identity. Like de los Reyes, Gurrea notices racial difference. Yet, rather than finding the roots of national identity in a common, pre-European, precolonial origin, Gurrea positions her construction of identity as one situated in the Philippines's transcultural legacy, as reflected in the *Cuentos*.

Additionally, Gurrea's decision to use Spanish in writing these stories differs from de los Reyes's. Due to her parents' background, Gurrea's first language was Spanish; her second language, due to her childhood home, was Hiligaynon. And, having been educated in the American educational system as a child, she also knew English, the language then imposed upon the archipelago (Álvarez Tardío 2009, 5). When considering that Gurrea lived and published her *Cuentos* in Madrid, it would not be surprising that she would use her first language to reach her immediate audience. However, the use of Spanish is not limited to our author. In her childhood home, Juana

> era una institución. . . . Hablaba el castellano, pero se olvidaba de él tan pronto como se la reprochaba alguna mala acción o falta en el cumplimiento de su deber. Entonces no se encontraba modo de evitar que diese sus pródigas explicaciones en el dialecto visayo.

> (was an institution. . . . She spoke castellano, but promptly forgot it as soon as she was reproached for some bad action or for not carrying out her duties. Then, there was no way to prevent her from giving her prodigious explanations in the Visayan dialect.) (Gurrea 2009, 48)

The fact that Juana was "an institution" in her home who spoke both Spanish and Visayan speaks to Gurrea's conceptualization of Juana as an authoritative figure and, in a sense, justifies the use of Spanish in the Philippine context. We also see this in reverse—Cruz-Lucero cites Perla B. Palabrica's work on the text, which demonstrates that certain Spanish words referencing Negros hacienda culture employed specialized meanings in the Hiligaynon language (2013, 108). In the same way that Juana—a "more native" Filipino—could recount her tales in Spanish, Gurrea likewise understood the specialized meanings of Spanish words in Hiligaynon. In addition to viewing Gurrea's use of the localized vocabulary as establishing her own authority and claim to Filipino identity, we can also consider it as a performative act that is generated by ongoing social interaction and that includes Gurrea within the boundaries of this identity. Therefore, for her, Filipino identity is inextricable from Spain's influence.

Yet, in describing Juana's storytelling, Gurrea recalled that "[en] el momento de las explicaciones, largaba su discursito en visaya; pero a veces se encontraba con réplicas que eran más que palabras. Cosas de la colonización. Para Juana no era denigrante el golpe en la mejilla" (at the time of her explanations, her chatter spilled out in Visaya; but sometimes she found herself with replies that were beyond words. Things from colonization. For Juana, a slap in the face was not denigrating) (2009, 50). As referenced earlier, Gurrea notes these uneven power relations as an everyday occurrence during her childhood (Villaescusa Illán 2020, 99). Further, one must recognize, with Gurrea writing toward the end of the United States' occupation of the Philippines (1935–46), the context in which she was attempting to configure her view of Filipino identity—that is, one in transition from the Spanish colonial state to the American neocolony and, at the same time, living in Madrid during the Spanish Civil War. Again, as Álvarez Tardío points out, Gurrea's works show a distinct disapproval of American culture, characteristic of the discourse promoted by the Franco regime (2009, 28–29). For her, as with de los Reyes, the use of Spanish likely emphasized the Hispanic influence on Philippine culture and simultaneously symbolized resistance to the imposition of the English language both in the archipelago and as an international language, likewise approved by Franco's Spain.

This transitory identity is likewise evident in the *Cuentos*. In all of Juana's stories, the characters are presented in states of ambivalence, suggesting Gurrea's own vacillation on Filipino identity and her own place within this framework. The text centers on five main figures, all variations of the Philippine aswang that generally represents an abstract malevolence: el tamao, el tic-tic, el camá-camá, el bagat, and el lunuk[9] del remanso verde (the lunuk of the green pool). The first two and the last two relate stories about vengeful spirits, with the good—albeit mischievous—spirit, the camá-camá, centering the text. Cruz-Lucero rightly states that, through the supernatural beings in *Cuentos de Juana*, Gurrea "presents the hybrid nature of Philippine postcolonial life, consisting of an indigenous system of thought that is the vital source of the natives' agency, on which was overwritten the hegemony of a Spanish plantation economy and the violent transition into American colonialism that they were undergoing at the time" (2013, 111). Likewise, as women's roles in Spain transitioned to one delimited by Franco's traditionalist regime, one could argue that Gurrea began to draw parallels between Spain's former colonial control of the archipelago and the contemporary one of its own people, using folklore to reflect on the dynamic processes of colonization and—like de los Reyes—as a form of literary subversion.

Cruz-Lucero's own literary analysis centers on the figure of the *tamao* in the first story, "La doncella que vivió tres vidas" (The maiden who lived three lives), and in the last story, "El lunuk del remanso verde" (The lunuk of the green pool). In these analyses, Cruz-Lucero aims to "distinguish the various voices constituting Gurrea's stories and the various ways in which each seeks to dominate, or silence, the others by turns" (2013, 111). In both, she outlines elements of Philippine mythic and epic tradition, situating the indigenous cultural heritage of these tales. Cruz-Lucero also draws attention to the sociopolitical critiques of both Spanish colonization and American imperialism. In "La doncella," Juana tells of a *tamao*'s abduction of a young girl, Pinang, whom he imprisons in the tamarind tree where he lives. Pinang is rescued by the household cook, who knows what ritual to use to overcome the *tamao*'s power. However, despite her release from the *tamao*, she continues living as though she were in a perpetual sleepwalking state: "muda, con los ojos muy abiertos, hipnóticos, ausentes" (mute, with her eyes wide open, hypnotized, blank) (Gurrea 2009, 72). The three lives of Pinang—before her abduction, imprisoned in the tamarind tree, and after her release—can be seen to represent precolonial Philippines, Spanish colonization, and American imperialism. The other story centered on the *tamao*, "El lunuk," likewise contains three parts. A vengeful *tamao* lives in a tree—el lunuk—by a green pool and, one by one, the Spanish masters across three generations are killed by the *tamao*. Each generation threatens to cut down the tree or otherwise do not leave it in peace, whereas none of the natives, who respectfully keep their distance, suffer any harm. In both stories, native, local knowledge is what comes to the rescue or keeps one safe, whereas foreign interference—or negligence in disregarding the *tamao*'s power—brings ruin. In recalling the stories of her childhood, Gurrea found in the folklore genre an avenue to examine the relationships between the social structures that she experienced in the Philippines, the bodies of knowledge that the native Filipinos used in developing strategies of resistance, and the ways that these contexts paralleled her situation in Spain at the time of the *Cuentos*'s publication.

In contrast to the vengeful nature of the *tamao* or the aswang, the camá-camá was a trickster. Juana tells the story of the relationship between the heron Mahamut and a mischievous son of a chief named Ino-Dactú, who became the original camá-camá. The camá-camá

es como un enanito con cabeza y patas de garza. No tiene muchas plumas; la cabeza, las patas y los brazos—que son como unas alitas con dos dedos—van cubiertos de ellas. El resto de su cuerpo es de persona.

(is like a dwarf with the head and feet of a heron. It does not have many feathers; the head, feet, and arms—that are like little wings with two fingers—are covered with them. The rest of its body is of a person.) (Gurrea 2009, 129)

One day, Ino-Dactú got lost during an adventure when the heron Mahamut found him and told him that he was far from home. Mahamut helped guide him to the village, which during his absence had been sacked and burned down, and he discovered that his parents had been kidnapped. Mahamut rallied the other animals to help Ino-Dactú rescue his mother.

Although heir to the chief of his village, Ino-Dactú longed for the freedom of his childhood and decided to abdicate the throne to his cousin, who was already ruling in his place until he came of age. Echoing de los Reyes's short story "¿El folk-lore administrativo?" in its treatment of a protagonist who flees their town to be free of corruption, Ino-Dactú told Mahamut that he wished to become a heron: "Los hombres son malos, yo prefiero ser ave. Me gustaría volar, tener plumaje, dormir en un nido. . . . Me gustaría ser garza como tú" (Men are evil, I prefer to be a bird. I would like to fly, have plumage, sleep in a nest. . . . I would like to be a heron, like you) (Gurrea 2009, 163). Mahamut threw a magic pearl into the air, which needed to be caught by a passing eagle; however, this only partially completed his wish. The eagle accidentally snapped the pearl in half, turning Ino-Dactú into a creature that was partly transformed—he became half heron, half human.

Beatriz Álvarez Tardío remarks in a footnote in her edition of *Cuentos de Juana* that, according to the references that Gurrea makes regarding the recent Spanish loss of its final colonies and the United States' growing influences in the archipelago, she would have been around five years old when this story was told to her (Gurrea 2009, 124). When considered in this light, I read Ino-Dactú as the native Filipino, cared for by Mahamut ("good" Spain) as he discovers his village has been destroyed by another oppressive group ("bad" Spain/America). The camá-camá may likewise reflect a native identity in Ino-Dactú that, on the one hand, recognizes the inextricability of Spain's influences on the archipelago—even expressing gratitude for this heritage— yet rejects the destructive mindset shared by the Spanish colonial project and the ensuing American imperialism. Ino-Dactú,

amante empedernido de la libertad, le horrorizaban los convencionalismos de la tribu, atada a leyes absurdas para su mentalidad, expuesta a ser arrasada por sus semejantes y obedeciendo siempre a un hombre.

(inveterate lover of freedom, was horrified by the tribe's conventionalism, tied to absurd laws for their mindset, at risk to be destroyed by their fellow peoples and always obeying a man.) (164)

Meanwhile, Mahamut expresses her love for Ino-Dactú but states that "mi amor eres tú, pero tú no sirves para el nido de una garza" (you are my love, but you are not fit for the nest of a heron) (163). His desire to become a heron, liberated from the colonial confines of his people, reflects his incorporation of these values and worldviews. Yet, Ino-Dactú never quite finishes the transformation. While his head, feet, and wings are mostly heron—perhaps suggestive of how foreign knowledges guide his thought and path—his body—wherein resides his heart—remains Filipino. This hybrid creature resulting from a native Filipino (Ino-Dactú) and the "foreign" influence of Mahamut perhaps embodies the transcultural Filipino identity at that point in time—a product of an "incomplete" assimilation that creates an entirely new, but no less authentic, being. If we consider Gurrea's own trajectory as the mirror image—a woman who saw her childhood Philippines being occupied by the United States, followed by her adulthood in Spain "at risk to be destroyed by their fellow peoples" while "always obeying a man"—it is not difficult to see how, despite Gurrea's Spanish background, her heart remained Filipino as she watched history repeat itself across the oceans. The artistic action of folklore opens up a space for Gurrea to explore these social structures and identities.

Conclusion

Folklore is a heterogenous space that allows for fluidity and change through its tellings and retellings. It avoids reductionist readings of culture and identity by using variability, change, and transformation precisely as its foundations. The heterogeneity of both de los Reyes's and Gurrea's texts therefore serves to acknowledge the multiplicity of perspectives and practices that existed before the arrival of the Spanish—and that continue to exist, alongside and beyond Spanish and American influences. The use of the Spanish language is both unifying and a tool for sociopolitical commentary. On the one hand, it unites the various types of folklore under one language and levels the field by not privileging one regional language over another (e.g., Ilocano, Tagalog, or Visaya). On the other hand, over 250 years of Spanish rule cannot help but impact the archipelago's stories. Folklore, for de los Reyes and Gurrea, serves as a fluctuating space with flexible boundaries, configuring and reconfiguring Filipino identity as it interacts with foreign influences, while establishing that it is precisely this plurality that makes up the roots of the nation.

Notes

1. References are made to Isabelo de los Reyes's original text published in Manila in 1889 by the publisher Tipo-Lithografía de Chofré y C. There is a 1994 reprint that combines the text with English translations by Salud C. Dizon and Maria Elinora P. Impson, and although this version is certainly valuable in making the text accessible to a wider audience of readers, one must be cognizant of errors in translation. While Dizon's and Impson's translations serve to get the broader point across, the translations in this chapter (and any errors or inaccuracies thereof) are mine.

2. All translations of Gurrea's *Cuentos de Juana* (2009) (and any errors or inaccuracies thereof) are mine.

3. And, by extension, Bauman's concept, as cited in Noyes 2012.

4. Here, I have in mind Benedict Anderson, Megan C. Thomas, Resil B. Mojares, and Ma. Diosa Labiste, among others.

5. Here, Aguilar references José Rizal's annotations of both Antonio Morga's *Sucesos de las Islas Filipinas* and *Historical Events of the Philippine Islands*.

6. While Gurrea's participation in feminist groups prior to the war, such as Lyceum Club Femenino, and the changing role of women during the context of the book's publication are certainly significant and worthy of study in and of itself, I will not focus on this theme here.

7. I thank Rocío Ortuño Casanova for her excellent comments in reviewing earlier versions of this chapter, one of which pointed out this detail that should have been obvious but that I entirely overlooked. To clarify: Álvarez Tardío's study focuses on these influences in Gurrea's poetry rather than in the *Cuentos*. Gurrea's poetry after 1954 was marked by discursive parameters outlined by Franco's regime, such as a love for the *patria*, defense of all things Spanish, triumphant nationalism, and a rejection of the United States and modernization (Álvarez Tardío 2009, 8). In the biographical introduction to her edition of *Cuentos de Juana*, Álvarez Tardío points out that, in contrast to Gurrea's poetry, *Cuentos* may have been written prior to this literary conversion, although it still maintained a strong criticism for the United States and a Hispanizing tendency (Gurrea 2009, 24).

8. Many thanks to Beatriz Álvarez Tardío for her generosity in consulting her files to confirm this information.

9. A tree that houses an exceptionally vengeful tamao.

References

Acuña, Arbeen R. 2017 "Portrait of the Cama-cama as Filipino: Adelina Gurrea's Image of Nation." *Humanities Diliman* 14 (2): 36–63. https://journals.upd.edu.ph/index.php/humanitiesdiliman/article/view/5761/5153

Aguilar, Filomeno V., Jr. 2005. "Tracing Origins: *Ilustrado* Nationalism and the Racial Science of Migration Waves." *Journal of Asian Studies* 64 (3): 605–37. https://doi.org/10.1017/S002191180500152X

Alburo, Erlinda K. 1992. "Continuing and Emerging Directions in Contemporary Philippine Folklore Studies." *Philippine Quarterly of Culture and Society* 20 (2/3): 210–25. https://www.jstor.org/stable/29792088

Álvarez Tardío, Beatriz. 2009. *Writing Athwart: Adelina Gurrea's Life and Works*. Quezon City: Ateneo de Manila University Press. http://www.cervantesvirtual.com/nd/ark:/59851/bmc224s0

Anderson, Benedict. 2000. "The Rooster's Egg: Pioneering World Folklore in the Philippines." *New Left Review* 2:47–62.

Colby Knowlton, Edgar. 1979. "Adelina Gurrea Monasterio and Philippine Folklore." *Proceedings of the International Symposium on Asian Studies in 1979*. Hong Kong: Asian Research Service, 3:643–49. http://www.cervantesvirtual.com/nd/ark:/59851/bmch72d9

Cruz-Lucero, Rosario. 2013. "Gods, Monsters, Heroes, and Tricksters in Adelina Gurrea's *Cuentos de Juana*." *Kritika Kultura* 20:99–128. https://journals.ateneo.edu/ojs/index.php/kk/article/view/KK2013.02006/843

de los Reyes, Isabelo. 1889. *El folk-lore filipino*. Manila: Tipo-Lithografía de Chofré y C. https://archive.org/details/aqq0261.0001.001.umich.edu/page/19/mode/2up

de los Reyes, Isabelo. 1994. *El folk-lore filipino*. With an English translation by Salud C. Dizon and Maria Elinora P. Imson. Quezón City: University of the Philippines Press.

Gallo, Andrea. 2007. "La herencia hispánica en dos autoras filipinas del siglo XX: Adelina Gurrea Monasterio y Elizabeth Medina." In *Escritoras y Pensadoras Europeas*, edited by Mercedes Arriaga Flórez, 297–320. Seville: Arcibel. http://www.cervantesvirtual.com/nd/ark:/59851/bmcz9159

Gurrea, Adelina. 2009. *Cuentos de Juana. Narraciones malayas de las Islas Filipinas*. Edited by Beatriz Álvarez Tardío. Manila: Instituto Cervantes. http://www.cervantesvirtual.com/nd/ark:/59851/bmcn0313

Labiste, Ma. Diosa. 2016. "Folklore and Insurgent Journalism of Isabelo de los Reyes." *Plaridel* 13 (1): 31–45. http://www.plarideljournal.org/wp-content/uploads/2016/06/2016-01-Labiste.pdf

Mojares, Resil B. 2006. *Brains of the Nation: Pedro Paterno, T. H. Pardo de Tavera, Isabelo de los Reyes and the Production of Modern Knowledge*. Manila: Ateneo de Manila University Press.

Noyes, Dorothy. 2012. "The Social Base of Folklore." In *A Companion to Folklore*, edited by Regina F. Bendix and Galit Hasan-Rokem, 13–39. 1st ed. Hoboken, NJ: Blackwell.

Rafael, Vicente. 2005. *The Promise of the Foreign. Nationalism and the Technics of Translation in the Spanish Philippines*. Durham: Duke University Press.

Thomas, Megan C. 2012. *Orientalists, Propagandists, and Ilustrados: Filipino Scholarship and the End of Spanish Colonialism*. Minneapolis: University of Minnesota Press.

Villaescusa Illán, Irene. 2020. "Nostalgia for the Orient: Images of the Philippines in the Work of Adelina Gurrea Monasterio." In *Transcultural Nationalism in Hispano-Filipino Literature*, 77–117. Cham, Switzerland: Palgrave MacMillan.

Villareal, Corazon D. 2010. "Demons, Saviours, and Narrativity in a Vernacular Literature." *Asiatic* 4 (2): 49–67. https://journals.iium.edu.my/asiatic/index.php/AJELL/article/view/522/489

La Sonoridad del Mundo en Manila del Siglo XIX

A Synesthetic Listening to Spanish Writings in 19th-Century Manila

meLê yamomo

Oye, ¡Tú Eres Testigo![1]

In the 19th century, Manila was an important cultural capital of the emerging modern global economy in the Asia Pacific. Global historians Dennis O. Flynn and Arturo Giráldez, as well as Luke Clossey, argue that the establishment of Manila as the Spanish Empire's capital in the Asia-Pacific was the beginning of globalization (see Flynn and Giráldez 1995, 201–21; 2002, 391–427; 2004, 81–108; Clossey 2006, 41). With the opening of the Suez Canal in 1869 and the arrival of new transportation and communication technology, Manila was interconnected to the rest of the world by steamships, telegraphs, and newspapers.[2] Nineteenth-century Manila newspapers not only provide us with a glimpse of the Philippine capital's vibrant cultural scene. An important function of newspapers of that time also places Manila within the larger public sphere of the Spanish Empire as it was entangled in inter-imperial and nascent "internationalizing" globality. The readers of these papers would have been acutely aware of their cosmopolitan position in the globalizing world.

Historian Mark Smith invites us to open our ears to history, which has conventionally been occularcentric (2004). Sound historiography methodologically allows us to open our ears to historical understandings that transpire in the ontological and metaphorical processes of sounding, speaking, musicking, noise making, and silencing. Engaging the sonic register in historiography allows us to observe how colonial urban planning or social relationships transpired in how sound and music in Manila were organized and governed. Who was allowed to speak, and who was not? Who was listened to, or who was even allowed to listen? How was globalization heard, and how was Manila entangled in this polyphony and counterpoints of global sound-ings and imaginations? In the absence of sound recording in the 19th cen-tury, this chapter relies on synesthetic listening to Spanish literature in 19th-century Manila. I hearken us to listen with our literary ear to reverberations of Manila's soundscape from newspaper writings, biographies, documenta-tions of theatrical performances, and José Rizal's novels—our "earwitnesses." In opening our ears to 19th-century Manila, I echo the notion of multiple modernities proposed by sociologist Shmuel Eisenstadt (1999, 283–95). How do we listen to Manilans' imagination of a cosmopolitan postcolonial Philip-pines interwoven with tapestries of European colonial encounters?

Like everywhere in the Spanish Empire, social lives in the cities and vil-lages in early modern Philippines were built *bajo de la campana*—under the bells. The pealing of the church bells governed the social, cultural, and polit-ical spheres of the colony. However, the 19th century would transpose how Manila would listen to itself and its entanglement with the rest of the world. The sound of new mechanized sea and land transportation technologies, the telegraph and telephone, the new architectural structures, and the arrival of international music, theater, and opera companies—all of these recomposed the sonicsphere of Manila.

By 1883, Manila was serviced by five tram lines, its first modern public transport. The horse-drawn streetcars whose hourly sounds of galloping, of wheels running on metal tracks, and of its arrival horn provided the rhythm of urban mobility in the city.[3] The steam engine tram line that ran through Malabon all the way to the working-class suburb of Caloocan opened in 1888 (Legarda 2002, 329). The first telephone line was installed in Manila in 1890. In 1892, the Manila-Dagupan steam train was inaugurated, extending the mechanized transportation farther out of the capital. The U.S. Bureau of Cen-sus documents Manila's population at 176,777 by 1887—twice as many peo-ple compared to the previous decade. Philippine theater historian Cristina Laconico Buenaventura also observed that the theaters in the city doubled in the last two decades of the 19th century, identifying 26 theaters operating all over Manila by 1896 (Buenaventura 2010, 48). These theaters catered to the Manilans with different entertainments ranging from "the usual *teatro español* and *teatro tagalo* to operas, concerts and bullfights" (49). Buenaven-tura notes that Teatro Circo de Zorillo as "the most elegant of them all, catered to the political and social elite" (49)—which would have also hosted the most extravagant performances of operas and zarzuelas of the visiting European opera companies. Manila's entanglement with the global economy created new polyphonies of transcontinental trading. Raw materials from the colonies were shipped to Europe, and manufactured goods, as well as the latest books, fashion, musical scores, and musical instruments, returned to colonial Southeast Asia on the opposite route. The postal ships that delivered the letters from Europe also brought concert musicians, dramatic and music theater companies, and circus troupes to Manila. In the second half of the 19th century, Manila would become a cultural nexus and an important destination of touring and peripatetic theater and music companies that found theater season ticket buyers, an organized musicians' union, and modern theater infrastructures. By the 1880s, Manila saw locally organized opera and zarzuela companies. The zarzuela would develop its own syncretic form—the *sarswela*—and would be crucial in the anti-colonial movement in the 20th century (see Fernandez 1996, 74–94; Tiongson 2010, 150–86; meLê yamomo 2018b).

These new sounds would not only resonate the soundscape of the city. They would also reconfigure how the citizens of Manila tuned their understandings of themselves within nascent globalizing modernities. However, sonic understandings of the modern and the global encountered conflicting receptions and perceptions from the sounding communities and the listening bodies. From reports, biographies, and literary texts by Europeans listening to the sounds of Manila, we hear responses ranging from appreciation and admiration to abjection and disgust. Visitors to the tropics express in different literature their distress toward the sounds of animals and insects, especially when the lights were turned out. An area of disharmony is the sense of familiarities in European music repertoire with the aesthetic difference in local sound culture in Manila. Attending a Catholic mass in suburban Manila in 1885, British Royal Navy officer Henry Ellis observed: "The music . . . is almost invariably very indifferent; the vocal part harsh and discordant" (1859, 243). Visiting Europeans found discordant perceptions in Catholic ritual practices, which they formally recognized but heard aesthetically different. The familiarity implies an uncanny colonial auditory recognition. The European musical form, conventions, and repertoire and the instruments that the native Filipinos had mastered through 300 years of Spanish and Catholic colonization would sound familiar to the European ear. However, the singing—which relies on the singer's body as its instrument—caused cognitive dissonance[4] in the ears and minds of the earwitnesses. Historical listeners also wrote of what to Europeans was discordant mixing of religious and profane music in Catholic rituals. Ellis observed that "the style of instruments that the natives excel in are much better adapted to a '*bayle*' [public dance] than a church" (243). Jesuit priest and historian J. Mallat also noted that "the choice of the airs which they play is not always the most edifying. We have heard in the churches the waltzes of Musard, and the gayest airs of the French comic opera" (quoted in Blair and Robertson 1906, 45:272).

   In this chapter, I will focus on two areas of sonic world making from two different sources. Newspaper reviews and newspaper features written in Spanish give us ears to what theatergoers and concertgoers in the 19th century were hearing. I survey how journalism and literature circulated auditory and musical discourse that were pedagogical in the forming of a listening public sphere in globalizing Manila. I also invite us to draw our ears to auditory reverberations within José Rizal's two novels, *Noli me Tangere* and *El Filibusterismo*, and listen to sonic expressions of how Manilans heard and auditioned their modernities in their global city.

De Todo un Poco

   Colla de espectáculos
   varia y divertida
   zarzuela, opereta
   Circo y mágia *Albina*,
   ¿Y dirán que hay crisis! [. . .]
   ¡¡Y que nos consume
   la Langosta china!!
   Dígalo *Chiarini*,
   y la Compañia,
   de ópera italiana
   (no sus contratistas),
   pues, si no los DIVOS,
   al menos las *divas*
   no pueden quejarse
   de estos suaves climas,
       Pues no digo nada
   de la troupe lírica
   que guía Navarro

á la gloria altísima.
    Ya han ganado tanta
nombradía y guita
que les vino estrecha,
su morada antígua
y se han ido á Tondo . . .
á espaciar la vista.
    Pero la infalible,
la mejor medida,
que pueda decirnos
de manera fija,
si estamos en alza,
si estamos en ruina,
es de Chiarini
la gran *Pitonisa*,
doctora en la ciencia
burlesco-satírica,
pues á la insinuante
llamada Mayística
se van los ahorros de las alcancías,
y puede decirnos
D. Giuseppe al dia
cuántos mejicanos
ruedan por Manila.[5]

In the last quarter of the 19th century, Manila was at the height of what historical musicologist William Summers calls the "golden age" of Manila's cultural scene (n.d.).[6] The poem above appeared in *La Oceañia Española* on April 7, 1889. The city was reverberating with musical activities. Theater managers were raking in fame and profit—amid the sugar crisis.[7] But, more than commenting on the economy, the poem humorously remarks on how the rise and fall of the city's morale were in the hands of the Compañía de Ópera Italiana and circus director extraordinaire Giuseppe Chiarini.

    In the absence of sound recording technology at the time, the primary sources in understanding the vibrant sounds and scenes in Manila are the numerous 19th-century newspapers. Former publisher of the *Manila Daily Bulletin*, which published *History of the Philippine Press*, Carlson Taylor traced the beginning of Philippine newspapers to 1843; many of the early publications, however, were short-lived (1927). These newspapers, written in Spanish, initially served the Hispanic and the Spanish-speaking elites of Manila. The first pages of these newspapers were devoted to reprinting news from Europe. The cover pages echoed the "news of the wars in Europe, debates about nationalism in Paris, the construction of the tunnel in the Alps connecting Bavaria, Switzerland, and Italy, as well as the latest gossips about the European royalties" (meLê yamomo 2018b, 93). Local Manila readers could also read "editorial essays on the issues of nationalism and democracy that were being debated by the rising middle classes in Europe" (93). The "Local" section was initially dedicated to announcements of the arrival of ships, the opening of new shops, or new legislations. By the 1870s, local news expanded into "multiple subsections which included weather forecast, dedicated local religious and military events, local advertisements, as well as announcements and reviews of local music and theatre performances" (93–94). The major dailies also began weekly serializations of Spanish novels or the popular fiction in Europe and the United States, translated into Spanish. In the last quarter of the 19th century, literary figures, scientists, and politicians published poetries and opinions, as well as political, artistic, and scientific treatises in the newspapers.

As Manila became enmeshed in the global network of traveling theater and music troupes, the advertisement sections were filled with announcements of opera, zarzuela, and theater productions and ticket subscriptions. Side by side the announcements, writings that discussed the history and contexts of pieces being performed in Manila—as well as performance reviews and criticisms—became standard fixtures in the newspapers. The rise of specialized sections in the papers also shaped how the Manila audiences listened to these modern musical compositions. Articles and columns were dedicated to biographies of composers and musicians, as well as philosophy and aesthetics of theater and music—particularly by shows running in Manila. An important columnist of the newspaper *El Comercio* was Oscar Camps y Soler. Soler was the organist at the Manila Cathedral and a teacher at the Colegio de Niños Tiples, a prestigious school for boy sopranos in Manila. He trained as a pianist and composer under the masters Theodore Bohler and Guiseppe Mercadante in Italy and was a music teacher in Madrid before moving to Manila (see Fox 1976, 266; "Oscar Camps y Soler" 2008).

Onstage, in the auditorium, on the streets, and on the pages of the newspapers and emerging literary culture, ways of listening were negotiated—from around the world into Manila and from Manila into the world. The traveling opera companies arriving in Manila would hire the local orchestras that previously serviced Manila's different churches. The rise in such demands led to the establishment of a union of musicians in 1885.[8] The negotiations between local and global listening practices also entailed the transculturization of sound cultures. The theaters built in tropical architectures, which enabled air circulation but not soundproofing, allowed the music to be heard from outside. For the *indios*—the natives of the Philippines who are the poorest in the Spanish colonial *casta* (race and class) system[9]—who could not afford the tickets, this allowed for them to hear the latest opera plots and melodies from Europe.[10]

In 1887, local composer and conductor Ladislao Bonus founded a local opera company that Spanish theater historian Wenceslao Emilio Retana described as composed entirely of singers and musicians from "*tagalos de la mas pura cepa*" (Tagalogs of the purest stock) (1909, 155–56). Bonus would also compose and perform the first Tagalog opera, *Sangdugong Panaguinip*, in 1904. The revival of the Spanish zarzuela in Madrid in the second half of the 19th century also found an enthusiastic audience in Manila. The scores and play-texts of the operas and zarzuelas, advertised in the newspapers, were also available to Manila's literate audiences. By the turn of the century, zarzuela was indigenized into the local *sarswela*—performed in the different vernacular languages in the Philippine archipelago—and would eventually become instrumental in the Philippine nationalist project (Tiongson 2010, 152–53; see also Fernandez 1977; 1993, 320–43).

In the novel *El Filibusterismo*, José Rizal takes us inside a Manila theater, which is probably based on Teatro de Variedades built in 1878 (Camagay 1992, 135). Zacarias Deplace leased the theater for his French theater company in the 1870s, which Rizal himself would have attended during his studies in Manila.

The interior of the theater presented a lively aspect. It was filled from top to bottom, with people standing in the corridors and in the aisles, fighting to withdraw a head from some hole where they had inserted it, or to shove an eye between a collar and an ear. The open boxes, occupied for the most part by ladies, looked like baskets of flowers, whose petals—the fans—shook in a light breeze, wherein hummed a thousand bees. However, just as there are flowers of strong or delicate fragrance, flowers that kill and flowers that console, so from our baskets were exhaled like emanations: there were to be heard dialogues, conversations, remarks that bit and stung. Three or four

boxes, however, were still vacant, in spite of the lateness of the hour. The performance had been advertised for half-past eight and it was already a quarter
to nine, but the curtain did not go up, as his Excellency had not yet arrived. . . .
In the reserved seats, where the ladies seemed to be afraid to venture, as few
were to be seen there, a murmur of voices prevailed amid suppressed laughter
and clouds of tobacco smoke. They discussed the merits of the players and
talked scandal, wondering if his Excellency had quarreled with the friars, if
his presence at such a show was a defiance or mere curiosity. Others gave
no heed to these matters, but were engaged in attracting the attention of the
ladies, throwing themselves into attitudes more or less interesting and statu-
esque, flashing diamond rings, especially when they thought themselves the
foci of insistent opera-glasses, while yet another would address a respectful
salute to this or that señora or señorita. (Rizal 1912a, 195–96)[11]

The restless auditorium is punctuated by the protestations of the gallery gods:
"Impatient and uncomfortable in their seats, [they] started a racket, clapping
their hands and pounding the floor with their canes. Boom—boom—boom!
Ring up the curtain! Boom—boom—boom!" (195).[12] We hear in this auditorium a polyphony of genders, classes, and races of Manila's listening public.
The opera would not begin until the fashionably late elite box subscribers had
taken their seats. In the meantime, the noise increased.

The orchestra played another waltz, the audience protested, when fortunately
there arose a charitable hero to distract their attention and relieve the man-
ager, in the person of a man who had occupied a reserved seat and refused
to give it up to its owner . . . The artillerymen in the gallery began to sing
out encouragement to the usurper. . . . Hisses were heard . . . the galloping of
horses resounded and the stir increased. One might have said that a revolution had broken out, or at least a riot, but no, the orchestra had suspended
the waltz and was playing the royal march: it was his Excellency, the Captain-
General and Governor of the islands, who was entering. . . . The artillerymen
then became silent and the orchestra tore into the prelude. (196–97)[13]

Here, we get aural impressions of Manila's colonial society inside the auditorium. The chapter allows us to hear the sounds made by the audiences from
different social hierarchies and places within the theater. We hear the orches-
tral waltz of placation, the silencing and social policing of human sounds in
the theater vis-à-vis the nonverbal sounds of protestations, and the auditory
imposition of state power through its anthem.

"¡Esta Noche Oirá Filipinas El Estallido, Que Convertirá En Escombros El Informe Monumento!"

The sonic experience of global modernities within Manila's theaters and in how its citizens heard their city as a stage of this global imagination resonated in the literature of the time. José Rizal's novels, in particular, made audible the sound of Manila's streets, theaters, and articulations and silencings of emergent anti-colonial voices. Rizal was a member of the Filipino Propaganda movement and a proponent of political reforms for the Philippines as a colony under Spain.

In the same auditorium in the chapter of *El Filibusterismo* above, everyone was listening to the operetta in French and to cancan music from Paris: the Spanish elites, artillerymen, mestizo university students, and, taking into account their inability to buy tickets, the Filipino working class, who were catching the free concert from outside the theater. "'Quoi v'la tous les cancans d'la s'maine!' sang Gertrude, a proud damsel, who was looking roguishly askance at the Captain-General" (Rizal 1912a, 199). Outside the theater, Rizal opens our ears in *Noli me Tangere* to Arroceros Cigar Factory, which "resounded with the noise of the cigar-makers pounding the tobacco leaves . . . [whose] strong odor which about five o'clock in the afternoon used to float all over the Puente de Barcas" (Jose Rizal 1912b, 211).[14] His aural accounts draw cosmopolitan comparisons between Manila and Madrid, where "the lively conversations and the repartee of the crowds from the cigar factories carried him back to the district of Lavapiés in Madrid, with its riots of cigar-makers, so fatal for the unfortunate policemen" (211–12).[15] In *El Filibusterismo*, the reader is taken on board the steamer *Tabo*, whose "whistle shrieks at every moment, hoarse and commanding like a tyrant who would rule by shouting, so that no one on board can hear his own thoughts" (Rizal 1912a, 6).[16] Or is brought to the Chinese *panciteria* (noodle restaurant), where the boisterous voices of the university students are punctuated by the "sizzling of the grease in the frying-pan" (233). As sounds of urbanity envelope 19th-century Manila, so do its citizens begin to hear and engage their understanding of noise. British physicist G. W. C. Kaye stated in 1931 that "noise is sound that is 'out of place'" (quoted in Bijsterveld 2008, 240). Such engagement, however, entails both its acoustic manifestation and how society understood it metaphorically. Sound historian Hillel Schwartz argues that the understanding of how "noise itself has been transformed this century from the acoustic to the metaphorical" helps us understand how societies organize sounds (2004, 53). In synesthetically listening further to sonic reverberations in Philippine

Spanish literature, John Cage makes an observation that attunes us to what the writers were listening to and how they were listening: "Wherever we are what we hear is mostly noise. . . . When we ignore it, it disturbs us. When we listen to it, we find it fascinating" (1991).

In *Noli me Tangere*, Crisóstomo Ibarra, the novel's protagonist, has just returned to Manila upon learning about his father's death after seven years of studying in Europe. In chapter 5, Ibarra sits in melancholic thought of his father's tragic death. Across the river from his hotel room, "gay strains of music, largely from stringed instruments, were borne across the river even to his room" (Rizal 1912b, 72). Through Ibarra, Rizal echoes scenes from his impressions of European opera productions: seeing "with his opera glasses what was going on in that atmosphere of light, he would have been charmed with one of those magical and fantastic spectacles, the like of which is sometimes seen in the great theaters of Europe" (72).[17] The spectacular musicscape and dramaturgy of an orientalist European opera are counterpointed with the specters of the empire in the abject scenario of the Spanish colonial capital: "To the subdued strains of the orchestra there seems to appear in the midst of a shower of light, a cascade of gold and diamonds in an Oriental setting, a deity wrapped in misty gauze, a sylph enveloped in a luminous halo, who moves forward apparently without touching the floor" (72).[18]

I drew from *Noli me Tangere* and *El Filibusterism*, Rizal's two novels, aural descriptions of Manila's entanglements with the globalizing circulation of music, opera, and zarzuela. Within the melodramatic convention of his time, Rizal crafts in *Noli me Tangere* a deftly written tragedy where the novel's personae follow their irreversible tragic fates within an inescapable colonial machinery in rural San Diego. In its sequel, Ibarra vengefully returns disguised as the wealthy jeweler Simoun. *El Filibusterismo* follows through the lives of *Noli*'s surviving characters. *El Filibusterismo* is published 14 years after *Noli* in Gent. *El Filibusterismo* pulsates with an urban tempo and a cosmopolitan outlook as its scenes unfold primarily in Manila and introduce new characters of young, vibrant university students. *El Filibusterismo*'s plot is a multi-gear engine of frustrated and disgruntled Manilans injured by the colonial system winding up toward an armed revolution financed by the vindictive Simoun.

In *El Filibusterismo*, we hear the polemics of reform and revolution. The idealist Isagani envisions: "Tomorrow we shall be citizens of the Philippines, whose destiny will be a glorious one" (Rizal 1912a, 225).[19] Effusing to his beloved Paulita Gomez, we hear from Isagani a sensuous dream of a modern

Philippines: "I hear the steam hiss, the trains roar, the engines rattle! I see the smoke rise—their heavy breathing; I smell the oil—the sweat of monsters busy at incessant toil" (225).[20] Influenced by Harriet Beecher Stowe's *Uncle Tom's Cabin* and the abolitionist movement, Rizal's reformist ideology advocates for the voice of the Philippines through its representation in the Spanish parliament. Through such reform, he envisions the abolition of the slave system of *polo y servicios* and the enactment of the legal treatment of Filipinos and Spaniards as equals, which would give Filipinos rights to participate in the government. Isagani elaborates this worldly vision:

> Free from the system of exploitation, without hatred or distrust, the people will labor because then labor will cease to be a despicable thing, it will no longer be servile, imposed upon a slave. Then the Spaniard will not embitter his character with ridiculous pretensions of despotism, but with a frank look and a stout heart we shall extend our hands to one another, and commerce, industry, agriculture, the sciences, will develop under the mantle of liberty, with wise and just laws, as in prosperous England. (225)[21]

Simoun's revolution, however, is brutal—accomplished with the modern warfare technology of the time, inaugurated by the deafening explosion of nitroglycerin. To Simoun, the dynamite disguised as a lamp symbolizes the "concentrated tears, repressed hatred, wrongs, injustice, outrage. It's the last resort of the weak, force against force, violence against violence" (290).[22] In his plan, "the most dangerous tyrants will be blown to pieces, the irresponsible rulers that hide themselves behind God and the State, whose abuses remain unpunished because no one can bring them to justice" (290).[23] He declares that the rebellion was to be announced by an "explosion that will convert into rubbish the formless monument whose decay I have fostered" (290).[24] The thunderous sound will resound through the city, and its report "will have been heard in the country round, in the mountains, in the caves" (290).[25] It would herald Simoun's war:

> Upon hearing the explosion, the wretched and the oppressed, those who wander about pursued by force, will sally forth armed to join Cabesang Tales in Santa Mesa, whence they will fall upon the city, while the soldiers, whom I have made to believe that the General is shamming an insurrection in order to remain, will issue from their barracks ready to fire upon whomsoever I may designate. Meanwhile, the crowed populace, thinking that the hour of

massacre has come, will rush out prepared to kill or be killed, and as they have neither arms nor organization, you with some others will put yourself at their head and direct them to the warehouses of Quiroga, where I keep my rifles. Cabesang Tales and I will join one another in the city and take possession of it, while you in the suburbs will seize the bridges and throw up barricades, and then be ready to come to our aid to butcher not only those opposing the revolution but also every man who refuses to take up arms and join us. (291)[26]

The mutiny, however, would be snuffed hastily, in silence. An unidentified figure swiftly seized the lamp and threw it into the river. "The whole thing happened in a second and the dining-kiosk was left in darkness. The lamp had already struck the water before the servants could cry out" (306–7).[27] We deduce the intruder to be Isagani trying to save the life of Paulita Gomez. "The figure, more agile than they, had already mounted the balustrade and before a light could be brought, precipitated itself into the river, striking the water with a loud splash" (307).[28]

Thus, rather than building toward a crescendo of a deafening explosion, it was in the muting of Simoun's bomb that the ideological dispute of diplomatic reform and armed revolution in Rizal's novel culminated.

Coda

Manila's 300 years of imperial relations to Spain and its long trading history in the Indian and Pacific Oceans made it an important cultural nexus by the 19th century connecting the Asia-Pacific to the rest of the world. Manila was the place to hear the European operas, zarzuelas, and concerts—in their full orchestration. Manila too was the source of musicians who played in the municipal bands in its neighboring Asian cities (meLê yamomo 2015, 2018a). The aural experience of 19th-century global modernities and Manila's role in it were documented in Spanish newspaper writings, poems, and novels. The local dailies published not just advertisements of upcoming music and theater performances. They were also sources of detailed background, dramaturgy, and history of the opera, zarzuela, and dramatic productions playing on the local stage. From Rizal's novels, we also hear reverberations of sonic world making by citizens of Manila in how they heard modernity and in how Manila was a stage in the performance of this early globalization. In reading Rizal's words in print, we listen to the auditioning of Philippine modernity inside the theaters, on the streets, and on the world stage. The competing sounds and noises were not necessarily harmonious in how anti-colonial voices were heard or silenced.

Notes

1. José Rizal, *El Filibusterismo* (Gent: Boekdrukkerij F. Meyer-van Loo, 1891), 466.

2. For a historical context of the sociopolitical and economic shift brought about by the opening of the Suez Canal, see Osterhammel 2014. Its impact on Philippine politics and economy is discussed in Chang 2016, 305–22; Legarda 2002. I discuss the Philippines' and Southeast Asia's interconnection with the 19th-century global cultural network from 1869 in meLê yamomo 2017, 2018b.

3. Dita Kinney, the superintendent of the US Army Nurse Corps, reported in 1902 her observations of the Manila public trams during a one-month visit to Manila: "Manila's rapid (!) transit facilities consist of a car drawn by ponies which, by contrast, look hardly larger than rats. The following graphically and truthfully describes this service: 'It starts nowhere, goes nowhere, and runs when and where it pleases. Nobody who is interested in reaching any particular point at any particular time ever thinks of using it.' The approach of the car is announced by a peculiar little whining whistle blown by the driver. To the uninitiated this sounds like one of those toy combination whistles and balloons which children inflate with breath." See Kinney 1902, 32–38.

4. The notion of cognitive dissonance is coined by Leon Festinger to refer to psychological discomfort felt in response to two or more conflicting cognitions, such as values, beliefs, ideas, or cultural practices. See Eysenck 1963.

5. *La Oceanía Española*, April 7, 1889.

6. I am grateful to Prof. William Summers for allowing me to use his digital archive of 19th-century newspapers in Manila housed at the University of Santo Tomas Heritage Library in Manila.

7. In the last decades of the 1880s, a sugar crisis hit the Philippines, causing the biggest American firm, Peele, Hubbel & Co., in Manila to declare bankruptcy in 1887 and face lawsuits for another two years. See Legarda 2002, 320–25.

8. Unión Artístico-Musical, "Reglamento De La Sociedad De Conciertos," 1885.

9. For further discussion on the class and race in the colonial Philippine society, see Agoncillo 1977.

10. An advertisement of *Las amazonas del Tormes* at the Teatro de Tondo indicated a ticket charge being imposed on audiences who were listening from outside the theater: "Los que vayan para oir la funcion desde la calle pagarán solamente una peseta, pero siendo oyentes en carruage, media entrada." (Those who go to hear the performance from the street shall pay only a peseta, but those listeners in carriages, half the entrance fee.) *La Oceanía Española*, January 10, 1885.

11. From the original Spanish: "El aspecto que ofrecía el teatro era animadísimo; estaba lleno de bote en bote, y en la entrada general, en los pasillos se veía mucha gente de pié, pugnando por sacar la cabeza ó meter un ojo entre un cuello y una oreja. Los palcos descubiertos, llenos en su mayor parte de señoras, parecían canastillas de flores, cuyos pétalos agitára una leve brisa (hablo de los abanicos), y en donde zumban insectos mil. Solo que

como hay flores de delicado y fuerte perfume, flores que matan y flores que consuelan, en las canastillas de nuestro teatro tambien se aspiran perfumes parecidos, se oyen diálogos, conversaciones, frases que pican ó corroen. Solo tres ó cuatro de los palcos estaban aun vacíos apesar de lo avanzado de la hora; para las ocho y media se había anunciado la funcion, eran ya las nueve menos cuarto, y el telon no se levantaba porque S. E. no había llegado todavía. . . . En las butacas—á donde parece que temen bajar las señoras tan no se ve á ninguna—reina un murmullo de voces, de risas reprimidas, entre nubes de humo. . . . Discuten el mérito de las artistas, hablan de escándalos, si S. E. ha reñido con los frailes, si la presencia del General en semejante espectáculo es una provocacion ó sencillamente una curiosidad; otros no piensan en estas cosas, sino en cautivar las miradas de las señoras adoptando posturas más ó menos interesantes, más ó menos estatuarias, haciendo jugar los anillos de brillantes, sobre todo cuando se creen observados por insistentes gemelos; otros dirigen respetuosos saludos á tal señora ó señorita." Rizal 1891, 380–82.

12. From the original Spanish: "impacientes é incómodos en sus asientos, armaban un alboroto pataleando y golpeando el suelo con sus bastones. '—¡Bum-bum-bum! ¡que se abra el telon! ¡bum-bum-bum!'" Rizal 1891, 380–81.

13. From the original Spanish: "La orquesta toca otro vals, el público protesta; afortunadamente se presenta un héroe caritativo que distrae la atencion y redime al empresario; es un señor que ha ocupado una butaca y se niega á cederla á su dueño. . . . Los guardias, teniendo en consideracion la categoría del rebelde. . . . Resuenan silbidos . . . se oye galopar de caballos, se nota movimiento; cualquiera diría que ha estallado una revolucion ó cuando menos un motin; no, la orquesta suspende el vals y toca la marcha real; es S. E. el Capitan General y Gobernador de las Islas el que llega. . . . Los artilleros se callan entonces y la orquesta ataca la introduccion." Rizal 1891, 382.

14. From the original Spanish: "oir el estruendo que hacen las cigarreras golpeando las hojas . . . acordándose de aquel fuerte olor que á las cinco de la tarde saturaba el Puente de Bargas." Rizal 1902, 132.

15. From the original Spanish: "Las animadas conversaciones, los chistes llevaron maquinalmente su imaginación al barrio de Lavapiés en Madrid con sus motines de cigarreras, tan fatales para los desgraciados guindillas, etc." Rizal 1902, 134–35.

16. From the original Spanish: "El silbato chilla á cada momento, ronco é imponente como un tirano que quiere gobernar á gritos, de tal modo que dentro nadie se entiende." Rizal 1891, 13.

17. From the original Spanish: "hubiese querido ver con la ayuda de unos gemelos lo que pasaba en aquella atmósfera de luz, habría admirado una de esas fantásticas visiones, una de esas apariciones mágicas que á veces se ven en los grandes teatros de Europa." Rizal 1902, 85.

18. From the original Spanish: "en que á las apagadas melodías de una orquesta se veía aparecer en medio de una lluvia de luz, de una cascada de diamantes y oro, en una decoración oriental, envuelta en vaporosa gasa, una deidad, una sílfide que avanza sin tocar casi el suelo." Rizal 1902, 85.

19. From the original Spanish: "Mañana seremos ciudadanos de Filipinas, cuyo destino será hermoso porque estará en amantes manos." Rizal 1891, 435.

20. From the original Spanish: "Oigo el vapor silbar, el traqueteo de los trenes, el

estruendo de las máquinas miro subir el humo, su potente respiración, y aspiro el olor del aceite, el sudor de los monstruos ocupados en incesante faena." Rizal 1891, 436.

21. From the original Spanish: "Libres del sistema de explotacion, sin despechos ni desconfianzas; el pueblo trabajará porque entonces el trabajo dejará de ser infamante, dejará de ser servil, como imposicion al esclavo; entonces el español no agriará su caracter con ridículas pretensiones despóticas y, franca la mirada, robusto el corazon, nos daremos la mano, y el comercio, la industria, la agricultura, las ciencias se desenvolverán al amparo de la libertad y de leyes sabias y equitativas como en la próspera Inglaterra." Rizal 1891, 381–82.

22. From the original Spanish: "¡Son lágrimas concentradas, odios comprimidos, injusticias y agravios! Es la suprema razon del débil, fuerza contra fuerza, violencia contra violencia." Rizal 1891, 563.

23. From the original Spanish: "¡Esta noche volarán pulverizados los tiranos más peligrosos, los tiranos irresponsables, los que se ocultan detrás de Dios y del Estado, y cuyos abusos permanecen impunes porque nadie los puede fiscalizar!" Rizal 1891, 563–64.

24. From the original Spanish: "¡Esta noche oirá Filipinas el estallido, que convertirá en escombros el informe monumento cuya podredumbre he apresurado!" Rizal 1891, 564.

25. From the original Spanish: "la detonacion se habrá oido en las comarcas próximas, en los montes, en las cavernas." Rizal 1891, 566.

26. From the original Spanish: "Al oirse el estallido, los miserables, los oprimidos, los que vagan perseguidos por la fuerza saldrán armados y se reunirán con Cabesang Tales en Santa Mesa para caer sobre la ciudad; en cambio, los militares á quienes he hecho creer que el General simula un alzamiento para tener motivos de permanecer, saldrán de sus cuarteles dispuestos á disparar sobre cualesquiera que designare. El pueblo entretanto, alebrestado, y creyendo llegada la hora de su degüello, se levantará dispuesto á morir, y como no tiene armas ni está organizado, usted con algunos otros se pondrá á su cabeza y los dirigirá á los almacenes del chino Quiroga en donde guardo mis fusiles. Cabesang Tales y yo nos reuniremos en la ciudad y nos apoderaremos de ella, y usted en los arrabales ocupará los puentes, se hará fuerte, estará dispuesto á venir en nuestra ayuda y pasará á cuchillo no solo á la contrarevolucion, ¡sino á todos los varones que se nieguen á seguir con las armas!" Rizal 1891, 566.

27. From the original Spanish: "Todo pasó en un segundo: el comedor se quedó á oscuras. La lámpara ya había caido en el agua cuando los criados pudieron gritar." Rizal 1891, 596.

28. From the original Spanish: "Pero la sombra, más ágil aun, ya había montado sobre la balaustrada de ladrillo y antes que pudiesen traer una luz se precipitaba al río, dejando oir un ruido quebrado al caer en el agua." Rizal 1891, 596–97.

References

Agoncillo, Teodoro A. 1977. *History of the Filipino People*. Quezon City: R. P. Garcia.

Bijsterveld, Karin. 2008. *Mechanical Sound: Technology, Culture, and Public Problems of Noise in the Twentieth Century*. Cambridge, MA: MIT Press.

Blair, Emma Helen, and James Alexander Robertson. 1906. *The Philippine Islands, 1493–1898*. Cleveland: Arthur H. Clark Company.

Buenaventura, Cristina Laconico. 2010. *The Theater in Manila, 1846-1946*. 2nd ed. Manila: De La Salle University Press.

Cage, John. 1991. "The Future of Music: Credo (1937)." In *John Cage: An Anthology*, edited by Richard Kostelanetz. New York: De Capo Press.

Camagay, Ma. Luisa T. 1992. *Kasaysayang Panlipunan Ng Maynila, 1765-1898*. Quezon City: Maria Luisa T. Camagay.

Chang, Julia. 2016. "Between Intimacy and Enmity: Spain and the Philippines Post-Suez." *Journal of Spanish Cultural Studies* 17 (4): 305–22. https://doi.org/10.1080/14636204 .2016.1240884

Clossey, Luke. 2006. "Merchants, Migrants, Missionaries, and Globalization in the Early-Modern Pacific." *Journal of Global History* 1 (1): 41. https://doi.org/10.1017/S174002 2806000039

Eisenstadt, S. N. 1999. "Multiple Modernities in an Age of Globalization." *Canadian Journal of Sociology/Cahiers Canadiens de Sociologie* 24 (2): 283–95. https://doi.org/10.23 07/3341732

Ellis, Henry T. 1859. *Hong Kong to Manilla and the Lakes of Luzon, in the Philippines*. London: Smith, Elder.

Eysenck, H. J. 1963. "A Theory of Cognitive Dissonance: Leon Festinger." *Journal of Psychosomatic Research* 7 (1): 66. https://doi.org/10.1016/0022-3999(63)90061-8

Fernandez, Doreen G. 1977. *The Iloilo Zarzuela: 1903-1930*. Quezon City: Ateneo de Manila University Press.

Fernandez, Doreen G. 1993. "Zarzuela to Sarswela: Indigenization and Transformation." *Philippine Studies* 41 (3): 320–43.

Fernandez, Doreen G. 1996. "Zarzuela to Sarswela." In *Palabas: Essays on Philippine Theatre History*, 74–94. Quezon City: Ateneo de Manila University Press.

Flynn, Dennis O., and Arturo Giráldez. 1995. "Born with a 'Silver Spoon': The Origin of World Trade in 1571." *Journal of World History* 6 (2): 201–21. https://www.jstor.org /stable/20078638

Flynn, Dennis Owen, and Arturo Giraldez. 2002. "Cycles of Silver: Global Economic Unity through the Mid-Eighteenth Century." *Journal of World History* 13 (2): 391–427. https://doi.org/10.1353/jwh.2002.0035

Flynn, Dennis, and Arturo Giráldez. 2004. "Path Dependence, Time Lags and the Birth of Globalization." *European Review of Economic History* 8 (1): 81–108.

Fox, Frederick. 1976. "Philippine Vocational Education: 1860-1898." *Philippine Studies* 24 (3): 261–87.

Kinney, Dita H. 1902. "Glimpses of Life in Manila." *American Journal of Nursing* 3 (1): 32–38.

Legarda, Benito J. 2002. *After the Galleons: Foreign Trade, Economic Change and Entrepreneurship in the Nineteenth Century Philippines*. 1st ed. Quezon City: Ateneo de Manila University Press, in cooperation with the Center for Southeast Asian Studies, University of Wisconsin–Madison.

"Oscar Camps y Soler." 2008. Recuperación del Patrimonio Cultural de Adra. http://www .adracultural.es/html/6personajes_ilustres/blasco/camps.shtml#

Osterhammel, Jürgen. 2014. *The Transformation of the World: A Global History of the Nineteenth Century*. Translated by Patrick Camiller. Princeton: Princeton University Press.

Retana, Wenceslao Emilio. 1909. *Noticias Histórico-Bibliográficas de El Teatro En Filipinas Desde Sus Origínes Hasta 1898*. Madrid: Librería de V. Suárez.

Rizal, José. 1891. *El Filibusterismo*. Gent: Boekdrukkerij F. Meyer-van Loo.

Rizal, José. 1902. *Noli Me Tángere*. Barcelona: Casa Editorial Maucci.

Rizal, José. 1912a. *The Reign of Greed: A Complete English Version of El Filibusterismo from the Spanish of José Rizal*. Translated by Charles Derbyshire. Manila: Philippine Education Company.

Rizal, Jose. 1912b. *The Social Cancer (A Complete English Version of Noli Me Tangere from the Spanish c. 1885)*. Translated by Charles Derbyshire. New York: World Book.

Schwartz, Hillel. 2004. "On Noise." In *Hearing History: A Reader*, edited by Mark M Smith, 51–53. Athens: University of Georgia Press.

Smith, Mark M. 2004. *Hearing History: A Reader*. Athens: University of Georgia Press.

Summers, William. *Repairing the Fractured Mirror: A Chronicle and Source Book Devoted to the Performing Arts in Manila, 1848–1898*. n.d.

Taylor, Carlson. 1927. *History of the Philippine Press*. Manila: Philippine Revolutionary Press.

Tiongson, Nicanor G. 2010. "A Short History of the Philippine Sarsuwela (1879-2009)." *Philippine Humanities Review* 11/12: 150–86.

yamomo, meLê. 2015. "Brokering Sonic Modernities: Migrant Manila Musicians in the Asia Pacific, 1881–1948." *Popular Entertainment Studies* 6 (2): 22–37.

yamomo, meLê. 2017. "Global Currents, Musical Streams: European Opera in Colonial Southeast Asia." *Nineteenth Century Theatre and Film* 44 (1).

yamomo, meLê. 2018a. "Echoing Musical Modernities: Filipino Migrant Musicians from the 19th Century to the Present." In *Saysay Himig: A Sourcebook on Philippine Music History 1880–1941*, edited by Arwin Q. Tan, 265–70. Quezon City: University of the Philippines Press.

yamomo, meLê. 2018b. *Theatre and Music in Manila and the Asia Pacific, 1869–1946: Sounding Modernities*. Cham: Palgrave Macmillan.

PART IV

Anti-Colonial Writings in the Colonial Language

Brazo, corazón, y lengua

Immigration and Anti-Colonial Biopolitics in the Spanish Caribbean and the Philippines

Ernest Rafael Hartwell

Embodied Synecdoches: An Introduction

Bodily metaphors are common in late 19th-century "national novels" of the Hispanophone Caribbean and the Philippines, two colonial regions that remained under Spanish rule long after the Latin American wars of independence, before each region was subsequently reassigned to the United States' sphere of influence around 1898. For example, José Rizal's novel *Noli me tangere* (1887) chronicles the "social cancer" that afflicts the colonial Philippines, and Manuel Zeno Gandía's novel *La charca: Crónicas de un mundo enfermo* (1894) uses sickness as a metaphor for social problems or "ills" that "plague" Puerto Rico.[1] Not surprisingly, extensive research exists on bodily metaphors, medical discourse, and projects of nation building in these regions.[2] This chapter, however, centers on a less studied form of figurative speech: embodied synecdoches employed to refer to immigrant bodies and politics of immigration used in the late 19th and early 20th centuries by anti-colonial writers from Puerto Rico, the Philippines, and Cuba. In particular, the following sections examine three synecdoches: *brazo, corazón, y lengua* (arm, heart, and tongue); not just the whole immigrant but entire communities of immigrants and related constructions of economics and culture and biology are evoked when these writers—José Julián de Acosta of Puerto Rico, Trinidad Pardo de Tavera of the Philippines, and José Martí of Cuba—refer to the aforementioned body parts. The synecdoches remain suspended between the literal and the figurative, between the part and the whole, just as these three regions remained suspended between colonized status and national ambitions, not to mention between emerging and receding empires.

These embodied synecdoches are different from the descriptive, corporeal metaphors of national novels, which are rhetorical and critical. In contrast, Acosta's, Pardo's, and Martí's embodied synecdoches about immigrants are prescriptive. They propose specific political projects and aim to dictate the movement and meaning of bodies along and across their countries' borders. The three synecdoches point to distinct yet interrelated biopolitical desires that respond to and redirect debates on immigration in these island regions, highlighting less evident continuity in anti-colonial writings from the still remaining Spanish colonies in the Pacific and the Caribbean. This chapter traces the intersection of biopolitics and anti-colonial thought in these turn-of-the-century writings about immigration, building off of the principle that the study of biopolitics would be incomplete without analyzing its function within colonial contexts. Furthermore, and more centrally, this chapter investigates contradictions in liberal politics by wielding the concepts of biopolitics to examine which aspects of colonialism are challenged and which are perpetuated through Caribbean and Philippine anti-colonial writing of the turn of the 20th century.[3]

Biopolitics and the Colonies

Biopolitics refers to the philosophical concept most prominently investigated by Michel Foucault and Giorgio Agamben. Foucault asserts that in 17th-century Europe a shift occurred from the rule of sovereign power to the regime of biopower, or from sovereignty's right "to take life or let live" to biopower's right to "'make' live and 'let' die" (2003, 240–41). The technologies that bolster biopower include treating man-as-body in order to discipline the individual and promote more efficient labor, and treating man-as-species, which seeks to regulate "the birth rate, the mortality rate, longevity . . . together with . . . related economic and political problems" (242–43).[4] Recent critics, including Achille Mbembe and Roberto Esposito, have challenged and translated these ideas from within colonial/neocolonial contexts, asserting that by overlooking the work of colonialism in regimenting races and bodies, Foucault and Agamben "dehistoricize" biopolitics.[5] This chapter builds off Mbembe's and Esposito's critiques of biopolitics, going beyond the examination of how colonizers enact biopolitical practices (for example, through the *encomienda*, slave trade and slavery, or the population control of the Bourbon reforms) and focusing on the role biopolitical discourse plays in anti-colonial politics, specifically in the cultural and political writings of educated elites.

Using the methods of close reading and historical contextualization of journalistic essays, historiographical writings, and politically infused travel narratives, I argue that despite surface-level divergences, anti-colonial discourses about immigration from the Spanish Caribbean and the Philippines are largely rooted in similar biopolitical debates and desires. Among the debates: Does immigration represent an act of disruption or restoration? Which immigrants help and which hurt the projects of anti-colonial resistance and nation building? Through examining three works of anti-colonial writing that redirect these debates, this chapter concludes that a paradoxical biopolitical desire consistent on the antipodal ends of Spain's waning empire was that ideal immigrants enhance a country not by bringing something new to it but rather by making the host country become more like itself.

Debates on Immigration

Responding to the independence of former Spanish colonies in Latin America, Spain sought to defray losses in three of its remaining colonies: Cuba, Puerto Rico, and the Philippines. In brief, the Spanish opened the previously limited tobacco cultivation and trade in the Philippines, a move called the "desestanco" (Pérez Serrano 1998, 29), while aggressively promoting the sugar industry in the Caribbean at first by increasing the importation of enslaved peoples and later by promoting immigration (Schmidt-Nowara 1999, 128). Economic restructuring led to the promotion of immigration by the colonial authorities in the Caribbean and the Philippines, which was met with ambivalence by anti-colonial critics.

In Cuba, there was a deep connection between projects of immigration and abolitionist discourse. Such a connection is made evident as early as 1809, when Juan José Díaz de Espada suggested that Cuba invite European immigration as part of a project of economic and demographic renovation, or, in other words, a project of agricultural diversification and racial uniformity rooted in whitening miscegenation. Espada was the bishop of Havana and director of the Sociedad Económica de Amigos del País, a group including the likes of José Antonio Saco and Ramón de la Sagra that promoted liberal ideas, seeking to distance Cuba from the plantation model and promoting "colonización blanca," or the settling of Cuba's interior by free, white laborers who cultivated more than just sugar (Naranjo Orovio and García González 1996, 54–56). A debate ensued about which white populations to allow to immigrate. While on the one hand, some championed "all kinds of immigrants or settlers provided they were white," on the other hand, the likes of Ángel Fernández-Caro asserted that the ideal immigrant worker came from a less "fair" white nation or a "golden-brown race," like the people of southern Spain and the Canary Islands; Fernández-Caro "proved" his point using scientifically inflected reasons involving immunology, climate compatibility, and appetite (Naranjo Orovio 1998, 309–11). Subsequent debates included the question of contracted Asian immigrant workers who had supplemented enslaved labor in Cuba since 1847, only to be banned from immigrating in 1871 (311–15). The question was not only if Asian immigration was profitable for Cuba but also which Asians to allow to immigrate, or as Consuelo Naranjo Orovio distills the question, which Asians were "barbarians" and which were "civilized": for example, the Buddhist Chinese mostly male immigrants versus the Christian Annamites who immigrated as families (314–15).

In total, the Cuban debate about immigration accompanied the rise of Darwinism in the 19th century, elites employing scientific discourse to shape politics in their favor (Naranjo Orovio 1998, 303–5). For example, scientific racial discourse was used to defend slavery up to the 1870s, with defenders of slavery arguing that white men were incapable of acclimating themselves to hard labor in the tropics. However, when the slave trade was limited and eventually prohibited, nearly identical scientific theories, not rooted in new evidence, defended specific white communities' strength at hard labor, suggesting even that the best workers were mixed-race "offspring" of immigrants systematically "breeding" with freed slaves (308). As Naranjo Orovio asserts, these dehumanizing debates illustrate how the science employed in such claims is often based more on convenience of argument than on scientific rigor.

Similarly, in Puerto Rico, elites debated on how to develop and adapt the economic apparatus of the island given the disintegration of the established order, which had been predicated on enslaved labor (Álvarez Curbelo 2001, 182). Through the 1815 "Real Cédula de Gracias," the Spanish colonial authorities aimed to attract European immigrants to Puerto Rico, guaranteeing them land, naturalization, freedom of return to Europe, reduced taxes, and the right to bring enslaved African people with them. Since the imposition of this colonial policy, debates emerged around the need for immigration to Puerto

Rico and which immigrants were ideal immigrants (Cifre de Loubriel 1964, 33). Many argued that the prohibition of the slave trade in the 1820s (Ramos Mattei 1981, 127) and the spread of disease on the island (Cifre de Loubriel 1964, 37) had led to a shortage of laborers, which necessitated, in addition to immigrants from Europe, the immigration of *"indios"* from the Yucatán peninsula, free black people from neighboring Caribbean countries or from Africa, and "coolies" from China and India (Ramos Mattei 1981, 129). Others contested this position, asserting that the work shortage was a misconception, that the free working class had grown since 1815, and that they would be victimized by the indolent immigrants "from other latitudes" (Ramos Mattei 1981, 129–30; García 2015, 48). These Puerto Rican opponents to nonwhite immigration compared themselves consistently with Cuba, which "benefitted" from greater white immigration and "suffered" from greater immigration from China and India (García 2015, 49).[6]

The debates about immigration in the Philippines featured the Chinese immigrant to an even greater extent. Imported Chinese laborers had played a role in Philippine politics since contracted rowers revolted against and killed the governor-general of the Philippines on a 1593 naval mission to Ternate (Morga 1609, 30; Hartwell 2018, 63). Despite the Chinese Filipinos developing over the centuries into a relatively powerful minority, the colonial authorities maintained a wariness before Chinese immigrants and settlers well into the 19th century. This wariness manifested itself through policies of limited entry, as well as social and political restrictions to the Chinese already in the Philippines (Fradera 1999, 148). Additionally, there was a limited number of intercolonial migrations mostly from New Spain—recruited Novohispanic soldiers, convicted criminals, and leaders of the Mexican independence movement like Epigmenio González (García de los Arcos 1996, 16–17). However, the opening of the Philippine tobacco industry, in combination with the difficulty of attracting European and intercolonial immigrants to the Philippines, led to a change in official colonial policy toward Chinese immigrants (Pérez Serrano 1998, 29–30). The colonial government shifted to a policy rooted in stimulating immigration, eliminating restrictions, and promoting economic opportunities for immigrating Chinese (Wickberg 1965, 48). Despite the colonial authorities shifting their position toward immigration, many *"naturales,"* or native-born peoples of mostly Malay descent, clung to xenophobia, critiquing Chinese behaviors and economics and any policies that might support them (Pérez Serrano 1998, 30).[7] These native voices made claims similar to those of pro-Spanish peninsular writers like Wenceslao Retana and Pablo Feced, both of whom also famously attacked the *ilustrados* throughout the Propaganda movement. Retana and Feced disparaged Chinese mestizos as an idolatrous racial menace, in part as a response to the Chinese mestizos having gained substantial political awareness and prestige throughout the late 18th and 19th centuries (Rodao 2018, 431). The polemical aspect of Chinese immigration is most clearly observed in journalistic debates carried out for months at a time in the 1880s between two local newspapers. *El Comercio* argued that Chinese immigrants and residents in the Philippines were victims of ostracization at the hands of the Spaniards and *"naturales,"* having to isolate themselves as a defense mechanism, while *La Oceanía Española* asserted that the Chinese enjoyed economic success, accumulated power, and refused to assimilate to local culture, displacing the *"naturales." La Oceanía Española* argued that these *"naturales"* were the "real" victims of the presence of the Chinese in the Philippines, in the workplace, in the neighborhoods of Manila, and in the arena of political influence (Pérez Serrano 1998, 22–23).[8]

This question of the politics of assimilation dominates Acosta's, Pardo's, and Martí's writings on immigration, which diverge in different ways from the terms of these debates established above. This can be seen in the following section on the Puerto Rican Acosta's writings about *brazos*. He is not entirely consistent in his responses to the question of *brazos*, a term commonly used in Spanish that symbolically reduces the human being to its function as laborer through the bodily synecdoche of the appendage that shoulders much of that work, the "arm." Tracing his use of the term over time, one observes a shift in Acosta's views on immigration, a shift, however, that never strays from racialized and biologically deterministic ideas about work, morality, and education.

Brazos and Biopolitics

José Julián de Acosta was a renowned Puerto Rican abolitionist, naturalist, education advocate, and political commentator who studied in Europe in the 1840s (Vázquez 1986, 261). Acosta's politics could be categorized principally as abolitionist and reformist, having represented Puerto Rico alongside 27 other Puerto Ricans, Filipinos, and Cubans on the 1866–67 Junta Informativa de Reformas, in which he advocated for abolitionism and participated in conversations about systemic change and self-government that would eventually evolve into the Autonomist Party platform of the later 19th century

(Vázquez 1986, 261; Ángeles Castro 1995, 10). Scholars, like Carmen Vásquez, traditionally consider Acosta a bold and progressive thinker, whose views on race, which were a product of his time, do not define his politics and legacy (1986, 265). Vásquez is correct in asserting that Acosta's ideas are progressive for 1853; they should not be dismissed just because the racial views that he espouses do not radically transcend those of his time. However, Acosta's contributions to debates on immigration show that race is not a sidenote but rather a central biopolitical legacy of colonialism that pervades his anticolonial writings.

In 1853, in the midst of a period of economic struggle for the Puerto Rican sugar industry, Acosta published an article in the *Boletín Mercantil de Puerto Rico* called "Cuestión de brazos." The economic problems, which began in the 1840s and continued through the 1860s, were rooted in the fact that Puerto Rico had consolidated its agricultural apparatus in sugar and global sugar prices had subsequently dropped, causing nearly all sugar plantations, except the largest, to disappear (Ramos Mattei 1981, 126). In "Cuestión de brazos," Acosta counters a popular narrative that the crisis, which reduced the number of plantations from 1,500 in 1830 to 500 in 1860, was due to a shortage in the workforce in Puerto Rico, which should in response either further import enslaved people, the trade of whom had been outlawed since 1820 in Puerto Rico, or promote the immigration of Chinese coolie laborers (Ramos Mattei 1981, 126–29). He deliberately presents a series of demographics and statistics, including the large number of urban slaves (whom he considered surplus agricultural workers, implying sufficient rural labor), free laborers' wages (which were low, indicating more supply than demand), and transport rates of enslaved people from Puerto Rico to Cuba (which remained steady throughout the mid-19th century, implying a surplus of workers in Puerto Rico). These numbers show that there are enough free workers in Puerto Rico to continue fighting for the abolition of the slave trade and avoid the importation of Chinese labor (Acosta 1997, 34). Any economic struggle of the island is rooted not in a lack of *brazos* but in a lack of education of those workers, whom Acosta also refers to as the "*jíbaros*," the idealized term for rural Puerto Ricans famously portrayed in verse by Manuel Alonso in 1845. What would happen to the *jíbaros* if the Chinese immigrated en masse, the "raza de Oriente, muelle por naturaleza, indolente por temperamento, y poco apta por sistema para la civilización occidental, que con la luz del evangelio recibimos de nuestros padres, los esforzados castellanos del siglo 15" (race of the Orient, soft by nature, indolent by temperament, and systematically not very apt for Western civilization, which with the light of the gospel we have received from our fathers, the hardworking Castilians of the 15th century) (34). Acosta was certain that the already difficult *jíbaro* life would only be aggravated by allowing them to work alongside or to be supplemented by the Chinese, who would corrupt and contaminate their morality, efficiency, and race, rooted in Catholic faith and Castilian descendancy.

Looking a little deeper into Acosta's logic, two interrelated biopolitical technologies are encrypted in his essay: the education of laborers to make them more efficient at their work and the preservation, strengthening, and restoration of the moral and racial integrity of the Puerto Rican working class. The education of free laborers, Acosta asserts, will bolster the moral well-being of the working class and make the *brazos* more efficient, increasing, of course, the agricultural output of the island (1997, 34). This prescription of education for the economic ills of Puerto Rico calls to mind Foucault's concept of "anatomo-politics," or the "techniques of power that were essentially centered on the . . . individual body . . . to ensure the spatial distribution of individual bodies . . . to increase their productive force through exercise, drill, and so on" (2003, 242). This education of *brazos* is different from the education of *cabezas*, or heads within Acosta's framework, because the *jíbaros* do not belong to the group of educated whites who, like himself, will "encabezar" or "head" progress through university study and political careers (García 2015, 49). The promotion of basic literacy through primary public instruction will change the attitude of the workers, responding to the complaints of plantation owners that these free workers do not fulfill their contracts for lack of the right attitude (49). In other words, education does not promote social mobility but rather allows for the control of the workers, the rendering of them more efficient, and the rejection of the belief that imported Asian workers will fix the problem. This rejection of coolie immigrant workers is rooted in a preventative form of biopower that considers men as species more than as individuals, Foucault's specific concept of "biopolitics" (2003, 242). Here, Acosta speaks of illness and contagion not on the level of the individual but on the level of the species and races, the Chinese posing a threat to the Puerto Ricans as a whole, "importing vices" and "corrupting" their morality, their efficiency, and their already fraught (in Acosta's view) racial makeup (1997, 34).

These views of the biopolitical effect of potential Chinese immigration to Puerto Rico are rooted in a consistent questioning in Acosta's writings about the possibility and politics of the assimilation of immigrants. In this

context, assimilation speaks to the potential to incorporate fully a new addition into an already existing body or community. The bodily synecdoche used
by Acosta highlights his views of assimilation: why incorporate *brazos* into
the Puerto Rican body when we already have *brazos* that simply need to be
harnessed and controlled through worker education? Too many *brazos*, especially *those brazos*, and your humanity will be compromised and deformed.
Not only do the Chinese immigrants not assimilate, but they do the opposite:
they negatively transform the races they interact with in the host country.
This is, however, not the case for all *brazos* and all assimilation according to
Acosta. In fact, he was an advocate for European immigration. In "Cuestión
de brazos," Acosta compares Puerto Rico with other Caribbean islands where
the prohibition of the slave trade had not "changed the nature of the races"
in those islands, while Puerto Rico, due to European immigration since the
"Real Cédula de Gracias," had expanded its free, white population (1997, 30).[9]
Acosta later changes his tune. In 1866, a series of endnotes, which Acosta
appends to an 18th-century official history of Puerto Rico that he republishes,
articulate abolitionist critiques of the colonial status quo that craftily sidestep
the colonial censor. Among these notes is one that uses demographic analysis
to illustrate how Puerto Rico lagged behind in literacy compared to Cuba
due to Cuba's greater white population and the greater intellectual culture of
these Cuban whites, as compared to Puerto Rican whites (Abbad 2002, 389).[10]
The conclusion he makes in this long endnote is that demographics do not lie,
and in order to increase the quality of life in Puerto Rico, linked inextricably
to its level of literacy, the workers the island imports should also increase the
island's social and intellectual capital (390).

Through this conclusion, Acosta racializes literacy as a uniquely white
capacity, a racialization upon which he structures his entire program for
national resurgence and economic restructuring. This also illuminates nuance
in his views on assimilation. For Acosta, the same phenomenon, the impos-
sibility of immigrant assimilation, leading to the radical, biopolitical transformation of the host country through immigration, can be seen as either a
contamination or a cure, depending on the race of the immigrant.

The politics of assimilation similarly dominates Trinidad Pardo de Tavera's article entitled "Recuerdos de Argentina" (Memories of Argentina), in
which the Filipino's travels to the Buenos Aires serve as a pretext for weighing
in on debates relevant to his home archipelago, debates on culture, modernity, and, of chief interest to this chapter, immigration.

Becoming *Patriotas de Corazón* (Patriots at Heart)

Trinidad Pardo de Tavera visited his brother Felix in Buenos Aires in 1914, publishing two years later a political memoir of his visit called "Recuerdos de Argentina" in the *Philippine Review*, a bilingual journal out of Manila.[11] This memoir includes extensive reflections on immigration that, on the one hand, implicitly dialogue with the reflections on assimilation in Acosta's writings, while diverging with regards to Pardo's inherent identification with the immigrant.

Pardo was the "quintessential Ilustrado" of the Philippines: wealthy, cosmopolitan, of Spanish descent, and controversial (Mojares 2006, 121). He lived his early adult years exiled in Paris in the 1870s and 1880s, due to his uncle's participation in the 1872 Cavite Mutiny (Gasquet 2019, 118; Mojares 2006, 126). Pardo was a subdued participant in the anti-Spanish Propaganda movement of the 1880s and 1890s (Mojares 2006, 132–133), while also collaborating extensively with the early US governorship over the Philippines until 1903 (146). Pardo is most celebrated for his diverse and rigorous contributions to emerging fields of social and natural sciences in the late 19th and early 20th centuries, including his extensive project of tracing the Sanskrit roots of Tagalog words (1887), his curating of the Philippine display at the 1889 Universal Exposition in Paris, his *Plantas medicinales de Filipinas* (1892), his editing and annotating of the 1589 manuscript *Las costumbres de los tagalos* (1892), and his founding of *La Democracia*, a Spanish-language journal out of Manila during the early years of US rule in the Philippines (Mojares 2006, 145).

A debate remains about the anti-colonial aspect of his research and writing, within the contexts of both Spanish and US rule. While Pardo remained on the margin of the Propaganda movement, or the "primary vehicle in creating Filipino national consciousness in the nineteenth century" (Schumacher 1997, quoted in Mojares 2006, 205), his participation in the resignification of the term "Filipino" from Spaniard born in the Philippines to a use that included mestizos and "naturales" and his research of cultural patrimonies with deeper roots than Spain's in the Philippines combined to undermine Spanish authority and the Spaniards' self-perceived centrality in cultural and political history. His writings were not explicitly political, as Arsenio Manuel notes, but nonetheless were resistant to dominant narratives about the dissemination of civilization through colonization, lending "substance to the assertions of the propagandists" (quoted in Mojares 2006, 208). Subsequently, with the fall of the First Philippine Republic in 1901 and the installation of US imperial power, Pardo became, according to US staffer Daniel Williams, the "right-hand man of Governor Taft in the establishment of civil government" (quoted in Mojares 2006, 147). Pardo resisted the Catholicism-centered colonial legacy of Spain by maintaining hope in and collaborating with the United States to promote education in self-government and eventually a "Philippines for the Filipinos." This hope faded in 1903, when William Howard Taft was replaced by a more transparently imperialist and authoritarian governor, Luke Wright, whom Pardo called "despotic" (150). The 1916 "Recuerdos de Argentina" continues Pardo's tradition of political evasiveness. On the one hand, he avoided polemical or pamphleteering statements and praised a project of assimilation similar to the ones he had supported in US rule before 1903. On the other hand, Pardo also lends substance to anti-colonial critiques of US rule in the Philippines, with which he had grown disenchanted, through his impatience with imperialistic and xenophobic discourses of yellow peril.

"Recuerdos de Argentina" is divided into more than 40 sections describing culture and politics in Argentina, with an eye to points that would be of interest to a Filipino reader (Gasquet 2019, 118). Pardo's strongest claim of the memoir is that "el origen de todo el progreso argentino es su *puerta abierta a la inmigración*" (the origin of all Argentine progress is its *open-door policy toward immigration*) (1916, 46), subsequently equating Argentina's capability of assimilating its new immigrants with the archetype for such assimilation, the United States (44). Assimilation includes "forgetting what you were" and adopting the language and "type of character" of the locals (44). Pardo underlines the strategies to transform all immigrants, even anarchists and thieves, into productive workers, which included giving the immigrants vaccinations and baths upon arriving, economic support and lodging, and a job provided by the Department of Immigration (47). "Argentinization" transforms the immigrant physically, socially, intellectually, and linguistically; in short, it produces "un hombre moderno del labriego mísero e ignorante de años atrás" (a modern man from an ignorant and miserable peasant from years ago) (46–47).

Pardo maintains a balance between the sentimental and the practical in this reflection on immigration to Argentina, a balance represented by the rival corporeal synecdoches he uses to talk about immigration: "corazón" (heart) and "mano de obra" (hand of labor), which is traditionally used in Spanish to speak about labor in general, as opposed to "brazo" (arm), which speaks specifically about the laborer (1916, 44, 50). The synecdoche "mano de obra" points to two different biopolitical phenomena. The above-mentioned procedure of sanitizing and directing the movement of immigrants to make them modern men and productive workers represents technologies of "anatamo-politics," or the regimenting of humans by treating them as bodies, much like Acosta's push for education. On the other hand, Pardo also notes how immigrant workers in Argentina have gained awareness that their bodies are merchandise and that the price of this merchandise—their wage demands—can be manipulated to preserve the wholeness and the function of these bodies.[12] This latter behavior suggests a form of grassroots anatamo-politics, the dictation of what one does with one's own body when one distances the body from the self, treating the body not as naked life but as business. When one objectifies oneself in such a way, she or he intervenes in the economic and cultural landscape of society. This form of self-determination contradicts, however, Pardo's claim that immigrants to Argentina immediately become "patriotas de corazón" (patriots at heart). This indicates not only that immigrants speak and act like Argentines, forgetting their homelands, but also that they consent to the hegemony of the established Argentine ruling class, the "hijos del país" (national sons) (51). Pardo says, "Naturalmente, los hijos del país no han tenido jamás motivos de celos ni temores de los recién venidos, que no han tratado ni por pensamiento de disputar el poder oficial sino de ganar dinero" (Naturally, the sons of the country have not had any motives to envy or fear the recently arrived, who have not tried or even thought about disputing the official power but only about earning money) (51). The disruptive self-determination that Pardo portrays does not combine seamlessly with the image of immigrants as consenting and politically passive "patriots at heart," suggesting an internal tension of identification, a doubt about whom Pardo identifies with, made evident through his wavering interpretation.

In fact, there are a number of "interpretive limitations" in Pardo's reflection on Argentine history, society, and politics (Gasquet 2019, 136–38). Argentine workers felt victimized by immigration, arranging a general strike in November 1902 demanding restrictions on immigration (Norambuena and Matamoros 2016, 55), and immigrants and their children began organizing in favor of their own rights ever since the end of the 19th century (Gasquet 2019, 129–30). Additionally, elites like poet Leopoldo Lugones saw even European immigration as a form of cultural contamination, as seen when immigrants "deform" the Castilian language spoken in Argentina and contribute to the country's disintegration (Ramos 2003, 276). The political and cultural order that Pardo describes as thorough, heartfelt assimilation and mutual appreciation between immigrants and locals is challenged by the historical record. This could be due to the fact that, as Pardo points out in the fragment of a letter to the *Philippine Review*'s editor that he includes to open the article, his visit was personal without a research agenda. The editor reached out to Pardo after he had already returned to Europe, Pardo having left Argentina in a rush, without his personal journals and notes, because of an "unexpected event" (Pardo 1916, 42). These moments of interpretive limitations suggest that the article informs the reader more about Pardo's personal experience, his process of perception, and the dimensions of his political beliefs and desires than about Argentina and its processes of assimilation.

Pardo clearly identifies with the "hijos del país," with whom his brother Felix associated and whose limited perspective on the realities of immigration are reflected in Pardo's Argentine memories. This constitutes, as Gasquet argues, "no sólo un reflejo clasista de filipino encumbrado, sino una identificación con un modelo de hispanidad existoso y moderno, que a sus ojos representaba 'el camino' a seguir por su propio país" (not only a classist reflection of the conceited Filipino but also an identification with a successful and modern model of Spanishness that in his eyes represented "the path" to follow for his own country) (2019, 130). Pardo's entire academic endeavor is predicated on exploring and defining the Philippines' history, nature, and language as cosmopolitan, while moving beyond the limitations of Spanish patrimony and inscribing the Philippines into emerging global debates about culture and science. It makes sense that these notions of immigration, the suggestion that through immigration Argentina can become more global and thus more like itself—Pardo sees Argentina as, by nature, cosmopolitan, welcoming, modern, and enterprising—would be attractive to Pardo for the Philippines. In fact, this highlights a striking consistency between Acosta's and Pardo's views on immigration. Despite dramatically different understandings of assimilation, both Acosta and Pardo view immigration as a biopolitical method through which a country can become more like itself, or at least more similar to the "true" national nature that these anti-colonial writers ascribe to their countries.

The difference between Pardo and Acosta has to do with nuances about race and identification between the writers and the immigrants. Acosta differentiates between different groups of immigrants, those who would promote intellectual and economic progress, and a return to Puerto Rico's true, white, literate identity due to their European race, and those who would disseminate moral and cultural plagues due to their Asian race. Pardo diverges here, critiquing Argentine president Roque Saenz Peña's notion of "humanity" in Pardo's moment of most emotionally stirred writing. His critique is of the phrase "Argentina para la humanidad," which responded to the United States' slogan about immigration, "America for the Americans." Pardo explains the error he sees in Saenz Peña's misinterpretation of the US phrase; it does not call to keep individuals out, just their previous nations. Upon immigrating to the United States, you must be loyal to the United States and not your previous country. The contradiction in the Argentine phrase is that, according to Pardo, their notion of humanity excludes whole races, especially "la raza amarilla," the yellow race (1916, 53). Their notion of humanity employs "poetic license," a euphemism to indicate that it is misleading and exclusive. And through his critique, Pardo reveals the schizophrenic nature of identification in this text; for a brief moment, his overarching identification with the "hijos del país" breaks down, revealing a competing identification with rejected Asian migrants. Put differently, Pardo identifies with the rejected Asian migrant to a greater degree than with European immigrants, whose struggles he glazes over while identifying with and assuming the perspective of the "hijos del país."

Pardo's writings about immigration in Argentina weigh in implicitly on the debates about Chinese immigration to the Philippines examined above. While his valuing of assimilation echoes aspects of anti-immigration critiques of Chinese mestizos in Manila like those of *La Oceanía Española*, his critique of Argentina's exclusion of "the yellow race" points to a fraternity among peoples from Asia. In fact, Pardo's complaint about the term "Argentina para la humanidad," as opposed to the phrase "America for the Americans," calls to mind a concept unmentioned in this text but discussed among Pardo and his *ilustrado* comrades: "Asia para los asiáticos" (Asia for the Asiatics). This redemptive regionalist sentiment, which mistrusted Eurocentrism, had been debated among *ilustrados* of the late 19th century and would continue to be deliberated up to the presidency of Manuel Quezón in the early 1940s. The central goal was to "resolve the contradiction between Enlightenment and Orient" (Blanco 2016, 73–74).[13] Taking this into account, Pardo's notes on Argentina can be understood as a compelling redirection of Filipino debates on immigration. Given that Pardo's identification with "the yellow race" insinuates fraternity with the Chinese, and following the logic Pardo attributes to "America for the Americans"—or that immigrants must not be loyal to their former countries—the burden of assimilation, he might argue, lies less on the Chinese in the Philippines and more on the Spaniards and North Americans who arrive to the Philippines with views on "fitness to rule," an innately biopolitical concept, that are entirely Eurocentric.

As stated above, Pardo praises Argentina's ability to fabricate through the anatamo-politics of immigration "un hombre moderno del labriego mísero e ignorante de años atrás." In similar terms, Cuban José Martí praises the United States: "How great a nation must be, to conduct in a quiet way, these bands of wolves, hungry and thirsty, these excrescences of old poor countries, ferocious and unuseful there—and here, under the influence of work, good, kind and tame!" (1880, 35). The crucial differences between these outwardly parallel claims, examined in the following section, are the use of irony and the estranged wielding of the English tongue, which point to a radical identification between Martí and the ferocious, thirsty immigrant.

Resistant *Lenguas*

José Martí was born in Havana in 1853, the son of humble Spanish parents. In 1868, Martí joined the popular Yara rebellion, and in 1870 he was imprisoned for anti-Spanish activities. Falling ill after six months of hard labor in prison, Martí was exiled to Spain, Mexico, Venezuela, and Guatemala, before he settled in the United States in 1880. During his years abroad, his writings included more than 500 travel narratives, literary portraits, and essays, in addition to renowned poetry that is said to have been the model for Latin American *modernismo* (Rotker 2006, 13). Beyond writing, he worked to organize the Cuban independence movement from abroad, eventually leaving the United States in 1895 in the hopes of liberating Cuba. Just four months later in Dos Ríos, Cuba, he charged Spanish troops that had established position around his group of Cuban rebels, engaging in combat for the first time in his life, and was killed (Hagimoto 2013, 152).

At first, Martí's interpretation of immigrants is cryptic, as seen in his 1880 first-person chronicle of his first sojourn in the United States, entitled "Impressions of America by a Very Fresh Spaniard" and published in English in a New York art weekly, *The Hour*. Martí appears to praise the US apparatus for domesticating immigrants through anatamo-politics similar to those desired by Acosta and Pardo, but Martí's readers are New Yorkers, and his hyperbolic tone suggests layers of irony and critique. In fact, as Julio Ramos asserts, as a rule, Martí's chronicles "subvert, with a literary look, the norms of the travel narrative historically linked to the project of modernization"

(2003, 195).[14] In part, this subversion has to do with Martí's view of and identification with the immigrant in these chronicles. Ariela Schnirmajer tracks
Martí's contradictory representations of Chinese immigrant communities
in the United States; in Martí's view, the Chinese in the United States are
victims of marginalization, while also trafficking opium and other social ills
(2011, 51–52). In general, Schnirmajer notes how Martí is critical of intol-
erance toward immigrants, how he recognizes his shared experiences with
many of the immigrants he portrays in his chronicles while also maintaining some prejudices of his era, specifically, the desire to determine which
countries produce the "inmigrante que ayuda" (immigrant who helps) and
which send forth the "inmigrante que daña" (immigrant who hurts) (55–58).
Similarly, another critique of Martí's writings on the United States is that
they are often rooted in a misogynistic biopolitical superiority of the southern countries, where classical gender norms—men being manly and women
being sensuous—are upheld, as opposed to the north, where economic desire
leads to deviations from "correct" gender performances.[15] On the other hand,
Laura Lomas rereads Martí's translations of Anglophone literature into Spanish as a practice of a "migrant intellectual worker," who aims to "provincialize"
the United States' notions of modernity and culture, staking "a claim to define
another American modernity beside that of the United States" (2009, 2–3).
Lomas analyzes Martí's intellectual production as that of a migrant, recen-
tering Ramos's reading of diverging modernities on the figure of the migrant.

Something none of the above-mentioned critics take into account is
Martí's employment of the immigrant's tongue, or *lengua*, in "Impressions
of America" to articulate these resistant cultural and political programs. A
caveat here is that while Acosta and Pardo do use the synecdoches *brazo*
and *corazón*, Martí does not explicitly invoke the whole immigrant by making reference to the immigrant tongue. However, the gesture of using the
immigrant's tongue and making reference to his own poor grasp of it, that
is, the self-consciously poetic and error-riddled English of "Impressions of
America," can be considered a synecdoche for Martí's entire anti-imperial,
early *modernista* aesthetic.

Martí's "Impressions of America by a Very Fresh Spaniard" is a series
of three travel chronicles published between July 10 and October 23, 1880.
Unlike many of his other chronicles' style, where disembodied bird's-eye perspectives are dominant and first-person narrators are scarce, "Impressions
of America" employs a hybrid structure where first-person narrations intervene in a structure of ethnographic critiques of North Americans that waver

between wonder and disavowal. There is disagreement among critics about the language in which Martí writes "Impressions of America." Some argue that he does so in French and subsequently has it translated into English by *The Hour* editor, as Martí has done with many other articles published in *The Hour* in 1880 (Rodríguez 2003, 9).[16] Others assert that Martí writes the chronicles in English, using errors and linguistic idiosyncrasies in the early chronicles as their evidence.[17] In a previous article, I argue, however, that not only did Martí write the chronicles in English but his errors were purposeful political statements:

> Martí plays with the English language with creativity and irreverence, wielding homophones, neologisms, and oxymorons with great savvy. See the phrase, ". . . these women, too richly dressed to be happy; these men, too devoted to business of pocket." With homophones ("too" and "to"), he creates internal rhythm. He coins new adjectives like "sobrious" and "candorous" to plant internal rhyme into a culturally devoid landscape. Through the clause, "with remarkable neglectness of the spiritual business," Martí explores paradoxes like "spiritual business" and experiments with cultured neologisms, such as "neglectness." In this way, he injects poetic energy into spaces, like "business," where it previously was not. (Hartwell 2019, 63)

The logic of these purposeful errors is encrypted in the vivid description of anatamo-politics in US immigration transforming a band of hungry wolves (European immigrants) into docile workers. Beyond using hyperbole to subtly critique the notion of such a "smooth" assimilation, Martí confronts the idea of assimilation by performing "ungovernability" through his wielding of the English language.

The "ungovernable" speaks to a concept coined by Ileana Rodríguez and used in the context of Philippine-Caribbean studies by Kristina Escondo, the "negating [of] his/her own negation within the established order" (2016, 53). Martí's prose performs "ungovernability" of the tongue, infusing poetry and culture in a language and landscape that are devoid of them and where they are not valued. While Pardo praises immigrants in Argentina for talking with perfect Argentine Castilian Spanish shortly after arriving, Martí wilds the tame, cultureless English language of North America, illustrating not only the failure of assimilation but also the harnessing of the disruptive power of the immigrant. This is similar to Walter Mignolo's concepts of "epistemic disobedience" and "delinking," only instead of distancing this intellectual framework from Western thought, Martí aims to highlight his proximity to classical traditions through his versifying prose and the United States' distance from them (2013, 141). Such a disobedient linking unsettles and disrupts US programs of assimilation and economic expansion, asserting that culture is the most important thing and that the immigrants, many of whom might belong to what Martí would later call "Nuestra América," have cultural authority and can call the shots. Thus, Martí responds to narratives of uncomplicated assimilation and the taming of wild wolves and tongues by insisting that his tongue, and by synecdoche all of him and all immigrants, can refuse to assimilate, refuse to be changed, refuse to be effaced and instrumentalized by mechanisms of US industrial anatamo-politics, insisting rather on being the active and purposeful agents of change.

Interestingly, when Martí identifies as immigrant, he does so as a Spanish immigrant and not a Cuban. So, while Acosta is unquestioning of Eurocentrism and Pardo critiques Eurocentrism by attempting to delink notions of civilization and scientific practice from a uniquely European patrimony, Martí provincializes Europe against the United States, the newer threat. Europe becomes a symbol of resistance: a fountain of indomitable immigrants and an alternative cultural and spiritual framework to the US cult of profit.

In this way, Martí, like the self-determining workers discussed by Pardo, performs a biopolitics of resistance. He stakes claim to his own body by poetically intervening in an imperial language with his own ungovernable tongue, as opposed to letting that tongue be disciplined by projects of linguistic and cultural assimilation. Therefore, when his piercing tongue resists the reduction of his body to naked life, Martí becomes a model of embodied subversion, countering the promise of assimilation with the threat of revolt.

Conclusions on Anti-Colonial Biopolitics and Immigration

How should we understand the intersection of biopolitics and anti-colonial thought in these turn-of-the-century writings about immigration? The answer is encrypted in the concepts of assimilation and disruption. Acosta and Pardo, for example, have dramatically diverging views of the function of assimilation. Acosta directly does not consider assimilation as a possible outcome of immigration; immigrants can cause either positive or negative disruption. Pardo, on the other hand, praises Argentina for fully assimilating their immigrants and transforming them into productive laborer-citizens.

Despite this difference, both writers frame ideal immigration as a demographic transformation without the "trans," that is, a change that does not cross over; good immigrants are new arrivals who do not add something "new" but rather paradoxically bring the host country closer to its "true" nature. Puerto Rico can become whiter, more productive, and more literate in line with Acosta's views on the true Puerto Rican identity, and Argentina, in line with Pardo's ideas of the Southern Cone country and his desires for the Philippines, can become more cosmopolitan and universal through immigration. Martí, on the other hand, asserts that immigration can be a form of disruptive resistance toward imperialism, identifying fully with the immigrant with his fresh—that is, both new and irreverent—use of the English tongue.

That said, while all three writers express biopolitical desires as a mode of critiquing colonial structures, they also maintain, to different degrees, a series of hierarchies established through the foundation of colonialism in the form of race, class, and gender discrimination, as well as Eurocentric notions about culture and civilization. This resonates with a claim by Walter Mignolo that a term previously coined by Aníbal Quijano, "coloniality," is the correlate for biopolitics in Latin America and other parts of the non-European world, or the regions that are alien to the "life experience, long and short-term memories, languages and categories of thought that brought about the concept of 'biopolitics'" (2013, 129–30). This fascinating assertion holds its weight when thinking about these discourses on immigration, especially when considering that "coloniality" speaks to the permanence in postcolonial society of mechanisms of control invented in the colony, specifically race, Eurocentrism, and capitalism (Quijano 2000, 533–34). Likewise, Acosta's, Pardo's, and Martí's writings on immigration show different forms of grappling with the colonial legacies of race and class hierarchies. They illustrate a tendency in anti-colonial Philippine and Caribbean writing to contest colonial structures that keep the educated elite out of power—like lack of political representation, Eurocentric notions of superiority of peninsular Spaniards over creoles, and protectionist, ancien régime, and slave-based economics—while not challenging to the same degree the biopolitical structures and processes of regimenting, categorizing, and disciplining bodies and races that tend to bolster creole elites' authority. Even the writer for whom this ambivalence is least applicable, Martí, still resorts on occasion to discriminatory notions about Chinese (and not European) migrants and discourses that regiment populations of immigrants via the dichotomy of help versus hurt. In sum, the three anti-colonial writers' outwardly diverging writings all rely heavily on an equation of immigration with disruption and a biopolitical impulse to diffuse or direct such disruption.

This convergence of biopolitical desires highlights a transoceanic emergence of fascination and wariness before the globalized modernity embodied by transnational migrants and migration, which leads to an identity crisis in both the Philippines and the Spanish Caribbean, a gradual and uneven shift from seeing migrants as "other" to identifying with them.

Notes

1. Even some non-novelistic prose from the era employed similar metaphors; as Puerto Rican Román Baldorioty de Castro put it in a report about what he saw as a pitiful display of Puerto Rico at the 1867 Universal Exposition in Paris, "Puerto Rico se arrastra penosamente como en una perpetua agonía entre el ser y el no ser" (Puerto Rico drags itself, huffing and puffing, as if it were in a perpetual agony between being and not being) (1867, 76–77). All translations are mine.

2. For research on medical discourse and nation building, see Gabriella Nouzeilles, "La esfinge del monstruo: Modernidad e higiene racial en La charca de Zeno Gandía" (1997); Lisa Nalbone, "Colonized and Colonizer Disjunction" (2010); and Warwick Anderson and Hans Pols, "Scientific Patriotism: Medical Science and National Self-Fashioning in Southeast Asia" (2012).

3. The term "anti-colonial" is used in an intentionally capacious way in this chapter as to include a broad series of political frameworks employed by colonized peoples who take stances against the colonial status quo. Just like there was no consensus about the future of the colonies vis-à-vis the decision to seek revolution or reform, both of these political frameworks are also schematic categories encompassing a series of specific political affiliations: reformism, liberalism, anti-clericalism, annexationism, nationalism, secessionism, abolitionism, autonomism, and krausism, among many others.

4. Agamben continues Foucault's probing of "the concrete ways in which power penetrates subjects' very bodies and forms of life" (1998, 5), centrally challenging Foucault's notion of a clean break between the "juridico-institutional and the biopolitical models of power" (6).

5. Esposito claimed that by focusing too much on the level of human nature and the plane of signification, Foucault and Agamben "dehistoricize" the biopolitical phenomenon, disregarding the work of colonialism in the universalization of biopolitical order and the proliferation of notions about entire races of "disposable subjects" (quoted in de Oto and Quintana 2010, 50). Achille Mbembe questions if "the notion of biopower sufficient to account for the contemporary ways in which the political, under the guise of war, of resistance, or of the fight against terror, makes the murder of the enemy its primary and absolute objective," especially in the context of wartime and colonized and postcolonial regions of the world, proposing a different framework to think about these problems within a colonial context: "necropolitics" or a "figure of sovereignty whose central project is not the struggle for autonomy but *the generalized instrumentalization of human existence and the material destruction of human bodies and populations*" (2003, 12–14; italics in origi-

nal). In 2019, Vicente Rafael published a fascinating article on Philippine president Duterte and US president Trump, employing reflections on Foucault "provincialized" in dialogue with Mbembe, in the *Journal of Asian Studies* called "The Sovereign Trickster."

6. Puerto Rico did receive over 1,300 contracted Chinese immigrant workers between 1855 and 1857 after the captain general recommended the introduction of 3,000 Chinese workers in 1854 (Cifre de Loubriel 1964, 38).

7. The use of the term "*naturales*" is an attempt to avoid anachronistic terminology. Before the latter half of the 19th century, "Filipino" had meant "creoles [or] Spaniards born in the Philippines" (Constantino 1975, 147). In the 1880s, the *ilustrados*, the "enlightened" wave of Castilian-speaking and reform-minded travelers, renovated this definition. They "first shared, then wrested the term Filipino from the creoles and infused it with national meaning which later included the entire people" (148).

8. Beyond racialized discourse used about Chinese and Chinese mestizos in the Philippines, one can look to the second chapter of Richard Chu's 2010 *Chinese and Chinese Mestizos of Manila: Family, Identity, and Culture, 1860s-1930s* for substantial research on their demographics, practices, and the legal systems designed to categorize and control them.

9. "Llegó el año de 1838 y con él una nueva legislación inaugurada por la Inglaterra, y la que continuada por la Francia en 1848, ha cambiado profundamente el estado social de las Antillas. Sin embargo esa misma legislación no ha sido ponderosa a cambiar la naturaleza de las razas y hoy más que nunca, ofrecen las colonias extranjeras en los elementos de su población . . . la falta de equilibrio enunciada. La isla de Puerto Rico por el contrario, ha visto aumentarse su población libre gracias a la cédula de Fomento de 1815 . . . y gracias también a las emigraciones de Santo Domingo y Venezuela" (The year 1838 arrived with a new legislation inaugurated by England, and which, when continued by France in 1848, has profoundly changed the social state of the Antilles. However, that same legislation has not been powerful enough to change the nature of the races and today more than ever, the foreign colonies show in the elements of their population a lack of the enunciated balance. The island of Puerto Rico, on the other hand, has seen its free population grow thanks to the "cédula de Fomento" of 1815 and thanks also to the emigrations of Santo Domingo and Venezuela) (Acosta 1997, 30).

10. "Una de las causas de la que la isla de Cuba haya importado y disfrute hoy en mayor número que la de Puerto Rico de las creaciones industriales y económicas, debidas al genio de los pueblos extranjeros, como los caminos de hierro, los telégrafos . . . consiste, aparte de haberla precedido en las vías del comercio libre, en el exceso de población blanca que hemos señalado y en la mayor cultura intelectual de esta" (One of the causes for which the island of Cuba has imported and enjoys today industrial and economic creations in greater number than Puerto Rico, due to the genius of foreign peoples, like the railroads and the telegraph . . . consists, aside from having come first to the path of free trade, in the excess of white population that we have underlined and their greater intellectual culture) (Abbad 2002, 389). In the same endnote, Acosta brags about having personally defended Puerto Rico from the "hijos degradados de la India oriental" (degraded sons of Eastern India) and the "viciosos súbditos del celeste imperio" (the vicious subjects of the Celestial Empire) (386). For more information on Acosta's endnotes to Fray Íñigo Abbad y Lasierra's 1788

Historia geográfica, civil, y natural de la isla de San Juan Bautista de Puerto Rico, see Gervasio Luis García's "Historia bajo sospecha" (2015) and my "Imperial Endnotes: The First Filipino and Boricua Historians" (2018).

11. The exact date of Pardo's visit to Argentina is not included in his article or biographies, but Axel Gasquet deduces the year 1914 due to references made in the article to who was president during his visit (Roque Saenz Peña) (Gasquet 2019, 140n).

12. "Como los inmigrantes no trabajan como máquinas, sino que tienen buen cuidado de conocer las circunstancias y condiciones de su mercancía que es *la mano de obra*, pronto se aperciben de que, siguiendo la misma suerte de toda mercancía, ésta también obedece la ley de la oferta y la demanda. Así resulta que todos los que trabajan tratan de nivelar el valor del trabajo" (Since the immigrants do not work like machines, but rather they make sure to know the circumstances and conditions of their merchandise, which is labor (the hand of work), soon they realize that, following the same fate as all merchandise, labor also obeys the law of supply and demand. Thus, in the end all who work try to balance the value of work) (Pardo 1916, 50).

13. Additionally, "Philippines for the Filipinos" was the strategy pursued by Taft in the early years of the US occupation of the Philippines. The US occupation would be a form of political education for the Filipinos in preparation for eventual independence. Pardo enthusiastically supported this policy, which was abandoned in 1903 by Taft's successor, Luke Wright (Mojares 2006, 149–50).

14. Ramos cites chronicles such as "El puente de Brooklyn" (1883) and "Coney Island" (1881) and even "Impressions of America" (1880) to show how through Martí's prose, the Cuban reorganizes what he perceives as lacking in spirit in the United States, which is obsessed with material wealth to a point of cultural blindness, using the poetic gaze that serves as the cultural advantage of his "Southern" countries, which are linked to classical traditions (2003, 195). Ramos asserts that through Martí's narrative voice, he orders the chaos of New York by contrasting "their" culture with "our" culture, by reconstructing challenged hierarchies in the space of the page, and by critiquing and reasserting gender roles that he perceives as faulty in the United States. Ultimately, by inflecting his prose with poetic energy, Martí responds to, on the level of literary form, the dry modernity put forth by the United States with a "modernismo" within which Latin Americans call the shots (Ramos 2003, 195).

15. See Julio Ramos's reading of "Coney Island" in *Desencuentros de la modernidad* (2003, 179).

16. Leonel-Antonio de la Cuesta asserts that the texts were written using a "strange linguistic exercise" (1996, 51), that is, the procedure of translating from a French text written by a Spanish speaker into English, and Pedro Pablo Rodríguez adds that Martí "still did not feel sure of his handle on English" and that *The Hour* did not yet employ a Spanish-to-English translator (2003, 9).

17. Mañach says that these were "published without correction, in Martí's own English . . . loaded and strange, these impressions 'of a Fresh Spaniard' must have seemed to The Hour's readers shockingly lacking of the usual timidity and flattery of the recently arrived foreigners" (1963, 152). Esther Allen adds, "Several months into his work for Dana, Martí seems to have decided to try his hand at writing in English for a three-part series

titled, 'Impressions of America by a Very Fresh Spaniard.' Its markedly eccentric prose includes a number of grammatical and spelling mistakes that make it rather unlike the polished translations from French previously published in *The Hour*. These errors alone indicate, to my mind, that this cannot simply be a poor translation (as Carlos Ripoll has maintained), but must be Martí's own often flawed but nevertheless spirited and forceful English which the editors and typesetters of *The Hour* decided to reproduce verbatim" (2018, 34).

References

Abbad y Lasierra, Íñigo. 2002. *Historia Geográfica, Civil y Natural de la Isla de San Juan Bautista de Puerto Rico*. Edited by José Julián de Acosta y Calbo. Madrid: Ediciones Doce Calles.

Acosta y Calbo, José Julián de. 1997. "Cuestión de brazos para el cultivo actual de las tierras de Puerto-Rico." In *Escritos de don José Julián de Acosta y Calbo: Tomo II*, edited by Jaime Alberto Solivan de Acosta. San Juan: self-published.

Agamben, Giorgio. 1998. *Homo Sacer: Sovereign Power and Bare Life*. Translated by Daniel Heller-Roazen. Stanford: Stanford University Press.

Allen, Esther. 2018. "'He Has Not Made Himself Known to Me': José Martí, U.S. History, and the Question of Translation." In *Syncing the Americas: José Martí and the Shaping of National Identity*, edited by Ryan Anthony Spangler and Georg Michael Schwarzmann. Lewisburg, PA: Bucknell University Press.

Álvarez Curbelo, Silvia. 2001. *Un País del Porvenir: El afán de modernidad en Puerto Rico (siglo XIX)*. San Juan: Ediciones Callejón.

Anderson, Benedict. 2004. *Under Three Flags: Anarchism and the Anti-Colonial Imagination*. New York: Verso.

Anderson, Warwick, and Hans Pols. 2012. "Scientific Patriotism: Medical Science and National Self-Fashioning in Southeast Asia." *Comparative Studies in Society and History* 54 (1): 93–113.

Ángeles Castro, María de los. 1995. "El autonomismo en Puerto Rico (1808–1898): La siembra de una tradición." *Secuencia* 31 (January–April): 5–22.

Blanco, John. 2016. "Oriental Enlightenment and the Colonial World: A Derivative Discourse?" In *Filipino Studies: Palimpsests of Nation and Diaspora*, edited by Martin Manalansan and Augusto Espiritu. New York: NYU Press.

Chu, Richard. 2010. *Chinese and Chinese Mestizos of Manila: Family, Identity, and Culture, 1860s–1930s*. Boston: Brill.

Cifre de Loubriel, Estela. 1964. *La inmigración a Puerto Rico durante el siglo XIX*. San Juan: Instituto de Cultura Puertorriqueña.

Constantino, Renato, and Letizia Constantino. 1975. *A History of the Philippines: From the Spanish Colonization to the Second World War*. Quezon City: Monthly Review Press.

Cuesta, Leonel Antonio de la. 1996. *Martí, traductor*. Salamanca: Editorial de la Universidad Pontificia de Salamanca.

Escondo, Kristina. 2016. "Alternative Orders and Revolution: The Anti-colonial *Grito* in the Manifestos of José Martí and Andrés Bonifacio." In *Trans-Pacific Encounters*, edited by Koichi Hagimoto, 51–73. Tyne, UK: Cambridge Scholars Publishing.

Foucault, Michel. 2003. *"Society Must Be Defended": Lectures at the Collège de France 1975–1976*. Translated by David Macey. New York: Picador.

Fradera, Josep M. 1999. *Filipinas, la colonia más peculiar: La hacienda pública en la definición de la política colonial, 1762–1868*. Madrid: Consejo Superior de Investigaciones Científicas.

García, Gervasio Luis. 2015. *Historia bajo sospecha*. San Juan: Publicaciones Gaviota.

García de los Arcos, María Fernanda. 1996. *Forzados y reclutas: Los criollos novohispanos en Asia (1756–1808)*. Ciudad de México: Potrerillos Editores.

Gasquet, Axel. 2019. "La hispanidad periférica en las antípodas el filipino T. H. Pardo de Tavera en la Argentina del Centenario." *UNITAS* 92 (1): 113–42.

Hagimoto, Koichi. 2013. *Between Empires: Martí, Rizal, and the Intercolonial Alliance*. New York: Palgrave Macmillan.

Hartwell, Ernest Rafael. 2018. "Imperial Endnotes: The First Filipino and Boricua Historians." *Latin American Literary Review* 45 (90): 53–67.

Hartwell, Ernest Rafael. 2019. "Bad English and Fresh Spaniards: Translation and Authority in Philippine and Cuban Travel Writing." *UNITAS* 92 (1): 43–74.

Kirk, John M. 1977. "José Martí and the United States: A Further Interpretation." *Journal of Latin American Studies* 2 (9): 275–90.

Lomas, Laura. 2009. *Translating Empire: José Martí, Migrant Latino Subjects, and American Modernities*. Durham: Duke University Press.

Mañach, Jorge. 1963. *Martí, el apóstol*. New York: Las Americas Publishing.

Martí, José. 1944. *Obras Completas de Martí*. Vol. 55, "Viajes I." Havana: Editorial Trópico.

Mbembe, Achille. 2003. "Necropolitics." Translated by Libby Meintjes. *Public Culture* 15 (1): 11–40.

Mignolo, Walter. 2013. "Geopolitics of Sensing and Knowing: On (De)Coloniality, Border Thinking, and Epistemic Disobedience." *Confero* 1 (1): 129–50.

Mojares, Resil B. 2006. *Brains of the Nation: Pedro Paterno, T. H. Pardo de Tavera, Isabelo de los Reyes and the Production of Modern Knowledge*. Manila: Ateneo de Manila University Press.

Morga, Antonio. 1958. *Sucesos de las Islas Filipinas* (1609). Edited by José Rizal (1889). Quezon City: R. Martínez and Sons.

Nalbone, Lisa. 2010. "Colonized and Colonizer Disjunction: Power and Truth in Zeno Gandía's La Charca." *Hispanófila* 159: 23–37.

Naranjo Orovio, Consuelo. 1998. "Immigration, 'Race' and Nation in Cuba in the Second Half of the 19th Century." *Ibero-amerikanisches Archiv* 24 (3/4): 303–26.

Naranjo Orovio, Consuelo, and Armando García González. 1996. *Racismo e Inmigración en Cuba en el siglo XIX*. Madrid: Ediciones Doce Calles.

Norambuena, Carmen, and Rodrigo Matamoros. 2016. "Política migratoria Argentina: Una mirada desde el institucionalismo histórico." *Si Somos Americanos. Revista de Estudios Transfronterizos* 16 (2): 45–72.

Nouzeilles, Gabriela. 1997. "La esfinge del monstruo: Modernidad e higiene racial en *La charca* de Zeno Gandía." *Latin American Literary Review* 25 (50): 89–107.

Oto, Alejandro de, and María Marta Quintana. 2010. *Biopolítica y colonialidad: Una lectura crítica de "Homo Sacer."* *Tabula Rasa* 12 (January–June): 47–72.

Pardo De Tavera, Trinidad H. 1916. "Recuerdos de Argentina." *Philippine Review (Revista Filipina)* 1 (2): 42–59.

Pérez Serrano, Julio. 1998. "Características de la población de las islas filipinas en la segunda mitad del siglo xix." Government of Spain, Ministry of Defense. http://www.armada .mde.es/archivo/mardigitalrevistas/cuadernosihcn/31cuaderno/01cap.pdf

Quijano, Aníbal. 2000. "Coloniality of Power, Eurocentrism, and Latin America." *Nepantla: Views from South* 1 (3): 533–80.

Rafael, Vicente L. 2019. "The Sovereign Trickster." *Journal of Asian Studies* 78 (1): 141–66.

Ramos, Julio. 2003. *Desencuentros de la modernidad en América Latina: Literatura y política en el siglo XIX*. San Juan: Ediciones Callejón.

Ramos Mattei, Andrés A. 1981. "La importación de trabajadores contratados para la industria azucarera puertorriqueña: 1860–1880." In *Inmigración y clases sociales en el Puerto Rico del siglo XIX*, edited by Francisco A. Scarano, 125–42. Río Piedras: Ediciones Huracán.

Rodao, Florentino. 2018. "'The Salvational Currents of Emigration': Racial Theories and Social Disputes in the Philippines at the End of the Nineteenth Century." *Journal of Southeast Asian Studies* 49 (3): 426–44.

Rodríguez, Pedro Pablo. 2003. "Nota editorial." In *Obras Completas: Edición Crítica*. Vol. 7, 1880–1881, by José Martí. Havana: Centro de Estudios Martianos.

Rotker, Susana. 2006. "Prólogo." In *Crónicas*, by José Martí, edited by Susana Rotker. Barcelona: Debate.

Schmidt-Nowara, Christopher. 1999. *Empire and Antisavery: Spain, Puerto Rico and Cuba 1833–1874*. Pittsburgh: University of Pittsburgh Press.

Schnirmajer, Ariela. 2011. "Minorías sociales y heterogeneidad: José Martí y la inmigración europea." *anclajes* 15 (1): 49–59.

Schumacher, John N., S.J. 1997. *The Propaganda Movement: 1880–1895: The Creation of a Filipino Consciousness, the Making of the Revolution*. Manila: Ateneo de Manila University Press.

Vásquez, Carmen. 1986. "José Julián Acosta, Abolicionista." *Anuario de Estudios Americanos* 48:259–74.

Wickberg, Eric. 1965. *The Chinese in Philippine Life, 1850–1898*. New Haven: Yale University Press.

The Sight of the Other

An Approach to the Inversion of the Colonial Discourse in Antonio Luna's Impresiones

Cristina Guillén Arnáiz

On November 9, 1889, Celso Mir Deas, Spanish editor of *El Pueblo Soberano*, dedicated the following words to the Filipino painter Juan Luna, believing that he was the author of the recently published article "Impresiones madrileñas de un filipino": "You who have received benefits from Spain, you who have been received by those in the Peninsula better than by your own people . . . have the nerve to insult those to whom you owe everything and who have given you much more than you deserve as an artist and a man" (1889).[1] To begin with, however, Mir Deas was bluntly mistaken about the text's authorship: it was not Juan Luna but his brother, Antonio, who published the article in *La Solidaridad* in October 1889, under the pseudonym "Taga-Ilog." Antonio Luna's article reflected a very critical first impression of a Filipino *ilustrado* upon his arrival in the Spanish Empire's metropolis. Despite the harsh words from the Spanish editor—signaling the ungrateful attitude of the Filipino toward his "Madre Patria"—Antonio Luna continued publishing his satirical and mordant descriptions of the city and Spanish society, which he eventually compiled in the book *Impresiones* (Madrid, 1891). This episode of the confrontation between Luna and Mir Deas—which culminated in several public accusations and even a challenge to a duel[2]—is a relevant anecdote as it illustrates the remarkable tensions existing at that moment vis-à-vis the relation between an already decadent imperial Spain and an emerging Filipino nation.

The last third of the 19th century was a period of approach and reinforcement of the means of communication—both literally and metaphorically—between the metropolis and the colony of the Philippines. This renewed contact also implied for Spain a rediscovery of its most remote colony. The Philippines archipelago, mainly considered by the Spanish governments a tactical port in Asia for decades (Fradera 2003, 107), needed to be known in that time of change in terms that would serve the objective of the successive Spanish governments in the last decades of the 19th century: to maintain and strengthen its power over the colony in a time when its overseas possessions had already been significantly reduced. For this reason, a Spanish colonial discourse toward the Philippines reemerged with vigor at that point in time. Politicians, journalists, and writers started to publish a wide variety of works describing the Asian colony as a territory that needed to be ruled by reformed colonial politics because of the plentiful resources offered by the land and the presumed incapacity of its native population to administrate them and even to account for themselves.[3] A conglomeration of Western colonial clichés—often mixed with reformist claims toward the Spanish colonial administration—spread among the Spanish population and also reached the Filipino *ilustrados* living in the metropolis. Predictably, the distorted image of their land and the racism deployed by these texts upset this "proto-nationalist group of urban and cosmopolitan Filipinos" (Rodao 2018, 427) and intensified their already initiated activism in regard to the construction of their national identity.

Antonio Luna's *Impresiones* has already been analyzed by a number of scholars as one of the literary works that contributed significantly to this national building process (José 1971, 2001; Reyes 2008). It was written and published in Spain—a liminal space for Luna in terms of Bhabha's conception (1994)—where the author strived to speak "from the twin position of the insider, as a Spaniard, and outsider, as a native Filipino" (Reyes 2008, 85). The argument of the present chapter is that the particularity of *Impresiones* resides in the discursive strategy used by its author to reach his purpose of national identity construction: an inversion of the Western colonial discourse. *Impresiones* can be read as an "autoethnographic text," defined by Mary Louise Pratt as an expression in which "colonized subjects undertake to represent themselves in ways that engage with the colonizer's own terms": a text in which "the others construct in response to or in dialogue with those metropolitan representations" (1992, 7). In *Impresiones*, the Filipino put himself in the position of the narrator—a Spanish position so far—as the Spaniard became the analyzed object. Thus, Antonio Luna came up with a brilliant response to the Spanish discourse about the Philippines: using the same narrative structures and literary images as its colonizers.

Through different examples of comparison between Spanish texts and Luna's equivalent, this chapter will provide an approach to the inversion of the roles in the narrative of the colonization proposed by the author: a compilation of texts where the Filipino colonial subject, always observed, takes on the voice of the narrator.

This chapter seeks to identify the features of Luna's autoethnographic expression as a response to a selection of colonial texts—these, too, being compilations of articles—written by Spaniards since the 1870s until the publication of *Impresiones*. For this purpose, the chapter analyzes Luna's work in comparison with Francisco Cañamaque's *Recuerdos de Filipinas* (1877, 1879), Francisco Vila's *Escenas Filipinas* (1882), Alberto Díaz de la Quintana's *Siluetas Filipinas* (1887), and Pablo Feced's *Filipinas: Esbozos y pinceladas* (1888). These works are considered in the context of the Spanish necessity of its reaffirmation as a colonial power. This chapter thus considers the Spanish colonial discourse as a discourse of nation construction—or reconstruction—at the end of the 19th century: a time of change when the Spanish fear of losing the control of one of its last colonies converged with growing demands of self-determination in the Philippines.

Spreading Knowledge about the Remotest of the Colonies: The Spanish Literary Reinvention of a Territory and the Filipino Resistance to It

During the last third of the 19th century—particularly since the 1870s—several administrative, economic, and social undertakings were brought into action by the Spanish government vis-à-vis the colonial administration of the islands. The combination of all these initiatives pursued common objectives, the first of them being to strengthen the relations between the metropolis and the colony, especially in the economic field (Fradera 2003). On the other hand, the reforms sought to reinforce the Spanish control of the territory, in order to prevent a possible revolution among the islands' population or a possible intervention of other imperial powers present in the region.[4]

During this period, in line with the administrative and economic initiatives, different actions came to occur in the Spanish social sphere with the common purpose of building links with one of the last colonies. It was also deemed necessary to spread knowledge about their *hermanos filipinos* to the Spanish public. As the Philippines were an almost unknown region up to that point, a considerable number of works containing factual information about the archipelago were published in Spain. Many of these texts were technical reports addressed to the colonial administration, the government, or specialized readers, in which their authors analyzed the current state of the colony and proposed necessary reforms.[5]

The Filipino colony was eventually consolidated as a matter for debate in the political and administrative sphere, but the islands also began to be present in the Spanish imaginary at the same time. This was the case not particularly by virtue of these official reports but thanks to another type of text that began to emerge at this very moment and that reached a wider range of public: the press reader. Within this early form of mass communication, politicians, journalists and workers for the Spanish administration in the Philippines wrote short articles describing their personal experience about their visits to the archipelago, pieces that were often later compiled in books.

These books narrating the personal Filipino experience of their authors share a range of common features. In organizational structure, all of them are divided into chapters suitable to be published as independent articles in the press; with the exception of *Escenas Filipinas*—published as a standalone book right away—all the articles appeared previously in newspapers from both Spain and the Philippines. They also share a common narrative structure: all of them start with the arrival of the author-narrator to the port of Manila, which constituted the first contact with other Spaniards in the colony. After, the authors described the trip to the *provincia* to which they were assigned and where they would usually get in touch with the respective Spanish *fraile* who showed them the everyday life of the Filipino native population.[6] Moreover, the short stories and anecdotes that riddled these narrations consider similar topics, and all of them emphasize the veracity and objectivity of their experience. It is difficult to subsume these works into one specific literary genre: Torres-Pou considers them a mix between "libro de viajes, cuadro costumbrista o tratado colonial" (travel book, *costumbrista* representation, and colonial treaty) (2013, 168), as they contain an itinerary structure, representations of *tipos* and scenes, and remarks about the colonial administration. But besides a classification in terms of genre, it is also important to signal their intentions: as Patricio de la Escosura pointed out in the prologue to *Recuerdos de Filipinas*, the compilation is "ligero en su forma" (light in its form) but "en su fondo grave e instructivo" (serious and instructive in its content) (in Cañamaque 1877, 20).

Beneath the entertaining and sometimes even fun stories, there was a hidden objective shared by all these works and their apparently lighthearted descriptions: in its *fondo grave* (serious content) the purpose remains of maintaining the Spanish hegemony over the islands to ensure the continuity of the colonial system. To attain this purpose, similarly to the rest of the colonial discourses, these texts affirmed a racial inferiority of the native Filipinos and stressed their incapacity to self-govern. Also, inviting Spanish investors to the land, these texts promoted an image of a docile native, easy to dominate, and a territory full of natural resources ready to be exploited.

The Spanish authors, despite their political differences—we may find both liberals and traditionalists among them—converged on a similar type of narrative to describe the Asian colony. This common writing resonates with the European imperial discourse as examined by Mary Louise Pratt (1992) and David Spurr (1993). Not all the Spanish writers represented the Philippines equally—which is unsurprising, given their political backgrounds—although the aim of this chapter is not to establish the differences existing between the four Spanish compilations but to display the imaginary present in Spain as a result of the combination of all these different representations. The whole variety of these images can be found in Luna's text, which collects and answers to the tradition of representing the Philippines in its entirety.

Focusing on the works itself, the two volumes of *Recuerdos de Filipinas* (1877 and 1879) by Francisco Cañamaque were one of the first and most polemic compilations. Deemed by some critics as one of the decisive causes of the Propaganda movement's emergence (García Castellón 2003, 41), *Recuerdos* is a satiric description of the archipelago through the personal testimony of its author-narrator. In his position as correspondent for the Ministerio de asuntos coloniales, this liberal politician exacerbated not just Filipinos but even the Spaniards living on the islands[7] with polemics statements like "lo único serio que hay en Filipinas son los terremotos y la disentería" (the only thing you can take seriously in the Philippines are earthquakes and dysentery) (Cañamaque 1877, 1).

Three years later, another employee of the Spanish colonial administration, Francisco Vila y Goyri, published the compilation *Escenas Filipinas* (1882). In the thought-provoking prologue by Rafael Ginard de la Rosa, the liberal politician wrote that "libros de la índole del que nos ocupa . . . libros acerca de países distantes casi desconocidos y en los que tremola la bandera española, son utilísimos, son necesarios para el conocimiento de su vida" (the kind of books that we are dealing with . . . books about distant countries almost unknown and where the Spanish flag trembles, are very useful, are necessary for the knowledge of its life) (in Vila 1882, 13). His words about "the kind of books" reveal an awareness about a certain kind of tradition in writing about the Philippines at that particular moment.

In 1887, coinciding with the Exposición de Filipinas held in Madrid, the physician and journalist Alberto Díaz de la Quintana, under the pseudonym Ximeno Ximénez, also published a compilation book: *Siluetas Filipinas*. In the author's own words, this book "viene a ser una colección de impresiones sentidas por mí en Manila, donde he trabajado literariamente unos años" (might be called a compilation of impressions felt by me in Manila, where I have worked in literary terms a few years) (1887, 5). Like some of his predecessors, Díaz de la Quintana waited for the precise moment when the interest in the archipelago was at a peak to make his personal experience about the colony known, which was also revealed in the representative style of some *siluetas*: projections that hide their real essence.

Ultimately, Pablo Feced y Temprado, forced to move to the Philippines for familiar issues, wrote similarly bitter articles for the Spanish newspaper *El Liberal* under the pseudonym Quioquiap. Like the ones before him, his articles were compiled in the book *Filipinas: Esbozos y pinceladas* (Manila, 1888). This work is the closest—in chronological terms—to the publication of *La Solidaridad* (1889–90), so Feced was in the spotlight of the Filipino *ilustrados* at the time he was publishing his articles. In fact, as Gloria Cano points out, there was an open war between the Spanish publication *La política de España en Filipinas*—directed by Feced—and *La Solidaridad*: "*La política de España en Filipinas* . . . became the antagonist of *La Solidaridad* with the prime objective of undermining the latter by pursuing a campaign based on discrediting Filipinos" (2011, 198). But the tensions between Spaniards defending the status quo of the colony and Filipino *ilustrados* fighting for the improvement of their political and administrative situation—and also for an end to the warped representation of their land—were a prevalent issue during these last decades of Spanish rule.

During the 1870s, a large community of Filipino *ilustrados* were living, studying, and working in the metropolis. The hope of modernity and reforms arrived in the colony inspired by the 1868 revolution in Spain. As García Castellón points out, "La clase mestiza . . . infunde a sus jóvenes vástagos la idea de liderazgo futuro y, a fin de prepararlos al efecto, comienza a enviarlos a las Universidades europeas. Hacia 1870 llegan a España los primeros estudiantes filipinos" (The mestizo class . . . instills in his youth the idea of future leadership and, in order to prepare them for it, starts to send them to European universities. Circa 1870 the first Filipino students arrived in Spain) (2003, 15). The so-called *ilustrados filipinos* soon realized the lack of knowledge about the Philippines among the Spanish population: what little information existed about the archipelago was provided by the tendentious impressions written by the Spanish travelers.

To fight this mangled image of their land, the Filipino *ilustrados* in Madrid and Barcelona initiated a propaganda campaign that would cast light on the appalling Spanish administration of the colony and present a more accurate image of the Filipino population: As Gloria Cano remarks (2011, 172) the freedom of the press present at that moment in the metropolis—yet unimaginable in the colony—protected Filipinos like Graciano López Jaena, Pedro Paterno, and José Rizal in their journalistic undertakings.

The irruption of Filipinos in the Spanish panorama press was welcomed yet at the same time ill received: some liberal journalists supported the Filipino cause and collaborated with Spanish liberal newspapers like *El País, El Liberal,* and *El Imparcial.* In contrast, however, a string of anti-reformist and pro-conservative journalists, such as Pablo Feced, began to attack the *ilustrados*: they did not consider that the Philippines was ready to become a Spanish province; they "believed they had not yet come of age" (Cano 2011, 199).[8] It was in this context that Luna's articles were published: the press became a battlefield where both Filipinos and Spaniards set out to defend their respective identities from different positions. In the case of the Filipinos, they were striving to achieve better political, administrative, and economic rights, first by looking for their recognition as Spanish citizens with equal rights as metropolitans but then, after several unsuccessful attempts, by finding their self-determination as an independent nation from Spain. In the same context but in the opposite way, Spaniards were struggling to maintain control over the archipelago, trying to retain their status as the biggest colonial power, injured at that time by the loss of continental America and stuck in an outdated colonial policy revealed as inefficient by the end of the 19th century.[9]

Luna's Answer to the Representation of the Philippines in the Spanish Compilations: Uses and Inversions of the Colonial Discourse

The first statement that characterizes the Spanish compilations is the condition of veracity of their testimonial texts: "Impórtame declarar que cuanto voy a decir en estas páginas, escritas a ratos perdidos, es exacto" (I want to declare that all I am going to say in these pages, written in spare time, is exact), says Cañamaque in the introduction of *Recuerdos* (1877, 1), while Feced adds: "¿Errores, omisiones o abultamientos hiperbólicos? Hay a veces fotografías sin acabado parecido, pero ni una siquiera sin un fondo general de verdad" (Mistakes, omissions, or hyperbolic exaggerations? There are sometimes photographs without similarity in its finish, but not a single one without a general content of truth) (1888, 6). The titles of the compilations themselves (*Recuerdos, Escenas, Siluetas,* and *Esbozos y pinceladas*) make reference to the intention of a close representation of reality, although they consider the inherent subjectivity of this testimonial action: as Feced points out, the image may be warped, but reality remains its backdrop.

Luna, too, will allude to the value of the representation, but in his first words an ironic reference to the Spanish works can be inferred: "Sobre los bocetos expuestos, me inspiré siempre del natural. . . . ¿Y bien? El arte pictórico ahora tiende a la realidad" (About the exposed sketches, I took live inspiration. . . . And so? Pictorial art now tends to reality) (1891, 9). This last sentence may be understood as a direct allusion to the presumed objectivity of the Spaniards describing the Philippines: if they are, supposedly, reflecting the reality of the colony, he is going to do the same with life in the metropolis.

These affirmations of veracity and objectivity of specific images able to represent a wider concept—*tipos,* traditions, landscapes, cities, and so forth— are common in the *costumbrismo* tendency of the 19th century (Fernández Montesinos 1960). But in this colonial context, in the case of the Spanish authors writing about the Philippines, the affirmation of the "I" may also be read through Pratt's concept of "monarch of all I survey": a European seeing man "whose imperial eyes passively look out and possess" (1992, 7). Cañamaque, Vila, Díaz de la Quintana, and Feced in essence were this kind of seeing men who, through their gaze and their writings, were possessing the Philippines, creating a new reality through their imperial eyes, conditioned by the context of an empire in decay.

Luna, in turn, will also occupy the place of the seeing man, though not in order to possess the metropolis: to put himself in the superior position of the observer allows him, contrarily, to uphold an independent position toward the Spaniards. This elevated position also serves Luna's intention to discredit Spain as a "capable" colonial power, a latent idea that will pervade the Filipino work.

The Natural Environment: Climate Conditions and Landscape

The four Spanish texts start at the same point: the arrival at Manila and the subsequent transfer to a *provincia*. For this reason, one of the first impressions captured by the travelers is the climatic conditions and the prospects over the rural landscape. In relation to the natural environment, there are two essential ideas that the Spanish travelers would spread: (1) the Philippines as a hostile space for Europeans due to their climate conditions and (2) the exuberance of the Filipino landscape, closely related to ideas about its economic exploitation.

Díaz de la Quintana, upon his arrival in Manila, writes: "suelo palpitante de calor y convulsiones, tierra fangosa donde los pies se pegan" (pounding soil by heath and convulsions, muddy land where the feet get stuck) (1887); Feced, on a journey to his rural hacienda, also complains: "La tierra parece hundirse bajo el peso de abrumadora carga. Y, allá arriba, un cielo a trozos de azul brillante, por donde el sol derrama rayos de fuego . . . y el silencio de la muerte aquí abajo" (The land seems to collapse under the weight of the overwhelming load. And, up there, a sky formed by pieces of shining blue, where the sun spills fire beams . . . and the silence of the death here below) (1888, 23). The authors describe the inclement weather and the Spaniards' difficulties adapting to the tropical territory. Cañamaque even goes as far as to criticize those from the metropolis who change their garments to be able to adapt to this climate: the "aplatanados . . . los que adquieren los hábitos del país y su calma inalterable" (*aplatanados* . . . the ones who acquire the country's habits and its unalterable calm) (1877, 221). In a conversation between a *vago* (newcomer) and a *matandá* (long-term Spanish resident of the islands), the second confesses to his countryman that he has ceased to wear "guantes" (gloves), a "chaleco" (vest), or even "calzoncillos" (underpants): "Aquí no guardamos la etiqueta de Europa, ciertas cosas están de más" (Here we do not keep the European protocol, some things are unnecessary) (221). In sum, the Filipino environment is portrayed as a negative influence that affects the decorum—in attire and in conduct—as it approximates the Spaniard to the native Filipino, transmitting to the former their uncivilized and even animalized features.

Against this extremely negative vision—which would discourage any immigrant from settling down in such a land—Rafael Ginard de la Rosa, in the prologue of *Escenas Filipinas*, writes:

Comprende el Archipiélago un territorio como la mitad de la Península
Ibérica, poblado por 5 millones de habitantes, y que puede sustentar a 20 millones. El clima tropical está templado por brisas constantes. Los aborígenes
no oponen obstáculos a la cultura, antes bien la mayor parte hace siglos que
forman una sociedad civil y política en la que reina el orden y la armonía.
Su suelo fecundísimo es de fácil rotación y cultivo; sus numerosos puertos
favorecen al comercio; sus productos naturales subministran a la industria
incalculables elementos.

(The archipelago comprises a territory as half of the Iberian Peninsula, with
5 million inhabitants, and able to sustain 20 million. The tropical climate is
tempered by steady breezes. Aborigines do not object to culture, rather the
majority has formed a civil and political society for centuries that maintains
the order and harmony. Its very fruitful soil is easy to rotate and cultivate;
its numerous ports facilitate trade; its natural products provide incalculable
elements to the industry.) (1882, 6)

Ginard's prologue is an ode to the Spanish immigration to the Philippines:
described as a land of opportunities, full of natural resources, and, furthermore, home to a native population living in perfect order and harmony, apparently far removed from any kind of revolt or revolution. As Spurr affirms
(1993, 125), it is not just the natural resources that are idealized in colonial discourse; the tradition of idealizing the "savage" has also been present since the
early stages of Western European imperial expansion. The Spanish journalist
draws the picture of an ideal territory to attract investors, thus backing the
economic reforms and other governmental initiatives aimed at encouraging
Spanish entrepreneurship in the colony, for instance, through the 1887 exhibition in Madrid. But the development of the Philippines had to be carried
out by the hands of a nation able to manage it efficiently, an argument that
serves once again the purpose of colonization. According to David Spurr, the
colonial narratives that underpin the appropriation of territory must portray
the land as of "natural abundance" but awaiting "the creative hand of technology" (1993, 28). The Spanish author Feced expresses both abundance and
said arrival of technology—or civilization, in his view—in one of his articles:

¡Perla española del Pacífico! Cuán grande será tu hermosura cuando a las maravillas de tu gigante flora se unan las maravillas del humano espíritu. Cuando

sobre la vegetación esplendorosa arroje la civilización su espléndido manto. Quiera el cielo que estos pobres escritores sean siquiera grano de arena del futuro templo.

(Spanish pearl of the Pacific! How great will be your beauty when the wonders of your gigantic flora join the wonders of the human spirit. When above the splendorous vegetation the civilization will throw its splendid cover. May heaven grant that these poor writers will be even a sand particle of the future temple.) (1888, 234–35)

Throughout his text, Feced seeks to aid in this necessity of bringing "civilization" to the archipelago, in order to capitalize on its natural resources since, as Spurr points out, in this kind of colonial narrative, "The writer literally sees the landscape of the non-Western world in terms of the promise of westernized development" (1993, 19).

The Spanish economic interest in exploiting the Philippines is precisely one of the first ideas to be found in Luna's text, as its author laments this by making an explicit reference to the Spanish texts spreading these ideas: "Prójimo hay que echa improvisado discurso sobre la naturaleza exuberante de aquellas tierras vírgenes, e introduciendo el si yo fuera allí, proyecta modificar la administración colonial española, etc., etc." (There are neighbors who talk about the exuberant nature of those virgin lands, and saying *If I went there*, projects to modify the Spanish colonial administration, etc., etc.) (1891, 5).

Antonio Luna thus expresses his indignation about this Spanish "improvisado discurso" (impromptu speech) on the Filipino landscape and the reformist initiatives that only seek to profit from the land's resources. Describing the archipelago as "tierras vírgenes" (virgin lands)—using the same expression as the Spanish authors (Cañamaque 1877, 160; Vila 1882, 5; Feced 1888, 215)—Luna's text exposes the colonial topic of the landscape written as uninhabited, unpossessed, unhistoricized, and unoccupied space (Pratt 1992, 50) according to the Spanish colonial discourse. The Filipino land, which "como Dios la hizo, . . . virgen se conserva a las avaricias del hacha y el arado" (as God did it . . . prevails virgin over the greed of the axe and the plow) (Feced 1888, 233) is described as ready and available for being possessed by the colonizer, reproducing the schema noticed by Anne McClintock in the English colonial discourse: the feminization of the land that would be ready for male exploitation (1995, 23–24). Moreover, the exhaustive descriptions of those spaces pictured by the Spanish authors are closely related, as in other European colonial discourses, with the economic possibilities of the land (Pratt 1992, 59–60) that Luna reports in his text: "La cabeza tira a la explotación" (The mind tends to exploitation) (1891, 5).

Reading the few lines of Ginard de la Rosa's prologue to Vila's *Escenas Filipinas* already referred (1882, 6), is easy to understand Luna's complain. That enumeration of the Philippines material wealth—including in this list the natives themselves—reflects the procedure described by Pratt in her study of English colonial texts, where the authors perform an "eye scanning" which prospects "possibilities of a Euro-colonial future coded as resources to be developed, surpluses to be traded" (1992, 59). All these resources, in colonizer's opinion, remain hidden in the lazy eyes of the natives—"¡Nosotros, añade, no sabemos las minas que allí tenemos ocultas!" (We, he adds, we do not know the hidden mines that we got there!) (1891, 5)—but the Filipino writer confronts this thought by revealing Spaniards' real ignorance about the Asian colony.

Spaniards, who seem to be exclusively concerned about the economic possibilities of exploitation, ignore basic information about the Philippines. As Luna exemplifies in various conversations with a number of inhabitants of Madrid, they are not even able to locate the Philippines on a map (1891, 4) or to identify the language spoken on the islands. Describing the character of the Spanish women, Luna reproduces the words of a young lady, stunned by her encounter with the author himself:

> —Pero qué bien habla usted el español. . . . Me extraña que usted lo posea tanto como yo.
> —Es nuestro idioma oficial en Filipinas, y por eso lo conocemos.
> —Pero, ¡por Dios! ¿en su país de usted se habla el español?
> —Sí, señorita.
> —¡¡¡Ahhh!!!

> (—You speak Spanish very well. . . . I am surprised that you master Spanish as I do.
> —It is our official language in the Philippines, that is why we can speak it.
> —But, in the name of God! Do you speak Spanish in your country?
> —Yes, lady.
> —Ahhh!!!) (1891, 22)

Luna uses several times the metropolitan's surprise in front of him—and his skills—as a technique to highlight Spaniards' lack of knowledge about the colony and its distorted image spread by the Spanish texts. In this case, Luna alludes to the preconception of the Filipino unable to speak proper Spanish, a vision that draws from the portrayals of the rural native population made by the metropolitan authors. In their works, the Spaniards often focus on rural areas—the *provincias* where they have traveled[10]—where the Spanish presence was scarce, sometimes only constituted by a single friar[11] who was also in charge of teaching the Spanish language.[12] The Spanish skills of the native population in these areas were thus limited, and the metropolitan authors took advantage of this situation for the benefit of their objective. By focusing their representations of the Filipino almost entirely in these spaces, they attempted to project a generalized representation of the Filipinos as primary people far from the European concept of civilization, expressed this time through the lack of mastery of "la riquísima y sabrosa lengua de Cervantes" (the rich and tasty language of Cervantes) (Díaz de la Quintana 1887, 6). For example, in the chapter "Prosa y versos" (Prose and verses), Cañamaque transcribes several texts originally written—according to him—by Filipinos in Spanish, letters and poems that are full of grammatical and spelling mistakes (1877, 121–30), and he uses these examples to ridicule their Spanish skills.

The same mockery is used by the authors in the other metropolitan texts. They focus specially on pronunciation errors, such as the confusion between the phonemes /f/ and /p/, apparently very common among Filipinos when they spoke Spanish. Pablo Feced transcribed in one of his articles the following words, spoken by a *gobernadorcillo*:[13] "Señor, dispense. El señor Capitán no sabe lengua prestada, quiero decir, español: pero yo sí, porque he estudiado *pilosopia* [sic] y un curso de la *pacultad* [sic] de *parmacia* [sic] en la real y *pontipicia* [sic] Universidad de Manila" (Sir, excuse me. Sir Capitan does not speak the borrowed language, I mean, Spanish: but I do, because I have studied philosophy and a year in the faculty of pharmacy in the royal and pontifical University of Manila) (1888, 68).[14] Feced ridiculed the *gobernadorcillo* because, despite all his qualifications, he was making basic mistakes of pronunciation in Spanish.

Antonio Luna, having read this kind of text and knowing the image of the Filipino present in the metropolis, changes the perspective to show this time the Spaniards as uninformed. Furthermore, in front of these allegedly instructed people, Luna uses himself—a Filipino native—as the figure of confrontation who stood in front of an amazed Spanish. Metropolitans and Filipinos are now on the same plane regarding the control of the language, a sign of civilization according to the Spanish texts. With this powerful image, Luna attempts to vindicate Filipino rights in a context of inequity: evidencing the equality of their language skills, the Filipinos move away from the position of inferiority that supposedly disables them from self-government.

After this blunt blow, it is Luna's opportunity to offer a sketch of the peninsular landscape. On his trip from Barcelona to Madrid, the Filipino observes and describes: "El país montañoso, árido y desierto, la naturaleza, raquítica y empobrecida, sin sembrados los campos y doquiera peñas y pedruscos. Bien decía un igorrote de la Exposición filipina de 1887: 'Aquí hay mucha hambre, porque no hay más que piedras'" (The mountainous, dry and desertic country, the nature, rachitic and impoverished, without seeded fields, and rocks and stones everywhere. As an Igorot from the Filipino Exhibition in 1887 said well: "There is real hunger, because there are only rocks") (1891, 3). Against the abundance and fertility of the Philippines, Spain is portrayed as a land of poor, barren soil. Using again his fine irony, Luna seems to imply that the real reason behind the colonial eagerness to possess and explore the natural wealth of the Philippines is actually the material poverty of the metropolis itself.

The misery and infertility of the Spanish countryside—expressed by Luna throughout the sum total of his articles—transcend natural space, as the image of Spain as a wasteland also impregnates the political and social sphere: a nation without resources, unable to carry out any meaningful reform. In conclusion, it is a fruitless country where all work or investment seems bound to fail. Moreover, by attributing the harsh statement "Aquí hay mucha hambre, porque no hay más que piedras" (There is real hunger, because there are only rocks) (1891, 3) to an Igorot of the Exposición, Luna magnifies the power of his attack: even one of the most "savage" inhabitants of the Philippines[15] has had the chance to utter a critical remark aimed at discrediting the alleged superiority of the colonizers' nation. Once again, the Filipino author uses *Impresiones* to expose the image of the primacy of the metropolis stated in the European colonial discourse in front of an enlightened, educated, and non-savage colonized subject. This strategy invalidates the logic of colonization where a civilized nation possesses the right to dominate another due to its assumed inferiority. This revelation also ensures and sustains the claiming of rights advocated by the Filipino nationalists, as this proved equality would allow them to claim equal rights in front of the Spanish authorities or even to uphold their capacity of self-government without Spanish tutelage.

The Other in Motion: Representing the Filipino, the Spanish, and Their Activities

From these first descriptions of the landscape, Luna moves swiftly toward the description of the inhabitants of Madrid and their customs. As an expert *costumbrista*, he paints the disappointing scene he observes in front of him in the heart of the city:

> De la Puerta del Sol solamente excitó mi curiosidad la muchedumbre de desocupados que van a tomar el sol y a calentarse en invierno en las aceras, esa apretada masa de seres vivientes de corto y de coleta que se sitúa frente al café Imperial, estorbando y molestando al pacífico transeúnte. ¿Qué hace allí horas enteras? No lo sé, ni lo he sabido nunca.

> (La Puerta del Sol only excited my curiosity for the careless crowd who go to sunbathe and to get warm on the pavement during winter, that tight mass of human beings *de corto y de coleta*, which is located in front of the café Imperial, disturbing and bothering the peaceful walker. What are they doing there for hours? I do not know, and I have never known.) (1891, 8)

According to Luna, the Spanish confine themselves to wandering around the square, as they seem to have no other occupation. This idea reflects what the Spanish writers called the *mal endémico* (endemic problem) of the Philippines: the laziness and the indolence of the *indios*. All four Spanish authors, at some point in their compilations, agree on this feature: Cañamaque has a whole chapter entitled "Pereza y abandono en los indios" (Laziness and neglect of the *indios*), and Díaz de la Quintana in "El trabajo en Filipinas" (Work in the Philippines) insists on the existence of "una mayoría de espectadores, personas hechas al orden, regimentadas sistemáticamente, y que ni hacen ni deshacen" (a majority of viewers, people used to rules, systematically ruled, and who do nothing) (1887, 101). Because of this particularity of the Filipino character, Spain has the duty to guide and teach those "mujeres y hombres" (men and women) with "ojos melancólicos" (melancholic eyes) and "aire perezoso y somnoliento" (lazy and sleepy appearance) (Cañamaque 1877, 18) in the "art" of labor. But in light of the picture Luna offers from the Puerta del Sol, the reader would surely call into question the Spanish nation's ability for this purpose. With this new comparison, the Filipino writer exposes again the fake discourse of European superiority that allows Spain to dominate the colony—Spaniards at the metropolis, as Luna portrays, endure the same *mal endémico* as the native population of the Philippines—discrediting once again the Spanish right to dominate the archipelago, as it would be unable to reform Filipinos from a misconduct suffered also by themselves.

Another scene that Antonio Luna will have the chance to sketch is a *ter-tulia* at a Spanish home. What was supposed to be an intellectual discussion turned into a *cursi*[16] meeting where, when the conversation falters, "doña Emerenciana invitaba a los concurrentes a jugar a la lotería, a céntimo por puesta, para que no se dijera que en su casa permitía el juego" (Mrs. Emer-encia invited everyone present to play the lottery, five cents as the bet so they could not say that gambling was allowed in her house) (1891, 165). The evening soon turns into unseemly small talk as the game seems to unleash a string of vices and frivolities. Gambling as a force of perversion in society also appears in the Spanish narratives. Díaz de la Quintana, for one, includes an entire chapter on "el panguingue," a Filipino type of card game (1887, 59). Astonished, the Spanish writer observes "la abundancia del sexo bello del propio país . . . y la infinidad de madres con críos que *panguinguean* toda la calderilla practicable con lacre de luto natural por el uso"[17] (the abundance of the fair sex from all over the country . . . and mothers with children that *panguinguean* all the possible loose change dirty from use) (1887, 63). The debasement of the human agents, exposing their weakness, their "filth and defilement," appears in these scenes as another feature of the colonial dis-course (Spurr 1993, 76). The addiction to gambling, which seems to affect the Filipino natives, used as an argument of their natural weakness, is all but overridden by the *lotería* scene in Luna's *Impresiones*: the Spanish mentality, too, is vulnerable to this kind of entertainment, present in both societies. In conclusion, gambling certainly seems to dominate in the Spanish home alluded to in Luna's text, and the Filipino writer even seems to associate the presence of this vice to all Spanish domains, including the colonies, with gambling not an endemic problem originating in the islands but an exported one from the metropolis.

Finally, we find two scenes that focus on yet another social activity of utmost importance in both societies, the illustration of which is particularly meaningful: dancing. In this type of cultural expression, the colonial narra-tives are highly significant. As shown in the following narrations, erotization and, worse, animalization (Spurr 1993, 170) are present in this cultural activ-ity, which involves a number of different agents and perspectives.

The first passage offering a description of a dance in the Philippines can be found in *Siluetas Filipinas* (1887). After the wedding ceremony between a *matandá* and a mestiza, the dance begins:

Del piano que hay allá en la sala, brotan alegres compases, que llaman incitando; crúzanse miradas de amor, los cuerpos se acercan, las cinturas se dejan abrazar, algunas cabezas se apoyan voluptuosas en hombros que se estremecen a tan grato contacto; queman los alientos, los nervios desfallecen de impresión, callan las lenguas, dejando toda su verbosidad a los ojos, que hablan rápidos, vehementes, apasionados.

(From the piano there in the room, cheerful rhythms fly out, which call incitement; loving looks are crossing, bodies are getting closer, waists allow the embrace, some heads lean voluptuous on shoulders that shudder with such a pleasing contact; breaths burn, nerves falter from impression, tongues remain silent, leaving all their verbiage to the eyes, which speak fast, vehemently, passionately.) (Díaz de la Quintana 1887, 69)

The erotic tension is palpable in this scene: a Spanish celebration held in the archipelago, a space where, as will be revealed in the course of this analysis, the decorum and formalism so present in the metropolis *se aplatanan*. This process of "adquisición de los hábitos del país y su calma inalterable" (acquisition of the habits of the country and its unalterable calm) (Cañamaque 1877, 221), as McClintock points out, is closely linked with the erotic power of the savage land, portrayed in the eyes of the colonizer as "a fantastic magic lantern of the mind onto which Europe projected its forbidden sexual desires and fears" (1995, 22). This idea permeates throughout the Spanish narrative, but Luna also will displace this concept to the land of the colonizer.

In *Impresiones*, Luna also represents several situations where dance is involved: parties, celebrations, festivities, and so forth. The most expressive instance is the one that takes place during a celebration of St. Joseph's Day, in the context of the lower social strata, *el pueblo llano* (common people):

Pepita, la incansable Pepita y una andaluza sensual, hermosa, provocativa, pusiéronse a bailar flamenco, y aquello fue la señal de la completa transformación. Las manos de ambas, como dislocadas, parecían describir raras figuras en el aire; las cabezas echadas hacia atrás, las bocas entreabiertas, los ojos entornados no eran capaces de ocultar el tinte voluptuoso de que estaban poseídas, las sacudidas eléctricas que hacían quebrar las cinturas, mover las caderas, y soltar de vez en cuando sonoras pataditas en el suelo. Aquello era la característica de grandes cantidades de sensualismo acumuladas.

(Pepita, the restless Pepita and a sensual Andalusian, beautiful, provocative, started dancing flamenco, and that was the sign of the complete transformation. The hands of both, as dislocated, seemed to represent strange figures in the air; heads thrown back, mouths ajar, the half-closed eyes unable to hide the voluptuous color of which they were possessed, the electric shocks that made the waists break, move the hips, and the sonic kicks on the floor. That was characteristic from large amounts of accumulated sensualism.) (1891, 242–43)

This flamenco show, a folkloristic representation of Spanish culture, is described by Luna through the eyes of a Western traveler. Flamenco lends Spain an air of "exotic sensualism," a key feature of the Orientalist discourse: "Orient seems still to suggest not only fecundity but sexual promise (and threat), untiring sensuality, unlimited desire" (Said 1978, 188). The Spanish particularity of the flamenco, with its roots in Arab culture, provides this chapter with a connection to the last element that Luna employs to discredit Spain as a capable colonial power.

Spain as a Non-European Nation: The Orientalization of the Country through Its Arab Past

Especially since the beginning of the 19th century, travel literature about Spain tended to display a Romantic vision of an exotic country. Geographically situated at the border of the civilized and the barbaric—Europe and Africa—Spain ensnared the Western traveler of the 19th century by its fascinating Arab past. During this period of a renewed interest in the "Orient," Spain came to be a space where Europeans could encounter a source of otherness, entailing a range of different reactions:

España había pasado de ser el límite temporal, por su decadencia, de una Europa a la que pertenecía por derecho, a convertirse ella misma en una frontera. En el siglo XIX era, a ojos de los europeos, el espacio en el que entraban en contacto Oriente y Occidente. Creo que es por ello, por el hecho de situarse justo en el límite, por lo que resultó tan interesante como un espacio en el que proyectar los deseos y los miedos del moderno yo masculino.

(Spain had moved from being the time limit, due to its decline from a Europe to which it belonged by right, to becoming a border itself. In the 19th century it was, in the eyes of Europeans, the space in which East and West came into contact. I think that is why, since it was right on the edge, it was so interesting as a space that projected the desires and fears of the modern masculine self.) (Andreu Miralles 2005, 206–7)

As Andreu Miralles specifies, the Romantic vision of Spain as an exotic, Orientalized—and possibly barbaric—country contributed to a growing chasm between the nation's image and the idea of modernity present at that time in Europe. Antonio Luna took advantage of this representation of Spain—already ingrained in the European imaginary—as his work underscores the distance between this particular nation and (his conception of) modern Europe, represented above all by capitals like London or Paris. During his strolls around the Spanish city, he wonders: "En vano buscaba ese algo poético y encantador que respiran los alrededores de París y Londres; en vano buscaba la coquetería de los chalets, de los jardines, de las praderas, que en estas grandes ciudades alegra el espíritu" (In vain I was looking for that something poetical and charming that you can breathe around Paris and London; in vain I was looking for the coquetry of the chalets, of the gardens, of the meadows, which in these big cities gladden the spirit) (1881, 12). In his opinion, Madrid could not compare to the genuinely modern cities around Europe that Luna had visited before.

To underline this impression, Luna introduces other elements that—in his view—betray the nation's "true" character into his discourse: "Muchas veces, al pensar en estas espontáneas manifestaciones [a reference to the aforementioned behavior of the Madrileños in the streets], me pregunto si estoy en Marruecos, en las peligrosas comarcas del Riff, y hasta llego a dudar si vivo en la capital de una nación europea" (Sometimes, when I think about these spontaneous manifestations, I ask myself if I am in Morocco, in the dangerous regions of the Riff, and I even doubt whether I live in the capital of a European nation) (1881, 4). These references to Morocco keep coming up: just a few pages after, Luna compares El Rastro, one of the principal street markets in Madrid, to one in Tangier, similar in its atmosphere and behavior of the vendors (6).

As these images evince, Spain is conceived as outside the European space, the space of modernity and civilization in the colonial discourse. Judging by the situation thus projected, the Spanish state seems all but unable to administrate its few remaining colonies in an efficient and just manner.

Conclusion

The objective of the Spanish "information campaign" about the Philippines was—despite the authors' personal and political differences—a clear one: to legitimize the Spanish colonial administration of the islands. The writers employed different strategies to advance this purpose: from the vision of the Philippines as an exuberant land of opportunities—seeking to attract Spanish immigrants to the islands—to the definition of the Filipino as inferior—Orientalized and barbaric—incapable of self-management and in dire need of the Spanish rule. In their sum, the images present in these works—essentializing and hardly representative, just like the Igorots at the 1887 exhibition—constructed an untrue, distorted notion of the colony: the result of an Orientalized and colonial discourse that Luna set out to fight.

In the articles that make up *Impresiones*, the author employed the very strategy of his adversaries to, in turn, attack and delegitimize the Spanish colonial power: an apparently innocent compilation of personal experiences in the guise of a travel diary but based on the representation of the Other. This time, the Filipino assumes the position of the "seer/civilized" in a colonial setting as he retorts the Spanish attacks by placing the ruling power in the position of the "seen/uncivilized." Through his sharp prose, permeated by a sarcastic and ironic tone, Luna offers the reader a picture of Spain as an Orientalized and uncivilized nation, a representation of the metropolis that clearly discredits its authority as a colonial power. Thus, the definition of otherness present in both Filipino and Spanish works eventually became the space of a struggle between an emerging nation and a decadent empire in which both sides sought to construct and reaffirm their identities.

Notes

1. Translation by Reyes (2008, 91).

2. More detailed information about the incident can be found in the works of Vivencio R. José (1971, 2001) and Raquel A. G. Reyes (2008).

3. During the last third of the 19th century, the Philippines, unlike Cuba and Puerto Rico, was still ruled through special laws. Directly given and applied by the Spanish government, these laws do not need to be approved by the Cortes (Elizalde Pérez-Grueso 2002a,

126), This situation of inequality in relation to the other colonies was justified by several Spanish politicians, given the special conditions and situation of the Asian colony and their native population. Manuel Azcárraga—Manila's civil governor during the 1890s—stated that the Philippines "puede considerarse aún en su period de educación" (can be still considered in their educational period) (quoted in Elizalde Pérez-Grueso 2002a, 130), and he said, according to this situation, "Filipinas no está preparada, como Cuba y Puerto Rico, para ejercer derechos políticos que no necesitan ni comprenden" (the Phipillines are not ready to exercise political rights that they do not need or understand) (quoted in Celdrán Ruano 2002, 130). This idea of an immature colony that needed to be tutored by a caring "Madre Patria" transcended the political sphere as it is shown in literary works. For example, the journalist Alberto Díaz de la Quintana portrayed Manila in his *Siluetas Filipinas* (1887) as a whimsical child who "grita, y grita rabiosamente . . . protestando amparo y protección; gritos que la madre escucha estremecida de dolor" (yells, and yells furiously . . . asking for refuge and protection; cries that the mother listens to, shaken by pain) (128).

4. Actions like the Motín de Cavite in 1872—the most significant uprising against the colonial power during the 19th century before 1896—warned the Spanish government about the discontent of the Filipino population and the need for change of the colonial policy toward the islands (Elizalde Pérez-Grueso 2002, 127). On the other hand, the presence in the Philippines of foreign investments and commercial traffic from other European powers—such as the United Kingdom, France, and Germany (Elizalde Pérez-Grueso 2002b; Rodao 2010, 448)—were perceived as a threat to the Spanish sovereignty of the islands (Celdrán Ruano 2002, 168; Elizalde Pérez-Grueso 2002a, 129).

5. The most widely known reports were Sinibaldo de Mas's *Informe sobre el estado de las Islas Filipinas* (1842) and the polemic *Apuntes interesantes sobre las Islas Filipinas* (1869) written by Vicente Barrantes, who entered a heated argument with Ferdinand Blumentritt (Torres-Pou 2013, 125). Despite their supposed objectivity and scientific data-based foundation, these reports are clear examples of the imperialistic rhetoric defined by Mary Louise Pratt and David Spurr in their respective works (Pratt 1992; Spurr 1993).

6. Cañamaque describes his arrival in "La noche de mi llegada al país" (1887) (The night of my arrival to the country), the first article of the compilation; also, Francisco Vila briefly relates his first steps at the beginning of "El crímen de Malmanic" (1882) (Malmanic's crime), the first chapter of his book. Díaz de la Quintana uses the article "Adios a Manila" (1887) (Goodbye Manila) to remember his arrival and first days in the city; and, finally, Pablo Feced in "En Manila" (1888) (In Manila) sketches the first days after his arrival. The chapters that follow—mainly former articles published in press—depicted different aspects of life in the islands, such as the structure of a tribunal (small units of government in the *provincias*), leisure activities (cock fights, theater performances, board games or life at the cafés), and rites (weddings and funerals).

7. As a response to *Recuerdos*, Francisco de Paula Entrala—himself, too, a Spaniard living in the colony—published the miscellanea *Olvidos de Filipinas* (1881). In it, Entrala tried to redefine the representation of the native—as far as the colonial conceptions allowed him—but particularly defended the image of the Spanish long-term dweller in the colony.

8. Apart from the mentioned confrontation between Feced and the *ilustrados*, the

open conflicts between José Rizal and Vicente Barrantes—an administration employee in
the Philippines and the editor of several publications in Spain (José 2001, 26)—or between
Rizal and Cañamaque are also noteworthy.

9. On the problems of the Spanish colonial policies at the end of the 19th century, see
Fradera 2002, 2004; Schmidt-Nowara 2005; Elizalde Pérez-Grueso 2009; and Rodao 2010.

10. Francisco Cañamaque avoids revealing the name of the province where he was
assigned, trying not to make it recognizable in order to prevent any problems that his portrayals may cause (1877, 8). Francisco Vila served as prosecutor and judge at the court of
first assistance in the districts of Bohol, Bataan, Leyte, Samar, and Quiapo (1882). Alberto
Díaz de la Quintana, according to his compilation, seems to spend his time in the Philippines almost entirely in Manila, but he also mentions the *provincias* omitting their names.
Finally, Pablo Feced settled in his brother's hacienda in Camarines del Sur (García Castellón 2001).

11. As several authors have pointed out (Pérez Serrano 1998; García Abásolo 2011;
Fernández Palacios 2011), the Spanish population was concentrated in urban areas, mainly
in Luzón and especially in Manila and its surroundings.

12. Since the first centuries of colonization, there was a broad discussion about education in the colony, especially regarding the teaching of the Spanish language among the
native population. It was not until 1863 that education in Spanish was institutionalized in
the colony and that the first schools opened in the archipelago. Before that, the friars, without any general law or system, were in charge of education in the Philippines. On education
and language instruction in the Philippines, see Donoso 2012.

13. A *gobernadorcillo* was a native authority introduced in Filipino society by the Spanish powers during the first years of colonization. His responsibilities were to manage internal issues in the Filipino community: administrative tasks, enforcement of the laws, and so
forth. These duties were always under the supervision of the Spanish authorities (Elizalde
Pérez-Grueso 2009, 55).

14. In the Spanish quote, the words in italics—used by Feced himself—indicate where
the confusion between /f/ and /p/ takes place: the Filipino says in Spanish "*pilosopia*"
instead of "*filosofía*" (philosophy); "*pacultad*" instead of "*facultad*" (faculty); "*parmacia*"
instead of "*farmacia*" (pharmacy); and "*pontipicia*" instead of "*pontificia*" (pontificial).

15. As Sánchez Gomez points out, Spaniards and *ilustrado* Filipinos used this term to
refer to "todos aquellos individuos de poblaciones no cristianizadas que vivían práctica-
mente al margen de la administración española, conservando con escasas variaciones los
modelos culturales existentes en los inicios de la colonización . . . negritos e 'igorrotes' de
Luzón. . . . En no pocas ocasiones, se aplicaba también a los moros, a los musulmanes de
Mindanao" (all those people from non-Christianized populations who lived practically on
the edges of the Spanish administration, preserving with few variations the cultural models
existing at the beginning of the colonization . . . Negritos and "igorrotes" of Luzón. . . . On
many occasions also applied to the Moors, the Muslims from Mindanao) (2001, 145–46).
The Filipino nationalist reactions to the exhibition of 1887 agreed that one of its most
deplorable features was the exhibition of *salvajes*. For example, the criollo Eduardo Lete
"insiste en que la presencia de 'igorrotes' y moros no es sino una maniobra de las órdenes
religiosas . . . para mostrar en la Península y a los peninsulares la necesidad de su presen-

cia" (insists that the presence of "igorrotes" and Moors is nothing other than a maneuver from religious orders . . . to show in the Peninsula and to the peninsular the need for their presence there) (Sánchez Gómez 2001, 155). In conclusion, *ilustrados* and criollos did not deem the exposition to be truly representative, as it did not reflect the actual social makeup of the islands, but just a number of native people seen to be the most removed from the colonial civilization model. This verdict did not, however, imply a feeling of solidarity among the fellow countrymen.

16. The *Diccionario de la Real Academia española* defines *cursi* as a person who intends to be elegant and sophisticated without success. On this word and its meaning in Spanish society in the 19th century, see Valis 2010.

17. The present analysis has no intention of omitting the relevance of the representation of "woman" in these types of colonial texts. However, as this is a highly interesting issue, it deserves an entire independent study in the near future.

References

Andreu Miralles, Xavier. 2005. "El triunfo de Al-Ándalus: Las fronteras de Europa y la '(semi)orientalización' de España en el siglo XIX." *Saitabi* 55:195–210. http://roderic .uv.es/handle/10550/27267

Bhabha, Homi K. 1994. *The Location of Culture*. New York: Routledge.

Cañamaque, Francisco. 1877. *Recuerdos de Filipinas*. Madrid: Librería de Anillo y Rodriguez.

Cañamaque, Francisco. 1879. *Recuerdos de Filipinas*. Madrid: Librería de Anillo y Rodriguez.

Cano, Gloria. 2011. "*La Solidaridad* y el periodismo en Filipinas en tiempos de Rizal." In *Entre España y Filipinas: José Rizal, escritor*, edited by María Dolores Elizalde Pérez Grueso and Beatriz Álvarez Tardío, 171–201. Madrid: Biblioteca Nacional de España.

Celdrán Ruano, Julia. 2002. "Instituciones hispano-filipinas: La representación parlamentaria filipina en las constituciones españolas del siglo XIX." In *Las relaciones entre España y Filipinas. Siglos XVI-XX*, edited by Dolores Elizalde Pérez-Grueso, 157–74. Madrid and Barcelona: CSIC and Casa Asia.

Díaz de la Quintana, Alberto (Ximeno Ximénez). 1887. *Siluetas Filipinas*. Madrid: Librería de robles y compañía.

Donoso-Jiménez, Isaac, ed. 2012. *Historia cultural de la lengua española en Filipinas: Ayer y hoy*. Madrid: Verbum.

Elizalde Pérez-Grueso, Dolores. 2002a. "La administración colonial de Filipinas en el último tercio del siglo XIX. Dos procesos contrapuestos: La reactivación del interés español frente a la consolidación de una identidad nacional filipina." In *Las relaciones entre España y Filipinas. Siglos XVI-XX*, edited by Dolores Elizalde Pérez-Grueso, 122–41. Madrid and Barcelona: CSIC and Casa Asia.

Elizalde Pérez-Grueso, Dolores. 2002b. "Comercio, inversiones y estrategia. Los intereses internacionales en Filipinas." In *Las relaciones entre España y Filipinas. Siglos XVI-XX*, edited by Dolores Elizalde Pérez-Grueso, 221–40. Madrid and Barcelona: CSIC and Casa Asia.

Elizalde Pérez-Grueso, Dolores. 2009. "Sentido y Rentabilidad. Filipinas en el marco del imperio español." In *Repensar Filipinas. Política, Identidad y Religión en la construcción de la nación Filipina*, edited by Dolores Elizalde Pérez-Grueso, 45–78. Barcelona: Ediciones Bellaterra.

Feced y Temprado, Pablo. 1888. *Filipinas. Esbozos y pinceladas*. Manila: Establecimiento Tipográfico de Ramírez y Compañía.

Fernández Montesinos, José. 1960. *Costumbrismo y novela. Ensayo sobre el redescubrimiento de la realidad española*. Madrid: Castalia.

Fernández Palacios, José María. 2011. "En los confines el mundo hispánico: Una propuesta para el estudio de la vida cotidiana de los españoles en Manila (1517–1898)." In *Fronteras del mundo hispánico: Filipinas en el contexto de las regiones liminares novohispanas*, edited by Luque Talaván and Manchado López, 109–34. Córdoba: Universidad de Córdoba.

Fradera, Josep M. 2002. "Filipinas en el siglo XIX: crecimiento económico y marco colonial." In *Las relaciones entre España y Filipinas. Siglos VXI-XX*, edited by María Dolores Elizalde Pérez-Grueso, 107–22. Madrid and Barcelona: Centro Superior de Investigaciones Científicas and Casa Asia.

Fradera, Josep M. 2004. "De la periferia al centro. (Cuba, Puerto Rico y Filipinas en la crisis del Imperio español)." *Anuario de Estudios Americanos* 61 (1): 161–99. https://doi.org/10.3989/aeamer.2004.v61.i1.146

García Abásolo, Antonio. 2011. "Filipinas. Una frontera más allá de la frontera." In *Fronteras del mundo hispánico: Filipinas en el contexto de las regiones liminares novohispanas*, edited by Luque Talaván y Manchado López, 71–88. Córdoba: Universidad de Córdoba.

García Castellón, Manuel. 2001. *Estampas y cuentos de la Filipinas hispánica*. Madrid: Clan.

José, Vivencio R. 1971. *The Rise and Fall of Antonio Luna*. Quezon City: University of the Philippines.

José, Vivencio R. 2001. "Literary Producers and the Construction of the Filipino Nation." In *Imperios y naciones en el Pacífico. Volumen II: Colonialismo e identidad Nacional en Filipinas y Micronesia*, edited by María Dolores Elizalde and Josep M. Fadrera y Luis Alonso, 21–45. Madrid: Centro Superior de Investigaciones Científicas and Asociación Española de Estudios del Pacífico.

Luna, Antonio (Taga-Ilog). 1891. *Impresiones*. Madrid: Imprenta de El progreso tipográfico.

McClintock, Anne. 1995. *Imperial Leather*. New York: Routledge.

Pérez Serrano, Julio. 1998. "Características de la población de las islas Filipinas en la segunda mitad del siglo XIX." *Jornadas de Historia Marítima* 22:5–36. https://armada.defensa.gob.es/archivo/mardigitalrevistas/cuadernosihcn/31cuaderno/01cap.pdf

Pratt, Mary Louise. 1992. *Imperial Eyes: Travel Writing and Transculturation*. London: Routledge.

Reyes, Raquel A. G. 2008. *Love, Passion and Patriotism: Sexuality and the Philippine Propaganda Movement, 1882–1892*. Singapore: National University of Singapore Press.

Rodao, Florentino. 2010. "Asia: Filipinas, percepciones y los empujes tardíos." In *La política exterior de España. De 1800 hasta hoy*, edited by Juan Carlos Pereira, 487–506. Madrid: Ariel.

Rodao, Florentino. 2018. "The Salvation Currents of Emigration: Racial Theories and Social Disputes in the Philippines at the End of the Nineteenth Century." *Journal of Southeast Asian Studies* 49 (3): 426–44.

Said, Edward W. 1978. *Orientalism*. New York: Vintage Books.

Sánchez Gómez, Luis Ángel. 2001. "'Salvajes e ilustrados': Actitudes de los nacionalistas filipinos ante la Exposición de 1887." In *Imperios y naciones en el Pacífico. Volumen II: Colonialismo e identidad Nacional en Filipinas y Micronesia*, edited by María Dolores Elizalde and Josep M. Fadrera y Luis Alonso, 145–72. Madrid: Consejo Superior de Investigaciones Científicas and Asociación Española de Estudios del Pacífico.

Schmidt-Nowara, Christopher. 2005. "Introduction." In *Interpreting Spanish Colonialism: Empires, Nations and Legends*, edited by Schmidt-Nowara and Nieto-Phillips, 1–18. Albuquerque: University of New Mexico Press.

Spurr, David. 1993. *The Rhetoric of Empire: Colonial Discourse in Journalism, Travel Writing and Imperial Administration*. Durham: Duke University Press.

Torres-Pou, Joan. 2013. *Asia en la España del siglo XIX: Literatos, viajeros, intelectuales y diplomáticos ante Oriente*. Amsterdam: Rodopi.

Valis, Noël. 2010. *La cultura de la cursilería: Mal gusto, clase y kitsch en la España moderna*. Madrid: Antonio Machado.

Vila, Francisco. 1882. *Escenas Filipinas*. Madrid: Librería de Fernando Fe.

PART V

Narratives of the Self and World War II

Writing a Spanish/Filipino Life

Travel, Trauma, and Disease in the
Works of Antonio Pérez de Olaguer (1907–68)

David R. George Jr.

On a spring afternoon in 1928, 21-year-old Antonio Pérez de Olaguer was invited to a poetry reading at the home of Filipino novelist, playwright, and poet Jesús Balmori. The lively recitations of poems by the national poet laureate and his contemporaries, Luis Planas Taverné and Manuel Bernabé, interspersed with performances by popular *declamadoras* Celia Canseco and Delfina San Agustín, enchanted the aspiring writer, who had recently arrived in Manila from Barcelona (fig. 1).[1] In his memories of the visit included in his 1928 travelogue *De Occidente a Oriente por Suez*, Olaguer exclaims:

> Y digo que en Filipinas se ama a España como a una madre. Que hubo una Guerra. Que hubo grandes errores y grandes mentiras. Que Filipinas se apartó del solar hispano, pero que ya no hay rencores ni prejuicios. Y que aquí—en Filipinas—el castellano triunfa como idioma. Y se miran las cosas de España con cariño.

> (And I say that in the Philippines, Spain is loved like a mother. There was a war. There were great mistakes and great lies. The Philippines moved away from the Hispanic world, but there are no more grudges or prejudices. I say that here in the Philippines, Spanish triumphs as a language. And they look at everything about Spain with affection.) (Pérez de Olaguer 1928, 195)

Balmori strikes a similarly celebratory tone in a bombastic sonnet with which he signed Olaguer's travel album. The poet exalts the resilient ties between Spain and the Philippines, and, more broadly, the global Pan-

Hispanic cultural tradition based on Spanish as a common language, in the final stanza:

Que el libro prisionera [*sic*]
Te dirá por donde quiera
Camines de cara al sol,
Que en la oriental patria mía,
Es flor de gloria y poesía
El dulce idioma español!

(May the book be a prisoner
He'll tell you that anywhere
You walk facing the sun,
That in my eastern homeland,
It's a flower of glory and poetry
The sweet Spanish language!)
(Pérez de Olaguer 1934, 177)

Born in 1907 in Barcelona to Filipino parents of Spanish descent, Olaguer was certainly ecstatic to discover that despite almost three decades of US colonial occupation, the Spanish language continued to be a vibrant vehicle of cultural life in Manila. His exuberance, though, should not be interpreted merely as an expression of nationalistic pride mixed with postcolonial nostalgia. Rather, the persistence of the language spoken by his parents and grandparents born in Manila in the 19th century, for him, also confirms the continuation of an unbroken affective tie to the country from which he and his forebears had been displaced by the circumstances of history.

In the 1967 biography of his father, Luis Pérez Samanillo (1868–1936), titled *Mi padre un hombre de bien*, Olaguer characterizes the movement for Philippine independence that dislodged his family from Manila as inevitable. Even so, on an affective level the writer cannot help lamenting the outcome that led to his displacement:

Mientras él [mi padre] permanecía en España, la guerra en Filipinas seguía su curso y se precipitaba su desenlace, que tenia que llegar inexorablemente como consecuencia de errores políticos de todo tipo y también, por así decirlo, porque Filipinas había alcanzado su mayoría de edad. Y cuando ello llega los pueblos se emancipan, en un ansia natural de independencia.

Fig. 1. Photo at the home of Jesús Balmori (*upper right*); also pictured are Antonio Pérez de Olaguer (*center front*), Delfina San Agustín (*left front*), and Celia Canseco (*right front*) (Pérez de Olaguer 1934, 193).

(While he [my father] was in Spain, the war in the Philippines was still going on and its outcome was fast approaching, which had to come inexorably as a result of political mistakes of all kinds and also, so to speak, because the Philippines had come of age. And when this happens, peoples emancipate themselves, in a natural yearning for independence.) (Pérez de Olaguer 1967, 109)

The rupture of the colonial bond is inevitable; however, for Olaguer, more painful is the interruption of the affective ties that bind him to the archipelago. The emotional pain he describes in this passage pushes him to join contemporary Filipino authors like Balmori and Bernabé, who chose to write in Spanish and thereby promote Hispanic culture as a means to resolder the relationship between the Philippines and Spain, as well as with the wider Spanish-speaking world.

Bella Brodzski notes, "Whether male or female, the autobiographer is always a displaced person. To speak and write from the space marked as self-referential is to inhabit, in ontological, epistemological, and discursive terms, no place" (1998, 156). In life writing produced in postcolonial contexts, Bart Moore-Gilbert adds, "feelings of being 'at home' or of displacement can be as much subjective and psychological as a function of the material (dis)location of the Subject" (2009, 66). Pervasive throughout Olaguer's life writing is just such a dual and contradictory sentiment of displacement: he expresses a sense of alienation in the familiar settings of Barcelona at the same time that he conveys an uncanny feeling of "being at home" in the transient state of homelessness that marks narrations of sojourns in the Philippines. The archipelago is a constant throughout Olaguer's autobiographical works: he dedicates one-third of both the above-cited *De Occidente a Oriente por Suez* and *Mi vuelta al mundo* (1934) to describing his first three-month visit in 1927 and roughly half of the sequel, *Mi segunda vuelta al mundo* (1943), to record a stop of just a few weeks in 1941. In his autobiography, *Hospital San Lázaro: Autobiografía novelesca* (1953), almost 300 pages are devoted to scattered recollections of the scant two years total he spent in Manila in 1946–47. Finally, the devastating Battle of Manila in the final months of World War II is the topic of *El terror amarillo en Filipinas* (1947), and the last decades of Spanish colonial rule figure large in the biography of his father cited above. The insistence on describing the Philippines as a real place, I contend, reflects the disjunctive and fractured nature of the writer's Spanish/Filipino identity that causes him to seek out there a sense of rootedness, security, and personal significance.

Even though Olaguer's life story begins nearly a decade after the end of Spanish colonial rule in the Philippines, his travelogues and auto/biographies are characterized by a double-voiced narration that Philip Holden observes is a mark of post/colonial travel writing as a particular mode of life writing: "They are colonizing with reference to the indigenous people who occupy the land of the settler colony, yet they also begin the process of claiming the

landscape as part of a process of gaining autonomy from the colonial center"
(2008, 113). Olaguer is proud of his Spanish heritage, yet as I elaborate here,
he does not reclaim the Philippines for Spain; instead, as in the episode of the
soiree at Balmori's home, from the start, he is inclined to lend his voice to the
Spanish-speaking chorus that called for the independence of the archipelago
from the English-speaking colonizer, the United States. The self-fashioning
act of his various autobiographical texts, I suggest, allows him to embed himself in a newly imagined community of the Philippines, not wholly at odds
with its Spanish heritage.

In this chapter, I examine the corpus of Olaguer's life writing and how he
employs accounts of travel, trauma, and disease, as subgenres of an autobiographical mode, to negotiate a hybrid Spanish/Filipino identity in the post/
imperial context of 20th-century Philippines. Geographical itineraries verte-
brate all these works, yet therein, as I explore here, the writer uses these three
tropes as frames to recall personal memories and to reflect on the histories
that confound Spain and the Philippines as points of origin and arrival in his
life journey. The result, as I argue, is a post/imperial self-portrait of Olaguer
that is compound and diffuse and so symptomatic of the fusion of identities
conditioning definitions of Philippine literature written in Spanish.

A Spanish/Filipino Writer?

The choice of a slash to denote Olaguer's identity as Spanish/Filipino is strategic: unlike the hyphen, which either divides or marries two terms, the slash
delineates a border and, therefore, the possibility of transgression, that is, of
crossing from one side to the other and back (see Tamburri 1991, 44). Olaguer
identifies himself as Spanish, given that he was born in Spain, yet throughout
his nonfiction, he also expresses an affinity with the term "Filipino," although
he never applies it to himself. During the Spanish colonial period, "Filipino"
was reserved for Spaniards born in the Philippines, so it makes sense that
he would identify with it, yet it also captures the evolution of the concept
during the US occupation when it came to encompass all of the peoples of the
archipelago collectively, both natives and those of European and East Asian
descent (Chinese and Japanese) (Thomas 2012, 54–55). Important here is how
Olaguer transits back and forth between Spanish and Filipino identities in his
writing and how, by doing so, he establishes an intersubjective relationship
between the two. The result, thus, as Pamela Cooper-White (2014) explains,

is "a more reciprocally influential and dynamic interaction" than one merely between subject and object—and so, as I argue here, one that disrupts the paradigm of the unidirectional imperial gaze typically used to interpret Spanish writings about the Philippines.

Olaguer's biography and family history reflect the intertwining flows of Philippine and Spanish history, from the end of the 19th century to the middle of the 20th. His parents were born in Manila, so by 19th-century definitions they were Filipino: his paternal grandfather arrived in the 1860s seeking the opportunities promised by the Suez Canal in 1869 and the establishment of a direct maritime link between Manila and Barcelona. His mother descended from a military family resettled in the Philippines in the 1820s from Argentina following the wars of independence in Spain and the Americas. The outbreak of rebellion against Spain in August 1896, and the ensuing Spanish-American War in 1898, led his father to move the family to Europe, first to Paris and eventually settling in Barcelona, where Antonio would be born 11 years later.[2] The armed conflict against colonial authorities and the economic uncertainties announced by US annexation no doubt spurred the real estate magnate to split his base of operations between the soon-to-be-former metropole and Manila. However, as Olaguer writes in *Mi padre, un hombre de bien*, alleged collaboration with the Filipino independence movement might also have motivated the move to Europe: "El confusionismo político en aquel tiempo debió de ser tan grande que, pese a la realidad de sentirse, aparte de serlo, españoles todos mis familiares, se les acusó también de traidores a la patria y de simpatizantes con la insurrección" (Political confusion at that time must have been so great that, despite the reality of feeling, apart from being, Spanish, all my relatives were also accused of being traitors to the country and of being sympathizers with the insurrection) (1967, 106). By the time Olaguer's family fled Manila, his father sat on a sizable fortune and left an enduring mark on the city.[3] The affluence of the Pérez Samanillo Company continued during the US occupation and is symbolized by the landmark Pérez Samanillo Building inaugurated in 1928 (see Rubio 2014). Wealth and position determined the series of misfortunes that befell the family in the 1930s and 1940s, which would have a profound impact on Olaguer's life and writing: his father and older brother Manuel were assassinated in Barcelona in July 1936 in the early days of the Spanish Civil War, and his brother Luis fell victim to the rampage of violence perpetrated by the Japanese army against the civilian population of Manila in February 1945.

In the literary panorama of the 20th century, Olaguer is a complicated and admittedly unsavory figure: he was renowned as a travel writer in his youth, but if not for his inflammatory pamphlets denouncing the violence of Republican factions during the 1936–39 Spanish Civil War and his tendentious journalism of the 1940s and 1950s, which aligned him with the Francisco Franco dictatorship, he might well be forgotten today. He began his literary career in 1926 with a short story collection, *Ensayos literarios*, but truly gained renown for the travel narratives studied here and for the cosmopolitan novels *Españolas de Londres* (1932) and *La ciudad que no tenia mujeres* (1934). In spite of being modern in form, style, and thematics, his early writings are tinged by Catholic sentimentality and laced with anti-Masonic, monarchist overtones that anticipate his affiliation with the recalcitrant Carlist movement after 1934.[4] From the 1940s until he died in 1968, he served as chief editor of the Catholic literary magazine *La familia*, and his short fiction and essays appeared in other Catholic magazines as well as in major Spanish newspapers, including *La Vanguardia*.[5]

Olaguer's conservatism locates him at the nexus of the redefined notion of *Hispanidad*, which, as Paula C. Park suggests, is key for describing and analyzing Filipino literature in Spanish within the larger field of Hispanic studies (Park 2018). Thanks to the prominent position of his family, from his first arrival in Manila in 1928 through his final visit in 1946–47, Olaguer had privileged access to the intellectual and social circles frequented by the writers of the so-called golden age of Philippine literature in Spanish (see Ortuño 2014). In addition to the aforementioned relationship with Jesús Balmori, he also maintained a long-standing friendship with the poet Manuel Bernabé, who wrote dedicatory poems for Olaguer's autobiography, *Hospital San Lázaro*. The Spanish/Filipino writer also corresponded with poet, playwright, essayist, and statesman Claro M. Recto, who supplied him with documentation and testimonial materials for *El terror amarillo*, and he was also a friend of Spanish/Filipino caricaturist Luis Lasa. Certainly, he also had access to the political and economic elite of the future independent Philippines: in 1928 he interviewed revolutionary general Emilio Aguinaldo; in 1940 he was entertained by sitting president Manuel L. Quezón at the Malacañang Palace; and in 1946 he recounted the war suffering of elite blended Spanish/Filipino families, including that of magistrate Vicente F. Francisco, industrialist Enrique Zobel, and President Sergio Osmeña.

Ultimately, Olaguer's identity as a Spanish/Filipino writer follows the contours of the shifting patterns of association between Spain and the Philippines from the 1920s to the 1950s. As a process of self-interrogation, that is, a question mark, he is forced to adjust claims of belonging as his racial and ethnic subjectivities become ever more fragile and unstable. In 1928, he embraces the inseparability of Hispanic heritage from definitions of being Filipino promoted by Recto and others. Later, in 1946, while he is still compelled to choose both attachments, the maneuver is complicated by circumstances and experiences that move the dwindling Spanish-speaking community to see itself as only Filipino within the newly founded nation and national identity.

A Traveling Life: *Mi vuelta al mundo* (1934) and *Mi segunda vuelta al mundo* (1943)

In his prologue to Olaguer's *Mi vuelta al mundo*, playwright Jacinto Benavente lauds the book for its honesty and candor as a tale of youthful discovery in the tradition of the bildungsroman (Pérez de Olaguer 1934, 9). *De Occidente a Oriente por Suez*, later incorporated as the first part of *Mi vuelta al mundo*, includes a prologue by another playwright, Enrique Estévez-Ortega, who also praises Olaguer for his youthful traveler's gaze and underscores his familiarity with Tagalog: "Con sus ojos, un poco de tagalo, ha sorprendido un vasto mundo, unos paises remotos, colmados de interés y de sugestiones diversos, y ha sabido comtemplar lo que se ofrecía a su vista y luego ha sabido contarlo" (With his eyes, a smattering of Tagalog, he has taken in a vast world, remote countries, full of interest and diverse suggestions, and he has been able to contemplate what was before his eyes and then he has known how to narrate it) (14). The comment Orientalizes the young Spanish writer by suggesting he possesses an insider's knowledge of Asia by virtue of his Filipino heritage, manifested in the language, and a "look" that allows him to blend in and see more than the average traveler. Estévez-Ortega explicitly differentiates Olaguer from other recent Hispanic visitors to Asia: Enrique Gómez Carrillo, Luis de Oteyza, Federico García Sanchiz, and Vicente Blasco Ibáñez (Pérez de Olaguer 1934, 14).[6] The note certainly anticipates the special attention paid to the Philippines in the second part of the volume but, more importantly, defines Olaguer's intersubjective position as a result of the processes of transculturation that shape both Spanish and Filipino identities.

Voluntary displacement and nomadism, Olaguer confesses, run in his family: as he makes his way from Barcelona to Marseille to embark for Manila in 1928, he states: "Ese viaje tiene también para mi algo tradicional" (This journey also has an aspect of tradition for me) (Pérez de Olaguer 1928, 17).

Even though it is his first journey to the Philippines, he claims it is not an unfamiliar experience: embarkation signals admission into a community of travelers composed of family members who share the experience of the voyage in the present, as well as of all those who have traveled similar routes across time, in both history and fiction. In *Mi segunda vuelta al mundo*, when his ship passes close to the rocky outcrop guarding the mouth of the expansive Bay of Manila, he traces his genealogy that stretches back and forth between Barcelona and Manila:

> ¡Corregidor! Para los que, por antecedentes familiares, conocemos desde niños el Archipiélago Filipino, la palabra Corregidor nos suena a resorte mágico, que nos abre la ciudad donde triunfaron nuestros abuelos y nos adelanta el paisaje soñado y la bellas realidades presentidas.

> (Corregidor! For those of us who are familiar with the Philippine archipelago from childhood, the word Corregidor sounds like a magic word that unlocks the city where our grandparents triumphed and provides us with a glimpse of our dreams and the beautiful realities we have experienced.) (Pérez de Olaguer 1943, 87)

Olaguer embraces travel as a form of detachment, yet even so, like every autobiographer, he cannot escape, as Sandra Paquet describes, "lineage in territory as a distinctive marker of individual identity that is coexistent with journey space [*sic*] and/or consciousness beyond regional space" (quoted in Moore-Gilbert 2009, 67). Amid travel, the binomial Spanish/Filipino is transposed to Spain/Philippines, and Barcelona/Manila, as the separations between self/Other and origin/destination, are muddled in the continuous layering of lives and experiences. In each set or pair, the slash makes visible the duplicity of Olaguer's territorial lineages between which he is forced to constantly transit back and forth to arrive at a notion of the self.

The sensation is vividly described in "En tierras filipinas," part two of *Mi vuelta al mundo*, when he describes finding himself alone in a bedroom in his father's mansion in Manila's Paco District. Curiously, he refers to the space as "mi cuarto" (my room) and then confesses: "Yo no he estado allí nunca. No conozco todo aquello. No obstante . . . Diríase que todo me es familiar, íntimo . . . Diríase que me he asomado muchas veces a esta ventana. Y, sin embargo, indiscutiblemente, es la primera vez que me acerco a ella" (I've never been there. I'm not familiar with all that. However . . . You might say that everything is familiar, intimate. . . . You might say that I've looked out this window many times. And yet, unquestionably, this is the first time I've been here) (Pérez de Olaguer 1934, 94). The family home, which heretofore could only be imagined by the writer, becomes a microcosm of the imagined home country that lies beyond its structure and formidable iron fence. The space, as he describes it, is a phantasmagoria of his family history confounded with that of the two nations therein intertwined: Spain and the Philippines. He sees the shadowy figures of his parents chatting in the moonlit garden and then envisions the turmoil of revolution and war that unfolds in the streets of Manila beyond the wrought-iron fences surrounding the mansion. In this hypnagogic state, he overhears his father announce the painful decision to uproot the family and move to Spain:

> Nacimos, tú y yo, en esta Filipinas de nuestros amores. Nuestros padres vinieron de España para hacer grandes estas tierras magníficas. Y lo lograron plenamente. Y he aquí que cuando nosotros, siguiendo su ejemplo, continuábamos laborando y empezábamos a recoger óptimos frutos, he aquí que surge la revolución.

> (We were born, you and I, here in our beloved Philippines. Our parents came from Spain to make these magnificent lands great. And they did it completely. And when we, following their example, continued to work and began to reap the best fruits, the revolution sprang up.) (Pérez de Olaguer 1934, 96)

From here, Olaguer continues with vague echoes of futile parliamentary debates in Madrid and images of the destruction of the Spanish fleet at Cavite that culminate in a vignette of his uncle José de Olaguer Feliú signing the articles of capitulation and surrender of Manila on August 11, 1898, which are included in the text (98–99).

"En tierras filipinas," hence, comprises a narrative of discovery of an unfamiliar homeland and the writer himself. In explorations of Manila and its environs, and adventures farther afield in the Ilocos region and Mindanao, Olaguer seeks out ties to bind himself to the land and the people he encounters. Pulsing throughout is a double current of nostalgia for the colonial and imperial past. Following Patricia Lorcin's definitions, on the one hand, the episode in the mansion cited above exhibits a restorative longing for the past lifestyle and idealized intercultural relations of the colony. On the other hand, allusions to the Spanish conquest of the archipelago and the humiliating defeat of 1898 represent a reflective yearning for Spain's hegemonic past position on the world stage (Lorcin 2013, 107). In the Spanish settlement of Cervantes, in Illocos Sur, for example, Olaguer is overtaken by both sentiments when he and his brother, having no place to overnight, are taken in by a humble mestizo family: "Yo siento en el alma una extraña melancholia. Me parece vivir en otros tiempos nunca conocidos y muy soñados" (I feel a strange melancholy in my soul. I seem to live in other times never known and very dreamed) (Pérez de Olaguer 1934, 113). He discovers in the simple gesture and generosity of the farmer and his wife traces of Spanishness: "¡Desinterés hidalgo de rancio abolengo español! Te encuentro ahora en mitad de los trópicos en la hondonada de un monte, al borde de la civilización" (Disinterested hidalgo of ancient Spanish ancestry! I find you now in the middle of the tropics in the hollow of a mountain, on the edge of civilization) (114). While it is disconcerting, he also finds solace in the persistent memory of Spain, as both Madre Patria and colonial oppressor, that continues to reside vividly in the Filipino demeanor and consciousness.

The mix of colonial and imperial nostalgia becomes furthermore apparent when Olaguer turns attention to the Spanish-speaking cultural life of the Philippines. The world of arts and letters he encounters during his sojourn is representative of the Filipino elite responsible for expressing nationalist ideologies and postcolonial modernity in the first half of the 20th century: he names principal composers and musicians, like José Estella, Nicanor Abelardo, and Calixto Llamas, and painters, Fabián de la Rosa and Fernando Amorsolo (Pérez de Olaguer 1934, 182). Obviously, Olaguer pays special attention to literati and, in particular, to the poets who dominate the golden age: in addition to Balmori, the list of names dropped includes Claro M. Recto, Manuel Bernabé, Adelina Gurrea, and Evangelina Guerrero (183). Following the general overview, he dedicates a full chapter to José Rizal, identifying him as both a national hero and a touchstone figure in Filipino letters, and then he narrates the previously mentioned evening of poetry readings at the home of Balmori.

At the gala dinner organized in Olaguer's honor at the Casa de España on the eve of his departure in 1928, he catches a glimpse of his future as a writer in the Philippines were he to heed his father's pleas to take his place alongside his brother in the family business. The anecdote depicted in a caricature by Luis Lasa is ironic and painful since it makes him vividly aware of the contradictions of such an existence. Feted as a Spanish writer, he sees himself therefore only as Spanish: "Se rendía allí homenaje a un escritor español. Y yo aceptaba ambos títutlos como el major galardón y como el triunfo mayor" (A Spanish writer was being honored there. And I accepted both titles as the greatest award and the greatest triumph) (Pérez de Olaguer 1934, 209). Playfully, he follows up with a self-deprecating claim that he is unworthy of neither accolade, suggesting he feels not quite a writer and not wholly Spanish. The humorous remark in response to the customary gesture indiscriminately bestowed by the Casa de España upon all who pass through Manila underscores nonetheless how he sees himself and the Philippines as contentiously Spanish.

In the first pages of the third part of the travelogue, "Rumbo a América," Olaguer reacts more solemnly as he bids farewell to friends and family on the pier by lamenting that the Philippines is no longer Spanish. Once again, his words are tinged with nostalgia for both colony and empire, first posed as an innocent yearning for a lost colonial home and then staged as a resounding lament for Spain's disappeared imperial power. Throughout the text, he moves freely across the border between Spanish and Filipino, until suddenly he finds himself completely displaced from the latter term. As his ship steams away from Manila, Olaguer evokes the final defeat of Spain and the loss of the colony: "¡Debió ser en un atardecer así, al caer de una noche como ésta, cuando se derrumbó, hecha astillas de maderas, cuerpos y almas, la vieja y mísera Escuadra Española! ¡Y con ella el ultimo baluarte del poder colonial más grande que existió en el mundo!" (It must have been on an evening like this, as the night fell, when it collapsed, shattered into splinters of wood, body, and soul, the miserable old Spanish Squadron! And with it the last bastion of the greatest colonial power that the world ever knew!) (Pérez de Olaguer 1934, 213).

A Traumatic Life: *El terror amarillo en Filipinas* (1947)

The retrospection of episodes of violence and suffering through life writing allows such events to be transmitted to the community and so to become available for recollection as collective memory by those who did experience the trauma firsthand (Gilmore 2001, 31–32). Individual narration is the first step in marking an event with a given community as cultural trauma, which Jeffrey C. Alexander defines as "a horrendous event that leaves indelible marks upon their group consciousness, marking their memories forever and changing their future identity in fundamental and irrevocable ways" (2003, 2). As Ron Eyerman elaborates, "Cultural trauma articulates a membership

Fig. 2. Caricature by Luis Lasa of dinner at the Casa de España in honor of Antonio
Pérez de Olaguer (Pérez de Olaguer 1934).

group as it identifies an event or an experience, a primal scene, that solidifies
individual/collective identity" (2001, 15). In *El terror amarillo en Filipinas*,
published in 1947, Olaguer narrates the atrocities committed by Japanese
soldiers during the Battle for Manila in February 1945. Based on firsthand
accounts and written testimonies of victims he gathered during his 1946–47
visit to the Philippines, the book employs trauma as a trope for resoldering
the fracture in the writer's Spanish/Filipino in the aftermath of civil and world
wars and for reconstituting the Spanish-speaking community decimated by
the brutal monthlong siege. The book takes the form of a conventional travel
book but amplifies the narrative perspective through the use of the testimonial form. Olaguer presents himself as a traveler on a mission to give voice to
the victims of the tragedy that befell Manila in 1945: as he wanders the ruins
of the city, he temporarily relinquishes his authority to capture the experiences of Spanish-speaking witnesses and victims, which he perceives are in
danger of disappearing altogether in the changed linguistic context of the
soon to be independent Philippines.

The inflammatory title of the 1947 book hearkens back to the series of
pamphlets he published during the Spanish Civil War denouncing similar
brutalities of a lesser scale committed by left-wing factions in Catalonia,
Andalusia, and Cantabria: *El terror rojo en Cataluña* (1937), *El terror rojo en
Andalucía* (1938), and *El terror en la montaña* (1939). Certainly, the use of the
word "red" in these titles carries similarly racist and incendiary overtones:

Olaguer openly subscribed to the discourse that attributed the political and social strife unleashed in Spain in the 1930s to an international conspiracy hatched by a coven of Zionists, Bolsheviks, and Anarchists. In the context of the Philippines, the derogatory term "yellow" adds a layer of complexity to the construction of the writer's Spanish/Filipino identity: first, it conflates the two as contiguous racial categories based on shared religion, Catholicism, language, and history; second, it separates the native population of the archipelago from the rest of Asia by virtue of its post/colonial status. The "yellow peril" trope, according to Abe Ignacio (2004), was reserved for Chinese and Japanese, whereas Filipinos regardless of their descent (European or Asian) were considered "brown" and so less threatening to the US colonial occupation. To be sure, the deployment of race in the title is a sign of self-differentiation from Asia and an attempt to vindicate the Filipinos as Hispanic and, therefore, aligned somehow with whiteness.

In 1946, the confluence of the postwar and recently gained Philippine independence obliged Olaguer to engage in a different form of self-representational storytelling by embedding the personal trauma of his brother Luis's death at the hands of the Japanese military within the larger narration of the experience of violence and destruction suffered by the population of Manila during the Japanese occupation and subsequent liberation. The description of his brother's violent demise collapses the writer's fractured identity and suspends, if only momentarily, the possibility of moving between Spanish and Filipino identities. Believing that he could save himself and his family from the house-to-house killing spree of marauding Japanese troops, Luis holds out his hand to display his Spanish identity card to prove that he is not a combatant and is a citizen of a "neutral" country, albeit one allied with Imperial Japan. The soldiers respond to his plea by first chopping off his hand, which falls to the ground still clutching the card, and then hacking him to death in the middle of the street (Pérez de Olaguer 1947, 18). The slashing blow of the saber severs the distinction of being Spanish such that all that remains is Filipino: the memory of Luis's death becomes embedded in the greater Filipino tragedy when he shares the fate of the more than 100,000 civilian victims killed by Japanese troops or American bombs. His Spanish identity no longer serves as a privilege, and he is thus only Filipino.

The murder of his brother culminates a set of prefatory stories of similar losses suffered by three of Olaguer's close friends, with whom he reunites and reminiscences upon arriving in Manila in 1946. From here, the narrative spins out to an expanding array of ever more sordid tales of rape, mutilation, and murder that concludes with an index of the names of the dead:

Insisto: la lista no sólo es larga, sino que es angustiosamente interminable. Cuatro amigos, reunidos en la bella casa de nipa, somos todo un símbolo de la tragedia de Manila. Cada uno de nosotros pasa recuento a sus distintas amistades, y el balance es sencillamente tremendo. A mi tenor, cuentan casos y casos.

(Let me insist: the list is not only long, but it is distressingly endless. Four friends, gathered in a beautiful nipa house, we are all a symbol of Manila's tragedy. Each of us takes stock of our different friendships, and the toll is simply tremendous. To me, they recount cases and cases.) (Pérez de Olaguer 1947, 23)

Narration, as Dori Laub argues, is a central part of the experience of trauma: the individual pain reenacted through storytelling reframes the traumatic episode not merely as personal history but also as a memory rooted in a collective history (quoted in Gilmore 2001, 32). Following this logic, by narrating the trauma of his brother's cruel execution, Olaguer can experience the event at the same time that he incites readers to do the same. Extending this moment beyond the personal and into the collective realm through a spreading network of connections weaves his personal memory into the memories of others and then into a larger collective Philippine history, which begs to be recovered. The result is that "his pain" becomes "our pain," where "our" connotes both Spanish and Filipino: "¡Ay, amigos! Yo no quisiera . . . Os lo juro por lo más sagrado. Yo no quisiera escribir esto. Mi gusto sería poder borrar esta página bochornosa de la Historia de Filipinas, de la Historia de la Humanidad, de la Historia de la Civilización" (Oh, my dear friends! I would not wish . . . I swear to you by what is most sacred. I would not wish to write this. I would like to erase this shameful page from the history of the Philippines, from the history of mankind, from the history of civilization) (Pérez de Olaguer 1947, 124).

The traumatic experience of the war, as Florentino Rodao observes, dealt a decisive blow to the Spanish community and to the broader identification of the new Filipino nation with Hispanic culture and Spain: "Lo español fue arrinconado a la comunidad española, mientras que los puentes con el resto de la sociedad se difuminaban cada vez más, tanto por ese decreciente papel de los mestizos o del lenguaje como por esa creciente asociación de los hispanos con lo rico" (Spanish culture was pushed into a corner in the Spanish community, while the links with the rest of society were becoming increasingly blurred, both because of the decreasing role of mestizos or language and because of the growing association of Hispanics with the rich) (Rodao 2009, 23). The outrage Olaguer expresses vis-à-vis the collective tragedy is aimed at vindicating personal ties to the archipelago at the same time that he seeks to make a universal claim upon which to identify the suffering of the Spanish community in the Battle of Manila with the greater cultural trauma endured by the Filipino nation and indeed the scope of humanity in the aftermath of World War II.

A Diseased Life: *Hospital San Lázaro: Autobiografía novelesca* (1953)

In his 1953 book *Hospital San Lázaro: Autobiografía novelesca* Olaguer takes up explicitly the autobiographical genre but does so with irony by appending the adjective *novelesca* to the title. He recognizes in the prologue, which is preceded by two poems composed by Manuel Bernabé, the inevitability of embellishing certain facts of his life story with notes of fiction and underscores how, as in life, the real and the fantastic are sometimes confounded: "Se funden, como en la vida también, el realismo más crudo, la fantasia más desbordada, la caridad más encendida, los sueños más quiméricos, los ideales más encontrados" (Just as in life, the rawest realism, the wildest fantasy, the most ardent charity, the most fanciful dreams, the most conflicting ideals, all merge) (Pérez de Olaguer 1953, 13). The first part of the title refers to the two leper hospitals dedicated to Saint Lazarus, one in Barcelona and the other in Manila, that anchor the narrative arc of Olaguer's life story, which he retells in four simultaneous tempos organized around his philanthropic service to sufferers of Hansen's disease (leprosy): (1) in 1915 when Olaguer is eight years old in Barcelona; (2) in 1940, at age 33, during his second visit to the Philippines; (3) in 1946–47 when he returns to Manila at age 40 to take care of family affairs; and (4) in 1953, as he writes the memoir in La Garriga (Barcelona). While the first and last moments unfold in Spain, the better part of the book, almost 400 pages, recounts the experiences of three years spent in the Philippines, where he reencounters the lepers he first met in Barcelona, at Manila's Hospital San Lázaro and at the Culión Island leper colony. Despite the playful subtitle, the author is careful to preempt possible critiques of his reference and usage of leprosy as a *tremendista* detail in the construction of the work:

> Mi libro escapa, en lo que puede, a toda cruda exposición, soslaya las lacras y las miserias de la terrible enfermedad. Sin divagaciones a lo Edgar Poe. Sin

extravagancias, como tantos autores que han tocado y aun apurado el tema. Incluso, he procurado emplear lo menos posible la palabra leproso.

(My book avoids, as much as possible, exposing the scourges and miseries of the terrible disease. No Edgar Poe digressions. No extravagances, like many other authors who have touched and even pressed the issue. I have even tried to use the word leper as little as possible.) (Pérez de Olaguer 1953, 15)

Indeed, the writer's engagement with victims of the debilitating disease is a biographical fact: he was first taken to the Barcelona hospital by his father in 1915 and became ever more deeply engaged with the cause as a means to carry on his father's legacy of Catholic charity (Pérez de Olaguer 1967, 282). Certainly, he avoided using the word "leper" to repair the centuries-old stigma attached to the disease as the quintessential marker of the social outcast, but as a macabre detail woven into the background of his life story, he nevertheless resorts to the long-established symbolism of the figuration as a way of reflecting on his life.

The image of disabling illnesses and diseases, as David Mitchell and Sharon Snyder note, serves as a metaphorical "crutch upon which literary narratives lean for their representational power, disruptive potentiality, and analytical insight" (2000, 49). Leprosy as a leitmotiv developed throughout Olaguer's autobiography elucidates his conception of the self as fractured and somehow incomplete. As in the case of war trauma, he does not suffer from the deforming disease himself, and so he can only be a witness to the pain of victims and express empathy toward them. His near-obsession with lepers in the Philippines, thus, becomes a metaphor for the continuous process of disintegration caused by the series of displacements his family suffers through the turmoil of the first half of the 20th century in Spain and the Philippines.

At the end of his 1946–48 stay in the Philippines, Olaguer made an eight-day trip to the leper colony established by the United States in 1907 on the Palawan island of Culión. In the episode, the writer describes communion with the patients of the remote hospital, and he revels in the fact that he can do so thanks to the recent discovery of a treatment for the disease. In the final scene of the narrative, he makes a noble attempt to bid farewell in Spanish to the English-speaking children of Culión; at the end of his speech he is heartened when the young audience shouts out to him in Tagalog, "Lolo!":

Es decir, diminutivo cariñoso, en Filipinas, de ¡abuelo! ¿Abuelo yo? / Siento en mi interior una mezcla de risa y de melancolia. De niño me llamaban Tono.

De joven, Antonio. Últimamente, don Antonio. Cada década de mi vida, salpicada de luchas y de tragedias, aumenta la gravedad de mi nombre. Al empezar la cuarta década me llaman ya abuelo.

(In other words, the affectionate diminutive, in the Philippines, for grandfather! Grandfather me? / I feel inside me a mixture of laughter and melancholy. When I was a child, they called me Tono. When I was young, Antonio. Lately, Don Antonio. With every decade of my life, dotted with struggles and tragedies, the seriousness of my name increases. At the beginning of the fourth decade they call me Grandfather.) (Pérez de Olaguer 1953, 398)

Michel Foucault observes: "One writes in order to become other than what one is" (quoted in Gilmore 2001, 11). Autobiography offers the writer an opportunity for self-transformation or, as Leigh Gilmore notes, a way to testify to "having lived" as a mode of claiming for one's self a condition of representativeness (2001, 12). The Tagalog word "Lolo" is of Hispanic origin, a duplication of the final syllable of the word *abuelo*, yet its usage in Filipino denotes an Asian-inflected notion of filial piety and respect for elders that instills a surplus of affective value. The first two syllables are not disappeared but merely elided; they are present at the affective level, and so they need not be pronounced. In the fragmented term, transformed but not deformed, Olaguer finds the realization of a Spanish/Filipino self that he had sought over two decades of travel and writing between Spain and Philippines. However, the writer's relationship as grandfather is metonymic rather than metaphoric; that is, he discovers himself as a Spanish part of a Filipino whole rather than as a representative stand-in for a higher experience of one or the other (Gilmore 2001, 78–79).

Conclusion

The Philippine archipelago lies at a double crossroads that defies unidirectional approaches and demands to be read back and forth, from East to West and from West to East. Introducing the varied corpus of Olaguer's life writing into conversations surrounding the scope and breadth of Philippine literature in Spanish further nuances the inseparability of the notions of the Filipino and the Hispano entailed by this intellectual project. In 1964, University of Santo Tomás professor Alfredo Panizo appealed for support from the Mexican Embassy for the creation of a Centro Filipino-Hispano-Americano that would reintegrate the Philippines as "la hija de America [*sic*], la nieta de España" (the daughter of America, the granddaughter of Spain), into the family tree of Hispanic nations.[7] As Paula Park points out, through the image of the Philippines as "a colony of a colony," Panizo's proposal recognizes the role of Spanish America in the formation and transmission of a global Hispanic tradition that at once includes and supersedes Spain (2019, 88). Notwithstanding the apparent ideological limitations of the familial metaphor as shorthand for describing the complexities of postcolonial relationships among former colonies and metropoles, it is certainly apt for locating Olaguer as a Spanish/Filipino writer in the scope of the emerging field of Hispanic-Asian studies. The dimensions of travel, trauma, and disease that define his life writing expose the difficulties of reconciling the inherent contradictions of an identity that is continuously in flux, wrought by violence and somehow permanently rendered deficient vis-à-vis normative definitions of nationhood.

Notes

1. As elsewhere in the Spanish-speaking world, the physical and aural enactment of poetry by declaimers was a key part of social gatherings and public events in early 20th-century Philippines; see Kuhnheim 2014. As for the *declamadoras*: performances by Canseco are referenced in conjunction with recitals in the Spanish-language newspaper *Voz Española*, and poet José Hernández Gavira evokes her name in two poems "Celia" and "El Madrigal," contained in his 1937 collection *Mi copa bohemia: poesias*; see Gavira Hernández 1937, 52, 57. San Agustín (1905–92), as Adam Lifshey points out, wrote a doctoral thesis on Hispano-Filipino literature, and recordings of her declamations can be accessed online via YouTube; see Lifshey 2012, 63.

2. In 1880, Luis Pérez was sent to study at the Jesuit-run Saint-Ignatius School for Higher Education in Commerce in Antwerp, Belgium, and in 1889, he returned to Manila to take his place alongside his father and brothers.

3. Pérez Samanillo real estate holdings included the emblematic Hotel de Oriente, large undeveloped parcels on Escolta Street, the center of the capital's new financial and shopping district, and tracts adjacent to the future site of the main train station in the Paco district.

4. His collaboration with Benedicto Torralba de Damas on the 1935 historical drama *Más leal que galante*, which is set during the Third Carlist War (1872–76), would become a kind of Carlist manifesto during the 1936–39 Spanish Civil War.

5. Notwithstanding affinities with the Franco regime, in the 1960s he played a pivotal role in the reconciliation among Carlist factions, eventually getting them to back the candidacy of Juan Carlos as the legitimate heir to the Spanish throne.

6. Estévez-Ortega refers to travel books by Enrique Gómez Carrillo about Japan, including *El Japón heróico y galante* (1912); Federico García Sanchiz's novels inspired by

travels in the Philippines, China, and Japan, *La ciudad milagrosa, Shanghai* (1926); and the round-the-world travelogues by Vicente Blasco Ibáñez, *La vuelta al mundo de un novelista* (1924), and Luis Oteyza, *De España a Japón* (1927).

7. Alfredo Panizo, Letter to José Muñoz Zapata, Ambassador of Mexico in the Philippines, 10 March 1964.

References

Alexander, Jeffrey C. 2004. "Toward a Theory of Culture Trauma." In *Cultural Trauma and Collective Identity*, edited by Jeffrey C. Alexander, Ron Eyerman, Bernard Giesen, Neil J. Smelser, and Piotr Sztompka, 1–30. Berkeley: University of California Press.

Brodzki, Bella. 1998. "Mother, Displacement, and Language." In *Women, Autobiography, Theory: A Reader*, edited by Sidonie Smith and Julia Watson, 156–59. Madison: University of Wisconsin Press.

Cooper-White, Pamela. 2014. "Intersubjectivity." In *Encyclopedia of Psychology and Religion*, edited by David A. Leeming. Boston: Springer. Accessed 30 November 2018. link. springer.com/referencework/10.1007/978-1-4614-6086-2

Eyerman, Ron. 2001. *Cultural Trauma: Slavery and the Formation of African American Identity*. New York: Cambridge University Press.

Giesen, Bernhard. 2004. "The Trauma of Perpetrators: The Holocaust as the Traumatic Reference for German National Identity." In *Cultural Trauma and Collective Identity*. edited by Jeffrey C. Alexander et al. Berkeley: University of California Press.

Gilmore, Leigh. 1994. *Autobiographics: A Feminist Theory of Women's Self-Representation*. Ithaca: Cornell University Press.

Gilmore, Leigh. 2001. *The Limits of Autobiography: Trauma and Testimony*. Ithaca: Cornell University Press.

Holden, Philip. 2008. *Autobiography and Decolonization: Modernity, Masculinity, and the Nation-State*. Madison: University of Wisconsin Press.

Ignacio, Abe. 2004. *The Forbidden Book: The Philippine-American War in Political Cartoons*. San Francisco: T'Boli.

Kuhnheim, Jill S. 2014. *Beyond the Page: Poetry and Performance in Spanish America*. Tucson: University of Arizona Press.

Lifshey, Adam. 2012. *The Magellan Fallacy: Globalization and the Emergence of Asian and African Literature in Spanish*. Ann Arbor: University of Michigan Press.

Lorcin, Patricia. 2013. "Imperial Nostalgia; Colonial Nostalgia: Differences of Theory, Similarities of Practice?" *Historical Reflections* 39 (3): 98–111.

Mitchell, David T., and Sharon L. Snyder. 2000. *Narrative Prosthesis: Disability and the Dependencies of Discourse*. Ann Arbor: University of Michigan Press.

Moore-Gilbert, Bart. 2009. *Post-Colonial Life-Writing: Culture, Politics and Self-Representation*. New York: Routledge.

Ortuño Casanova, Rocío. 2014. "Literatura filipina en español. Introducción temática." *Literatura filipina en español*. Biblioteca Virtual Miguel de Cervantes. Accessed 30 November 2018. www.cervantesvirtual.com/portales/literatura_filipina_en_espanol/ literatura_filipina_espanol/#n3

Park, Paula C. 2018. "La ruta del tornaviaje: En torno a una redefinición de Hispanidad desde Filipinas y México." Presentation delivered at the Filipino Literature in Spanish in the Context of Hispanic-Asian Studies conference, 3–5 December 2018, University of Antwerp, Antwerp Belgium.

Park, Paula C. 2019. "Transpacific Intercoloniality: Rethinking the Globality of Philippine Literature in Spanish." *Journal of Spanish Cultural Studies* 20 (1–2): 83–97.

Pérez de Olaguer, Antonio. 1928. *De Occidente a Oriente por Suez.* Barcelona: Rafael Casulleras.

Pérez de Olaguer, Antonio. 1934. *Mi vuelta al mundo.* Barcelona: Juventud.

Pérez de Olaguer, Antonio. 1943. *Mi segunda vuelta al mundo.* Barcelona: Juventud.

Pérez de Olaguer, Antonio. 1947. *El terror amarillo en Filipinas.* Barcelona: Editorial Juventud.

Pérez de Olaguer, Antonio. 1953. *Hospital De San Lázaro: Autobiografía novelesca.* Barcelona: Editorial Juventud.

Pérez de Olaguer, Antonio. 1967. *Mi padre, un hombre de bien.* Barcelona: Ediciones La Familia.

Rodao, Florentino. 2009. *Gerónimo de Uztariz* 25:9–26.

Roger Kurtz, J. 2018. "Introduction." In *Trauma and Literature,* edited by J. Roger Kurtz, 1–18. Cambridge: Cambridge University Press.

Rubio, Paúlo. 2014. "Pérez Samanillo Building." *Arquitectura Manila,* 29 March. Accessed 30 November 2018. arquitecturamanila.blogspot.com/2014/03/perez-samanillo-building.html

Tamburri, Anthony Julian. 1991. *To Hyphenate or Not to Hyphenate: The Italian/American Writer: An Other American.* Montreal: Guernica.

Thomas, Megan C. 2012. *Orientalists, Propagandists, and Ilustrados: Filipino Scholarship and the End of Spanish Colonialism.* Minneapolis: University of Minnesota Press.

The Ethnology of the Atomic

Gender, Japanese Occupation, US Empire, and the
Testimonio Filipino *of José Reyes's* Terrorismo
y redención *(1947)*

Sony Coráñez Bolton

Testimonio Filipino: Atomic Futures, Racial Pasts

Filipino novelist and essayist José Reyes's book-length testimonial essay *Terrorismo y redención: Casos concretos de atrocidades cometidas por los japoneses en Filipinas* (Terrorism and redemption: Concrete cases of atrocities committed by the Japanese in the Philippines) (1947) rescues a Philippine modernity from the caustic fires that engulfed Manila during World War II. Little known to many Americans is that the Japanese attack on the military outpost of Pearl Harbor, Hawaii, which brought the United States into the global conflict, also coincided with Japan's attack on Manila. Reyes illuminates the Pacific theater in World War II as a pivotal arena in which the injurious effects of technological advancement, human rights abuses, genocide, civilization, and barbarism played out on a global stage.

Terrorismo is a collage of sociopolitical testimonials giving account of the genocidal campaign of Japanese occupation of the Philippine archipelago from 1942 to 1945. The essay is structured around and through tactically placed personal testimonies. Despite such journalistic elements, *Terrorismo* is a hybrid document integrating various literary elements and styles: personal eyewitness accounts, photography, poetry, and hyperbolic prose. This document would fall within the genre of reportage literature typically known as *testimonio*. *Testimonio* is a genre of autobiographical literature wherein the author or authors recount their firsthand experience of human rights abuse or trauma during times of war, extreme violence, and political oppression. It has been largely associated with modern Latin American literature (Beverley 2004, 31).[1] Some of these debates are instructive for understanding what I call *testimonio Filipino*.

In the case of Reyes, the protraction of a Philippine Hispanic modernity into the midcentury demonstrates the ways that mestizo Spanish-speaking *ilustrados* ("enlightened") were not merely outdated historical artifacts from the 19th-century Spanish colonial period later eclipsed by the advent of the modern; rather, they had a unique stake in the meanings of Asian modernity in a world fatigued by the power plays of European and American political actors. While Reyes is not part of the cadre of 19th-century Philippine *ilustrados*, I suggest that he is inclusively part of a Hispanized elite culture in the archipelago that navigated the intersections of Spanish, US, and Japanese imperialisms. Reyes anticipates how the economic and political center of world affairs would incrementally shift toward Asia. And yet this shift is not understood outside of a telos of US political supremacy. What exactly is "redeemed" in *Terrorismo y redención*? The atom bomb and the scientific acumen that made it possible seem to hold a partial answer.

Reyes redeems and even legitimizes the catastrophic violence that leveled the cities of Japan: "Las dos primeras bombas atómicas que cayeron sobre Hiroshima y Nagasaki, que determinaron la *rendición* del Japón . . . han demostrado plenamente al mundo el inmenso poder destructivo de esta arma que, afortunadamente es susceptible, según los científicos, de aplicación constructiva en tiempos de paz" (The first two atomic bombs that fell over Hiroshima and Nagasaki, which brought about the surrender of Japan . . . have demonstrated clearly to the world the immense destructive power of this weapon that, fortunately, according to scientists, is susceptible to constructive application in times of peace) (1947, 105).[2] Out of the fires of war, Reyes attempts to chart a path forward emphasizing the generative possibilities of atomic energy. Despite Reyes's preference for the constructive over the destructive, atomic violence is further inoculated in a section entitled "La energía atómica para usos constructivos." Reyes writes:

> La bomba atómica es el arma formidable que dió [*sic*] fin en 1945 a la guerra del Pacífico. Dios quiso que el perfeccionamiento de esta invención y su secreto se hallen ahora en manos de América, país cristiano, que por la magnífica e insuperable posición en que le han colocado las circunstancias de la segunda guerra mundial, está ahora llamado, más que ninguna otra poten-

cia del mundo, a ser el supremo dirigente en la tierra de los destinos de la
humanidad.

(The atomic bomb is the formidable weapon that ended the Pacific War in
1945. God wished that the development of this invention and its secrets be,
in this moment, in the hands of America, a Christian country, that because of
the magnificent and undeniable position which the circumstances of World
War II have placed it, is now called on, more than another world power, to be
supreme leader of the world and human destiny.) (104–5)

The atomic future and "human destiny" are in the hands of the United States.
In this chapter, I claim that the atomic apotheosis of the United States as a
world power after World War II is dependent on the further consolidation
of unequal racial hierarchies that inhere within Reyes's narrative account of
"committed atrocities." Nevertheless, atomic violence is only a platform that
is used to bookmark which country is a deserving leader with moral virtue
(the United States), while the recipient of this violence (Japan) is highlighted
for its barbarity and thus deserving of this violence.

In the first section, I outline the literary genre of *testimonio Filipino*. I suggest in this section that Spanish colonial heritage, through the frame of US
imperialism, paradoxically and problematically animates a critique of Japanese imperialism. In the second section, I describe the ways that the moral
suasion that Reyes employs to demonize the Japanese relied on gendered representations of sexual violence and trauma. The Filipina body takes on central
importance in Reyes's documentation of Japanese *atrocidades*. I suggest that
the barbarism that characterizes Japanese occupation and victimization of the
Filipina body draws on ethnological tropes of savagery. In this way, I claim
that atomic violence and ethnological violence unexpectedly connect in the
airing of grievances constitutive of *testimonio* writing. Thus, in the third section, I demonstrate how Reyes's allusions to the splitting of the atom and the
new technological frontier of atomic science center for him a new world order
captained by US imperialism. Stunningly, Reyes tactically misremembers US
colonization of the archipelago through the use of a localized and Philippin-
ized Spanish Catholic morality. However, by reading against the grain of the
Spanish colonial and the US imperial, I argue that we can see how the "atomic
age" of the postwar era inescapably relies on allusions to the race science of
ethnology to distinguish between civilized and uncivilized Asian subjects.

Bearing Witness to US Imperialism

Reyes furnishes for us an archival text that offers us a "witness" to developments of postwar economics and politics. This becomes especially evident in *Terrorismo*'s ending thoughts on what the author predicts to be the new kinds of political and economic rationalities characterizing the rise of atomic science and technology. Writing in the atomic wake of the annihilation of Hiroshima and Nagasaki, Reyes lauds the United States' destruction of a mortal enemy. While the kinds of political rationalities undergirding Reyes's takes on the global are open to interpretation, two things become supremely clear through even a cursory reading of the document. The first is that the atomic keys to the kingdom are in the hands of the United States. The United States is represented as the rightful moral and political center of the new world order following the devastations of the European continent. Despite the Hispanic Philippine context of *Terrorismo* and its author, a key thesis is the deeply desired apotheosis of a US empire. The second topic that emerges as noteworthy for Reyes is the representation of a moral Asian modernity juxtaposed with the barbaric cruelty of the terroristic regime of Japan. Thus, we have a tale of two imperialisms whose polarity is adjudicated by the unique intellectual tools of the Hispano-Filipino, known to many as the *ilustrado*—tools that are emblematized by the documentarian genre of the *testimonio* queerly articulated in Filipino Spanish (Mojares 2006; Reyes 2008).

The Spanish colonial emerges through multiple citations and understandings of the traumas of war allegorized through the "Calvario," or Calvary of Christ. The Philippines during a time of war becomes an allegory for "El Cristo que murió en el Calvario . . . el Héroe del Drama de la Redención" (Christ, who died on the Calvary . . . the Hero of this Drama of Redemption) (Reyes 1947, 8). The Calvary, or the biblical site of Christ's crucifixion, is representative of a religious rhetoric leveraged by Reyes, which permeates the modern postwar period with Filipino intellectual tools resonant with the Spanish colonial period. That is to say, Filipino historical memory of the Spanish colonial informs understandings of the 20th-century advent of the US imperial. Catholic metaphor is mobilized by the *ilustrado* to construct a moral universe in which the modern Asia of the Philippines, ravaged by the cruelty of the Japanese, locates a moral empire of the United States whose own historical Pacific military interests are downplayed. Indeed, US colonization of the Philippines is minimized when it is even mentioned at all (only *once* in the entire 120-page document, and even so its mention is the tangent of a tangent):

> Durante el tiempo en que estuvo [las Filipinas] bajo la soberanía Americana, antes de estallar la guerra del Pacífico, disfrutó de una vida nacional, feliz y progresiva, habiéndose registrado en sus ciudades y pueblos un progreso verdaderamente asombroso, digno del renombre y prestigio inmortal de que gozan hoy día en el concepto universal de los nobles, bravos y humanitarios hijos de la América del Norte. En todos los órdenes de la vida se observó este progreso, sobre todo en lo referente al embellecimiento de las ciudades, como lo demostraban los hermosos y magníficos edificios, que han sido destruídos [*sic*] por los japoneses, de construcción moderna en su gran parte, que constituían el orgullo y atractivo de nuestras urbes, aparte de los otros muchos de arquitectura antigua, entre los cuales se contaban nuestros templos y monumentos levantados en tiempo del gobierno español, que eran igualmente el orgullo y ornato del pueblo de estas islas.

(During the time in which [the Philippines] was under American sovereignty, before the war burst across the Pacific, it enjoyed a national life that was happy and progressive, which spread an astounding progress to its cities and villages, consistent with the renowned and immortal prestige of the universal concept (of progress) which the noble, bold, and humanitarian children of North America enjoy today. This progress was observed in every aspect of life, above all in regards to the beautification of the cities, as was demonstrated in the magnificent and beautiful buildings, which have been destroyed by the Japanese, that were of modern construction and were the pride and opulence of our cities, apart from the many others of older architecture, among which were our temples and monuments constructed during the period of Spanish government, which were also the pride and beauty of the nation of these islands.) (Reyes 1947, 10–11)

We see the ways that Reyes makes sense of the intersection of Spanish colonialism and US imperialism by marking a Philippine modernity that is at odds with the destructive and anti-modern ethos of "los japoneses." It becomes clear that the US colonial period for the Philippines was a period of *progress* for a deserving country with a rich European heritage monumentalized through its ornate "arquitectura antigua" built during the "tiempo del gobierno español" (the era of Spanish government). This misremembering of colonial history renders the trope of the Calvary a curious one. The Philippine experience of war is allegorized as Christ's own suffering inoculating the Spanish colonial period from moral concern or judgment; indeed, Reyes monumentalizes the "templos y monumentos levantados en tiempo del gobierno español" (the temples and monuments constructed during the time of Spanish government) as the "orgullo" (pride) of the Philippines. Spanish colonialism, and the Catholic sacrificial allusions it implanted in the archipelago, provides the moral tools of suasion that the Oriental menace of the Japanese cannot ever hope to access. Indeed, reading the above description you might not even think that you were reading about an "Asian" nation or "Asian" heritage. The Philippines then becomes another kind of Asia altogether, articulated in a modern Spanish discourse that is activated by contemporaneous Orientalism. The effect? The praise of the "los nobles, bravos y humanitarios hijos de la América del Norte" (the noble, bold, and humanitarian sons of North America).

What then do we make of this comingling of the Spanish colonial as the source of the moral tools of enlightenment that then are used to welcome the imperialism of the United States? In the antinomy that Reyes constructs between the civilization of the United States and the barbarism of the Japanese, the *ilustrado* deploys racial, gendered, and sexualized discourses to crystallize a morally persuasive logic. This logic constructs a modern, Hispanic Philippines as war victim *and* intuitive political interlocutor for a Western order of things.

And, nevertheless, it seems that the Philippines holds untold importance for the United States' imperial century. At the turn of the 20th century, the archipelago was part of the Pacific front that indexed the United States' shifting foreign policy to build strategic military outposts particularly in Asia. The mestizo *ilustrados* known as the "Propagandists" or "Hispanistas" had the dubious position of navigating the transition from a fervent revolutionary period historically marked by the execution of one of its luminaries, namely, José Rizal, in 1896, to what several scholars have characterized as a period of imperial accommodation to US interests and internal colonial bureaucracy (Go 2008; Kramer 2006). However reformist scholars might characterize the Philippine Enlightenment of the late 19th century's epoch of "national consciousness" articulated through a textual nucleus of Philippine writing in Spanish, mestizo illustration in the postwar period decidedly shifted from ambiguous anti-colonial vanguard to unequivocal American endorsement at least in the case of Reyes. Philippine Hispanic letters, at least where Reyes's surprising postwar publication of *Terrorismo* is concerned, evince a demonstrable shift in political consciousness. My point is that the central importance of the Philippines is re-semanticized during World War II from initial front of a burgeoning American imperial power to the much-needed debut of a fully realized US empire endowed with the political clout and will of a newly enshrined center of global gravity in the atomic age. The atomic is never too distant from the anthropological, however. Gender and racial discourses work together in *Terrorismo* to link ethnological race science to atomic science. This starts with Reyes's characterizations of the Filipina woman. Gender becomes the political and moral terrain upon which a curious racial logic is articulated.

The Filipina during the War

Sexual and gender-based violence is excruciatingly prominent in Reyes's work. Nevertheless, for the reader to best understand the horror of such violence, Reyes establishes the value of feminized labor for the nation—a value measured via patriarchal logics. One of the antepenultimate sections of *Terrorismo*, entitled "La mujer en la pasada guerra," hones in on the role of Filipina women during the occupation. Much of Reyes's past moralist work on the debilitated moral state of Philippine society focused on retrenching typical gendered divisions of labor revolving around the traditional heteronuclear family. While the exigencies of war certainly put pressure on the kinds of normativities that circumscribe the social, it is still unsurprising that we see the same kinds of traditional outlooks on gender in *Terrorismo*. Entrenched normative gender ideals around women's labor still manifest despite moments of abject crisis. The abjection of imperial cruelty and femininity intersect in disturbing, traumatic, and yet illuminating ways for the current analysis.

Reyes's earlier work coincides with shifting global gender dynamics pertaining to women's liberation and suffrage in the early 20th century—what is typically called the "First Wave of Feminism."[3] For instance, in the 1930 publication of Reyes's novel *Novela de la Vida Real*, there are extensive representations of the "madre modelo" (model mother) sacrificing everything for the betterment and reproduction of the nation (1930). This included not an insignificant representation of the Filipina nurse, indeed the anglicized "la 'nurse,'" who seemingly emblematized a compromise between the "New Woman" and the needs of patriarchal society.[4] "La nurse" is professionalized, and yet she dutifully serves the nation through the feminine labor of care and nursing. I was unsurprised then to see that in the pages of *Terrorismo* the Filipina *enfermera* also showed an effusive "ternura maternal" (maternal tenderness) to wounded or fallen Filipino soldiers, "dulcificando los últimos momentos de los moribundos" (easing [literally, "sweetening"] the last moments of the dying) (Reyes 1947, 95–96). The figure of the Filipina as caregiver/nurse was clearly one that Reyes was concerned with for many decades. The motif of care as an extension of feminine duty to the nation, however, is not the central animating representation of Filipina femininity in *Terrorismo*. Filipina women's representation and embodiment *as* care is certainly eclipsed by them being an *object* of care and protection unto themselves. Filipina women are the singularly most affected victims of war.

Reyes's essay features graphic and harrowing depictions of sexualized and gender-based violence. To my mind, the rhetorical and political effect of these representations is twofold. The first is that the representation of these gender violences is to effectively render the Japanese an abject savage. The second is the ways that the paternal care that Reyes evokes through the documentation of these atrocities creates a space in which heterosexuality becomes a "foundational fiction" for Philippine society (Sommer 1991). Heteronormativity, I claim, becomes one of the main structuring logics of the *testimonio* genre as it is expressed in *Terrorismo*. And while it is not the depiction of the heterosexual marriage per se that signals national unification, the representation of a dastardly manliness in the form of the Japanese rapist creates a space for the articulation of a Filipino masculinity that embodies the manly virtues of respectability and modernity. The spatial dimensions of Spanish colonialism play a significant role in fleshing out this intervention. It is then the physical site of the Catholic heterosexual marriage (among other sacraments) that indicates the vicious perversity of Japanese soldiers through their defilement of the Filipina body in the sacred location of the church. Gender shifts our understanding of the incessant use of the Calvary motif especially in one of the most graphic scenes documented by Reyes. A subsection entitled "Orgía en plena iglesia" (Orgy in the middle of the church) is particularly insightful because in it we see how Japanese barbarity obtains meaning through religious heresy and sexual violence:

Orgía en plena iglesia.—La iglesia de San Agustín en Intramuros, que tiene fama de ser la más sólida construcción arquitectónica en la ciudad murada, que ha resistido los embates de los siglos y las conmociones sísmicas de los terremotos tristemente memorables de los años 1863 y 1882, en una de cuyas primarias criptas yacen los restos de Legazpi y Magallanes, ha sido testigo mudo de las orgías vesánicas perpetradas por los japoneses durante los 17 días mortales en que las preciosas y desventuradas mujeres de Intramuros estuvieron recluídas [sic] dentro de ese histórico templo, donde fueron víctimas del ultraje más vil y demoniaco.

(Orgy in the middle of the church.—The church of Saint Augustine in Intramuros, which is famous for being the solidest architectural construction in the walled city, which has resisted the passage of the centuries and the seismic events of the earthquakes tragically remembered from 1863 and 1882, and in whose first crypts lie the remains of Legazpi and Magellan, was made silent witness to senseless rapes perpetrated by the Japanese over 17 harrowing days wherein the precious but hapless women of Intramuros were kept imprisoned inside this historic temple, in which they were victims of rape most vile and demonic.) (Reyes 1947, 63–64)

The terror of the "orgía vesánica" (horrific orgy) of sexual violence is set into stark relief juxtaposed with the pure and virtuous walls of the church made "testigo mudo" (silent witness). Intramuros then becomes a focal point in his testimonial treatment of war's effect on Philippine society. This society is inevitably shaped by a Spanish colonial patrimony that is a testament itself to a Philippine civilization that paradoxically demonstrates a historical and colonial claim to a modern subjectivity in the service of an anti-imperial critique of Japan. The San Agustín Church survived the march of time and natural disaster ("conmociones sísmicas"). This survival describes a building that serves the function of an archival repository attesting to a Spanish colonial history that is spoken of fondly and admirably. Indeed, its "criptas" house the remains of Legazpi and Magellan, conquistadores that "discovered" and colonially administered the Philippines.[5] The church, its crypts, and its architecture are certainly testaments to a colonial heritage that Reyes wants to preserve. They also serve as witness ("ha sido testigo") to a society imperiled by the torturous regime of Japanese occupation. This sets the Calvary trope of Christian sacrifice into painful relief. San Agustín and all that it embodies and whose cultural heritage is in danger of extinction converges with the perils that are inflicted on the Filipina body; indeed, the church is the place where Filipinas were "víctimas del ultraje más vil y demoniaco . . . durante 17 días mortales" (victims of rape most vile and demonic . . . over the course of 17 harrowing days) (Reyes 1947, 64). The harrowing tale that Reyes documents continues with *testimonio* from a "Doña Isabel Benitez," who suffered "torturas más horrorsas en manos de aquellos abortos de Satán" (horrific tortures committed by those abortions of Satan) or of the Japanese. Reyes recounts her experience thusly:

> Yo, dentro de la iglesia,—dice esta señora—presencié actos espeluznantes cometidos por los japoneses en las pobres mujeres. Allí vi a algunas madres jóvenes de tiernas criaturas que, antes de ser ultrajadas y matadas, contemplaron el tremendo espectáculo que ofrecían aquellos sayones amarillos lanzando al aire a las pobres criaturas para recibirlas con la punta de la bayoneta. Hubo un caso en que un bárbaro nipón ensartó a tres chiquillos en una sola bayoneta.
>
> Las violaciones se consumían en plena iglesia y en presencia de ellas. Algunas de las víctimas eran arrastradas al patio de la iglesia que también fue testigo de aquella orgía infernal. Por las noches, los japoneses entraban con su *flashlight* en la iglesia y allí escogitaban [*sic*] a sus víctimas, alzando la sábana que cubría las cabezas femeninas, para ser llevadas después al lugar del sacrificio las damas de su gusto.

(I witnessed within the church,—the lady says—horrific acts committed by the Japanese against those poor women. There I saw some young mothers of tender infants which, before themselves being raped and killed, regarded the tremendous spectacle performed by the yellow executioners who flung these babies into the air only to catch them on the end of their bayonets. There was even a case in which one Japanese barbarian skewered three on a single blade.

The rapes were committed right in the middle of the church in front of all the women. Some of the victims were dragged to the patio of the church, which was also witness to such a hellish orgy. During the nights, the Japanese would enter the church with their flashlights and from there would select their victims, lifting the sheets that covered their heads, to be taken afterward to the place to sacrifice the ladies that whet their appetites.) (Reyes 1947, 64–65)

The act of catching three babies on a single blade ("hubo un caso en que un bárbaro nipón ensartó a tres chiquillos en una sola bayoneta") furnishes an important and vital critique of the horrors of war even if the scene's verisimilitude could be debated. It is curious that the extent to which this critique is convincing and the moral powers that it commands both rely on the sanctity of a synthetic articulation of Spanish-Philippine Catholicism in which the Church is always a witness.

The remnants of Spanish colonialism, indeed, the tomb in which "yacen los restos de Legaspi [sic] y Magallanes" (the remains of Legazpi and Magellan rest), are considered hallowed ground by Reyes. The religious language used to depict the heresy committed by Japanese infidels ("aquellos abortos de Satán") coincides also with a racialized language of classification ("sayones amarillos"); the Japanese not only are blasphemous but are also depicted as apostates of the modern itself. The terrifying scene of San Agustín, the "orgía vesánica," and the murdering of infants all tactically render an image of a ritualistic sacrifice. The syncretic colonial culture of a mestizo Philippines emblematized by the Catholic Church within the colonial fortifications of Intramuros sets the stage for the representation of a primitive people and culture (the Japanese) located far from the state of the divine grace of God. What I suggest is that this war scene of sexualized violence draws on a racialized language that alludes to the ethnological categorization of humanity.

The Japanese are not only apostate pagans; they are *primitive savages*. This turns Japanese imperial propaganda on its head. The racial and territorial language that was used by Japanese imperialists to justify their annexation of various territories of sovereign states across Asia—described as a reclamation of Asia to protect it from Western imperial interests, an Asia for Asians—falls on deaf ears for the mestizo Filipino who has a different civilizational genealogy of Spanish colonial culture to draw on. The appearance of this racialized religious language pokes holes in the Japanese imperial logic by tactically drawing on Spanish heritage, a territorial claiming of space tied to Spanish colonial architecture ("sólida construcción arquitectónica en la ciudad murada"), and Catholic identity to distance Filipino Asianness from putative Japanese barbarity. Gendered and sexual violence seems to be at the heart of this, but really it is also significantly about the desecration of a holy monument that bears witness to such violence. But what do we make of a critique of Japanese imperialism through moral persuasive logic rooted in Spanish colonialism? I do not dispute Reyes's important criticism of the war crimes committed by Japan in the Philippines. Rather, it is interesting to see how multiple colonial histories overlay one another in Reyes's *testimonios* in furnishing a critique that stiches together past and contemporaneous ideologies of colonialism. The savage acts and war crimes committed by the Japanese as they are witnessed by the sectors of Philippine society that Reyes accesses draw on a gendered grammar. The gendered representations of *Terrorismo* nevertheless obtain within a framework of racial science. In the next section I attempt to chart the ways that the atomic apotheosis of world events in Reyes's worldview cannot be understood absent an engagement with the political genealogies of ethnological human development.

Cannibalizing the Colonial

My preceding analysis of the horrific scene of San Agustín as relying on ethnological tropes of racial hierarchy is not meant to be an interpretative leap. Immediately following the harrowing and deleterious traumas of San Agustín is a treatment of Japanese "cannibalism." The rendering of the Japanese as barbaric cannibals does much work in creating a hierarchy of different Asias articulated on a spectrum from premodern to modern. In a chapter titled "Versiones cogidas al vuelo" (Accounts taken on the fly), Reyes reflects on human development through all too familiar themes of death and the moribund. He writes:

> Canibalismo.—En algunos barrios de Filipinas, particularmente en el Centro de Luzon [*sic*], se han observado actos de canibalismo en algunos japoneses remontados que al bajar al llano se dedicaban a secuestrar niños de tierna edad. Devoraban con ansiedad increíble los miembros de los tiernos infantes para aplacar el hambre que devoraba sus entrañas.

> (Cannibalism.—In some neighborhoods in the Philippines, particularly in Central Luzon, acts of cannibalism were observed in some of the Japanese stationed there and upon coming down into the plains dedicated themselves to kidnapping children of a young age. Anxiously they would devour the limbs of these tender infants in order to sate the hunger that ate at their insides.) (Reyes 1947, 65–66)

The Japanese are cannibals according to Reyes's observations. There is an explicit connection between the sacrificial scene of San Agustín and the miserable description of the cannibalistic behaviors that seem more germane to an ethnological framework. Not to belabor the obvious, but it might be useful to recapitulate Reyes's narration: the Japanese soldiers murder infants in the house of God, skewering them on their bayonets, and then Reyes describes

that "actos de canibalismo en algunos japoneses . . . [devorando] los miem-
bros de los tiernos infantes" (acts of cannibalism were observed in some of
the Japanese . . . [devouring] the limbs of those tender infants) (Reyes 1947,
65). The behavior as it is described and its strategic location in the text draw
on tropes of the ethnological description of a primitive tribe far from civilized
humanity. Given the context of the San Agustín scene, his is a description of
demons exhibiting absolutely inhumane behaviors akin to human sacrifice
and anthropophagy. The gendered dimensions of the ways that the Catholic faith, the imperiled Filipina, and the Filipino child create indelible links
between gender and the racial discourses certainly were deployed by Reyes
in his descriptions of cannibalism. Naturally, I do not suggest that the ascrip-
tion of anthropophagy is somehow an accurate description of "primitive" or
"tribal" life; rather, it is used as a problematic trope to consolidate the poles
of the modern and the anti-modern. I suggest that this project of consolidation represents a racialized and gendered relationship rooted in the unspoken
structure of the Filipino family as a "foundational fiction" attenuating anti-
Japanese sentiment (Sommer 1991). Heterosexuality becomes the tacit value
around which race and gender circulate.

I suggest that the heteronuclear family is the unspoken center of Reyes's
rhetoric, which ligaments the desecration of the Church with the ethnological evaluation of the Japanese. For this reason, the ample description of the
role of Filipina women as agents and objects of care becomes important in the
rhetorical structure of the *testimonios* of *Terrorismo*. For an educated mestizo
Filipino invested in textually representing a Philippine society structured by
traditional gendered roles—roles that become increasingly more important
due to the instabilities inaugurated by war—it is not too far-fetched to suggest that the extent to which Japanese barbaric behavior distances Japanese
men from the civilized human *also* distances them from the respectable subject position of the responsible patriarch whose duty is to protect women and
children. Many scholars have argued that race achieves its ordered categorization of human persons through the "accurate" cataloging of sexual and gendered perversity (Ferguson 2004; Somerville 2000; Hong and Ferguson 2011).
For my purposes, I claim that the extent to which an ethnological comparison
of Japanese barbarism with Philippine modernity obtains as meaningful is
through allusions to the failure to comply with responsible and respectable
masculinity. Eating the babies of women skewered on the blade of a bayonet
counts as a failure of manhood consonant with neither the virtues of Christianity nor the "humane" rules of proper warfare. Despite the induction of

the Philippines into the thoroughly modern age of the atom bomb, I would suggest that the reader need not feel badly about the atomic annihilation of an enemy as perverse and savage as the Japanese described in *Terrorismo*. The Japanese are not the object of the redemption (*rendención*) that Reyes's *testimonio* seeks.

I find it curious the connections between the racial sciences of ethnology and atomic science. The splitting of the atom and the racial categorization of humanity comingle in this *testimonio*. What do we make of the ways that Spanish coloniality and racial, eugenic, and atomic science intersect? Racial science is the categorization of humanity into discrete groups in a hierarchical relationship through a logic of evolutionism and development with European whites on the top. Such a connection becomes historically relevant in *Terrorismo* given the political and ethical debates around eugenics in Nazi Germany. The intended effect is a Filipino claim to the moral side of the conflict and to modernity itself. While Nazi eugenics are not explicitly mentioned in Reyes's text, there are clear mentions of the kinds of deprivations that occur with military occupation; given the historical environment in which *Terrorismo* is situated, it is difficult to completely disarticulate it from allusions to concentration camps. Citing the *testimonio* of congressional representative José P. Fausto, in a speech he gave to "la Cámara de Resprentates del Congreso de Filipinas, el 25 de Septiembre de 1945" (The representative body of the Congress of the Philippines, the 25th of September, 1945), Reyes quotes: "He visto esqueletos con vida moverse lentamente, con ese andar fatigoso del que solo está a pocos pasos de la tumba, y al llegar a este punto yo quisiera hacer una comparación entre el generoso americano y el cruel japonés" (I have seen live skeletons move slowly, with that lugubrious pace evincing that they were close to death's door, and upon arriving at this point I would like to make a comparison between the generous American and the cruel Japanese) (Reyes 1947, 75). Indeed, with this very sentence we might have the ultimate thesis of Reyes's *Terrorismo y redención*: the Americans are saviors, the Japanese are barbaric, and the modern Filipino is uniquely positioned to bear witness to this truth.

I find so striking the ethnological allusions describing the "cruel japonés" as a barbaric cannibal, feasting on Filipino children, while "generous" American liberators save them. Reyes through Fausto explicitly celebrates that "América [como] el pueblo escogido por la Providencia para desempeñar el papel principal de héroe en el sangriento drama que acabamos de presenciar" (America is the nation chosen by Providence to carry out the role of hero in the bloody drama that we have just witnessed) and that "El pueblo americano ha contribuido mayormente al triunfo de la libertad en la pasada guerra" (The American nation has contributed chiefly to the triumph of freedom in the past war) (Reyes 1947, 71). Through the prominence, however furtive, of ethnological comparativism ordering humanity hierarchically, we see how the atomic age in which the United States "justly" used atomic bombardment to defeat an evil enemy contours technological advancement through a racial logic. My claim is that in Reyes's text, "redemption" not only rescues a Philippine modernity from Japanese occupation but also secures the morality of a US imperialism as savior and legitimate executor of rational violence through atomic science. The context of atomic war and violence highlights the United States as a modern empire. Meanwhile, the testimonial representation of gender-based violence situates the Japanese as anti-modern racialized savages. Ethnology and racial comparison form the rational basis through which atomic advancement can structure a new world with the United States in the driving seat.

Conclusion: The Ethnology of the Atomic

Reyes braids the modernity of atomic science with the primitivity indexed by race science. In *Terrorismo*, even superficial gestures to racial science condition the ways that an atomic future is mapped out by Reyes with the United States at its center. Reyes's *testimonio* presents valuable evidence demonstrating a transition from ways of racial thinking based on evolutionary science to an era of atomic science in which humanity would transcend and subvert the bodily limitations of the human. Nevertheless, it is Orientalist and savage tropes of ethnological primitivism that were initially used to oppress Filipinos in their own home that find their way into Reyes's understanding of Philippine modernity—an assimilable Asia that is modern insofar as it can tether itself to an American order.[6] Rather than a radical break from racial science, Reyes shows how the ethnological and the atomic intersect within the genre of *testimonio* as a form that catalogs wrongs and past traumas occasioned by oppressive colonial regimes. We can see that *testimonio* can compulsively omit that to which it can ethically bear witness. Here *testimonio* as the giving of an account of trauma attempts to repair and heal by obfuscating US racial-colonial power even through a critique of Japanese imperialism. Historical memory becomes selective.

I have been arguing that these racial descriptions of the Japanese and the gendered descriptions of the Filipina obtain within an ethnological framework of human development. Immediately following the horrendous scene of the "orgía" in San Agustín are quasi-anthropological explications of why the Japanese would behave in such a "cannibalistic" manner. I have attempted to shed light on the bizarre use of anthropological discourses in thinking through the atomic age in which humanity is supposedly on the verge of transcending the containments of the body (Meyerowitz 2004; Stryker 2009). The ways in which ethnological thought structures Reyes's understanding of the atomic take on special meaning during an age in which the body is taking on new meanings and rendered mutable because of the advances of technology and the sciences. While faith is a large undercurrent of the moral universe constructed in *Terrorismo*, the specter of ethnological science furnishes for us a developmentalist logic rooted in coloniality (Quijano and Ennis 2000). The fact that these ethnological depictions appear in the same section that Reyes elaborates a seemingly gender-progressive critique of Japanese barbarism demonstrates the extent to which the gendered dimensions of imperialism are co-constituted with the ethnological power/knowledge networks of colonialism. This is a barbaric and savage depiction of a perverse Japanese masculinity juxtaposed with the civilized, respectable masculinity of the *ilustrado* Filipino. The ethnological subtends the articulation of the atomic. That is, allusions to atomic modernity become an illusory vanguard dependent on developmentalist discourses captured in the colonial project. Splitting the atom and the divisions of humanity into hierarchical racial categories complements each other in telling narratives on human progress.

Notes

1. As John Beverley has defined: "By testimonio I mean a novel or novella-length narrative in book or pamphlet (that is, printed as opposed to acoustic) form, told in the first-person by a narrator who is also the real protagonist or witness of the events he or she recounts, and whose unit of narration is usually a 'life' or a significant life experience" (2004, 31). Because of Latin America's history of consistent US intervention, violent dictatorial authoritarianism, and political oppression of various kinds, the *testimonio* has emerged as a truth-telling genre proliferating narratives from the margins that get overwritten by more "official" accounts. Despite the activist and documentarian ethos of *testimonio*, its position within the category of "literature," i.e., more fictional accounts and representations of social reality, is seen as dubious by some.

2. All translations of the original Spanish of *Terrorismo y redención* are my own. All English translations will be accompanied by the original Spanish.

3. "Second Wave feminism" describes the political efflorescence of feminist activism in

the 1960s and 1970s. Third Wave describes the critiques of women of color feminism of the poverty of racial analysis in the Second Wave, which typically only focused on white and Western women's issues.

4. For more on the "modern girl" or "New Woman" in a transnational context, see the excellent anthology by Alys Eve Weinbaum, *The Modern Girl around the World: Consumption, Modernity, and Globalization* (2008).

5. Miguel López de Legazpi (ca. 1502–72) was governor-general of the Philippines and the Spanish East Indies from 1565 to 1572. The first colonial settlement was established in the Philippines in the island of Cebu in 1565, at which time the Philippine islands were administered through the viceroyalty of Mexico. While the first official colonial settlement was established under Legazpi, the Philippines was "discovered" by Portuguese navigator Ferdinand Magellan (1480–1521; Spanish: Fernando de Magallanes). He is famous for being the first explorer to have circumnavigated the globe. However, this is apocryphal, as he died in the Philippines in 1521 before he could complete the journey.

6. I have written about comparative civilizations in "Asia" in another context: see Bolton, "Cripping the Philippine Enlightenment: Ilustrado Travel Literature, Postcolonial Disability, and the 'Normate Imperial Eye/I'" (2016).

References

Beverley, John. 2004. *Testimonio: On the Politics of Truth*. Minneapolis: University of Minnesota Press.

Bolton, Sony Coráñez. 2016. "Cripping the Philippine Enlightenment: Ilustrado Travel Literature, Postcolonial Disability, and the 'Normate Imperial Eye/I.'" *Verge: Studies in Global Asias* 2 (2): 138–62. https://doi.org/10.5749/vergstudglobasia.2.2.0138

Ferguson, Roderick A. 2004. *Aberrations in Black: Toward a Queer of Color Critique*. Critical American Studies Series. Minneapolis: University of Minnesota Press.

Go, Julian. 2008. *American Empire and the Politics of Meaning: Elite Political Cultures in the Philippines and Puerto Rico during U.S. Colonialism*. Politics, History, and Culture Series. Durham: Duke University Press.

Hong, Grace Kyungwon, and Roderick A. Ferguson, eds. 2011. *Strange Affinities: The Gender and Sexual Politics of Comparative Racialization*. Perverse Modernities Series. Durham: Duke University Press.

Kramer, Paul A. 2006. *The Blood of Government: Race, Empire, the United States, and the Philippines*. Chapel Hill: University of North Carolina Press.

Meyerowitz, Joanne J. 2004. *How Sex Changed: A History of Transsexuality in the United States*. Cambridge, MA: Harvard University Press.

Mojares, Resil B. 2006. *Brains of the Nation*. Quezon City: Ateneo de Manila University Press.

Quijano, Aníbal, and Michael Ennis. 2000. "Coloniality of Power, Eurocentrism, and Latin America." *Nepantla: Views from South* 1 (3): 533–80.

Raquel, A. G. 2008. *Love, Passion and Patriotism: Sexuality and the Philippine Propaganda Movement, 1882–1892*. Critical Dialogues in Southeast Asian Studies Series. Seattle: University of Washington Press.

Reyes, José G. 1947. *Terrorismo y redención: Casos concretos de atrocidades cometidas por los japoneses en Filipinas*. Manila: Cacho Hermanos.

Reyes, José G., and Teodoro M. Kalaw. 1930. *Novela de La Vida Real*. Manila: self-published. https://catalog. hathitrust. org/Record/000480508

Somerville, Siobhan B. 2000. *Queering the Color Line: Race and the Invention of Homosexuality in American Culture*. Series Q. Durham: Duke University Press.

Sommer, Doris. 1991. *Foundational Fictions: The National Romances of Latin America*. Latin American Literature and Culture Series, 8. Berkeley: University of California Press.

Stryker, Susan. 2009. "{We Who Are Sexy}: Christine Jorgensen's Transsexual Whiteness in the Postcolonial Philippines." *Social Semiotics* 19 (1): 79–91.

Weinbaum, Alys Eve. 2008. *The Modern Girl around the World: Consumption, Modernity, and Globalization*. Next Wave Series. Durham: Duke University Press.

CONTRIBUTORS

John D. Blanco is Associate Professor of Comparative Literature, Spanish, and Cultural Studies at the University of California at San Diego. His research interests concern the colonial roots of globalization between the 16th and 19th centuries. He is the author of *Frontier Constitutions: Christianity and Colonial Empire in the Nineteenth Century Philippines* (2009).

Luis Castellví Laukamp is Associate Professor (lecturer) in Hispanic Cultural Studies at the University of Manchester. His research has recently focused on the analysis of colonialism and postcolonialism in the 19th century, especially in relation to the Philippines. He is the author of *Hispanic Baroque Ekphrasis: Góngora, Camargo, Sor Juana* (2020).

Sony Coráñez Bolton is Associate Professor of Spanish and Latinx and Latin American Studies in the Department of Spanish at Amherst College in Massachusetts. His first book, *Crip Colony: Mestizaje, US Imperialism, and the Queer Politics of Disability in the Philippines* (2023) crips and queers transpacific Borderlands and Filipinx cultural production to understand the architectures of disablement that constitute overlaps of Spanish and US imperialisms.

Kristina A. Escondo is Associate Professor of Spanish in the Department of Modern Languages at Otterbein University (Ohio). Her main research interest focuses on connections between Latin America and Asia, especially between Cuba, Puerto Rico, and the Philippines. Her current work focuses on exploring women's insurgency and women's conceptualizations of nation and citizenship in Cuba and the Philippines in 19th- and 20th-century revolutions.

Axel Gasquet is Professor of Latin American Studies at the University Clermont Auvergne, France, and principal researcher at IHRIM of the French National Council for Scientific Research (CNRS). He has published twelve monographs, including *Hispanoamérica, Filipinas y las culturas de Asia* (2023), *Argentinean Literary Orientalism, from Esteban Echeverría to Roberto Arlt* (2020), and *El llamado de Oriente* (2015); coedited eleven essay collections and edited six critical editions, including *El desafío de la modernidad en la literatura hispanofilipina (1885–1935)* (Brill 2022), *Cultural and Literary Dialogues between Asia and Latin America* (2020), José Rizal's *Noli me tangere* (2019), and world edition of Benigno del Río, *Cuentos filipinos* (2023).

David R. George Jr. is Senior Lecturer in Spanish in the Department of Spanish at Bates College (Maine). He has published articles and book chapters on a variety of aspects of 19th and 20th-century Spanish literature, film, and television, including on issues of cultural exchange and travel between Spain and Asia. He is coeditor of the volumes *Historias de la pequeña pantalla: Representaciones históricas en la televisión de la España democrática* (2009), and *Televising Restoration Spain: History and Fiction in Twenty-First Century Costume Dramas* (2018). He is also author of annotated editions Leopoldo Ala's *Doña Berta* (2008\) and Benito Pérez Galdós's *Tormento* (2012).

Cristina Guillén Arnáiz is a joint PhD candidate at the Universidad Autònoma de Barcelona (Spain) and Universiteit Antwerpen (Belgium). Her dissertation focuses on Spanish 19th century reports written by travelers to the Philippines, the connections with other European travelogues on Asian colonies at the time, interactions with Filipinos writing in Spanish, and the discussions on modernization of the archipelago and on a shift of the colonial model that are developed in her corpus.

Ernest Rafael Hartwell is Associate Professor of Spanish at Western Washington University. His research is on Philippine and Caribbean prose from the end of the 19th century. Specifically, he addresses problems of authority in anticolonial writing in terms of language, race, and intellectual patrimony.

Rocío Ortuño Casanova works currently at UNED (Spain) and is Associate Professor of Spanish-speaking literatures at the Universiteit Antwerpen. She specializes on cultural and literary relations between the Philippines and the hispanophone. She is author of *Mitos cristianos en la poesía del 27* (2014) and coeditor of *El desafío de la modernidad en la literatura hispanofilipina (1885–1935)* (2022). She has coordinated several projects on Philippine printed culture, including the Portal on Philippine literature in Spanish at Biblioteca Virtual Miguel de Cervantes, the virtual exhibit PhilPeriodicals, and the database Filiteratura.

Paula C. Park is Associate Professor of Spanish and Latin American Studies at Wesleyan University. Her research areas are Latin American and Hispanic Caribbean literatures and Philippine literature in Spanish and English from the 20th and 21st centuries, with a focus on Orientalism and Asian diasporas, exile writers, and media culture. She is author of *Intercolonial Intimacies: Relinking Latin/o America to the Philippines, 1898–1964* (2022).

Ana M. Rodríguez-Rodríguez is Associate Professor specializing in Early Modern Spanish literature at the University of Iowa. She is the author of *Letras liberadas. Cautiverio, escritura y subjetividad en el Mediterráneo de la época imperial española* (2013), exploring Spanish textual manifestations of the phenomenon of captivity during this period. In 2020 she curated the exhibition "Tan sabia como valerosa: mujeres y escritura en los Siglos de Oro" (Wise and Valiant: Women and Writing in the Spanish Golden Age) at Instituto Cervantes (Madrid).

Marlon James Sales is Associate Professor of Spanish and Translation Studies at the University of the Philippines at Diliman, researching the history of translation in the Philippines, Tagalog missionary linguistics, literary multilingualism, and religion, colonialism, and knowledge in the early modern Iberian world. He has curated the virtual exhibit *The Literary Worlds of the Spanish Philippines* at the University of Michigan, where he previously worked as a postdoctoral fellow.

meLê yamômo is Assistant Professor of Theatre, Performance, and Sound Studies at the University of Amsterdam, and the author of *Sounding Modernities: Theatre and Music in Manila and the Asia Pacific, 1869–1946* (2018).

INDEX

Abad, Antonio M., 59, 110, 116, 122, 127–28, 132, 137, 145–48
Abbad y Lasierra, Iñigo, 121n2, 122, 215
Achen, Dato, 105
Acosta, Fr. José de, 34–35, 38, 45–46
Acosta, José Julián de, 122, 193, 198–201, 205, 207–8, 210, 213nn9–10, 215, 217
Acquaviva, Claudio, 109
Aetas, 159
Africa, 4, 8, 51, 69–70, 197, 235
Agrava, Leonor, 13, 24
Aguinaldo, Emilio, 14, 251
Alfonso X "the Wise," 54
Alinea, Estanislao B., 51, 54, 58, 66
Almonte, Pedro de, 104
Alta California, 31
Amazonian, 31
Amboina, 145
America, 4–5, 21, 70, 80–81, 83–84, 84n2, 87, 89, 93, 96, 104, 121n2, 124, 130, 133, 169, 206–10, 214n14, 215, 224, 256, 263–64, 267–68, 270–71, 279, 282
American imperialism, 116, 168–69
Americanization, 12
Ángel, Fr. Francisco, 103
Anti-Colonial, 12, 17, 155–56, 158, 161, 175, 181, 185, 191, 193–95, 199, 202–3, 205, 210–11, 212n3, 215, 271
Apóstol, Cecilio, 14, 20, 127–29, 137, 140–44, 147, 147n4, 148
Aquino de Belén, Gaspar, 15, 57, 59, 69
Arab(s), 5, 94, 100, 235
Arellano, Alonso de, 85n14

Argensola, Bartolomé Juan Leonardo de, 111–12, 115, 117, 122,
Argentina, 22, 24, 70, 201–7, 209–11, 214, 250
Asia, 4–5, 7–8, 10, 20, 39, 51–52, 68–69, 75, 80–81, 95, 104, 107, 110, 112, 119, 124, 130, 138, 173, 206, 212n2, 219, 240–42, 252, 258, 267, 269, 271, 276, 280, 282
Asia Pacific, 184
Atienza, Francisco de, 107
Atomic modernity, 281
Attila, 139
Austria, Don Juan de, 136
Ávalos, Melchor de, 96–97, 107
Ayamontes, Martín de, 85–86
Azores, 33

Bahamas, 33
Balagtas, Francisco, 55
Balmori, Jesús, 5, 13, 22, 58, 62–63, 72–79, 82–85, 85n7, 148, 245, 247–49, 251, 255
Barcelona, 18, 68, 107, 189, 217, 224, 231, 240–41, 245–46, 248, 250, 252–53, 260–61
Barrantes, Vicente, 15, 20, 104, 107, 135, 148, 238–39
Battle of Manila, 11, 14, 18, 145, 248, 260
Bazán, Francisco de, 134–35, 139
Bernabé, Manuel, 14, 20, 58, 76, 78, 245, 248, 251, 255, 260
Bernal, Rafael, 81, 86, 87
Billy, Fr. Jacques de, 56
Biopolitics, 193–94, 198, 200, 210–11